Constitutionalism in the Americas

STUDIES IN COMPARATIVE LAW AND LEGAL CULTURE

In today's shrinking world it's important to extend our horizons and increase our knowledge of other people's laws. This series publishes in-depth volumes covering various aspects of private and public law in diverse legal traditions. Additionally, it seeks to encourage improved techniques and methods of comparative legal research, including the use of interdisciplinary studies. Individual volumes may deal with the law and culture not merely of well-known and frequently studied countries, but also with lesser-known, mixed, religious, and plural systems of the world. The focus ranges from important aspects of legal history, culture, and institutions to local experience and evolving legal trends.

Titles in the series include:

Order from Transfer
Comparative Constitutional Design and Legal Culture
Edited by Günter Frankenberg

Corruption and Conflicts of Interest
A Comparative Law Approach
Edited by Jean-Bernard Auby, Emmanuel Breen and Thomas Perroud

Legal Innovations in Asia
Judicial Lawmaking and the Influence of Comparative Law
Edited by John O. Haley and Toshiko Takenaka

Rights-Based Constitutional Review
Constitutional Courts in a Changing Landscape
Edited by John Bell and Marie-Luce Paris

Constitutionalism in the Americas
Edited by Colin Crawford and Daniel Bonilla Maldonado

Constitutionalism in the Americas

Edited by

Colin Crawford

Tulane University, USA

Daniel Bonilla Maldonado

Universidad de Los Andes, Colombia

STUDIES IN COMPARATIVE LAW AND LEGAL CULTURE

Edward Elgar PUBLISHING

Cheltenham, UK • Northampton, MA, USA

Published by
Edward Elgar Publishing Limited
The Lypiatts
15 Lansdown Road
Cheltenham
Glos GL50 2JA
UK

Edward Elgar Publishing, Inc.
William Pratt House
9 Dewey Court
Northampton
Massachusetts 01060
USA

A catalogue record for this book
is available from the British Library

Library of Congress Control Number: 2017953162

This book is available electronically in the **Elgar**online
Law subject collection
DOI 10.4337/9781788113335

MIX
Paper from responsible sources
FSC® C013056

ISBN 978 1 78811 332 8 (cased)
ISBN 978 1 78811 333 5 (eBook)

Typeset by Servis Filmsetting Ltd, Stockport, Cheshire
Printed and bound in Great Britain by TJ International Ltd, Padstow

Contents

List of figures and tables vii
List of contributors ix
Acknowledgment x

1 Introduction 1
Daniel Bonilla Maldonado and Colin Crawford

PART I THE RELATIONSHIP BETWEEN LATIN AMERICAN AND U.S. CONSTITUTIONALISM

2 The political economy of legal knowledge 29
Daniel Bonilla Maldonado

3 The geopolitics of constitutionalism in Latin America 79
Jorge L. Esquirol

PART II LATIN AMERICAN CONSTITUTIONALISM

4 Constitutionalism in the Americas: a comparison between the U.S. and Latin America 111
Roberto Gargarella

5 Back to the future? The return of sovereignty and the principle of non-intervention in the internal affairs of the states in Latin America's "radical constitutionalism" 140
Javier Couso

6 Constitutionalism old, new and unbound: the case of Mexico 155
Francisca Pou Giménez

7 Socioeconomic rights and majoritarian courts in Latin America 188
David Landau

PART III U.S. CONSTITUTIONALISM IN THE 21ST CENTURY

8 Constitutional drafting in Latin America: a quantitative perspective 217
David S. Law and Tom Ginsburg

9 The global diffusion of U.S. legal thought: changing influence, national security and legal education in crisis 240
Fernanda Nicola

10 The limits of U.S. racial equality without a Latin American constitutional "right to work" – a thought experiment 258
Tanya Katerí Hernández

Name index 287
Subject index 288

Figures and tables

FIGURES

2.1	Eugène Delacroix (1798–1863): *Chasse aux lions* (*Lion Hunt*)	54
2.2	Théodore Chassériau (1819–1856): *Tepidarium*	55
2.3	Henri Regault (1843–1871): *Exécution sans jugement sous les rois maures de Grenade* (*Execution without Trial under the Rule of the Moorish Kings in Granada*)	56
8.1	Similarity between Latin American constitutions and the U.S. Constitution over time	220
8.2	Constitutional similarity to the United States in Latin America and the rest of the world	221
8.3	Constitutional similarity between Argentina and the United States	222
8.4	Growth in the average number of index rights	223
8.5	Constitutional similarity between Chile and the United States	225
8.6	Constitutional similarity between Venezuela and the United States	226
8.7	Constitutional similarity between Brazil and the United States	226
8.8	Constitutional similarity between Colombia and the United States	227
8.9	Constitutional scope and detail, by region and over time	230
8.10	Extent of executive power found in constitutions, by region and over time	231
8.11	Extent of legislative power found in constitutions, by region and over time	232
8.12	Details of executive tenure, by region and over time	233
8.13	Details of executive selection specifity, by region and over time	233
8.14a	Overall level of rights protection, by region and over time	234
8.14b	Criminal procedure rights, by region and over time	235

8.14c Economic rights, by region and over time 235
8.14d Civil and political rights, by region and over time 236

TABLES

4.1 Constitutional models: autonomy and self-government 116
8.1 Latin America's rank in each category among all eight regions 224
8.2 Latin American constitutions ranked by similarity of rights provisions to the U.S. Constitution as of 2012 227
8.3 Regional differences in constitutional content 229

Contributors

Daniel Bonilla Maldonado, Associate Professor, Universidad de los Andes School of Law, Colombia.

Javier Couso, Professor, Universidad Diego Portales School of Law, Chile.

Colin Crawford, Robert C. Cudd Professor of Law, Tulane Law School, USA.

Jorge L. Esquirol, Professor of Law, Florida International University College of Law, USA.

Roberto Gargarella, Professor, Universidad Torcuato Di Tella School of Law, Argentina.

Tom Ginsburg, Leo Spitz Professor of International Law, University of Chicago Law School, USA.

Tanya Katerí Hernández, Archibald R. Murray Professor of Law, Fordham Law School, USA.

David Landau, Mason Ladd Professor, Florida State University College of Law, USA.

David S. Law, Charles Nagel Chair of Constitutional Law and Political Science, Washington University in St. Louis, USA; Sir Y.K. Pao Chair in Public Law, University of Hong Kong, Hong Kong.

Fernanda Nicola, Professor of Law, Washington College of Law, American University, USA.

Francisca Pou Giménez, Assistant Professor, Instituto Tecnológico Autónomo de México School of Law, Mexico.

Acknowledgment

The editors would like to thank Anthony Cooper for his invaluable work in the preparation of the indices.

1. Introduction

Daniel Bonilla Maldonado and Colin Crawford

Latin American constitutional law has undergone a profound transformation in the last twenty-five years. On the one hand, a significant number of countries in Latin America reformed or issued new constitutions in order to consolidate or expand their liberal democracies.[1] The constitutional transformations in Brazil (1988), Colombia (1991), Paraguay (1992), Peru (1993), Argentina (1995), Ecuador (1998) and Chile (2005) had, among other objectives, the aim of re-legitimizing their political systems, establishing a new balance between the branches of the government, expanding their bills of rights or modernizing their political and legal institutions.[2]

On the other hand, the new constitutions of Venezuela (1999), Ecuador (2008) and Bolivia (2009) aimed to move away from the liberal model that had historically been the norm of the majority of the States in the region.[3] The constitutions of these three countries were issued in order to materialize a new political model that would allow for efficiently attacking the problems of poverty, inequality and exclusion that affect the majority of

---

[1] Roberto Gargarella (2013), *Latin American Constitutionalism, 1810–2010. The Engine Room of the Constitution* (Oxford: Oxford University Press), Ch. 9.

[2] Rodrigo Uprimny (2011), "The recent transformation of constitutional law in Latin America: Trends and challenges", *Texas Law Review*, **89** (7), 1587–1610. An exception to this trend may be the Dominican Republic's 2010 Constitution which, among other things, decrees that abortion is banned under any circumstances, including when the mother's life is at risk (Article 37) and bans any form of same-sex union (Article 55). In addition, the 2010 Constitution denied citizenship and its attendant rights to those living "illegally" in the country (Article 18), a provision that, as confirmed by the nation's Constitutional Tribunal, prohibited descendents of those born to Haitian parents illegally in the country after 1929 to the benefits of citizenship. See Kristymarie Shipley (2015), "Stateless: Dominican-born grandchildren of Haitian undocumented immigrants in the Dominican Republic", *Transnat'l L. & Contemp. Probs.*, **24**, 259.

[3] Javier Couso (2014), "Radical democracy and the 'new Latin American constitutionalism'", at: https://www.law.yale.edu/system/files/documents/pdf/sela/SELA13_Couso_CV_Eng_20130516.pdf (accessed 5 September 2017).

their citizens.[4] At least partially inspired by what has been called twenty-first-century socialism, these constitutions have sought to erect a radical democracy in these three South American countries.[5] To achieve this objective, these constitutions granted extensive powers to the executive branch, weakened the powers of the judicial branch, issued a notable number of social and economic rights, recognized a broad range of rights to cultural minorities, and transformed some of their political and legal institutions to make them compatible with their version of a principle of cultural diversity.[6]

Finally, Latin American constitutional law has become more robust and international in nature.[7] In turn, academic production on the topic has increased in the region. Not only has the number of publications increased, but so also has their quality; many Latin American constitutional law scholars and law schools have inserted themselves into the international academic networks of constitutional law.[8] Likewise, some Latin American legal interventions have drawn regional and international attention. The decisions affirming social and economic rights by the Constitutional Court of Colombia,[9] the efforts by the Brazilian Public Ministry to affirm socioenvironmental rights at both the federal and state levels,[10] the rights of nature set forth in the Ecuadorian Constitution,[11]

---

[4] Roberto Viciano and Rubén Martínez Dalmau (2010), "Aspectos generales del nuevo constitucionalismo latinoamericano", in *El nuevo constitucionalismo en América Latina* (Quito: Corte Constitucional del Ecuador).

[5] Rickard Lalander (2011), "¿Descentralización socialista? Reflexiones sobre democracia radical, participación política y el neoconstitucionalismo del siglo XXI en Bolivia, el Ecuador y Venezuela", *Politeia*, **34** (47), 55–88.

[6] Javier Couso (2017), "Back to the future? The return of sovereignty and the principle of non-intervention in the internal affairs of the states in Latin America's 'radical constitutionalism'", Ch. 5 in this volume.

[7] Roberto Viciano and Ruben Martínez Dalmau (2010), "¿Se puede hablar de un nuevo constitucionalismo latinoamericano como corriente doctrinal sistematizada?", in *El nuevo constitucionalismo en América Latina* (Quito: Corte Constitucional del Ecuador).

[8] See, for example, the Instituto Iberoamericano de Derecho Constitucional, at: http://www.juridicas.unam.mx/iidc/ and the Seminario en Latinoamericano de Teoría Constitucional (SELA), at: http://www.law.yale.edu/intellectuallife/SELAoverview.htm (both accessed 5 September 2017).

[9] See, in general, Manuel José Cepeda-Espinosa (2004), "Judicial activism in a violent context: The origin, role, and impact of the Colombian Constitutional Court", *Wash. U. Global Stud. L. Rev.*, **3**, 539.

[10] Lesley McAllister (2008), *Making Law Matter: Environmental Protection and Legal Institutions in Brazil* (Stanford, CA: Stanford University Press).

[11] Eduardo Gudynas (2009), "La ecología política del giro biocéntrico en la nueva Constitución de Ecuador", *Revista Estudios Sociales*, **32**, 34–47; and Marco Aparicio (2011), "Nuevo constitucionalismo, derechos y medio ambiente

or the Bolivian interpretations of the principle of multinationality,[12] for example, have become valuable and original objects of study for students and legal academics around the world.

However, the results of Latin American constitutionalism are varied.[13] While in some countries there have been advances on issues like the stability of the democratic processes, the protection of civil and political rights and the limiting of presidentialism, not surprisingly perhaps, all of the promises of Latin American constitutionalism have not been fully realized. Notably, the promises of equality, inclusion, dignity and autonomy of persons made by these new constitutions have not been delivered fully.[14] Similarly, in spite of the achievements mentioned above, outside the region Latin American academia and legal institutions largely remain on the margins of the discussion about the present and future of constitutionalism, and they continue to be considered secondary interlocutors on these matters.[15] In particular, their relationship with U.S. legal academia remains predominantly vertical and one-sided.[16] Latin American academia tends to be considered a space for reproduction and diffusion of the constitutional law products generated in countries of the Global North, like the United States. But as the articles gathered demonstrate, which form the basis of the chapters in this book, that need not be the case.

In contrast, U.S. constitutionalism has historically occupied a central position in the world.[17] The United States' legal and political institutions have long been considered paradigmatic examples of liberal theory and practice. The influence of the Constitution of 1787 is undeniable and its achievements on matters of the stability and prosperity of the political

---

en las constituciones del Ecuador y Bolivia", *Revista General de Derecho Público Comparado*, **9**, 1–24.

[12] Jorge Lazarte (2009), "Plurinacionalismo y multiculturalismo en la Asamblea Constituyente de Bolivia", *Revista Internacional de Filosofía Política*, **33**, 71–102.

[13] Roberto Gargarella (2017), "Constitutionalism in the Americas. A comparison between the U.S. and Latin America", Ch. 4 in this volume.

[14] Guillermo O'Donnell (1998), *Polyarchies and the (Un)Rule of Law in Latin America* (Notra Dame, IN: Helen Kellogg Institute for International Studies).

[15] Daniel Bonilla (2013), "Introduction", in Daniel Bonilla (ed.), *Constitutionalism of the Global South: The Three Activist Courts of India, South Africa and Colombia* (Cambridge: Cambridge University Press).

[16] Daniel Bonilla (2013), "Legal clinics in the Global North and South: Between equality and subordination", *Yale Hum. Rts. & Dev. L.J.*, **16**, 176.

[17] See Ugo Mattei (2003), "A theory of imperial law: A study on U.S. hegemony and the Latin resistance", *Ind. J. Global Legal Stud.*, **10**, 383, at 447; Wolfgang Wiegand (1996), "Americanization of law: Reception or convergence?", in Lawrence M. Friedman and Harry N. Scheiber (eds), *Legal Culture and the Legal Profession* (Boulder, CO: Westview Press), p. 137.

community it regulates are broadly admired.[18] Countries from all regions of the world have been inspired by (or have reproduced) much of its content.[19] U.S.-based academic production on constitutional law is also vast and often of high quality, and has permeated global discussion on the topic. The work of authors like Ronald Dworkin, Cass Sunstein and Bruce Ackerman, to name only three widely known professors, is discussed around the globe.[20]

However, over the last few years, there has been discussion of the weakening of the U.S. constitutional model,[21] or its decreased relevance in the international context.[22] For example, Supreme Court Justice Ruth Bader Ginsburg affirmed that, if a country were drafting a new constitution today, she would recommend that it look not towards the United States, but towards Canada, South Africa or Europe.[23] Her colleague

---

[18] Heinz Klug (2000), "Model and anti-model: The United States Constitution and the 'rise of world constitutionalism'", *Wis. L. Rev.*, **3**, 597; Louis Henkin and Albert J. Rosenthal (eds) (1990), *Constitutionalism Rights: The Influence of the United States and Constitution Abroad* (Columbia: Columbia University Press).

[19] George Athan Billias (ed.) (1990), *American Constitutionalism Abroad: Selected Essays in Comparative Constitutional History* (New York: Greenwood Press); George Athan Billias (2009), *American Constitutionalism Heard Around the World, 1776–1989: A Global Perspective* (New York: New York University Press); Duncan Kennedy, "The globalizations of law and legal thought", in David Trubek and Alvaro Santos (eds) (2006), *The New Law and Economic Development: A Critical Appraisal* (Cambridge/New York: Cambridge University Press), pp. 19, 57.

[20] Ugo Mattei (1994), "Why the wind changed: Intellectual leadership in western law", *Am. J. Comp. L.*, **42**, 195.

[21] Bruce Ackerman (2013), *The Decline and Fall of the American Republic* (Cambridge, MA: Belknap Press); Immanuel Wallerstein (2003), *The Decline of American Power: The U.S. in a Chaotic World* (New York: The New Press); Randall L. Schweller and Xiaoyu Pu, "After unipolarity: China's visions of international order in an era of U.S. decline", *International Security*, **36** (1), 41.

[22] David S. Law and Mila Versteeg (2012), "The declining influence of the United States Constitution", *New York University Law Review*, **87** (3), 762; Tom Ginsburg, Zachary Elkins and James Melton (2012), Response: "Comments on law and Versteeg's 'The Declining Influence of the United States Constitution'", *New York University Law Review*, **87**, 2088; and Fernanda G. Nicola (2017), "The global diffusion of U.S. legal thought: Changing influence, national security and legal education in crisis", Ch. 9 in this volume.

[23] In an interview in Egypt, Justice Ginsburg said: "I would not look to the U.S. constitution, if I were drafting a constitution in the year 2012. I might look at the constitution of South Africa. That was a deliberate attempt to have a fundamental instrument of government that embraced basic human rights, had an independent judiciary. It really is, I think, a great piece of work that was done. Much more recent than the U.S. Constitution: Canada has a Charter of Rights and

Justice Stephen Breyer recently explored the obligations of U.S. jurists to look beyond U.S. laws in arriving at their constitutional judgments.[24] More concretely still, recent research shows that the influence of the U.S. Constitution has decreased notably since the 1980s.[25] The contribution in this volume by Law and Ginsburg yet further endorses that conclusion. Ever fewer constitutions show the imprint of the Constitution of 1787.

Many arguments are offered to explain the supposed decline in its influence. Included among them are the argument that the U.S. Constitution does not serve modern constitutional needs because it recognizes very few rights, does not mention collective or social, economic and cultural rights, and is tremendously difficult to reform, impeding the flexibility needed in a rapidly changing world.[26] Political and economic arguments have been added to these explanations based on issues of constitutional theory and practice, including the weakening of the U.S. economic system, the problems of bipartisanism the United States faces, and the country's decreased political prestige.[27]

Furthermore, the emphasis that some prominent voices in U.S. constitutionalism put on issues such as originalism[28] or the right to bear arms[29] also leads to indifference in many international academic circles. These and other issues reveal a provincialism of some U.S. constitutionalism that also leads to a certain degree of rejection (or disinterest) by judges

---

Freedoms. It dates from 1982. You would almost certainly look at the European Convention on Human Rights . . .". The interview is available at: http://www.memritv.org/clip/en/3295.htm (accessed 5 September 2017).

[24] Stephen Breyer (2015), *The Court and the World: American Law and the New Global Realities* (New York: Knopf).

[25] Law and Versteeg (n 22).

[26] James Allan and Grant Huscroft (2006), "Constitutional rights coming home to roost? Rights internationalism in American courts", *San Diego L. Rev.*, **43** (1), 2.

[27] The literature about the decline of the U.S. is today wide and amply debated. Some of the most well known publications are Paul M. Kennedy (1987), *The Rise and Fall of the Great Powers* (London: Random House); Joseph S. Nye, *Bound to Lead: The Changing Nature of American Power* (1990) (New York: Basic Books); Niall Ferguson (2004), *Colossus: The Rise and Fall of the American Empire* (New York: Gardners Books); and Kevin Phillips (2006), "American theocracy: The peril and politics of radical religion, oil, and borrowed money in the 21st century", *Society and Business Review*, **4** (1), 82–83.

[28] Antonin Scalia (1989), "Originalism: The lesser evil", *U. Cin. L. Rev.*, **57**, 849 and Antonin Scalia (1997), *A Matter of Interpretation* (Princeton, NJ: Princeton University Press).

[29] See the second amendment of the U.S. Constitution where the right to bear arms is recognized.

and legal academics from other parts of the world.[30] Moreover, the fact that the greater part of U.S. constitutionalists have little interest in the constitutional theory and practice of other countries leads to a perception of superiority and isolation that is questioned in various academic spaces around the world.[31]

DOMINANT NARRATIVES: DEVASTATED LEGAL LANDSCAPES AND LIBERAL PARADISE

One might imagine that, given the immense geographical territory occupied by the Americas, in addition to the rich and complicated political, social and economic history of the continent since its colonization, the political and constitutional history of the United States and Latin America would, in turn, be constituted of both light and shadows, strengths and weaknesses. Surprisingly, however, these nuances are frequently lost in the dominant interpretations of the political and legal past and present of the countries forming the Americas. Thus, in the dominant narrative, Latin American history is homogenized, and its identity and history are both presented as single and continuous, and viewed negatively. U.S. history, by contrast, is presented as a unit without discontinuities that is viewed positively.[32] In this telling, Latin American constitutional history is typically described as a succession of dictatorships or *caudillo* and authoritarian governments. Its constitutions are conceived as mere rules on paper, legal norms that do not have application in the daily life of its citizens. Latin American law is thus commonly perceived by U.S. constitutionalism as a body of "failed law".[33]

---

[30] Ran Hirschl (2014), *Comparative Matters: The Renaissance of Comparative Constitutional Law* (Oxford: Oxford University Press), pp. 192–223. Justice Scalia's position on the role of comparative and international law in the U.S. legal system is a paradigmatic example of this argument. See, David C. Gray (2007), "Why Justice Scalia should be a constitutional comparativist sometimes", *Stanford Law Review*, **59** (5), 1249.

[31] A paradigmatic example is *Knight v. Florida*, 528 U.S. 990, 997 (1999). See also David S. Law and Wen-Chen Chang (2011), "The limits of global judicial dialogue", *Wash. L. Rev.*, **86**, 523, 525–27.

[32] See Keith Rosenn (1990–91), "The success of constitutionalism in the United States and its failure in Latin America: An Explanation", *University of Miami Inter-American Law Review*, **22**, 1 and Miguel Schor (2006), "Constitutionalism through the looking glass of Latin America", *Texas International Law Journal*, **41**, 1. For a critical view, see Jorge L. Esquirol (2013), "Legal Latin Americanism", *Yale Hum. Rts. & Dev. L.J.*, **16**, 145–70.

[33] Jorge L. Esquirol (2008), "The failed law of Latin America", *Am. J. Comp. L.*, **56**, 75.

Moreover, to the extent that it has an identity, Latin American constitutionalism is oftentimes seen as a mere replica of U.S. or European constitutionalism.[34] Latin American constitutional law is in this way interpreted as a derivative product that has little to offer to the global legal discussion, one that lacks great value as an object of academic study.

This narrative was synthesized powerfully in *Zappa v. Cruz*,[35] a 1998 decision from the United States District Court for the District of Puerto Rico. The decision merits interest for at least two reasons. First, the context for a lengthy interrogation of the understanding of law in Latin America as opposed to the United States is, at first glance, quite ordinary. In *Zappa*, the plaintiffs, non-Spanish speaking persons of Anglo descent, successfully argued that the circumstances of administering the exam to receive a license to sell real estate in Puerto Rico violated their constitutional Equal Protection rights, claiming that the English-language exam was more difficult than the Spanish-language exam and that, in any case, the exam was graded to give preference to native-born Puerto Ricans. As will be examined below, this led the U.S. District judge to explore the meaning of "culture" as it relates to law. In the end, as will be seen, the judge resoundingly affirmed the identity of Puerto Ricans as heirs to an enlightened U.S. legal traditon and not a dark, personality-driven Latin American legal tradition, proudly declaring that Puerto Ricans "live in a culture of personal freedom. That culture of freedom has nothing in common with any so-called Latin American culture and everything in common with the culture of the United States."[36] Second, and notably, the decision was issued by a Spanish-speaking federal judge from the United States born in Puerto Rico – by some estimations part of Latin America – but trained as a lawyer in the United States.[37] In the relevant part, the Court observed as follows:

> The political history of Latin America is one of dictatorship and its concomitant evils, corruption and civil war. Deriving from the notion of *caudillismo*—the distinctly Spanish philosophy of the ordering of man and his universe under which the individual's ego is so strong that it preempts broader concepts like community or nation—Latin American political systems have been little more than personality cults paying homage to political leaders, from the conquistadors, like Pizarro and Cortés, to the leaders of independence, like Bolívar and Hidalgo, to more recent heirs to power like Santa Ana, Perón, Castro, and

[34] Bonilla (n 15).

[35] *Zappa v. Cruz*, 30 F. Supp. 2d 123 (1998).

[36] *Zappa v. Cruz* (n 35), at 140.

[37] For a biography of Justice Jaime Pieras, see: http://www.prd.uscourts.gov/?q=node/208 (accessed 5 September 2017).

> Pinochet. Under political systems based on *caudillismo*, the governed in Latin American [*sic*] have placed less importance on ideals like liberty and justice than in the leader who is to incarnate those ideals. And the governing dictators have, also in the spirit of *caudillismo*, emphasized political separation over unity as a means of distinguishing and aggrandizing their personae. Employing personalistic political systems and elevating men over ideas have led to, in contrast to the United States, nations of men, not laws.[38]

The above-quoted language shows how the *Zappa* Court's interpretation of Latin American constitutionalism revolves around a set of ideas that homogenizes and impoverishes its history. Latin America is described as a devastated political and legal landscape. In particular, at least four aspects of the quoted language deserve emphasis. First, Latin America is seen as a geographically indistinct region. For the Court, Latin America constitutes a single space with no relevant borders. Mexico and Argentina, Ecuador and Brazil, or Costa Rica and Chile are thought of as a single space where there is no difference in terms of legal history. The issue here is not that there are no similarities between the region's countries. Among other things, of course, these countries share a colonial past, the Roman Catholic religion, language, traditions from the Iberian peninsula (Spanish and Portuguese), as well as notable levels of inequality, poverty and violence. To be sure, their multicultural populations constantly struggle to materialize the ideals of liberal democracies. Of course, one could cite as many differences, beginning with differences of geography and climate to resulting differences in immigrant populations and their contributions to the history of individual countries. The fact that the Court does not do so, however, highlights its preference for the narrative that prefers to see Latin America as a region of failed law.

Second, the Court's ruling assumes that Latin America is characterized by a unified and continuous regional history. In this view, the region is characterized by a single political and constitutional history, and it is rated negatively. In this telling, the region's history has an established beginning, the Conquest and European colonization, and it has a common present, the end of the twentieth century. The political and constitutional history of the countries that form Latin America is irrelevant. The Court identifies no appreciable differences; there are no nuances that must be explained.

Third, the quoted language is noteworthy because its tale of a Latin American history without discontinuities or differences is also marked by the idea that culture, on the one hand, and law and politics, on the other, have an organic relationship. Thus, Latin American authoritarianism is

---

[38] *Zappa v. Cruz* (n 35), at 138.

the fruit of a distinctly "Spanish philosophy": *caudillismo*. For this U.S. Federal Court, Spain-derived cultures have as one of their political products the cult of the charismatic leader and his prioritization in the legal order. In this narrative, Latin America is a region that inherited a lack of respect for the law from its Spanish forebears. Thus, Latin American culture is also characterized as a single culture emanating from a single source: Spain.[39] The Court also ascribes a static quality to this intertwined Latin American culture–law narrative. The description, finding that *caudillismo* is the essential characteristic of Latin culture, does not seem to allow, for example, the possibility of citizen-led change. Instead, it suggests that Latin America can only reach liberal democracy if the region stops following its essential ways of being and existing.

Fourth, the Court assumes a particular position between structure and contingent exception. Structurally, Latin America is an authoritarian culture. It we dig deeply, the Court argues, it would be possible to find some exceptions to the rule in its history, for example, democratic movements and successes in political and legal experimentation. Nevertheless, for the *Zappa* Court, these exceptions would only confirm the existence of the rule.

In contrast, the Court presented U.S. constitutionalism and political history in radical opposition to those of Latin America. If South and Central America is an example of a devastated legal and political landscape, the United States is the promised land, a liberal paradise incarnate. In the words of the Court:

> In the United States, on the other hand, we have struggled to ensure that both the letter and spirit of our Constitution, and especially the guarantees of individual liberty contained in the Bill of Rights, have been upheld and left unmolested by the government. While we have not won every battle, as various unhappy chapters in U.S. history attest, we continue to win the war and the United States remains a bastion of liberty, justice, and opportunity. The tenets of our political system are well-known and much imitated—it is a government of "we the people," by "we the people," and for "we the people." The people have retained the power by limiting that of the government. First, the Constitution enumerates the powers of the national government, establishing a federal system under which the individual states, within their jurisdictions, both share concurrent authority with the national government and enjoy powers not given the national government. Second, the enumerated powers of the national government are divided amongst the legislative, the judicial, and the executive branches. By that system of checks and balances, our founding fathers ensured that those who might have

[39] One has to wonder where this narrative leaves Portuguese-speaking Brazil or, for that matter, the English- and Dutch-speaking former colonies in the northeast of the continent and the Antilles.

> in mind dictatorial authority within the national government would be hobbled in any attempt to consolidate power. Third, and perhaps most importantly, the Constitution ensures that certain individual liberties may not be infringed upon by either the national or, via the Fourteenth Amendment, the state governments. These individual liberties, aside from abridging the governments' ability to impose upon individual citizens . . . enhance the citizenry's ability to police the government . . . Under this system, the citizens of the United States have the right to pursue the ends they desire, subject only to the laws created by those they elect, whose powers are cabined as described by the Constitution.[40]

For the Court, the United States is, in short, the conceptual and material opposite of Latin America. The Court suggests this is so for at least four reasons. In each instance, notably, the United States and its legal and constitutional traditions are placed in opposition to those alleged to be the Latin American way. First, the Court celebrates the United States for its tolerance of diversity, as follows: "[a]lthough often given the moniker, 'melting pot,' the United States is perhaps better described as a mixing bowl, a place where many 'cultural' elements coexist to form a whole without losing their individual flavors." In the United States, declares the Court, "classifications based on such criteria [i.e. ethnic or racial or other identity factors] are considered wrong, both morally and legally. Indeed, such classifications are wrong precisely because they do not work . . . [and] the nation as a whole has generally strived to rise above such classifications, especially during the last century." [41] By implication, as the Court's opinion goes on to demonstrate, this is the opposite of Latin America, where diversity and difference are not tolerated.[42] The fact that this ignores the cultural, social and political diversity of Latin America, a region whose history is as heavily marked as that of the United States by diverse waves of immigration from Africa, Asia and Europe,[43] only

---

[40] *Zappa v. Cruz* (n 35), at 139, affirmed by *DiMarco-Zappa v. Cabanillas*, 238 F.3d 25 (1st Cir., 2001).

[41] *Zappa v. Cruz* (n 35), at 135–36.

[42] See, e.g., *Zappa v. Cruz* (n 35), at 138.

[43] See generally, for example, Teresa A. Meade, *History of Modern Latin America: 1800 to the Present* (2016), 2nd edn (Chichester: Wiley-Blackwell). Specifically, it can be noted, for instance, that in addition to receiving more African-born slaves than any other country, Brazil has the world's largest communities of expatriates from Japan and the Levant. See, e.g., Walter Hawthorne (2010), *From Africa to Brazil: Culture, Identity, and an Atlantic Slave Trade, 1600–1830* (Cambridge: Cambridge University Press) (on forced African immigration to Brazil); Jeffrey Lesser (2013), *Immigration, Ethnicity, and National Identity in Brazil, 1808 to the Present* (Cambridge: Cambridge University Press) (on Asian, European and Middle Eastern immigration); Stewart Lone (2001), *The Japanese Community in Brazil, 1908–1940: Between Samurai and Carnival* (Basingstoke:

underscores the surprising power of this trope. Yet each of the Court's categories used to evaluate Latin America, when employed to evaluate the United States, renders positive conclusions.

Second, the history of the United States as a geographic and political entity is characterized by unity and continuity, but one where that unity and continuity represents a progressive movement and process of constant improvement. In this account, since it was founded, beginning with the Revolution and the proclamation of the Constitution of 1787, the U.S. political community has been, in the Court's narrative, committed to and worked to materialize liberal ideas. As the Court sees it, the U.S. liberal Constitution is a set of rules in action, not rules on paper. The principles of popular sovereignty, legality, separation of powers and individual rights do not exist merely in the Constitution's text, but form part of the daily life of all U.S. citizens. This stands in sharp contrast for the Court with the history of Latin America, which has suffered the imposition of "personalistic [*sic*] political systems and elevating men over ideas", creating "nations of men, not laws".[44]

Fourth, in the United States, regardless of their moral convictions, the Court argues that U.S. citizens are committed to a series of political values that allow for protecting their differences. According to the Court, the U.S. political community distinguishes between morality and justice. In the private sphere, U.S. citizens can construct their moral projects without the undue intervention of the state. There they can believe whatever they think is relevant, provided that they do not violate the rights of others by doing so. In the public sphere, however, there is a consensus around liberal values. Political values are clearly distinguished from the moral values that guide the life projects of the individuals that form the political community. While the Court recognizes that there have been some dark times in the political and constitutional history of the United States, these are presented as an exception to the rule. In stark contrast, in Latin America, explains the Court, the rule of men and not laws resulted in a situation

---

Palgrave Macmillan). Argentina's history also is marked by heavy immigration from Italy and other European countries (see, e.g. May E. Bletz (2010), *Immigration and Acculturation in Brazil and Argentina: 1890–1929* (Basingstoke: Palgrave Macmillan). The entire region has witnessed waves of Chinese immigration (see, e.g., Walton Look Lai (2010), *Indentured Labor, Caribbean Sugar: Chinese and Indian Migrants to the British West Indies, 1838–1918* (Baltimore: Johns Hopkins University Press) and Robert Chao Romero (2012), *The Chinese in Mexico, 1882–1940* (Arizona: University of Arizona Press)). These examples are merely illustrative, but make clear that the region has as much a claim to be a "melting pot" or "mixing bowl" as does the United States.

[44] *Zappa v. Cruz* (n 35), at 137–38.

in which "few Latin American leaders have felt themselves bound by any constitutional restraints. The result is a national history filled with poverty, suffering, repression, corruption, sycophancy, torture, assassination, and death in the field of battle."[45] In this last quotation, the Court thus again affirms not only the image of Latin America as a devastated legal and political landscape, but also betrays a willingness to disregard difference and nuance: Latin America has "a" national history.

Admittedly, *Zappa* is but one example of a narrative imagining Latin America as a devastated legal landscape in contrast to the U.S. realization of a liberal paradise. There are, no doubt, more complex narratives about U.S and Latin American constitutional law. However, it is our suggestion that the views expressed in *Zappa* are hardly the imaginings of one rogue federal judge. Indeed, the opinion was positively cited subsequently by other federal courts, repeating some of *Zappa*'s stereotypes of Latin American *caudillos.*[46] But our suggestion is that it may be a paradigmatic example, one that attests to widely held views of "failed" Latin American law.[47] One premise that underlines the chapters that appear in this volume is the view that this interpretation, one that idealizes U.S. constitutionalism and underrates Latin American constitutional achievements, is radically flawed. The authors whose work appears here strive, from a variety of perspectives and angles, to erode the dominance of a view like that

---

45 *Zappa v. Cruz* (n 35), at 138.

46 See *American Civil Liberties Union of Florida, Inc. v. Miami-Dade County School Bd.*, 557 F.3d 1177 (11th Cir., 2009), a case involving a history textbook's description of Cuba as not being sufficiently critical of the Cuban government, quoting *Zappa* (n 35), at 139, to the effect that "[s]ince 1898, Cuba, without benefit of the United States Constitution, has wallowed in poverty and corruption, mostly under dictatorial rule." Or consider the positive treatment of *Zappa* in a 2000 case involving a challenge to the inability of Puerto Ricans to vote, in which the Federal District Court for Puerto Rico lamented that "the United States citizens residing in Puerto Rico, who sit in the farthest frontier of the United States in the Atlantic and who have been U.S. citizens in good standing for close to 100 years, have embraced and made theirs a political culture similar to that of the United States and different from the political culture of other Latin American countries, and yet have not enjoyed the rights that go hand-in-hand with their political culture". *Igartua de la Rosa v. U.S.*, 107 F.Supp. 2d 140 (D.C.P.R., 2000). The *Igartua de la Rosa* Court positively quoted the *Zappa* decision, 30 F.Supp. 2d at 140, as follows: "If there is no political freedom, there can be no economic freedom where individuals can develop their innate abilities. That is why the United States' main claim to glory is not predicated upon the powerhouse of Wall Street but the Bill of Rights that protected the rights of citizens in a free society which created a society of equals devoid of the caste system and made possible a Wall Street and the American Dream."

47 Esquirol (n 33).

expressed in *Zappa*. In the process, the articles collected here together reveal some of the many achievements, innovations, challenges, weaknesses, and struggles of Latin American constitutionalism in particular and Latin American law in general.

THE GENERAL AND SPECIFIC OBJECTIVES OF THE BOOK

The articles collected, which form the chapters in this volume, cover a wide range of topics, dealing with the constitutions, law and constitution, and law-making histories and processes in countries across the Americas. The chapters offer a rich tapestry of analysis and reflections about constitutionalism in the abstract; they also contain specific and comparative case studies. In the process, the collection, taken together, reveals not only the strengths and ambitions of modern constitutional practice, but also its challenges and debilities. In this, the chapters contribute to debates about constitutionalism in ways both general and more specific. On the one hand, the authors in this volume are concerned not only with constitutionalism in the Americas but with modern questions of constitutionalism and constitution-making in general. On the other, the authors are concerned with specific, regional ambitions, tensions, conflicts, and contributions.

CONSTITUTIONALISM IN THE AMERICAS AND GLOBAL CONSTITUTIONALISM: GENERAL THEMES

At the most general level, the chapters reveal many of the concerns and preoccupations that characterize much debate about the role of constitutions in modern democratic states, and not only in the Americas. The shared concerns in the chapters can thus be divided into four aspects. First, the chapters reveal a consistent focus on the central question of what *interests* constitutions serve to protect. "Interest" in this context refers to the individuals and groups that constitutional (or any legal) provisions seek to support and promote. Second, they demonstrate a concern about the *functions* of constitutions in democratic societies; they ask about the aims pursued by constitutions. For example, should a constitution serve as a general outline of what individuals may do within a given social order and, conversely, what the government should not do? Or should constitutions be more aggressive statements of policy commitment, detailing the substantive protections a nation will provide its citizens? Third, they evidence engagement with the question of what *form* of constitution or constitution-making best serves the aims of governmental stability and prosperity in modern democracies. This aspect follows directly from the question of function. Thus, for example, a constitution mostly dedicated to the articulation of political and civil rights (such as the U.S. Constitution) will likely have a shorter form and leave more questions of governance unspecified than a constitution that consists of a charter of a wide range of social, economic and other positive rights (as is the case in most Latin American constitutions). Fourth and finally, the chapters address questions of the reach and the limits of *context*, and specifically the implications of – and reasons for – borrowing from one constitutional model and tradition and importing it into another. This is to recognize that different social systems, cultures, histories and related concerns inevitably affect the situations in which constitutions are prepared, making it a risky proposition to introduce wholesale large sections of the legal charters of other countries, where words and concepts may have an entirely different valence, and so different effects. As a consequence of this focus on context, a final concern seen in these chapters is comparative.

Interests

The Federalist Papers written by Alexander Hamilton, John Jay and James Madison addressed the question of what interests constitutions protect. For example, in Federalist No. 84, Alexander Hamilton famously objected to the inclusion of a Bill of Rights in the U.S. Constitution, when he affirmed as follows: "it is evident, therefore, that . . . [bills of rights] have no application to constitutions professedly founded upon the power of the people, and executed by their immediate representatives and servants. Here, in strictness, the people surrender nothing, and as they retain every thing, they have no need of particular reservations." What is of interest here in the quoted language is Hamilton's concern with the question of whether and how to protect the interests of the many as against the few. More than two centuries later, as some of these essays demonstrate, that continues to be a central question that constitutions are meant to address. Thus, for example, Roberto Gargarella examines constitutional "*organization of powers*, and . . . the *structure of rights* – and the way in which they relate to each other", first in the U.S. context and then in the case of some Latin American constitutions. In his account, the U.S. constitutional model effected a high degree of what he calls "internal consistency" by organizing governmental powers in the service of comparatively modest rights' provision goals, namely "the promotion of individual freedom and the limitation of power". Thus, the interests protected by the the U.S. Constitution are largely limited to individual ones and, at the time of its drafting, largely the individual rights of white males. (Notably, in this context, Gargarella labels the "constitutional failure" to address slavery to constitute "the main omission – the main internal inconsistency – of the U.S. Constitution"). By contrast, in Gargarella's telling, many Latin American constitutions are much more inclusive and generous in terms of their rights' structures, although powers are not organized in such a way as to permit those rights to be fully exercised. He therefore finds them to be less internally consistent – the generous rights structure is not balanced by an organization of powers that facilitates that structure. The consequence, for Gargarella, is that the organization of powers in most Latin American constitutions is "characterized by its verticalism and its hostility towards democracy and popular participation in politics". Simply put, the interests the constitutions say they protect are held at bay by other aspects of the same documents.

For contributor David Landau, the key question to ask in terms of the interests protected by constitutions is whether the document protects what he labels the "majoritarian" or "counter-majoritarian" interests. Landau's analysis suggests, somewhat in contrast to Gargarella, that constitutions generally tend to serve majoritarian goals. The "myth of the heroic court" in cases like *Brown v. Board of Education*[48] aside, suggests Landau, courts up and down the Americas tend on balance to favor majoritarian interests: "courts in the United States are likely to be the voice of the marginalized in the face of a hostile or indifferent political system". Despite the wide menu of socioeconomic rights contained in most post-colonial Latin American constitutions, Landau suggests that majoritarian tendencies tend to dominate in Latin America as well.

In contrast to Gargarella and Landau, however, Tanya Katerí Hernández finds some promise for counter-majoritarian (or minority interests) in constitutional structures that contain a menu of explicit socioeconomic rights. Hernández suggests that the right to work contained in the Brazilian national charter may serve to protect more vulnerable groups in society, and specifically Afro-Brazilians, whereas the lack of such an articulated right in the United States prevents mostly Anglo, male judges from having to consider its dimensions and value.

Functions

Another question central to the concerns animating the contributors to this volume is that of the functions of a constitution in a modern democratic

48 *Brown v. Board of Education*, 347 U.S. 483 (1954).

society. This is to ask, for example, whether a constitution is to be only, in Michael Dorf's memorable phrase, "aspirational" in character, or if it is a grounded legal tool, the ultimate authority for resolution of disputes about the limits and extents of rights and obligations of the members of modern democratic societies. The authors assembled here approach this question in different and provocative ways. Importantly, too, the juxtaposition of the chapters reveals to careful readers a robust debate about the answer to this and related questions. Jorge Esquirol, for example, challenges the orthodoxy that Latin American constitutionalism (and law) constitutes a failed project merely because Latin American constitutions are constantly being reworked and amended. Perhaps, Esquirol asks readers to consider, Latin American (or other, non-U.S.) constitutional practice needs to be evaluated on its own terms. By this logic, frequent rewriting may be a sign of success, a willingness to change with the times and not a consequence of a failure effectively to draft a document that will stand the test of time. As Esquirol notes, despite the myth that the U.S. Constitution persists because of its clarity and consistency, in fact there exist "numerous gaps, ambiguities, and contradictions within the U.S. Constitution – or other constitutions for that matter – concerning executive powers, states' rights, international treaties, and other anomalies not usually highlighted in uncritical accounts of U.S. law". Thus, Esquirol pushes us to question whether the U.S. Constitution – so often held as a model of thoughtful, succinct drafting – in fact serves the comprehensive function in defining the U.S. political and social order that it is sometimes alleged to do.

Similarly, Daniel Bonilla, in his contribution, among other things asks readers to consider why dominant narratives emerge that control the way we think about legal subjects over time and in different locations (what he calls "spaces"). These narratives, Bonilla warns, can occlude other legal traditions, practices and habits that may be useful – or, one might even posit, necessary – for the functioning of particular societies and legal cultures. In terms of function, then, Bonilla asks readers to reflect on how laws and constitutions are produced as a consequence of legal epistemologies that may not align with the histories, needs and characteristics of different societies and political orders. As a consequence, his contribution suggests, uncritically inherited legal epistemologies may function to determine legal content in less-than-ideal ways.

Applying a more historical method, Gargarella's contribution raises related concerns about constitutional function. Looking at examples of constitution-writing practice in Latin America back in the nineteenth century, Gargarella prods readers to consider the ways in which some constitutions can almost deliberately tolerate contradictions and opposing interests, so that constitutions become very conscious expressions of political consequences. Consistency, Gargarella's piece suggests, may be an appealing criterion by which to evaluate constitutions as written instruments, but to insist upon it as the only way to read constitutional practice may leave us with an impoverished understanding of the role, of the function, constitutions play in state creation and self-articulation – not just of law, but in processes of social and political ordering.

A darker, more alarmed view of the dangers of leaving well enough alone and *not* rewriting is contained in Francisca Pou's historical and legal analysis of the Mexican constitution. Mexico has, Pou shows, one of the most stable constitutional frameworks known. The 1917 Constitution remains in force, although constantly revised and amended. Thus, as Pou Giménez demonstrates, the Mexican Constitution functions both as a symbol of historical stability in a system that simultaneously values the function of reform. "Reformism", she explains, "is a badge of Mexican constitutional life: it speaks of the deep bonds the Mexican legal system retains with the past, but it should equally convey the idea of permanent, never-ending adjustment of basic rules and institutions." But Pou also questions whether a commitment to – or a tolerance of – stability in the form of adherence to the historical document – is a net positive for a dynamic and conflictual social and legal order. That is, Pou's chapter implicitly implores readers to compare the benefits of deliberate, comprehensive revision of constitutional structures at moments of change or crisis. Whole scale revision, she suggests, may direct societies to reflect on the function constitutions can serve to articulate values and priorities.

Still yet another view of the function of constitutions is provided by Javier Couso. Couso provocatively argues that Venezuela's rejection of and withdrawal from the Inter-American Human Rights System, rather than being viewed as an impetuous, heretical move, may be thought of as a carefully considered political and legal act in service of protection of Venezuelan sovereignty and its constitutional values. While critical of the Venezuelan action, Couso further locates the decision to withdraw within a longer reactive tradition in Latin American constitutional and legal argument aimed to protect state sovereignty in the face of U.S. imperialist or neocolonial moves.

Form

The question of form, of what shape constitutions should ideally take, is another longstanding issue addressed both explicitly and implicitly by many of the contributions assembled here. To be concerned with form is not, to be clear, merely a matter of being concerned with the cosmetic aspect of a constitution. On the contrary, as the debate in the Federalist

Papers mentioned above illustrates, the question of form is intricately connected to that of substance (which embraces both questions of interests and function).

Pou's analysis of Mexican constitutionalism is a case in point. As indicated above, Pou documents the fact that a notable feature of the Mexican Constitution is to respect its revolutionary roots – leaving much of the original document intact – while simultaneously committing to change with endless amendment. In this way, form follows function, producing a document that, in her telling, combines "length, detail, and other traits . . . [so as to] render the Mexican Constitution overweight and a bit oppressive as a directly enforceable charter, and makes it difficult for citizens to 'appropriate' it". By contrast, Esquirol suggests that the very "malleability" of Latin American constitutions (meaning documents susceptible to frequent revision) may reflect a form that more closely reflects social and political values – revision and amendment may thus be viewed as evidence of social and legal dynamism rather than as signs of confusion and disorder – than a document written centuries ago. In this way, both authors engage critically with a question that has long bedeviled constitutional theory.

For their part, Law and Ginsburg, in their contribution, arrive at an interesting conclusion with respect to the amendments characteristic of Latin American (and other, again non-U.S.) constitutions. Specifically, Law and Ginsburg suggest that the different waves of constitution-rewriting that have swept Latin America since the nineteenth century have resulted in constitutions that "exhibit growing dissimilarity to the U.S. Constitution in both their scope and their substantive content". Moreover, they suggest, the form and substance of Latin American constitutions is not only evermore unlike the U.S. charter, but is also distinctive as compared to other parts of the world. Like many of the other papers in this volume (Bonilla and Esquirol, notably), this conclusion opens the door for further research into how these new forms both shape and reflect the societies in which they are produced. That is, their research demonstrates the need for further examination of the ways in which constitutional forms are changing, in Latin America and elsewhere, and to question the consequences of that change.

Context

Many of the articles collected here reflect the changing context in which constitutions are made and amended. With regard to the Americas, most prominently, the articles both document a waning dependence on or the utility of the U.S. model, for at least three reasons. First, as

Bonilla's chapter notes, the insularity that often characterizes U.S. legal production may not always serve a region increasingly accustomed to engage in plural and global legal debate. Second, several of the authors touch on the fact that developments in the region such as the positive constitutional treatment for indigenous and other world views (features not characteristic of U.S. constitutional practice, despite the presence of significant indigenous minorities in the United States) may in fact be leading to a new context and habit of constitutional practice. The region thus, through constitutional practice, may be seen to be demonstrating confidence in its own values and contributions – a vote in favor of acknowledging local and national social, political and, thus, legal context. Moreover, in different ways, both Couso and Fernanda Nicola address these positive changes and also trace the consequences of illiberal tendencies in U.S. political and social life so as to turn Latin American (and other) countries elsewhere in their search for new legal ideas, arguments and ways of doing. For Couso, continuing imperialist and neocolonial tendencies – one could simply call it arrogance – of U.S. legal actors, especially notable in the post 9/11 clamp-down on some civil liberties, is forcing the hand of Latin American constitutionalists to forge a distinct path in defense of national interests. Nicola, by contrast, examines the consequences of 9/11 and other international events to transform the focus of U.S. constitutional and legal work into the creation of a semi-autonomous discipline of National Security Law, rendering the United States more isolated and backward than its Latin American neighbors (and again, other countries). Third, the chapters themselves demonstrate a deep, critical trend in thinking about constitutions in the region. Thus, for instance, while Gargarella laments the failure of "internal consistency" in Latin American constitutional structures in which substantive rights are not supported by an organization of powers that allows for their ready exercise, the identification of the problem (one echoed, for example, in Pou's contribution) must constitute a positive step in the possible resolution of the conflict.

In sum, this section has endeavored to demonstrate that the chapters assembled here do far more than merely document trends in Latin American or U.S. constitutionalism. To be sure, they do that, as will be explored presently. But they also engage powerfully with longstanding and modern trends in constitutional debate and argument, including questions of what interests constitutions protect (and how), constitutional function and form, and the context in which constitutions are produced and used.

CONSTITUTIONAL ANALYSIS IN THE AMERICAS: THE SPECIFIC AIMS OF THE BOOK AND ITS STRUCTURE

The volume also, of course, grapples specifically with questions of constitutional analysis in the Americas. In this regard, three features of the chapters, taken as a whole, merit attention. First, the volume seeks to question arguments and readings that constitute the homogenizing view of U.S. and Latin American constitutionalism, arguments and readings lacking in recognition of nuance and difference. Second, this volume also seeks to contribute to the construction of more subtle and complex interpretations of constitutionalism throughout the Americas, interpretations that can shed light on both successes and failures of the political and legal projects of countries in the Americas. Third and finally, this volume seeks to contribute to an effort to produce more rich, textured descriptions and evaluations of the relationships between U.S. and Latin American constitutionalism, as well as to the creation of more horizontal and more fluid exchanges between them.

To meet these objectives, the book is divided into three sections. Section I examines the relationship between Latin American and U.S. constitutionalism. In particular, it examines the widely held idea that Latin America is a mere space of reproduction and diffusion of U.S. constitutional production (or that of some continental European countries, like Germany or Spain), while the United States is a context-universal original legal knowledge production suitable for export the world over. Two chapters form this first section of the book. In the first, Daniel Bonilla argues that the production, exchange, and use of legal knowledge are subject to a political economy. These processes, he explains, are governed by a series of rules and principles that determine the conditions of possibility for the creation of, commerce in, and consumption of legal theory, doctrine and practices. For Bonilla, this political economy is not neutral. It constructs a specific subject of knowledge that acts within a particular space and time.

This first chapter therefore has a double objective. On the one hand, it seeks to describe and analyze the political economy model that dominates the contemporary legal imagination. In this sense, it seeks to examine the conceptual structure of what Bonilla calls the free market of legal ideas model. This is the model that typically serves to explain the prevalence of U.S. constitutionalism in Latin America. On the other hand, it seeks to describe and analyze an alternative, peripheral political economy model that would best explain the real dynamics that regulate the creation, trade, and use of legal knowledge. To reach this objective, Bonilla sheds light on the conceptual structures that form what he calls the colonial model of legal knowledge production. In practice, this is the model that regulates key components of the relationships between Latin American and U.S. constitutionalism. His chapter thus aims to shed light on the types of subject that the models of legal knowledge production lead to, as well as the way they imagine the time and space in which these subjects are situated. Likewise, it seeks to shed light on the most precise rules and principles that determine how these models imagine the production, exchange, and use of legal knowledge.

In the second chapter, Jorge Esquirol argues that the relationship between Latin American and U.S. constitutionalism is not horizontal. Esquirol argues that the vertical nature of the relationship is illustrated particularly well in the relative importance of the Latin American constitutional courts and the Supreme Court of the United States. While the U.S. Supreme Court enjoys broad prestige in Latin America, Esquirol explains, Latin American courts have a questionable reputation in the United States (when they are visible at all). While the U.S. Court is widely cited by Latin American court and academics, the case law of Latin American courts is not known and rarely cited by U.S. law professors and courts. For Esquirol, this relationship of subordination of Latin American to U.S. constitutional law is explained by two variables that have contributed to creating a negative image of Latin American constitutional law in the United States, variables that have been instrumental in constructing an idealized image of U.S. liberal constitutionalism and a hyper-realist image of the failures of Latin American constitutionalism.

The first variable is the concept of "obstruction of justice" in international law. This concept presents Latin American justice systems as radically dysfunctional. The second variable is the law and development movement and its impact on contemporary comparative law. Esquirol argues that for the law and development movement Latin American constitutionalism has failed. This movement explains the failure by the great number of constitutions that have governed the countries of the region, because their constitutions are easily changed and because constitutional law is viewed as indistinguishable from politics in the region. Given the vertical nature of the relationship between U.S. and Latin American constitutionalism and the imbalance of power that exists between the two regions, Esquirol also questions whether the construction of a global constitutional law would be desirable for Latin America, wondering whether global constitutionalism would be a more subtle but equally effective instrument for preventing the emergence or consolidation of a truly Latin American constitutionalism.

Section II of the volume, "Latin American Constitutionalism", provides a critical examination of Latin America's experience with both liberal and radical constitutionalism largely over the last twenty-five years, a period that represents the most recent wave of constitutional rewriting amidst the consolidation of democratically elected regimes. On the one hand, it analyzes the experience of countries like Colombia, Mexico and Argentina with the liberal constitutional model; on the other hand, it evaluates some dimensions of the Ecuadorian, Bolivian and Venezuelan experiences with what is commonly known as twenty-first-century socialism or radical constitutionalism. This part of the book assesses some of the costs and benefits of these two models and their future.

In the first chapter of this section, Roberto Gargarella examines the similarities and differences between U.S. and Latin American constitutional law. Gargarella indicates that, although U.S. constitutionalism has influenced Latin American constitutionalism in some circumstances, these two traditions constitute somewhat different ways of understanding constitutional law. Gargarella argues that Latin American constitutionalism has departed from U.S. constitutionalism on three significant points: it has incorporated a much broader list of rights than the U.S. Bill of Rights (which he says has the effect of allowing more substantive protection of egalitarian principles), it has favored hyper-presidential systems, and it has centralized territorial organization and the exercise of state political and legal power. Gargarella also states that these differences make the Latin American constitutional model more conservative and less consistent with respect to the exercise of power but more progressive on social, economic and cultural matters than the U.S. constitutional model.

In the section's second chapter, Javier Couso concentrates on the radical democracies of Venezuela, Ecuador and Bolivia. Couso's argument revolves around three axes. First, he argues that one of the innovative elements of Latin American constitutionalism has been its receptiveness to international human rights law and its commitment to the Inter-American Human Rights System. Second, he indicates that one of the characteristics of radical constitutionalism has been its staunch defense of the principle of national sovereignty. Finally, he states that the defense of national sovereignty has gone hand-in-hand with a constant defense of two principles of international law: the principle of self-determination of peoples and the principle of non-intervention.

Couso then argues that the defense of these three principles has ended up pitting radical constitutionalism against international human rights law. For Couso, for instance, Venezuela's denunciation of the American Convention on Human Rights is not a consequence of a circumstantial political situation, but an effect of the defense of the abovementioned three legal principles. This situation also allows for thinking that other countries of the Bolivarian block could make a similar decision in the near future. Finally, Couso argues that the illiberal turn taken by U.S. constitutionalism, shown in the violations of due process in the Guantanamo prison, selective assassinations, and the practice of torture, has facilitated the questioning of the Inter-American Human Rights System by radical constitutionalism.

In the third text of this section, Francisca Pou provides a critical analysis of Mexican constitutionalism. For Pou, this is characterized by "reformism", i.e., the capacity simultaneously to maintain close ties with the political/legal past and also to present itself as a system in continuous and uninterrupted transformation. The analysis of Mexican reformism advanced by Pou is both static and dynamic and is materialized in the following four steps: first, she presents the basic structure of the Mexican constitutional model; second, she provides an analysis of its key content: the standards, institutions, and substantive rules that form its backbone; third, she provides an assessment of the decision-making processes permitted and promoted by the Constitution; fourth and last, she evaluates what she calls the frequency variable, which is nothing other than weighing the effects that living under a constantly changing constitutional regime have had on Mexicans. Pou concludes that, in a context of institutional fragility and social and political exclusion, the reformism that characterizes the Mexican system has allowed profound institutional change to be perpetually controlled and prevented from above. Pou likewise concludes that the Mexican legal and political system will only be successful if there is a radical qualitative change in its institutions, rules, and principles.

In the last chapter of this section, David Landau provides an analysis of the judicialization of socioeconomic rights in Latin America. Landau argues that over the last few decades, the courts of the region have made it possible for socioeconomic rights to be judicially enforced. Nevertheless, Landau also indicates that the effect of this judicial application of socioeconomic rights has had little impact on the levels of social justice in the region. For Landau, this paradox could be explained if, as indicated by the specialized U.S. literature, it becomes evident that the courts are institutions that usually protect the positions of the social majorities and therefore tend to favor the interests of the politically powerful sectors. For Landau, this pattern of behavior has two primary components in Latin American constitutional courts: the model of individual application of socioeconomic rights and negative judicial requirements. This allows claimants, generally middle-class citizens, to realize their rights. However, this kind of decision does not attack the underlying problem preventing the solidification of socioeconomic rights for broad layers of the population. Negative judicial requirements allow for declaring the unconstitutionality of legal norms that convey public austerity policies. Nevertheless,

Landau argues, these decisions do not contribute to the realization of socioeconomic rights for the majority of the population; they only eliminate a norm that is considered unconstitutional from the legal system.

Landau finds, however, that some patterns of Latin American case law go against the arguments that are typically presented in the dominant constitutional doctrine on socioeconomic rights. One the one hand, for Landau, the Courts fill the void left by institutions that defraud the population by noncompliance with their duties with respect to socioeconomic rights. On the other hand, the Courts block unpopular measures taken by governments as a consequence of pressure from powerful national and international interests. Finally, Latin American case law on socioeconomic rights contributes to the creation of a constitutional culture that brings constitutions closer to the citizens, making law relevant in their daily life. However, Landau argues that the Latin American courts cannot easily be converted into institutional vehicles that are effective in materializing the social and economic rights of the region's citizens.

Section III of the volume, "US Constitutionalism in the 21st Century", examines some of the strengths of the U.S. constitutional model, the idea that its global influence has supposedly weakened, and some of the paths it could take in the future. In the first chapter, David Law and Tom Ginsburg provide a quantitative, comparative analysis of Latin American constitutionalism over the last 60 years, aiming to examine the following three recurring legal and political concerns: the enormous influence of U.S. constitutional law, the excessive control of power by the executive branch, and the high level of human rights violations. This analysis focuses on the content of the constitutional texts taken from the quantitative data of "big n" or big data, and it seeks to question the stereotypes of and preconceptions about the creation of constitutional norms in the region.

With respect to the first issue, Law and Ginsburg argue that Latin American constitutions have increasingly moved away from both the U.S. model and models from other regions of the world, such as Europe and Asia. With respect to the second issue, they argue that over time Latin American constitutions have decreased the formal powers granted to the executive branch and have been generous in the recognition and application of human rights. Finally, Law and Ginsburg argue that over the last two decades the distance between the rules recognizing human rights in Latin American constitutions and the social reality has become shorter. For these two authors, the differences between the constitutional promises and the daily life of common people in Latin America have decreased over the last twenty years.

In the second chapter, Fernanda Nicola questions those who affirm that the influence of U.S. legal thought is currently in decline. For Nicola, the diffusion of legal ideas that originate in the United States remains the rule, although the content exported and the procedures for doing so have changed. This transformation of the forms and content of U.S. legal ideas spread around the world can be seen on three intersecting axes: first, rights-centered U.S. constitutionalism has given way to the exportation of legal products related to national security law. The latter consists of a set of theories and practices that justify and indicate the means for adequate development of timely military interventions, actions against terrorism, and war between nations. Second, legal education focused on training critical students, social justice, and full-time professors is being questioned in the United States by those who, after the crisis experienced by law schools, think that legal education should aim to train attorneys to pass the bar exam, advance transactions that are useful for local businesses, and be taught by part-time professors. Finally, the exportation by U.S.-educated foreign legal elites of the most conservative interpretations of the educational model dominant in the United States. Nicola concludes, then, that the influence of U.S. legal ideas remains as notable around the world as it was in the twentieth century.

In the volume's final chapter, Tanya Hernández argues that the U.S. legal system's failure to recognize the right to work has negatively impacted the case law on racial issues issued by the Supreme Court, unlike Latin America where this right has been recognized formally. For Hernández, the lack of a right to work does not allow U.S. judges to examine the specific contexts in which work spaces are immersed. In these spaces, racial prejudice and the vulnerability of workers are the rule. Hernández concentrates her critical analysis on three key labor case law rulings of the U.S. Supreme Court: *Vance v. Ball State University*,[49] *University of Texas Southwestern Medical Center v. Nassar*[50] and *Ricci v. De Stefano*.[51] From Hernández's perspective, these three rulings show the disconnection between the Supreme Court and the realities of the U.S. labor market in paradigmatic fashion.

In sum, the chapters seek to provide a varied and useful primer to the robust debates and struggles over constitutionalism in the Americas today – not just in the United States but also and indeed, even more so, in Latin America. We hope that your review of these chapters will prove instructive and prompt further work and discussion in the area.

---

49 *Vance v. Ball State University*, 133 S. Ct. 2434 (2013).

50 *University of Texas Southwestern Medical Center v. Nassar*, 133 S. Ct. 2517 (2013).

51 *Ricci v. De Stefano*, 557 U.S. 557 (2009).

PART I

The Relationship between Latin American and U.S. Constitutionalism

2. The political economy of legal knowledge

Daniel Bonilla Maldonado

INTRODUCTION

The production, exchange, and use of legal knowledge are subject to a political economy.[1] These processes neither happen in a vacuum, nor are they developed in a venturesome manner. They are governed by a series of rules and principles that determine the conditions allowing the creation, commerce and consumption of legal theories, doctrines, and practices. These rules and principles specify where and who can create legal knowledge, how this knowledge is legitimized, which channels are appropriate for its dissemination, who may use it adequately, and how it may be used effectively. The political economy of legal knowledge contributes to the creation of our legal and political imagination, and therefore conditions the way we construct, perceive, and describe legal knowledge. As a consequence, this political economy is not neutral; it constructs a specific subject of knowledge[2] that acts within a particular space[3] and time.[4] More precisely, this political economy presupposes a subject, a space, and a time that determine the way we understand the processes that allow for the emergence, trading, and consumption of legal knowledge.

However, the political economy of legal knowledge is not only a set of abstract concepts, rules, and principles. This set of ideas and norms determines the way people perceive legal knowledge, and therefore the types of

---

[1] I understand "political economy" as the description and analysis of a system of production, distribution, and trade. In this case, the good that is produced, distributed, and exchanged is legal knowledge. *See* Barry Stewart Clark (1998), *Political Economy: A Comparative Approach* (New York: Greenwood Publishing), pp. 18–20.

[2] Paul Khan (1999), *The Cultural Study of Law* (Chicago: University of Chicago Press), pp. 77–86.

[3] Id. at 55–77.

[4] Id. at 43–55.

behavior considered appropriate within this social field.[5] Consequently, these concepts, rules and principles carry the important effects of enabling, while simultaneously limiting the actions of legal actors. Which context for the production of legal knowledge may be considered rich or poor, what value should be granted to legal ideas produced, what direction does the exchange of legal knowledge take, what issues are considered valuable objects of study, how and where this knowledge may be made public, and who can make appropriate use of the knowledge, are questions conditioned by the political economy of legal knowledge that dominates our legal and political imagination at a given moment in time.

Understanding, analyzing and evaluating this political economy will thus allow us to grasp some practical questions that affect our political communities on a daily basis. This will allow us to understand issues such as why legal transplants are typically exported by Global North countries and imported by Global South countries; why the grammar of modern constitutionalism is primarily created and managed by a small group of European and North American political theorists; why the constitutional products of the Global South appear on the margins of the global market of legal ideas;[6] why an important number of legal scholars from the Global South can now speak knowledgeably of cases like *Roe v. Wade*[7] but few can mention the ruling that decriminalized abortion in Canada,[8] and much less the ruling that partially decriminalized abortion in Colombia.[9]

Analyzing the political economy that controls the production of legal knowledge also allows us to understand why the work of authors such as Ronald Dworkin, John Rawls, H.L.A. Hart, and Richard Posner is widely known in the Global South and influences courts' holdings, as well as the way in which Global South scholars structure legal theory courses and research projects that are considered prestigious and useful. Finally, as to the micro-consequences of these concepts, rules and principles, we can better understand why for several years, U.S. immigration officers would not believe I was a visiting professor at a U.S. law school, as indi-

---

[5] About the relationship between concepts and practices, *see* Paul Khan (2011), *Political Theology: Four New Chapters on the Concept of Sovereignty* (New York: Columbia University Press), p. 93.

[6] Daniel Bonilla (2013), "Introduction", in Daniel Bonilla (ed.), *Constitutionalism of the Global South: The Three Activist Courts of India, South Africa and Colombia* (Cambridge: Cambridge University Press).

[7] *Roe v. Wade*, 410 U.S. 113, 153 (1973).

[8] *R. v. Morgentaler* [1988] 1 S.C.R. 30.

[9] Corte Constitucional Colombiana, Sentencia C-355/06, M.P. Jaime Araujo Rentería and Clara Inés Vargas Hernández.

cated in my immigration form, and not an intern; or why at a seminar on experiential education at an elite Brazilian university the main presenters were professors from weak U.S. law schools and with fragile academic production, while there were Latin American professors in the audience with much richer academic and professional experience.

Consequently, this chapter has two objectives. First, it seeks to describe and analyze the political economy model that dominates our legal and political imagination. As such, it aims at examining the conceptual structure of what I call the free market of legal ideas model. More precisely, it seeks to specify the subject of legal knowledge production established by the model, as well as its concepts of time and space. Likewise, it seeks to specify the precise rules and principles that determine the ways in which this model imagines the production, exchange, and use of legal knowledge, and the reasons that explain why this model has managed to capture our imagination.

Second, this chapter aims at describing and analyzing an alternative model of political economy that, from my point of view, would best explain (but would not justify) the real dynamics that regulate the generation, exchange, and use of legal knowledge. To achieve this objective, I highlight the conceptual structures that form what I call the colonial model of the production of legal knowledge. Therefore, I will (1) present the type of subject constructed by the model, (2) describe the time and space in which this subject is situated, (3) state the rules and principles that control the processes of production, exchange, and use of legal knowledge, and (4) specify the reasons for the existence of the model and its practical impact.

The subject created by the free market of legal ideas model, which I will present in the first part of this chapter, is an abstract, autonomous, and rational subject that can be materialized in any individual. This subject has the potential to create, exchange, and use legal knowledge in the same way that it has a sense of justice and the capacity to articulate and transform moral projects. This subject evolves in a globally open space, free of state borders; a free space where the egalitarian and fluid exchanges of legal knowledge are the rule, and the limits to the creation of knowledge are set by individual effort and talents.

The time in which this subject is situated is linear but infinite. Past knowledge is the basis for the creation of new knowledge, the objective of which is to apprehend the truth or face the fundamental challenges of a political community: how to achieve peace and prosperity. Nevertheless, this is a never-ending process, as nature and society's continuous changes require that we constantly adapt our legal knowledge, and humans' finite nature results in the incorrect or imprecise use of reason. This model is guided by the meritocracy principle, which explains the creation of legal ideas in a specific context as a result of the sum of a series of individual decisions that are intertwined with the discipline and work of those who generate them. The triumph of an idea is the result of its explanatory, analytical or normative power. The pre-eminence of an argument in the academic debate also has to do with the utility it demonstrates in resolving the community's legal and political problems. This model occupies a predominant place in our legal imagination given that it intersects, nurtures, and serves the liberal and enlightened modern values we are committed to: truth, objectivity, science, equality, autonomy, and the conviction that law is a necessary condition for political stability, and social and individual wellbeing.[10]

The colonial model of legal knowledge exchange that I explain in the second part of this chapter conceives the subject, time and space in alternative ways. The subject of this model is territorialized and racialized. It is a subject whose identity is defined by its geographic location, typically mapped as the Global South or the Global North, the colony or the metropolis. The Global South (or the colony) is the space occupied by the non-whites whereas the whites occupy the Global North (or the metropolis). Depending on its identity, this subject is also historicized, implicitly considered ahistorical or a secondary component of a legal tradition to which she arrived late.[11] Therefore, this subject may be considered a subject of rights with the capacity to create legal knowledge, or a legal barbarian with the sole ability to disseminate, reproduce or apply locally the knowledge created elsewhere.

The time in which this colonial model of the production of legal knowledge evolves is linear but finite. Time is a chain composed by a series of moments that end in the law of the metropolis, and in its dynamics for the production of legal knowledge. The generation, exchange, and use of legal knowledge in the colony are marked by its interaction with the law of the metropolis. The colony's legal past does not exist; it is irrelevant to the creation of legal knowledge. The present is a continuous effort to add a new link in the chain; an effort to reach the same status as the law of the metropolis, and to create the type of legal knowledge produced in the metropolis. The future is conceived as the ultimate point at which the colony is identified with the metropolis, that is, when the conditions for

---

[10] *See generally*, Alpana Roy (2008), "Postcolonial theory and law: A critical introduction", *Adelaide Law Review*, **29** (1/2), 315–57.

[11] *See generally*, Rosalind Morris and Gayatri Chakravorty Spivak (2010), *Can the Subaltern Speak?: Reflections on the History of an Idea* (New York: Columbia University Press).

the creation of legal knowledge that exist in the metropolis are reproduced internally. The metropolis is therefore situated at the end of history; it represents the last moment of development. The past and future of the metropolis collapse in an eternal and unitary present; its time is not fragmented, but perceived as one.

The conceptual geography of the colonial model of production of legal knowledge is binary. The space of this model is composed of the Global North and South.[12] This space is conceptual; it is not defined by geographical locations. Global North and South refer to the unequal distribution of power to create and exchange legal knowledge.[13] This unequal distribution of power is not isolated, but intersects with the unequal distribution of political, economic, military, and cultural powers.[14] The Global North denotes countries that, due in large part to their imperial past, are politically stable, relatively rich, militarily powerful, and culturally hegemonic. The Global South denotes a group of countries that, partly due to its colonial past, is politically unstable, relatively poor, militarily weak or at least not as strong as Global North countries, and culturally subordinate. Thus, the space of the colonial model of the creation of legal knowledge constructs a unidirectional model of exchange: the Global North creates and

---

[12] Global North and Global South are, no doubt, general categories. They name a heterogeneous reality constituted by groups of very different countries. Neither with regard to political or economic issues, nor with regard to legal knowledge it is the same talking about Germany and the United States or Spain and Portugal. Similarly, it is not the same talking about China and India or Surinam and Malaysia. Yet, these categories are useful to name the unequal relationship that exists between Western Europe and North America, on the one hand, and Latin America, Asia (excluding Japan) and Africa, on the other hand. These categories are more useful than the trite "developed and underdeveloped countries" or "first, second, and third worlds". Also, Global North and Global South are as general as other categories that we accept peacefully like "West" and "East". The critiques offered against the use of Global North and Global South can also be used against other general categories like "Latin America" or "United States". These categories are used not only for naming a geographical or legal and political fact, that is, a subregion of the American continent or a nation-state. They are used to give social, political and economic unity to a very heterogeneous reality. Mexico is not the same as Brazil and Ecuador is not the same as Belize. The east and the west or the north and the south of the United States are notably different. Some sections of the south have more similarities with Latin America than with the north east of the United States. However, we use these categories daily and accept their descriptive limits peacefully.

[13] Karin Mickelson (2009), "Beyond a politics of the possible? South–North relations and climate justice", *Melbourne J. of Int'l L.*, **10**, 411–23.

[14] Ibid.

exports legal knowledge, while the Global South imports, disseminates, reproduces, and applies this knowledge locally.

The rules and principles regulating the model are born out of a series of conceptual oppositions that describe and evaluate the spaces of our legal imagination occupied by the categories Global North and Global South. The four main conceptual oppositions are the following: (1) mimesis/autopoiesis; (2) local knowledge/universal knowledge; (3) culture/law; and (4) languages appropriate for legal knowledge/languages inappropriate for legal knowledge. These conceptual oppositions go hand-in-hand with a set of arguments that aim at explaining why the Global North is a rich environment for the production of legal knowledge, whereas the Global South is a poor context for the production of legal knowledge. These arguments make reference to the formalist nature of Global South legal communities;[15] to the fact that these communities are minor iterations of the great legal families of the world, the Romano-Germanic and the Anglo-American;[16] to the weaknesses of the legal academic communities of the Global South;[17] to the enormous influence that U.S. law has had on this part of the world;[18] to the presumed self-sufficiency of the Global North legal communities;[19] and to the direct or indirect imperial relationships that have existed between Global North and South countries.

As explained above, this chapter has descriptive, analytical and critical objectives. The first part of the chapter presents and examines the model that controls the way we imagine the production of legal theory, doctrine,

---

[15] *See* Bonilla (n 6).

[16] *See* Boaventura de Sousa Santos (1995), "Three metaphors for a new conception of law: The Frontier, the Baroque and the South", *Law & Soc'y Rev.*, **29**, 569, 579–82; Mark van Hoecke and Mark Warrington (1998), "Legal cultures, legal paradigms and legal doctrine: Towards a new model for comparative law", *Int'l. & Comp. L.Q.*, **47**, 4, 95, 498–99.

[17] *See* Daniel Bonilla (2013), "Legal clinics in the Global North and South: Between equality and subordination", *Yale Hum. Rts. & Dev. L.J.*, **16**, 176.

[18] *See* John Henry Merryman and Rogelio Pérez-Perdomo (2007), *The Civil Law Tradition: An Introduction to the Legal Systems of Europe and Latin America*, pp. 57, 60 (Redwood City: Stanford University Press); R. Daniel Kelemen and Eric C. Sibbitt (2004), "The globalization of American law", *Int'l Organization*, **58**, 103, 103–36; John Henry Merryman (1977), "Comparative law and social change: On the origins, style, decline, and revival of the law and development movement", *Am. J. Comp. L.*, **25**, 457, 484–89; Kerry Rittich (2006), "The future of law and development: Second-generation reforms and the incorporation of the social", in David Trubek and Alvara Santos (eds), *The New Law and Economic Development: A Critical Appraisal* (New York: Cambridge University Press), pp. 203–52.

[19] Ugo Mattei (1998), "An opportunity not to be missed: The future of comparative law in the United States", *Am. J. Comp. L.*, **48**, 712.

and practices. The second part highlights and evaluates the model that determines the real practices of production and exchange of legal knowledge. Therefore, the chapter's main objective is to understand the conceptual structure that determines how we interpret the creation, exchange, and use of legal knowledge. Critical statements will be presented exceptionally, mostly through illustrations of the general arguments. The chapter does not pretend to state the ideals towards which legal actors should gravitate. The aim of the chapter, I would like to emphasize, is not normative. The reform of questionable practices and concepts is valuable and very common in legal academia.[20] However, any (good) reform must be based on a sound diagnostic of the matter under study. Description and analysis must not necessarily go hand-in-hand with critique and reform proposals. A plausible division of academic labor promotes theoretical and methodological diversity. Reform should not be the sole objective of legal scholarship.

This chapter does not argue that the free market of legal ideals model is only a normative model without any practical implications, nor that the colonial economy model occupies no space in our legal and political imagination. This chapter argues that both models exist through our legal theories and practices in profound cognitive dissonance. The two models occupy a place in how we conceptualize, produce, exchange, and use legal knowledge. The market economy model is at the center of our normative legal imagination, while the colonial economy model is at the periphery. Our legal imagination is therefore not coherent. It is composed of diverse elements organized hierarchically that respond to different and often contradictory justifications.

The free market of legal ideas model, moreover, works as a conceptual cover that obscures the existence of the colonial model in our practices and discourses. The central position that the former occupies in our normative legal and political imagination tends to hide the dynamics of the former. The free market of ideas model does not aim at concealing the colonial model. Yet, in practice it tends to achieve this objective. Values like individual autonomy and meritocracy, that supposedly explain the creation, legitimation, and use of legal knowledge, hinder describing and evaluating the vertical power relations that exist between the legal academia of the Global North and South.

The two models, it is important to note, are not peacefully accepted by the legal academia of the Global North and South.[21] Surely, there are

---

[20] *See* Khan (n 2), at 7–30.

[21] *See generally*, Fernando Rubio Dominguez and Patrick Baert (eds) (2012), *The Politics of Knowledge* (London: Routledge).

spaces of critique, resistance, and epistemological emancipation. Legal academics from both regions have criticized the two models and have created alternative practices for the production, exchange, and use of legal knowledge. Groups of academics or intellectual movements like Third World Approaches to International Law (TWAIL)[22] and the postcolonial studies of law,[23] for example, question the colonial model of production of legal knowledge and intend to create original legal products taking into account the interests and contexts of the Global South. However, these spaces of resistance and emancipation will not be examined in this chapter. They will be analyzed in another paper, part of a larger research project, of which this piece is a chapter.

THE FREE MARKET OF LEGAL IDEAS

The Subject of Knowledge

An abstract, autonomous and rational subject lies at the center of the market economy of legal ideas model. This disembodied subject has the capacity to create, exchange and use legal knowledge. It is a type of individual committed to the search for truth and the solution of the political community's fundamental problems: violence and the creation of conditions that will allow for prosperity of all members of the polity. This subject does not have a particular identity. What is relevant is that as a member of the species, the subject has the capacity to create legal knowledge by using reason. The subject's ethnicity, gender, race or nationality does not matter. The capacity to create, exchange and use legal knowledge is beyond the incidents that constitute the subject's individuality. However, putting this power into action in ways that effectively create legal knowledge is a consequence of the free decision of each subject. The products generated, as well as their quality and utility, will fundamentally depend on the subject's work, discipline and commitment to truth and the flourishing of its political community. Therefore, the model is also committed to the principle of equality; all subjects of knowledge are equal in their capacity to create legal knowledge. A priori, there are no mandarins of legal knowledge. The recognition given to the subjects is a consequence of the truth-value and the utility of the knowledge they produce. The modern

---

[22] Makau Mutua (2000), "What Is TWAIL?", *Am. Soc'y of Int'l L. Proc*, **94**, 31–39.

[23] Teemu Ruskola (2002), "Legal Orientalism", *Mich. L. Rev.*, **101**, 179–234.

political community formally recognizes this value through intellectual property rights, where individuals must be compensated. Nevertheless, the returns that this generates must be weighed against the social utility of the product generated and with the possibility that everyone may use it. Hence, intellectual property rights are typically limited temporarily.

The subject created by the market of legal ideas model is captured paradigmatically in Charles Degeorge's sculpture titled Young Aristotle.[24] At the center of the image lies Aristotle, a young man seated in a chair, reading. In one hand, he holds a book; in the other hand, he holds a metal sphere. Below, there is a large plate, also made of metal. If the man falls asleep, the ball will fall from his hand and hit the container, making a noise that will wake him up. The search for knowledge, or for legal knowledge in our case, is the result of individual effort and commitment. The young man represents any human being. The truth and the production of knowledge that is useful for our political community is within reach of any individual. The only thing needed is an act of will that enables and sustains the capacity that every human being has to create legal knowledge. The young man sits on the chair voluntarily, plans, and implements a strategy that will allow him to advance his intellectual work; to advance his search for truth. His commitment to science, or the science of law in our case, does not have a limit distinct from his intellectual capacity and work.

The subject of knowledge of this model is also committed to the idea that law is a necessary condition for the order and prosperity of the political community. Contractualism, fundamental to justify modern political communities, reflects the above argument in a paradigmatic manner. The free market of legal ideas model is clearly only one component of a much wider and more ambitious political model: liberalism. The move from the state of nature to the civil state must be done so that life and the integrity of the people and of their goods can be guaranteed.[25] As argued by Hobbes,[26] violence is the rule in the state of nature or, as argued by

---

[24] Charles Degeorge (1875), *Jeunesse d'Aristote*. The sculpture is on display at the Musée D'Orsay. A photograph of the sculpture can be found at: http://www.musee-orsay.fr/fr/collections/catalogue-des-oeuvres/notice.html?no_cache=1&zoom=1&tx_damzoom_pi1%5Bzoom%5D=0&tx_damzoom_pi1%5BxmlId%5D=006426&tx_damzoom_pi1%5Bback%5D=%2Ffr%2Fcollections%2Fcatalogue-des-oeuvres%2Fnotice.html%3Fno_cache%3D1%26nnumid%3D006426%26cHash%3D66848a1aa7 (accessed 1 October 2017).

[25] *See generally*, David Boucher and Paul Kelly (1994), *The Social Contract from Hobbes to Rawls* (London: Routledge).

[26] Thomas Hobbes (2003), *Leviathan* (London: Penguin), pp. 205–13.

Locke,[27] violence is always latent in spite of the relative isolation in which individuals live. The natural rights we have over our body and our goods are always in danger of being violated during this pre-political time. The fundamental problem faced by the subjects that we imagine living in this situation is that no impartial third party exists that could resolve their conflicts.[28] Hence, the subjects decide to create the state through a free agreement, and to submit themselves to its power. However, positive law becomes a necessary tool to ensure the life and property of the members of the polity.[29] This specifies the content of natural rights and makes them demandable before the state and other citizens. Without law, there would be no political community, and without political communities there would be no life, personal integrity, stability, or prosperity.

Contractualism, then, identifies law with the polis and the polis with civilization. Outside of the polis, beyond the walls protecting the political community there is no positive law, only violence. Thus the "other" of law is violence.[30] The "other" of the citizen is the barbarian, or he who does not have a state that applies the positive, clear, and precise law that it generates. Hence, the subject of knowledge that the free market of legal ideas model creates is inescapably related to its other, the barbarian – he who lives in the state of nature.

The Time

The time in which the subject evolves is linear and infinite. Modern law is structured around two values: will and reason,[31] which are presupposed by the free market of legal ideas model. For the law to be valid and legitimate, it must be simultaneously the result of popular sovereignty and human reason. However, the popular will continually change (p. 38, par. 3), the natural and social circumstances in which human beings live are in constant flux, and people frequently fail in their use of reason. The past is thus fundamental for the creation, exchange, and use of legal knowledge. New knowledge is based on past successes and lessons learned from mistakes. Similarly to any other knowledge, legal knowledge is cumulative. It is

---

[27] John Locke (1991), *Ensayo Sobre el Gobierno Civil* (Madrid: Espasa Calpe), pp. 205–13.

[28] Id. at 294.

[29] *See* Hobbes (n 26), at 233–52.

[30] *See generally*, Paul W. Khan (2000), *Law and Love: The Trials of King Lear* (New Haven, CT: Yale University Press); Paul W. Khan (2008), *Sacred Violence: Torture, Terror, and Sovereignty* (Ann Arbor: University of Michigan Press).

[31] *See* Khan (n 2), at 7–30.

always an attempt to satisfy both will and reason. It is a trial and error process that simultaneously seeks to obtain the approval of the members of the polity, and arrive at the truth. The future, therefore, has no end. The creation, exchange, and use of legal knowledge never ends. The future is presented as always open, given the characteristics of nature, human finiteness, and the moral and political values we are committed to.

Congress of modern liberal democracies produces laws in a systematic and continual manner. For their citizens, this is something obvious that is accepted peacefully; however, the conceptual axes that motivate this dynamic are not commonly known. Will and reason are constantly correcting themselves.[32] Reason amends the errors of will, which may not be any different from vested interests or from temporary or permanent passions.[33] Will constantly reminds reason that without the agreement of the members of the polity, which is usually manifested through their representatives, we would only have a set of invalid and illegitimate norms.[34] Both reason and will are attentive to social changes, transformations in the natural environment, and human failures, such that the law may respond adequately to the needs or challenges that all of these circumstances generate.

If reason could lead to legal truth and legislators could make adequate use of reason, congress would only legislate once on each issue. The sovereign would only have to accept the conclusions that reason inescapably leads her to and vote in favor of the bills that best articulate these conclusions. This was the idea behind the Napoleonic Civil Code.[35] The legislator would accept the products of a group of experts who, by making use of reason, would create a set of legal standards to regulate all aspects of the field of study (the relationships among private parties) in a permanent manner.[36] The legal standards created had a vocation of eternity. This is why these standards could also be imposed on the peoples that were conquered during the Napoleonic military campaigns. We cannot forget that Napoleon advanced his military campaigns with a sword in one hand, and

---

32 Id.

33 Jon Elster (1998), "Régimen de Mayorías y Derechos Individuales", in Stephen Shute and Susan Hurley (eds), *De Los Derechos Humanos: Las Conferencias Oxford Amnesty de 1993* (Madrid: Editorial Trotta).

34 *See* Khan (n 2), at 7–30.

35 M.C. Mirow (2001), "Borrowing private law in Latin America: Andres Bello's use of the 'Code Napoleon' in drafting the Chilean Civil Code", *LA. L. Rev.*, **61**, 291; M.C. Mirow (2005), "The Code Napoleon: Buried but ruling in Latin America", *Denv. J. Int'l L. & Pol'y*, **53**, 179–94.

36 Julián Bonnecas (1944), *La Escuela de la exégesis en derecho civil* (Puebla: Cajica).

the civil code in the other.[37] Law, the fruit of reason, was immune to cultural differences and to the fact that the communities defeated militarily perceived law as heteronomous.[38]

If the will of the sovereign is the only element guiding the creation of legal norms, we would be subject to the rule of whim, intuition, factional interests or passions.[39] Legal norms would probably be based on incorrect empirical arguments or would be morally or politically questionable. Will, even if it is the will of the sovereign, must always be guided and limited by reason. Hence, for example, U.S. legal realism was committed to the idea that social sciences should guide the creation of legal norms in both the legislature and the judiciary.[40] Economy and sociology, among other fields, would contribute to the creation of statutes and rulings with solid, rational arguments. These processes of legal creation should not be guided by intuition, good faith, or moral commitments of legislators and judges. Thus, the economic analysis of law emphasizes that legislators and judges should base their decisions on a cost/benefit analysis that prioritizes the value of efficiency and is guided by mathematical models.[41] Science, or the social sciences in this case, should guide the will of the people that is manifested through the legislator or the judge who interprets their mandates.

The Space

The model conceives a global space. This space is imagined as an open geography where national borders are fundamentally irrelevant. The only spatial limit that the subject of knowledge has is that of the material edges of our planet. Legal knowledge can be created, exchanged and used in any part of the globe. The flow and use of this knowledge is multidirectional and decentralized. Legal knowledge has the potential to emerge in any part of the world, and has no predetermined channels or patterns of dissemination. The importation and exportation of legal knowledge may occur from and towards any point. The issues researched, the ideas that

---

37 Napoleon noted to this effect, "My true glory is not that I have won forty battles. Waterloo will blow away the memory of these victories. What nothing can blow away, what will live eternally is my Civil Code." Jean Louis Bergel (1988), "Principal features and methods of codification", *LA. L. Rev.*, **48**, 1073, 1078–79.

38 *See* Merryman and Pérez-Perdomo (n 18), at 29.

39 *See* Elster (n 33).

40 Karl N. Llewellyn (1949), "Law and the social sciences: Especially sociology", *Harv. L. Rev.*, **6**, 1286–305.

41 Richard A. Posner (1973), *Economic Analysis of Law* (Boston: Little, Brown and Company), Ch. 1.

end up dominating people's imagination, and the media and language that are the vehicle for the knowledge created, among other things, are the result of an immense set of small decisions made by the members of the community creating knowledge. Also, they are the consequence of the power that the legal products constructed have to approach truth or solve problems faced by political communities.

These exchanges with multiple trajectories that are not guided by a centralized power occur in principle between equal subjects of knowledge. The model is firmly committed to the principle of equality. The subjects of knowledge are fundamentally equal; they have the same capacities to create, exchange, and use legal knowledge. The legal products generated can certainly have a monetary value. This can create differences with respect to the real capacities that subjects have for the exchange and use of legal knowledge. However, this is not always the case, knowledge can be offered freely, and when knowledge does have a price, it is defined by the market. Therefore, the price is fair as it is determined by a great number of autonomous decisions made by those who produce legal knowledge, and by those who need it.

The productivity and capacity for exchange and use of legal knowledge by the subjects of legal knowledge are, in practice, determined by a set of institutional conditions. The production of knowledge does not occur in a vacuum. The subject of knowledge can be situated in any part of the world but is always localized. When the subject conceived by the model acts in the real world, it is affected by a series of material circumstances. The existence of comprehensive libraries, public funding for research, good universities accessible to all, and full-time positions for professors, among other things, affect the quality and systematic nature of the legal products generated. Save for exceptional case of great solitary creators, the existence and vigor of this type of institution conditions the subjects of knowledge. However, the institutional strength in one context of production or another is directly related to a series of decisions made by a set of individuals. For the free market of legal ideas model, institutional strength is the result of individual autonomy, creativity, discipline, and work of the members of the political community. In practice, then, inequalities can be generated between private subjects of knowledge, their institutions, and the political communities they are immersed in. However, these are legitimate inequalities in that they are the consequence of the autonomy of members of one scientific and political community or another.

RULES AND PRINCIPLES

The free market of legal ideas model is centered on the principles of truth, utility and meritocracy. The best legal ideas, the ones that capture our legal and political imagination, triumph. Truth and utility are the criteria that determine what these ideas are. The most powerful ideas are those that are understood as true, whatever may be the set of first-level criteria that determine what is true, and those that have the potential to describe, analyze, evaluate and, principally, solve the challenges that political communities face. The people that generate this type of product and achieve recognition of their peers and communities are those who have the discipline, commitment, creativity, and dedication to generate legal products with high levels of quality.

The innate talent that some subjects have is certainly a variable beyond the autonomy of these subjects. Fate granted them some advantages for creating legal knowledge. Thus, for example, they may have minds with greater capacities for analysis and abstraction than an average person, they may have a powerful imagination or a capacity for free association that allows them to make innovative connections between known and accepted phenomena. However, natural talents do not act on their own. They need the will of those who possess them to be put into action. Talented but lazy subjects of knowledge usually do not get very far.

The expansion of the adversarial criminal model in Latin America,[42] the flexibilization of labor markets in the region,[43] the omnipresence of the positivist liberal model to describe and substantiate the law,[44] the quasi-universal priority given to individual rights over economic, social and cultural rights,[45] the importation of *pro bono* theory and practice around

---

[42] Pilar Domingo and Rachel Sieder (2001), "Rule of law", in Pilar Domingo and Rachel Sieder (eds), *Rule of Law in Latin America: The International Promotion of Judicial Reform* (London: Institute of Latin American Studies, University of London), p. 1; Andrés Torres, *From Inquisitorial to Accusatory: Colombia and Guatemala's Legal Transition* 2 (Law and Justice in the Americas Working Paper Series, Paper No. 4, 2007), available at: http://lawdigitalcommons.bc.edu/ljawps/4 (accessed 9 September 2008).

[43] María Victoria Murillo (2005), "Partisanship amidst convergence: The politics of labor reform in Latin America", *Comparative Politics*, **37**, 441, 441–43; Graciela Bensusán (2007), *La efectividad de la legislación laboral en América Latina, Instituto de Estudios Laborales* (Ginebra: Organización Internacional del Trabajopp), pp. 13–22, available at: www.ilo.org/public/spanish/bureau/inst/download/dp18107.pdf (accessed 8 September 2017).

[44] Brian Leiter (2013), *Why Legal Positivism (Again)?*, 9 September, University of Chicago, Public Law Working Paper No. 442.

[45] Jack Donnelly (2003), *Universal Human Rights in Theory and Practice* (Ithaca, NY: Cornell University Press), Ch. 2.

the globe,[46] and the inclusion of clinical legal education in the curricula of law schools,[47] for example, are explained by the free market of legal ideas model by appealing to the idea of meritocracy that presupposes the concepts of subject, time, and space described above. For the model, these legal theories, doctrines, and practices have been regionalized or globalized because they describe reality in a better way, they are better substantiated than the rival perspectives, or allow for facing the common challenges of contemporary political communities in a superior way. These legal theories can tell us how to try criminal cases in a fair and effective way; what the criteria are to determine the validity and legitimacy of legal norms; how to increase productivity and levels of employment; how to enhance individual autonomy and enable citizens' representatives to make decisions on how they should invest communities' economic resources; how to face the problems of access to justice; and how to educate attorneys who are socially responsible and have the skills to perform efficiently in professional practice.

The case of *pro bono* legal work can help illustrate the model in a more detailed manner.[48] Latin American attorneys have performed free legal work for low-income people or the public interest for decades, if not centuries.[49] However, this work was informal in its proceedings and individual in its materialization, i.e., it depended on the good will of each attorney for its execution. For the last fifteen years, in contrast, attorneys at large Latin American law firms have promoted the institutionalization of *pro bono* work within their organizations.[50] This process was promoted by the importation/exportation of descriptive and normative practices

---

[46] Maya Steinitz (2009), "Internationalized pro bono and a new global role for lawyers in the 21st century: Lessons from nation building in southern Sudan", *Yale Hum. Rts. & Dev. L.J.*, **12**, 205.

[47] Richard J. Wilson (2004), "Training for justice: The global reach of clinical legal education", *Penn St. Int'l L. Rev..*, 22, 421, 427; Frank S. Bloch (2011), "Introduction", in Frank S. Bloch (ed.), *The Global Clinical Movement: Educating Lawyers for Social Justice* (New York: Oxford University Press).

[48] *See generally*, Scott L. Cummings and Deborah L. Rhode (2010), "Managing pro bono: Doing well by doing better", *Fordham L. Rev.*, **78**, 2357, 2364 and Lucie E. White (2000), "Pro bono or partnership: Rethinking lawyers' public service obligations for a new millennium", *J. Legal Educ.*, **50**, 134, 140.

[49] Daniel Bonilla, Luis Calvo and Belén Fernández, *El trabajo pro bono en Colombia*, manuscript.

[50] *Report on the Buenos Aires Conference on Pro Bono and Access to Justice* (2002), The Committee on Inter-American Affairs, The Association of the Bar of the City of NY, *The Record*, **57**, 479; for an analysis of the institutionalization of *pro bono* work in the United States, *see* Cummings and Rhode (n 48).

and theories articulated by U.S. legal academia and large law firms in the United States, primarily those in New York.[51]

The free market of legal ideas model would explain this legal transplant by appealing to its concepts of subject, time and space. The arguments that substantiate *pro bono* legal work in the United States and the practices that put them into action in an institutionalized manner are the consequence of a relatively broad group of entrepreneurial, disciplined, and creative attorneys who were seeking to face the problems of access to justice by the poorest in their political community. The practices and justifications for institutionalized *pro bono* emerge in the context of the large law firms in cities like New York and Washington.[52] These solid and powerful institutions, which create the conditions of possibility for formalized *pro bono* work,[53] are the result of the effort and creativity of these same attorneys. In addition, the academic discourse on *pro bono* work in the United States emerges from a group of disciplined and hardworking law professors who find the social responsibilities of attorneys to be a valuable object of study. Thus, they articulate a descriptive, analytical, and normative discourse on the practices and arguments of their colleagues. The discourse and practice of *pro bono* work is consequently a result of the autonomy of a set of subjects that put their capacity to create legal knowledge into action. Reason is their instrument; truth and utility are their primary guidelines.

The model indicates that the importation/exportation of U.S. legal practices and discourses on *pro bono* work are a consequence of the strength of the arguments that substantiate them and of the utility to face a common problem like the lack of access to justice by the lowest socioeconomic layers of the population. Historically, Latin America has articulated and

---

51 "The Cyrus R. Vance Center for International Justice Initiatives of the Association of the Bar of the City of New York, as one of its programs, has been collaborating with lawyers, bar associations and non-governmental organizations (NGOs) in South America to support local efforts to promote and institutionalize pro bono legal services. The Vance Center co-sponsored conferences on this subject in Argentina (2001), Chile (2002), and most recently, this past month, in São Paulo, Brazil. S. Todd Crider, a partner at Simpson Thacher & Bartlett, who chairs the Association's Committee on the Vance Center, says that in South America, until recently, 'Pro bono was not part of the legal lexicon. Now most significant-sized firms in these three countries have developed a pro bono policy, or are in the process of doing so. The Vance Center, working with colleagues in Argentina, Chile and Brazil, has contributed to this development.'" William Dean (2004), "Pro bono: A professional and ethical obligation", *N.Y.L.J.* (2 January).

52 *See generally*, Scott and Rhode (n 48).

53 *See generally*, Scott L. Cummings (2004), "The politics of pro bono", *UCLA L. Rev.*, **52**, 1.

enacted strategies to solve its problems of access to justice, such as, for example, the establishment of the public defender's office.[54] Nevertheless, Latin American countries had not articulated strong institutional strategies in the private sector to raise levels of protection of the individual right to access to justice. The legal knowledge created around *pro bono* work emerges in the United States due to the conditions of the legal market that allowed for the creation of law firms formed by hundreds if not thousands of attorneys. It also emerges due to problems of inequality the country faced, which prevented poor citizens from satisfying their legal needs, and due to the existence of morally responsible, academically well-trained attorneys that connected one situation with another.

However, this legal knowledge could have emerged in any part of the world where the same institutional conditions were in place. In this case, the United States is the source of the legal knowledge that moves towards the South (Latin America), but it could also have moved in other directions. The United States could have been the receptor of similar legal knowledge. The channels of exchange of legal knowledge are multidirectional, and those who issue and receive the legal knowledge are autonomous and equal. As receivers and issuers of legal knowledge, Latin American and U.S. attorneys are peers who maintain a horizontal relationship.

The interaction between reason and will has particular characteristics in this case. Reason, in this instance in the form of *pro bono* legal knowledge, seeks to solve a problem partially created by the law of the states receiving this knowledge: the legal institutions and strategies they adopted have not been sufficient to face the deficit of the right to access to justice for their populations. However, the solution does not seek a legal change, but a change in the private sector, that of the legal market, within the existing legal frameworks. In this case, the aim is not to create a new legal norm but to bring about a change in the practices of attorneys acting within the standards of professional ethics established by their political communities.

The case of the importation/exportation of clinical legal education to Latin America is useful to continue with the exercise of specifying the explanatory and analytical power of the free market of legal ideas model. During the 1960s and 1970s, various Latin American countries like Colombia, Chile, and Peru faced problems related to the efficacy and future of their development model.[55] The levels of economic growth,

---

[54] *See generally*, Mauro Capelleti and Bryant G. Garth (1996), *El acceso a la justicia: la tendencia en el movimiento mundial para hacer efectivos los derechos* (Mexico City: Fondo de Cultura Económica).

[55] David Trubek and Marc Galanter (1974), "Scholars in self estrangement: Some reflections on the crisis in law and development studies in the United

inequality and employment were not desirable. In dialogue with the United States, the diagnosis that these Latin American governments reached was that one of the reasons that limited the economic development of Latin American countries was directly related to the formalism that characterizes their legal systems. From a theoretical point of view, these types of systems are described as closed, complete, coherent and univocal.[56] It was argued that this characterization of the law had little to do with the legal reality in the region: systems that, like any other, constantly interact with other sets of norms such as morality and are characterized as being incomplete, contradictory and polysemic. In addition, the formalist concept of law gives way to a type of education that is encyclopedic, based on memorization, de-contextualized, acritical and legocentric.[57] This edu-

---

States", *Wis. L. Rev.*, **4**, 1062, 1066; Hugo Frühling (2000), "From dictatorship to democracy: Law and social change in the Andean region and the southern cone of South America", in Mary McClymont and Stephen Golub (eds), *Many Roads to Justice: The Law-Related Work of Ford Foundation Grantees around the World* (New York: The Ford Foundation), pp. 55, 56.

[56] About legal formalism in Latin America, *see* Rogelio Pérez-Perdomo (2005), "Rule of law and lawyers in Latin American", *Annals of the American Academy of Political and Social Science*, 603 (1), 110; Merryman and Pérez-Perdomo (n 18), at 66; Manual Atienza (2003), *El sentido del derecho* (Barcelona: Ariel, Editorial S.A.), pp. 276–79.

[57] *See*, for example, the articles published in (2008), *CuadernosUnimetanos*, **15**: Juny Montoya Vargas, "La reforma a la enseñanza del derecho en la Universidad de Los Andes", at 63–90; Andrés Cuneo Macchiavello, "Una experiencia de reforma curricular: el plan de estudios de Derecho de la Universidad Diego Portales", at 33–43; Mauricio Duce, "Enseñando destrezas de litigación en procesos orales en la Universidad Diego Portales: experiencias y aprendizajes", at 91–107; Horacio Spector, "The academic study of law in Argentina", at 6–15; Conrado Hübner Mendes, "La escuela de Derecho de São Paulo de la Fundación Getulio Vargas Caio Farah Rodriguez Joaquim Falcão", at 16–32; Caio Farah Rodriguez y Joaquim Falcao, "O projeto da escola de Direito do Rio de Janeiro da FGV", at 44–50. *Also see*, Luis Fernando Pérez Hurtado, "Content, structure, and growth of Mexican legal education", *J. Legal Educ.*, **59** (4), 567; Héctor Fix Fierro and Sergio López (2006), "La educación jurídica en México, un panorama general", in Nuria González Martín and Marta Morineau Iduarte, *Estudios jurídicos en homenaje a Marta Morineau: Sistemas jurídicos contemporáneos, derecho comparado, temas diversos* (Mexico City: Universidad Nacional Autónoma de México); Juny Montoya Vargas (2009), "Educación jurídica en Latinoamérica: dificultades curriculares para promover los temas de interés público y justicia social", El Otro Derecho, **38**, 29–42. *See also*, Mauricio Duce Julio, *Desafíos para la educación legal en América Latina*: *Documentos de trabajo del Encuentro de Educación Legal en América Latina: nuevos desafíos a las facultades de derecho* (2003) (Santiago: Universidad Diego Portales, Facultad de Derecho).

cation also trains students with few skills for professional practice[58] and no greater awareness of their social responsibilities. From a practical point of view, the legal orders of the region were seen as excessively ritualistic and slow systems that were not very attentive to citizens' real needs.[59]

This description of Latin American legal systems allowed for the conclusion that if one wanted to increase the levels of development of these countries it was necessary to change their laws and legal teaching.[60] The premise from which this conclusion stems was that an efficient liberal law system was a necessary condition for development.[61] To reach this objective, the origin of the problem, law schools, needed to be attacked. Working under this premise, U.S. politicians, technocrats and academics offered, among other things, the Socratic method and legal clinics.[62] The United States had faced similar challenges and had articulated the solutions that they then introduced as a product of exportation.[63] Decades

---

58 *See, e.g.*, Alfredo Fuentes Hernández (2003), "Globalization and legal education in Latin America: Issues for law and development in the 21st century", *Penn St. Int'l L. Rev.*, **21**, 40, 46.

59 Rogelio Pérez-Perdomo (2011), "Legal education in late twentieth-century Latin America", in Lawrence Friedman, Rogelio Pérez-Perdomo and Manuel Gómez (eds), *Law in Many Societies* (Stanford: Stanford Law Books), p. 63 ("During the entire period that we are examining, the perception has existed in certain universities that law schools had lost step with social changes and that legal studies had been left behind. This perception may have come from the perceived speed of the social change as opposed to the much slower and more difficult changes in the curricula and teaching methods in law schools. Latin American societies have continued to face severe problems of poverty, marginality, criminality, and police brutality, at the same time that political transformations, which were sometimes quite rapid, a communications revolution, and greater integration into the global economy took place – yet these problems and changes did not seem to affect the majority of law schools, which appeared secluded in a culture of codes and old books."). It is important to note that Pérez-Perdomo also argues that there have been changes on these issues (id.).

60 James A. Gardner (1980), *Legal Imperialism: American Lawyers and Foreign Aid in Latin America* (Madison: The University of Wisconsin Press), p. 43 and Laura Kalman (1996), *The Strange Career of Legal Liberalism* (New Haven, CT: Yale University Press).

61 David M. Trubek (2006), "The 'rule of law' in development assistance: Past, present, and future", in Trubek and Santos (n 18), at 74, 77.

62 Peggy Maisel (2008), "The role of U.S. law faculty in developing countries: Striving for effective cross-cultural collaboration", *Clinical L. Rev.*, **14**, 465.

63 Legal formalism was strongly attacked and weakened by legal realism. *See, e.g.*, John Dewey (1924), "Logical method and the law", *Cornell L.Q.*, **10**, 17; Karl Llewellyn (1931), "Some realism about realism—responding to Dean Pound", *Harvard Law Review*, **44**, 1222. *See also* Brian Leiter (ed.) (2007), *Naturalizing Jurisprudence: Essays on American Legal Realism and Naturalism*

earlier, the U.S. had faced problems related to formalism in theory, professional practice, and legal education.[64] Latin American politicians, technicians and academics concluded that these tools were adequately conceived and substantiated. They also concluded that if they had been successful in the United States, they would also produce positive results in Latin America. Hence, countries like Colombia issued statutes making legal clinics obligatory for all law students.[65] Forty-three years after they were issued, these legal rules still remain in effect.[66]

The free market of legal ideas model would describe and explain this process of creation, exchange and use of knowledge in the following manner. First, a set of subjects (political, academic and technical) situated in one area of the globe has created legal knowledge that seeks to address a particular legal and political problem (the inversely proportional relationship between formalist law and development). These subjects offer this product to another set of subjects situated in another area of the globe that face a similar problem. The value of this legal knowledge is a result of the strengths (work, discipline, creativity) of the individuals that created it and of the academic and state institutions in which they are immersed. The subjects receiving this legal knowledge find that this is the best product offered in the market of legal ideas, and decide to import it. Both those issuing and receiving this knowledge are therefore equal, and their flow of exchanges, fluid.

Second, the areas of the globe where these different sets of individuals are located are not particularly relevant. In this case, the flow of legal knowledge had a North–South direction. Nevertheless, it is not necessary that that be the case. Legal knowledge may also move South–North or East–West. The place of creation of the legal theory or practice is irrelevant. What matters is its truth-value and utility. What is significant is that

---

in Legal Philosophy (New York: Oxford University Press); Brian Leiter (2010), "Legal formalism and legal realism: What is the issue?", *Legal Theory*, **16**, 111.

[64] M.H. Hoeflich (1986), "Law and geometry: Legal science from Leibniz to Langdell", *Am. J. Legal Hist*., **30**, 97.

[65] *See*, *e.g*., Edward A. Laing (1974), "Revolution in Latin American legal education: The Colombian experience", *Lawyer of the Americas*, **6**, 307, 372–76. This article explains the influence of legal formalism in Colombian legal education and the "revolution caused by experiential learning".

[66] Legal clinics were created by Decree No. 196 of 1971 and developed by Decree No. 765 of 1977, Law No. 23 of 1991 and Law No. 583 of 2000 (Colombia). Beatriz Londoño Toro (2003), "Las clínicas jurídicas de interés público en Colombia. Retos y posibilidades de una naciente experiencia", in F. González (ed.), *Clínicas de Interés Público y Enseñanza del Derecho* (Chile: Facultad de Derecho, Universidad Diego Portales), pp. 9–47.

it is the best product available on the market of legal ideas. The market of legal ideas is an open space only limited by the borders of our globe.

Finally, the interaction between will and reason that is the engine of the continual transformations experienced by modern law is shown both at the point of issuance and the point of reception of legal knowledge. The confrontation between the dominant visions of law, represented as expression of both the sovereign and reason, and the critical visions, represented as the voice of reason, are adequately understood and used. In the United States, we have the meeting between the classical liberalism of the Lochner era and the interventionist liberalism of the New Deal.[67] Similarly, we have the confrontation between the classical vision of legal academia[68] represented in paradigmatic fashion by Dean Langdell, and the alternative perspectives on the teaching of law offered by legal realism.[69] All of these visions are articulated and implemented legally or through "private" norms, such as the mandatory ABA norms. In Latin America, there is a conservative interpretation of political liberalism that does not believe in a close relationship between efficient liberal law and economic development, and a new vision that offers the law and society movement where the former is a necessary precondition for the latter. Therefore, we find the tension between a vision of legal academia that combines German historicism with the French school of exegesis,[70] and the interpretation that the law and development movement offers of U.S. legal realism.[71]

The pre-eminent place that the free market of legal ideas model occupies in our legal imagination is not accidental. It is another piece in the horizon of understanding we are immersed in. This horizon is formed in large part by the central ideas of liberal modernity. It is formed by concepts like individual autonomy, equality, science, objectivity, progress, truth, merit and market.[72] The supply and demand of this legal knowledge model is an

---

[67] Jack M. Balkin (2011), *Constitutional Redemption* (Cambridge, MA: Harvard University Press).

[68] Oliver Wendell Holmes (1897), "The path of the law", *Harv. L. Rev.*, **10**, 457 (articulating the anti-formalist bases for which legal realism came to be known).

[69] Jerome Frank (1933), "Why not a clinical lawyer-school?", *U. Pa. L. Rev.*, **81**, 907.

[70] Diego Lopez Medina (2004), *Teoría Impura del Derecho. La transformación de la cultura jurídica latinoamericana* (Bogotá, Legis-Universidad de Los Andes-Universidad Nacional de Colombia), pp. 129–233.

[71] David M. Trubek and Alvaro Santos (2006), "Introduction: The third moment in law and development theory and the emergence of a new critical practice", in Trubek and Santos (n 18), at 1, 2–3.

[72] *See generally*, Louis Dupre (2004), *The Enlightenment and the Intellectual Foundations of Modern Culture* (New Haven, CT: Yale University Press).

application and adaptation to the legal field of the central ideas to which many citizens of the contemporary liberal democracy are already committed. The autonomy, rationality, and equality that characterize human beings for liberalism, qualities that are then transferred to citizens,[73] now move towards the subject of legal knowledge.

Legal knowledge is seen as a product that does not escape the laws of supply and demand; the products that are generated, the place where they are created, their value and the flows of dissemination and exchange of these products are a consequence of the sum of a series of decisions made by a multitude of anonymous individuals around the world. The political economy of legal knowledge is also committed to the idea of progress, which can be reached through science, or legal science in this case. Knowledge is the expression and development of reason that in a trial and error process leads us to the legal truth and shows us the ways in which it can be socially useful.

THE COLONIAL MODEL OF PRODUCTION, EXCHANGE AND USE OF LEGAL KNOWLEDGE

The Subject of Knowledge

The subject constructed by the colonial model is dual but interdependent. On the one side, we have the subject of legal knowledge of the metropolis; on the other, the subject of legal knowledge of the colony. Both are defined positively and negatively; they are constructed based on what they are and what they are not. The first is a subject that is understood to have the capacity to create, exchange and use legal knowledge. The second is conceived as a subject that only has the capacity to reproduce, disseminate, and apply locally the legal knowledge created in the metropolis. The metropolis subject defines her identity based on what she is not: a barbarian. The colonial subject derives her identity from her antonym, the *homo ius*. The metropolis subject is understood to be a political subject, i.e., she no longer belongs to the state of nature; she has a state and a law. The colonial subject is still situated in the state of nature. She has not been able to construct a polis to rise above the violence that puts her life and property in continuous danger. What is called law is only that in appearance.

These subjects of knowledge are therefore territorialized and racialized

---

[73] John Rawls (1996), *Political Liberalism* (New York: Columbia University Press), pp. 29–65.

and have a particular relationship with history. The identity of the metropolis subject and of the colonial subject is defined in part by the place where these subjects are located, the metropolis or the colony, the Global North or the Global South. The first is understood as a rich context for the production of legal knowledge while the second is understood as a poor context for (the production of) legal knowledge. The legal community and tradition in which these are immersed determine the way their identity is constructed. The process of constructing the identity of these subjects is consequently dialogic. They are created from the interaction with those who conceive their other and with their political and legal community. One cannot exist without the other.

The metropolis subject and the colonial subject have a skin color. The territory they inhabit and that defines them is conceptually, not materially, racialized. In the metropolis, the subject of knowledge is white; in the colony, non-white. The construction of rich or poor legal traditions is partially related to the amount of melanin that the subjects have in their body. The dark-skinned subject lives in the colonial South, the light-skinned subject lives in the imperial North. In the colonial model, the imperial subject has been identified as Caucasian; the colonized subject as black, brown, red or yellow. In addition, the first is a legally ahistorical subject. Before contact with the metropolis, she did not have law. The subject was not immersed in a legal tradition on which she could rest and that was her basis for constructing new and truly original legal knowledge. The subject's legal knowledge begins when she is conquered and colonized. Contact with the law of the metropolis allows the subject to enter into the history of law. However, the subject enters into this history, not as a maker but as a reproducer or a minor actor. The law of the metropolis replaces the native law or tolerates it, provided that it does not contradict its presuppositions.[74] The pre-historic moment is therefore lost in time; it returns to being inaudible and ungraspable. It is not a valuable object of study; it is neither narrated nor written about. The colonial subject does not have access to its legal past. The metropolis subject, on the other hand, is a subject with history and a historicized subject. It is part of an intergenerational chain that connects it with its past, that explains its present and that launches it towards multiple possible legal futures. Its legal past and present are significant objects of knowledge. They deserve to be known,

---

[74] The *Leyes de Indias* enacted by the Spanish empire, for example, recognized the laws of indigenous peoples if they did not violate imperial norms. *See* Recopilación general de las Leyes de Indias, Libro Segundo, Título Primero, Ley iii.

narrated, and kept in written language. Consequently, the identities of these subjects of legal knowledge are created from the way in which their law and legal traditions (or lack thereof) are narrated.

J.M. Coetzee presents these subjects in a paradigmatic fashion in the novel *Waiting for the Barbarians*.[75] The protagonist is the magistrate of a metropolis who exercises his functions in the colony, in a desert, surrounded by barbarians of color. The empire does not have a name; nor does the colony or the magistrate. They are expressions of the idea of empire and of colony. The magistrate is the guardian of civilization; the one who brings law into a no-man's land. The territory is one where violence and love, the opposites of law, rule. The barbarians rob, injure, and kill each other; the barbarians are flesh, and they love each other. Through law, the magistrate seeks to resolve conflicts that emerge between the barbarians. These conflicts create instability and poverty. The magistrate also protects his own people from this state of nature. The town that he runs is an extension of the polis he represents. Its wood and mud walls materially separate civilization from barbarism. Nevertheless, law constitutes these walls conceptually. The law is what separates the ones from the others.

The symbolic and material power that the magistrate concentrates is also at the service of the citizens of the metropolis, particularly of its functionaries. They represent other facets of the civilization; they bring civilization to the colony. When the metropolis has news that the natives want to emancipate themselves, it acts immediately. Colonel Joll, who interrogates a group of natives seeking information on the rebels, in spite of his cruel methods (torture), wants nothing but to bring order and stability to these no-man's lands. These are the preconditions for the magistrate to be able to exercise his functions as an impartial third party between the savages and to protect the other representatives of the metropolis. Merchants, tax collectors and artists also play a role in this civilizing process and must be protected.

The magistrate defines himself through what he is but also what he is not. He is the law and, consequently, he is the civilization. He embodies a legal tradition that he now seeks to apply in the territories. However, he is also defined in contrast to the other, the natives with whom he interacts on a daily basis, and whom he rules and resolves their conflicts. He is not them; they are not him. His occasional native lover and the young woman who was tortured by the colonel and whom he protected remind him of

---

[75] J.M. Coetzee (2003), *Waiting for the Barbarians* (London: Secker & Warburg).

this constantly. They represent love and desire. They represent the incarnated body with its own norms, distinct from legal norms. In contrast, despite his cruelty, the official shares a part of his identity; his belonging to the metropolis makes him a part of the same imagined community. When the magistrate decides to return the tortured young woman to her people, he is then accused, detained, and condemned by the metropolis. Colonel Joll accuses him of "cooperating with the enemy". The laws of the metropolis, "the law", confront the norms of love, in this case a combination of romantic love and love for your fellow human being.

These dual but interdependent subjects are also shown in a powerful manner in the Orientalist paintings of the nineteenth century.[76] These artists were simultaneously fascinated and disturbed by the barbarians. They were great masters of European art from the period in question and they synthesize a particular gaze upon Europe's other. In the works of Delacroix, Chassériau, Regault, Guillaumet, Tournemine and Barrias, the colonial subject is identified with the other of law: violence and love.[77]

Always dark, the other is a bloodthirsty warrior who inhabits extreme environments like the desert or the jungle; it is a body, in particular, an erotized female body, and it is friend or husband who defends his loved ones.[78] The recurring themes of these painters are scenes of war, hunting, wild animals and harems or naked female bodies placed in sumptuous spaces.[79] The colonial subjects are not normalized bodies who are guided by law. They are bodies that are outside of the law: they are desire, nature, violence, fraternal or romantic love. They are those who the law wants to control, dominate, and marginalize.

---

[76] *See generally*, Gerard-Georges Lemair (2001), *The Orient in Western Art* (Columbia, NY: Konemann).

[77] Some of the most well-known orientalist paintings by these artists are in the Musée d'Orsay, *see*: http://www.musee-orsay.fr/fileadmin/mediatheque/integration_MO/PDF/Orientalism.pdf (accessed 8 September 2011). The images reproduced in this chapter are located in this museum. The three images have creative commons licenses: https://commons.wikimedia.org/wiki/File:Eug%C3%A8ne_Delacroix_-_Chasse_au_tigre_(1854).jpg; https://commons.wikimedia.org/wiki/File:Th%C3%A9odore_Chass%C3%A9riau_-_Tepidarium_-_Google_Art_Project.jpg; https://commons.wikimedia.org/wiki/File:Henri_regnault_maures_grena.jpg.

[78] *See generally*, Donald A. Rosenthal (1982), *Orientalism, the Near East in French Painting, 1800–1880* (Rochester, NY: Memorial Art Gallery of the University of Rochester).

[79] Mary Anne Stevens (1984), *The Orientalists: Delacroix to Matisse: European Painters in North Africa and the Near East* (Exhibition catalogue, Royal Academy of Arts).

Source: https://commons.wikimedia.org/wiki/File:Eug%C3%A8ne_Delacroix_-_Chasse_au_tigre_(1854).jpg (accessed 1 October 2017).

Figure 2.1 Eugène Delacroix (1798–1863): Chasse aux lions *(*Lion Hunt*)*

Legal Knowledge's Time

The time that the colonial model of production of legal knowledge creates is linear but finite. The time of the metropolis is interpreted as a valuable and solid chain that is lost in the past, experienced in the present and maintained in the future. The legal tradition that the metropolis belongs to is presented as undoubtedly fertile. This legal tradition is connected with a complex and immemorial culture that is embodied in the law. For example, the civil tradition is typically presented as the result of the genius of the Romano-Germanic culture.[80] The contributions that colonial

[80] P.G. Monateri (2006), "Gayo el Negro: una búsqueda de los orígenes multiculturales de la tradición jurídica occidental", in P.G. Monateri and Samuel Geoffrey, *La Invención Del Derecho Privado* (San Diego, CA: Estados Unidos de America), p. 67.

Source: https://commons.wikimedia.org/wiki/File:Th%C3%A9odore_Chass%C3%A9riau_-_Tepidarium_-_Google_Art_Project.jpg (accessed 1 October 2017).

Figure 2.2 Théodore Chassériau (1819–1856): Tepidarium

Source: https://commons.wikimedia.org/wiki/File:Henri_regnault_maures_grena.jpg (accessed 1 October 2017).

Figure 2.3 *Henri Regault (1843–1871):* Exécution sans jugement sous les rois maures de Grenade (Execution without Trial under the Rule of the Moorish Kings in Granada)

subjects have made to this tradition – Jews, Egyptians, for example – are made to be invisible.[81] The interaction with the other is understood as a contamination. Cultures are organized hierarchically in direct relation to their capacity to create true law. There are cultures that have the potential to create law; others that can only reproduce their backwardness.

The legal tradition of the metropolis begins in a remote past that is retrieved through constant reinterpretations. This tradition, the time in which the metropolis subject lives, is conceived as a unit. It has no solution of continuity; it is not fractionated; it is one. The metropolis subject experiences it as a whole in the present. The future of this legal subject is to maintain her present indefinitely; to maintain the metropolis as the metropolis, which will always be defined by its other, the colony. In a way, the history of the metropolis has ended; it is already the metropolis. The time of the metropolis subject is a function of the time of the colony and the colonial subject. Without a doubt, it will keep facing legal challenges and difficulties. Nevertheless, these are presented as having as background a legal tradition, and on the basis of a set of institutions and a legal order that were reached after a long historical process, and presumed to be solid. It does not make sense to change them radically; they form the "metropolis" law, that which the colonies aspire to reach some day.

The time of the colony, its history and its legal past, begin with its interaction with the metropolis. The colonial subject's past has a clear and distinct origin. For the colonial subject, there is no time before this encounter. Prior to the zero moment there is a temporal void; it is known that there was something before the beginning of history but the model chooses to ignore this fact. The low legal value of what precedes history does not merit attention. The law, the legal tradition of the colony, begins with the imperial conquest. The history of the colonial subject is therefore a continuous effort to be like its other, to experience and overcome each of the stages that will lead it to the end of history: the moment when it cannot be distinguished from the metropolis. The present is always shown as a link in a chain that ends at a defined point, while the future is shown as the ever-open possibility of arriving at the end of history.

The Latin American experience with its legal past is illustrative in this respect. Our legal tradition, the one that we now ignore or try to apprehend halfway (our production on the history of law is insufficient),[82] begins with the moment that our interaction with Europe begins. Historically, we

---

81 Id.

82 Matthew C. Mirow (2004), *Latin American Law: A History of Private Law and Institutions in Spanish America* (Austin: University of Texas Press).

have identified ourselves as part of the Romano-Germanic tradition.[83] The colonial laws, Spanish or Portuguese, determine the beginning of our legal history. The laws of the recently created republics did not break with that tradition. The civil code of Andrés Bello, the legal document par excellence in the region, which determines a central part of our legal identity, is evidence of this fact.[84] Bello's Code is in large part a synthesis of the Napoleonic Civil Code, the Seven Items of Alphonse X the Wise and the Digest.[85] We enter the history of law as secondary members of a tradition that we did not create. We have certainly appropriated this tradition and transformed it. However, it is not interpreted, we do not interpret, that these appropriations and transformations have changed the course of the tradition or have become first-order representations of the values that it promotes.

The situation is made even more complex if we attend to the influence that the Anglo-American legal tradition has had on the region in the last few decades.[86] Anglo-Saxon liberal and critical legal theory, the value of case law in the legal system, adversarial criminal law, neoclassical labor law, U.S. teaching methods and ways of doing legal academia, among many other things, have entered into our legal history subtly or abruptly.[87] Again, we interact with the metropolis and the history of law in an uncomfortable manner. These creations are ours in many senses. They form part of our legal reality. We have used, interpreted, and adjusted them. However, once again we get on the train car of legal history without having been able to reach its locomotive. We are not in control of the tradition, and we (and others) perceive our products as minor expressions of the same. The hybrid character of our legal tradition is not a problem; rather, it is an opportunity. Nevertheless, as subjects of knowledge we enter this history being perceived and internalizing that our legal history begins when we make contact with the other; being interpreted and interpreting as minor iterations of a past that does not belong to us and to which we have made no significant contributions.

When we try to look beyond the zero moment of our legal history we are left with our hands nearly empty. The Pre-Hispanic legal/political past is almost completely unknown; we have not made it part of our present. This does not mean that normatively we should defend a kind of nativism that

---

[83] David Clark (1990), "The idea of the civil law tradition", in John Henry Merryman and David Scott Clark, *Comparative and Private International Law* (Berlin: Duncker and Humblot), pp. 11–23.

[84] Mirow (n 35).

[85] Id., at 304, 309.

[86] Kelemen and Sibbitt (n 18).

[87] Merryman (n 18); Rittich (n 18).

only values that which would be perceived as original: the legal and political traditions of the Pre-Hispanic indigenous peoples. These traditions may be useless for contemporary societies, questionable morally or politically, or there simply may not be sufficient information to evaluate and reinterpret them. This nativism would also negate our Creole legal being. Part of what we are legally is already conditioned by the civil law and Anglo-American legal traditions; the axes that constitute these traditions form part of our legal identity and have an undeniable richness.

Nevertheless, it would seem useful for Latin America to reconnect critically with this other part of its legal past that has been made invisible.[88] For example, some of the experiments we have seen in Bolivia and Ecuador may be promising. The idea that nature has rights, that human beings can have a non-anthropocentric relationship with nature, and the recognition of the cultural diversity within institutional structures, among other things, can generate valuable reinterpretations of the traditions of indigenous peoples that allow the states of the region to fulfill their purposes adequately.[89] This knowledge may intersect richly with legal knowledge that already forms part of our history and generate innovative legal products that are politically useful. These experiments may also lead us to rethink ourselves as subjects of legal knowledge, and rethink the concept of time we move in.

Legal Knowledge's Space

The space of the colonial model of knowledge production is also dual. It is mapped as a hierarchized North–South space. The space is not horizontal, and it is not perceived as equal. The content of each of these geographies is different and is qualified in distinct ways. The Global North, the metropolis, is the legal promised land; the Global South, the colony, is scorched legal earth. The former is a rich context of legal production; it has the conditions to create, exchange, and use legal knowledge. It has a rich tradition, solid academic, legal and political institutions and subjects that are adequately trained. Its history shows the countless original legal products that it created and exported, or could export. In contrast, the colonial territory is described as a poor context for the creation of legal knowledge. It is a space

---

88 Alejandro Medici (2010), "El nuevo constitucionalismo latinoamericano y el giro decolonial: Bolivia y Ecuador Revista", *Derecho y Ciencias Sociales*, **3**, 3–23.

89 *See* Eduardo Gudynas (2009), "La ecología política del giro biocéntrico en la nueva Constitución de Ecuador", *Revista Estudios Sociales (Bogotá)*, **32**, 34–47 and Marco Aparicio (2011), "Nuevo constitucionalismo, derechos y medio ambiente en las constituciones de Ecuador y Bolivia", *Revista General de Derecho Público Comparado*, **9**, 1–24.

of reproduction, dissemination, and local application of knowledge from the metropolis. In this conceptual geography, original knowledge is not constructed, and the minimum requirements for this to happen are not met. Its legal tradition is nonexistent, poor, or a marginal piece within the tradition of the metropolis; its legal and political institutions are weak and unstable; and its subjects and institutions of knowledge are poorly trained and fragile.

For example, until recently, comparative law courses and materials in U.S. law schools did not include countries of the Global South in their legal analyses.[90] Still today, it is unusual to find syllabi that include countries other than Germany, France, the United Kingdom, and perhaps Canada.[91] Courses on Latin American, Asian or African law are the exception in U.S. law schools.[92] When they are occasionally given, they usually depend on what is known as *area studies*. Studying the law of a Global South country may be relevant for understanding its main structures, dynamics, and characteristics. Thus, it may be relevant for social scientists and humanists that belong to departments of area studies. However, the law of the Global South is not significant for law professors. It is not a legitimate object of study in Global North law schools.

However, the space of the colonial model is also internally hierarchized. The South also exists in the North, and not all southern colonies are equal. For the model, put into operation, Germany, France and the United States are not the same as Spain, Portugal, and Greece; nor is India the same as Vietnam, South Africa the same as Namibia, or Argentina the same as Nicaragua. The flow of exchange of legal goods in this space is therefore unidirectional. The movement of legal theory, doctrine and practices is always North–South; it occurs in a single direction between the binary space that is the axis of the model or within each of the spaces that constitute this axis.

THE RULES AND PRINCIPLES

The General Conceptual Oppositions

The rules and principles that guide the model revolve around the following four general conceptual oppositions: (1) mimesis/autopoiesis; (2) local

---

[90] Ran Hirschl (2014), *Comparative Matters: The Renaissance of Comparative Constitutional Law* (Oxford: Oxford University Press), pp. 192–223.

[91] Id. Hirschl discusses the world-series syndrome that affects comparative constitutional law in the Global North.

[92] *See* Bonilla (n 6), at 11.

knowledge/universal knowledge; (3) culture/law; and (4) useful languages for legal knowledge/languages not useful for legal knowledge. These oppositions go hand in hand with another four particular conceptual oppositions: (1) high academic capital/low academic capital; (2) high-quality academic products/low-quality academic products; (3) rich academic institutions/poor academic institutions; and (4) experience in the use of legal knowledge/inexperience in the use of legal knowledge. All of these conceptual oppositions intersect, creating a system that guides the subjects of legal knowledge in their processes of production, exchange, and use of legal knowledge. These conceptual oppositions also give rise to five assumptions that specify the ways the metropolis subject and the colonial subject must behave. In previous publications, I have called these presuppositions[93] "academic capital hierarchy", "he who pays decides", "production well", "protected geographical indicator" and "effective operator".

The first general conceptual opposition, mimesis/autopoiesis, describes the contents of the colonial legal systems as representations of the legal systems of the metropolis. The colony therefore aspires to represent the theories, doctrine and practices of the metropolis. In the best cases, the law of the colony is a copy of the law of the metropolis. This is the highest aspiration of the colony. In as much as its legal and political reality does not meet the necessary conditions for the creation of legal knowledge, it has no option but to imitate the legal products generated by its other. Its greatest achievement, therefore, is to faithfully copy the original. The problems and challenges that the colony and the metropolis face are similar. They are a consequence of the fact that human beings pursue similar purposes, for example, peace and prosperity, and that nature generates similar challenges for them both.[94] The legal knowledge of the metropolis may therefore be exported from the metropolis to the colony. Legal transplants can, and should, be the rule.[95] The mimetic colony is therefore the space where the original knowledge emerging in the metropolis is disseminated and applied locally.

Part of the Latin American literature on legal theory follows this pattern.[96] Publications in the area are often attempts to explain the argumentative

---

[93] *See* Bonilla (n 17), at 6–13.

[94] To understand this argument adequately it might be useful to appeal to the analogous argument offered by functionalism in comparative law. *See* Mark Tushnet (1999), "The possibilities of comparative constitutional law", *Yale L.J.*, **108**, 1225–39.

[95] Id.

[96] For an analysis of Latin American legal theory and its relationship with the Global North's legal theory, *see* Lopez Medina (n 70).

structure of the work of the great Anglo-American philosophers of law to the local public.[97] In this sense, legal theory texts are presented as a sum of literal interpretations and explanatory glosses that allow new generations of theorists to learn and have access to the canon. Thus, it is not surprising to find that the shelves of legal theory in Latin American law libraries contain a significant number of books on the theory of Ronald Dworkin, H.L.A. Hart or Richard Posner, among others. Many of these books are not horizontal dialogues between Anglo-Saxon and Latin American authors. The text is not an effort to think about a theoretical or practical problem together. The U.S. author is the reference around which the explanatory efforts of the Latin American author revolve. From the start, there is an epistemic subordination of the latter to the former. The point is not to deny that the work of one may be broader and more solid than that of the other. The Anglo-Saxon authors named certainly have a tremendously rich production. The point is the attitude with which the Latin American academic assumes his interaction with the U.S. academic. He is not a peer attempting to describe, analyze or evaluate the legal realities of contemporary states. He is a disseminator of legal knowledge created by others.

On other occasions, Latin American works on legal theory seek to apply the theories of the metropolis authors to their own realities. The theoretical framework is given by the production of the Anglo-Saxon author, and the colonial authors seek to specify the consequences that using it has for describing, analyzing and evaluating the local reality. The argument is not that making use of foreign theoretical frameworks to understand Latin America is problematic in and of itself, although it may be so when these frameworks emerge from contexts that are very different from the contexts where they are intended to be applied. Nor does the argument intend to deny that the discourse might be transformed when used, and therefore, that innovation might be a consequence of interpretation. The argument is that the attitude with which this enterprise is often assumed illustrates the mimesis/autopoiesis conceptual opposition. The Latin American author does not enter into dialogue with the theoretical framework. She does not understand herself as part of a narration that may transform, or that may contribute to developing or criticizing; her role is to apply and disseminate pre-existing knowledge in a precise manner. She is outside of the narration.

In contrast, the law of the metropolis is understood as an original system that emerges as a consequence of and simultaneously reflects metropolitan culture. The rich and complex culture of the metropolis

---

97 Id.

gives way to a particular kind of law that has the objective of solving a series of social and political problems. Culture and law in the metropolis have an organic relationship.[98] Legal rules, principles, theories and practices express and confirm their culture. At the same time, the autopoietic character of the system alludes to its capacity to reproduce and transform itself. The legal order has the tools to continue existing as an original product and to transform itself without losing this originality. The system certainly has the capacity to enrich itself with foreign elements (and does so effectively). However, it also has the power to appropriate these elements, and transform them into an additional component of its conceptual machinery.

The local/universal conceptual opposition intersects with the mimesis/autopoiesis pair. The knowledge of the colony is interpreted as spatially limited knowledge. It only has application within the borders of the colony; it only attends to its challenges and realities. It is not reproducible in other contexts. An article about Mexican or Brazilian labor law, for example, is only relevant for Mexico or Brazil, not for Colombia, South Africa, India or the United States. The realities of Global South countries cannot be generalized. Due to their specific character, they are not useful for other Global South countries, and much less for those of the Global North.

In contrast, the knowledge of the metropolis is understood as universal. It has a relevance and value that transcend national borders. Hence the knowledge of the metropolis is considered *ex ante* transplantable while the knowledge of the colonies, *ex ante*, is considered rooted in local realities and therefore incapable of crossing their borders. The colonial model's concept of time explains this fact. As the time of the colony is linear and is formed by a set of links that end at the law of the metropolis, the legal knowledge it generates is only applicable to its particular conditions. It is only relevant for the stage of legal development in which the colony is found. The time of the metropolis, the eternal present it experiences at the end of history, enables the knowledge it generates to spread and to be applied to all links of the chain that precede it. The knowledge of the metropolis can contribute to the colony's advancement, to its progress, and to the materialization of its objective: be like the metropolis.

The reception that the work of Ronald Dworkin and John Rawls has had in much of the Global South may be useful for illustrating this

---

98 To understand this argument adequately it might be useful to appeal to the analogous argument offered by expressivism in comparative law. *See* Pierre Legrand (1997), "The impossibility of 'legal transplants'", 4 *Maastricht J. Eur. & Comp. L.*, **4**, 111.

argument. The two philosophers explicitly recognize that their work is based on U.S. law and political culture.[99] However, their words are read, commented on, and applied throughout the Global South without there usually being a reference to the close relationship they have with a particular context.[100] Consequently, the connection between context and the knowledge created in the metropolis is lost in the colonial model of legal knowledge production. This knowledge would seem to exist in a cultural vacuum, and is therefore immediately exportable and applicable in any other cultural context. This point becomes even more telling when this knowledge is composed by a set of local rules or practices. An article on U.S. commercial law, intellectual property or constitutional law is also understood as having immediate relevance in the Global South. The fact that the article refers to particular rules or practices that are only valid in the United States is irrelevant.

In contrast, Latin American, Asian or African legal knowledge is presumed to be attached to its specific cultural context. The titles and content of articles produced in these regions always clarify that they are referring to Chilean, Egyptian or Korean law. It is made clear from the beginning that it refers and applies only, or fundamentally, to one country. Nevertheless, it is not very common to find that the title of a publication authored by a U.S. law professor states something like "Freedom of Expression in the United States" or "Intellectual Property in the United States". When commenting on one of my papers, a colleague from the United States told me that if I wanted to publish it in a law journal in his country I should add a reference to Colombia in the title. In his opinion, which was certainly useful from a strategic point of view, it should be clear what national context it came from and where my analysis was developed. Paradoxically, none of the various papers that this professor published in Latin America made reference to the United States in the title. Neither he nor his editors or publishers felt the need to make the clarification.

The argument that presupposes the universality of the Global North's

---

[99] John Rawls (1971), *A Theory of Justice* (Cambridge, MA: Harvard University Press) and Ronald Dworkin (1986), *Law's Empire* (Cambridge, MA: Harvard University Press).

[100] About the relationship between U.S. legal theory and the Global South, *see generally*, Ugo Mattei (2003), "A theory of imperial law: A study on U.S. hegemony and the Latin resistance", *Ind. J. Global Legal Stud.*, **10**, 383, 447; Ugo Mattei (1994), "Why the wind changed: Intellectual leadership in western law, *Am. J. Comp. L.*, **42**, 195; Wolfgang Wiegand (1996), "Americanization of law: Reception or convergence", in Lawrence M. Friedman and Harry N. Scheiber (eds), *Legal Culture and the Legal Profession* (Boulder: Westview Press), p. 137.

legal knowledge can also be illustrated by appealing to the minor role that empirical legal research has historically played in Latin America. This may be explained by the lack of empirical research tools that characterize Latin American law professors and the legocentrism that has identified an important part of the legal academia of the region. Law schools do not usually teach quantitative and qualitative empirical research methods. As a consequence, legal academics are not typically familiarized with these methods or do not have experience in using them. In as much as the paradigmatic object of study of the Latin American legal scholar has been the law (*la ley*),[101] the main type of academic product has been the treatise. In the best of cases, this kind of academic product aims at systematizing the rules that constitute a specific area of the law.[102] In the worst case, unfortunately very common, it aims at presenting the basic contents of the law and adding a few glosses that are usually directed to solving practical problems.

Yet, these arguments only tell one part of the story. The lack of empirical research in Latin American legal academia is also related to the use of Global North theoretical frameworks that are assumed to be universal. Thus, many Latin American legal scholars presuppose that they can apply these conceptual tools without taking into account the particularities of the legal contexts where they are located.[103] Theoretical knowledge, given its general character and rationality, may be used to describe, analyze or evaluate any political community. Consequently, the empirical work that would allow knowing the dynamics and characteristics of the contexts in which Latin American legal norms are created and applied becomes irrelevant.

The conceptual opposition between culture and law suggests that in the colony there is really no law, only a particular type of culture. The law in the colony has failed[104] or is useless. The culture of the colony does not have the characteristics that would enable it to create a legal system that could achieve the objectives that legal systems usually attempt to achieve, order and justice, for example. In this way, the law of the colony and

---

[101] *See* Pérez-Perdomo (n 56), at 103–104.

[102] *See* Alejandro Madrazo (2008), "From revelation to creation: The origins of text and doctrine in the civil law tradition", *Mexican Law Review*, **1** (1).

[103] The way in which the work of Jürgen Habermas is used in Latin America makes explicit how the argument operates. Although Habermas states that his work refers mainly to Western Europe, in Latin America, many times, we use his work mechanically to examine and evaluate our social and legal reality.

[104] Jorge L. Esquirol (2008), "The failed law of Latin America", *Am. J. Comp. L.*, **56**, 75.

the legal knowledge that has it as an object of study is irrelevant for the metropolis. The levels of impunity, for example, are so high that criminal law is considered irrelevant or marginal for maintaining social order. The degrees of security that the colony may have must therefore be explained by appealing to other normative orders, secular morality or religion, for example. No subject of knowledge of the metropolis would be interested in studying this set of paper legal rules.

This argument can be illustrated by referring to the descriptions made in asylum petitions by many Latin Americans to the United States.[105] The strategy that attorneys and social organizations articulate so that their client may be able to stay in the United States legally consists of showing that the client's country of origin of is scorched legal earth.[106] In this country, there are no functional legal and political institutions and the law is only a form with minimal consequences, if any, for social reality.[107] Human rights violations are thus systematic and form a continual pattern that affects the entire social reality. There are no areas where law and legal and political institutions function. The issue is not that attorneys or social organizations describe the reality of Latin American law in the above manner for strategic reasons that may be understandable and laudable, nor is the issue the fact that human rights violations are not common in the region. The matter I want to call attention to with this example is that these descriptions end up constructing the general representation that the metropolis has of the law of the colony. The courts accept this generalization, politicians use it to generate public policies, and Latin American academics benefit from it when they serve as attorneys in the proceedings.[108] These kinds of situations contribute to creating and promoting a homogenizing vision of the Latin American legal and political reality that qualifies it negatively in an absolute way. This vision also helps with the consolidation of the idea that Latin American law is not an object of valuable study, even if its shipwreck is.

However, if the failed law of the colony becomes a second-grade object of study for attorneys and legal academics of the metropolis, it also becomes a valuable object of study for social sciences like the anthropology and sociology of the metropolis.[109] For these sciences, the failure of law in the colony

---

[105] Jorge L. Esquirol (2013), "Legal Latin Americanism", *Yale Hum. Rts. & Dev. L.J.*, **16**, 145–70.

[106] Id.

[107] Id.

[108] Id.

[109] *See* Brian Z. Tamanaha (2009), *The Primacy of Society and the Failures of Law and Development* 6 (St John's University Legal Studies Research Paper Series,

generates a descriptive and explanatory challenge that may produce notable epistemological results. Therefore, the supposition that stems from this conceptual opposition is that there is a close relationship between culture and law, and that there are some cultures that can create law and others that cannot. Hence, the civilizing process that has gone hand-in-hand with many imperial enterprises starts with a cultural change: the barbarians will have to adopt the religion, language and mores of the metropolis. Legal barbarism has cultural barbarism as one of its primary causes.

In contrast, in the colonial model of legal knowledge production, the metropolis has law, not only an appearance of law. This legal order also reflects and is an effect of its culture. A rich, complex and solid culture is a precondition for the existence of a true legal order. The relationship between law and culture in the metropolis is therefore symbiotic. Culture gives way to law but law confirms and protects culture. This relationship is firmly rooted in comparative law. The civil tradition is understood as a consequence, principally, of the Romano-Germanic culture; the common law of the Anglo-American culture.[110] The two dominant families in the theory and practice of comparative law are the results of two cultural traditions of European origin.[111] The two have been (or were) relevant in the imperial projects of the United Kingdom as well as of those of Italy, Germany, France and Spain.[112]

The last general conceptual opposition, languages apt for legal knowledge/languages that are useless for legal knowledge again makes reference, but in a more specific manner, to a central element of all cultures: language. The colonial model of legal knowledge production understands that the languages of the metropolis, Spanish, Portuguese and English, among others, were or are adequate tools to express the legal truth.[113] The model argues that this is particularly true with respect to English nowadays,[114] given the enormous influence that Anglo-Saxon

---

Paper No. 09-0172), available at: http://papers.ssrn.com/sol3/papers.cfm?abstract_id=1406999 (accessed 8 September 2017); Jorge L. Esquirol (2009), "Writing the law of Latin America", *Geo. Wash. Int'l L. Rev.*, **40**, 693, 706, 731.

110 John R. Schmidhauser (1992), "Legal imperialism: Its enduring impact on colonial and post-colonial judicial systems", *International Political Science Review*, **13** (3), 321–34.

111 Mariana Pargendler (2012), "The rise and decline of legal families", *Am. J. Comp. L.*, **60**, 1043.

112 John R. Schmidhauser (1989), "Power, legal imperialism, and dependency", *Law & Society Review*, **23** (5), 857–78.

113 Theresa M. Lillis and Mary Jane Curry (2010), *Academic Writing in a Global Context: The Politics and Practices of Publishing in English* (London: Routledge).

114 Id.

legal theories, doctrine and practices have on the legal communities of the Global South. English is understood as a direct, precise and flexible language that enables the creativity of its speakers.

Legal English names realities in an exact and concise manner. It makes efficient use of its resources: its sentences are short; its paragraphs adequately distinguish between the ideas they present and they have a convenient length so the reader does not lose the driving thread. English is also presented as a language that is flexible in the face of the reality that names or qualifies, for example, when allowing for the verbalization of nouns. This, in turn, enables and promotes the creativity of its users. Users can easily invent words to name the reality they are perceiving or evaluating, to capture their nuances or to design a new phenomenon, for example. In contrast, languages like Spanish are understood as imprecise and inefficient. For example, Spanish is described as a language that does not know the principle of economy of means: its long sentences, interminable paragraphs, descriptions that make use of an infinite number of words. In sum, Spanish is thought to be a language that is not very useful for expressing legal knowledge. As can be seen, these descriptions of English and Spanish are sometimes presented as central components of the language itself; other times, as conventions on the ways these languages are used in legal academia.

Latin Americans who have studied or worked in a U.S. law school have probably heard these kinds of descriptions of Spanish. In this sense, many of these practitioners or academics invest a great amount of time and effort in modifying the conventions for the expression of the ideas they were educated with. Without a doubt, this can be helpful. It allows these Latin American attorneys to approach different forms of expression that can generate returns distinct from those created by the linguistic conventions and conventions of academic locution that they know. The problem arises when these conventions and practices are essentialized and naturalized. The issue would probably be explained better by saying that the Latin American attorney simply does not have adequate mastery of English and is expressing his ideas by making use of words in this language but with grammatical forms from Spanish. Without a doubt, this is an error that must be corrected. Nevertheless, this situation is not presented as a practical problem that can be solved with work and effort by the Spanish writer, but as characteristics of her language and therefore her culture. On the above-mentioned situation, we cannot conclude that Spanish cannot be an adequate vehicle for the expression of clear and precise legal knowledge.

This problem becomes more acute when we realize that most prestigious academic discussions and publications have English as their sole official language and are primarily located in the United States.[115] The academic from the Global South who does not have English as her native language has a double challenge: to become competent in a language that is not her own, and to learn U.S. norms as to research, writing and submission of legal academic works. In verbal academic debates, this burden is particularly onerous. First, the lawyer from the Global South who does not speak English is required to speak a language that is not her own because it is the "international" language; second, in order to be taken moderately seriously, she is asked to have the same linguistic competencies as her English-speaking colleagues. Slowness, imprecision or poor pronunciation is barely tolerated. Again, those who have studied or worked in a U.S. law school will probably have seen how their English-speaking colleagues disperse, get anxious or roll their eyes at times when, upon presenting their ideas, sentences become very long, their words become vague or mistakes in pronunciation become recurrent. This situation contrasts with the fact that the number of U.S. law professors who speak a second language is quite limited. In this sense, most U.S. professors have not had to experience the effort involved in learning another language, assimilating the academic norms through which other communities of knowledge express themselves, or feel the uneasiness that arises when making a mistake or being imprecise when speaking a language that is not your own in professional circles.

The Particular Conceptual Oppositions

The four particular conceptual oppositions make direct reference to and specify the contexts for the creation of knowledge in the colony and in the metropolis. These conceptual oppositions are nurtured by and also feed the four general conceptual oppositions. All of these constitute a conceptual network that should explain and guide subjects of legal knowledge. These specific conceptual oppositions are the following four: high academic capital/low academic capital; high-quality academic products/low-quality academic products; rich academic institutions/poor academic institutions; and experience in the use of legal knowledge/inexperience in the use of legal knowledge.

The first conceptual opposition makes reference to the differences that exist between the metropolis and the colony with respect to their respective academic capital. The former is understood as a space with high academic capital. Its universities are more solid than those of the colony. This solidity

---

115 Id.

is shown in both quantitative and qualitative dimensions:[116] on the one hand, the number of full-time professors, number of databases, quantity of books in the libraries, wealth of publications and high number of academic exchanges with national or international networks; on the other hand, the quality of the academic production, internalization and systematic application by members of the legal academic community of a series of dynamics for the production, discussion and dissemination of legal products, and quality of the infrastructure that law professors have available. In contrast, in the colony, the model assumes that the academic capital available is low, for quantitative and qualitative reasons.[117] The professionalization of legal academia is recent and thus there are very few full-time professors and the number of books, publications, and national and international networks available are low. Likewise, the dynamics of production and critique that allow for the systematic creation of legal knowledge does not exist or has not been systematized or internalized by the colonial legal academia. The quality of the material structure that law professors have access to, buildings, computers and databases, among other items, is inadequate.

This first conceptual opposition goes hand-in-hand with the following two: rich academic institutions/poor academic institutions and high-quality legal products/low-quality legal products. In part, the academic communities of the metropolis owe their high academic capital to the great quantity of economic resources they have at their disposition. For example, this allows for covering notable costs, such as hiring full-time professors, having good libraries and constructing and participating in national and international academic networks. Likewise, this allows them to make greater contributions to academic projects advanced jointly with Global South institutions, including the organization of seminars, research including field work or the publication of books. The lack of economic resources partially explains the weaknesses of Global South law schools and their lesser material contribution to projects that advance partnership with academic institutions of the metropolis.

It is therefore no surprise that, for the model, the quality of products from the colony is presumed to be low and the quality of products from the metropolis is presumed to be high. The material and immaterial (academic culture) conditions available for each of these regions are different. Fruit that is appetizing for the intellect cannot emerge from an academically barren land; wonderful harvests for restless and active minds will emerge from an academically fertile and well-cultivated land.

---

116 *See* Bonilla (n 17), at 6–9.

117 Id.

In turn, these three conceptual oppositions generate three premises that guide, and should guide, the subject of knowledge of the colonial model: production well, protected geographical indicator, and he who pays decides.[118] These premises indicate that the only possible source for the creation of legal knowledge is the Global North; that legal products of the metropolis should be presumed to have a high quality because they come from the metropolis; and that he who contributes more resources to the financing of a joint South–North project should enjoy greater decision-making power over its purposes and development.

The first premise, the production well, would explain why in the construction and interpretation of the grammar of modern constitutionalism, Global South academia and courts have played a marginal role.[119] Both are at the margins of the global dialogue that occurs around the meaning and practical consequences that concepts like people, sovereignty, citizenship, rights, equality and autonomy should have.[120] These concepts, constructed by a relatively small set of modern and contemporary theorists, like Thomas Hobbes, Jean Jacques Rousseau, John Locke and Immanuel Kant, on the one hand, and John Rawls, Charles Taylor, Robert Nozick and Jürgen Habermas, on the other, form the axes around which the modern legal and political imagination revolves.[121] Nevertheless, the subjects of colonial knowledge barely appear within those that are presumed to be legitimate interpreters of these categories. When we speak of legitimate contemporary interpreters of this constitutional grammar, institutions like the Supreme Court of the United States, the European Court of Human Rights or the German Constitutional Court come to mind. Authors like Ronald Dworkin, Cass Sunstein and Richard Posner also appear. Nevertheless, few would think that institutions like the Supreme Court of India, the South African Constitutional Court or the Colombian Constitutional Court, among the most solid legal academies of the Global South, have played or might play a similar role to that played by Global North authors or institutions.

The second premise would explain why it is common that in conferences on legal issues in Latin America, professors from the U.S. are invited as key speakers or play a de facto capital role. It does not matter what institution they belong to, or if these institutions are solid. Nor does the

---

118 *See* Bonilla (n 17), at 7–13.

119 *See* Bonilla (n 17), at 6–9.

120 James Tully (1995), *Strange Multiplicity: Constitutionalism in an Age of Diversity* (Cambridge: Cambridge University Press), pp. 62–79.

121 Id. *at* 42, 59–60, 79–80; Charles Howard McIlwain (1940), *Constitutionalism: Ancient and Modern* (Ithaca: Cornell University Press), pp. 3–24.

quality of their academic production matter much. It is not common to have precise information about U.S. law schools in Latin American legal academia. The information that they have about schools other than those that occupy the first few positions in the academic rankings is minimal. All Latin American law professors know Yale, Harvard, Stanford or Columbia, but very few have precise knowledge of the greater part of law schools that occupy the middle and lower levels of the U.S. academic hierarchy. Nor do they have much precise information about the work of academics who do not belong to Ivy League universities.

In these cases, what is important for the organizers of many conferences is the context of the production of knowledge where the professors come from, and that their production is written in English and published in U.S. journals. Like wine from Burgundy, these professors and their production enjoy a presumption of quality that protects and values them even before their works are read and evaluated. However, the issue is that once they are tried, these wines (these works) may be sour or have high degrees of acidity or an excessive degree of tannins. To be more concrete, and to go back to the introduction of this chapter, this premise also explains why at the conference on experiential legal education at an elite Brazilian university, key invitees were two U.S. professors who belonged to a weak institution and whose academic production was not particularly notable. The fundamental criteria that determined their invitation and privileged position at the event, above Latin American professors with a more solid academic background and production, was the context of production of legal knowledge that they came from, i.e., putting the production well and protected geographical indicator presuppositions into effect.

These three presuppositions, along with the conceptual oppositions universal knowledge/local knowledge and autopoiesis/mimesis, also explain why a ruling like *Roe v. Wade* is recognized and positively valued as a legal product in a good part of the Global South. It can be argued that this ruling is not formal or substantively better as a product of legal knowledge than the German or Colombian rulings that partially decriminalize abortion or the Canadian one that does so fully. Without a doubt, the historical moment in which *Roe* is issued is a factor that allows for its recognition: it is one of the first rulings in the world that decriminalized abortion. However, these variables only explain part of the history. It is common for both defenders and opponents of abortion in colonial academia to refer to *Roe*. Nevertheless, it is not common for academics not experts in the subject to be able to allude to German, Canadian or Colombian rulings on the subject. To explain the very broad recognition that the ruling has achieved, we would also have to indicate that it was issued by the U.S. Supreme Court and that it has been described and evaluated an infinite number of times by U.S. professors. Likewise, we would have to mention that the United States has been understood as the production well of legal knowledge par excellence for at least the second half of the twentieth century.[122]

The premise of he who pays decides, following with the illustration of the presuppositions of the colonial model of the production of legal knowledge, is continually put into operation in the joint projects by professors at U.S. and Global South law schools.[123] Clinical projects like the so-called *fact-finding missions* are useful to show how this premise functions. Typically, the objective of this kind of project is to describe the violation of human rights in an area of the Global South in a precise and comprehensive manner.[124] In these projects, a U.S. law school and a social organization or a law school from the South partner up to complete this work. Usually, however, decisions are made by the party contributing a greater amount of financial resources. For example, the money to finance the fieldwork generally comes from the academic institution in the North. The premises of the colonial model of legal knowledge therefore accept and promote the notion that, given these circumstances, the institution of the metropolis is the one that decides on the project's basic structure and scope. However, this situation hides the contributions that the colonial institutions make, which are necessary for the program's success: contact with local populations and academic information that describes, analyzes and evaluates the project's object of study.

The last particular conceptual opposition, experience in the use of legal knowledge/inexperience in the use of legal knowledge, makes reference to who is considered a legitimate agent to put the legal products that are generated in the metropolis and the colony into operation ethically and efficiently. This conceptual opposition generates the presupposition of the effective operator.[125] For the colonial model of the production of legal knowledge, the subject of the knowledge of the metropolis has the *know-how* to make effective use of legal products, claims, reports and articles, for example. In parallel fashion, it is understood that this subject has internalized the rules of professional ethics of her legal community. In contrast, the colonial subject is understood as an ineffective, ingenuous or ethically weak subject for the use of legal knowledge. She does not have contacts

---

[122] *See* Maximo Langer (2004), "From legal transplants to legal translations: The globalization of plea bargaining and the Americanization thesis in criminal procedure", *Harv. Int'l L.J.*, **45**, 1.

[123] *See* Bonilla (n 17), at 21–25.

[124] Id.

[125] Id.

in national or international networks so that the knowledge created may have an impact. His or her legal communities do not have or do not apply rules of professional ethics, and the communities do not have the capacity or the will to do so.

The conceptual oppositions and the concepts of subject, time and space of the colonial model of the production of legal knowledge described are explained by the set of reasons presented below. The first of these is the direct or indirect relationship between the Global North and South.[126] The imperial relationships of Spain, Portugal, the United Kingdom, Germany, Italy, France, Belgium and the United States, among others, with Latin America, Asia and Africa are well known and have used law as one of their primary instruments for their consolidation and development.[127] The *Leyes de Indias* and the concept of *terra nullius* are good examples of the role of the law in the processes of conquest and colonization of the Global South.[128] The idea that the colonial empires are the trunks from which the primary legal traditions emerge also plays an important part in explaining the existence of the colonial model of the production of legal knowledge.[129] Latin America is understood as a minor member of the civil law tradition,[130] whereas Africa[131] and Asia,[132] depending on the empire that controlled the different territories that formed them, are understood as marginal iterations of the common or civil law traditions. Likewise, Eastern Europe is understood as a minor reproduction of obsolete socialist law and contemporary importations of law from Western Europe or

---

[126] *See generally*, Anthony Anghie (2004), *Imperialism, Sovereignty and the Making of International Law* (Cambridge: Cambridge University Press); *see also* Karin Mickelson (2000), "South, north, international environmental law, and international environmental lawyers", *Y.B. of Int'l Envtl. L.*, **11**, 52.

[127] *See generally*, Martti Koskenniemi (2001), *The Gentle Civilizer of Nations: The Rise and Fall of International Law 1870–1960* (Cambridge: Cambridge University Press).

[128] *See generally*, Jérémie Gilbert (2006), *Indigenous Peoples' Land Rights under International Law: From Victims to Actors* (Ardsley, NY: Transnational).

[129] *See* Boaventura de Sousa Santos (1995), "Three metaphors for a new conception of law: The frontier, the Baroque and the South", *Law & Soc'y Rev.*, **29**, 569, 579–82; Mark van Hoecke and Mark Warrington (1998), "Legal cultures, legal paradigms and legal doctrine: Towards a new model for comparative law", *Int'l. & Comp. L.Q.*, **47**, 495, 498–99.

[130] *See generally*, Jorge L. Esquirol (1997), "The fictions of Latin American law (Part I)", *Utah L. Rev.*, 425, 427–28; Jorge L. Esquirol (2003), "Continuing fictions of Latin American law", *Fla. L. Rev.*, **55**, 41, 42; Esquirol (n 104).

[131] *See* Kwame Nkrumah (1962), "Law in Africa", *African L.J.*, **6**, 103, 105.

[132] Lama Abu-Odeh (2004), "The politics of (mis)recognition: Islamic law pedagogy in American academia, *Am. J. Comp. L.*, 52, 789, 806–8.

the United States.[133] In some countries of these regions, the tradition of the metropolis, transformed and reinterpreted, coexists with a native law. Typically, however, this is subordinated to the legacy of the metropolis or is considered to be of a lesser quality.

This explanation has a powerful epistemological consequence: it causes the law of the Global South to be considered not a valuable object of study and causes the legal knowledge focusing on it to be considered marginal or irrelevant. If you want to describe, analyze or evaluate the great legal traditions of the world, you would have to examine the law of the countries that gave rise to, developed or transformed them. It is not useful to analyze legal orders that are mere copies or minor reinterpretations of these traditions.

This perspective is strengthened when connected with the enormous influence that U.S. law has had in recent decades throughout the Global South.[134] This second argument again points to the fact that legal theory, doctrine, and practices of the Global South are more or less faithful copies of Global North law. The exportation of legal packages by the United States has meant that a significant part of Latin American, Asian and African law cannot be fundamentally distinguished from U.S. law. Adversarial criminal law,[135] classical liberal labor law,[136] the standards of intellectual property that are adopted as a consequence of free trade agreements[137] and the corporate law that protects multinational companies[138] are just a few illustrations of this argument. All of these are legal transplants that come from the United States and have a North–South direction.[139] As a consequence, the law of the Global South is again

---

133 Rene David and J.E. Brierley (1978), *Major Legal Systems in the World Today: An Introduction to the Comparative Study of Law*, 2nd edn (London: Free Press), pp. 222–24.

134 Merryman and Pérez-Perdomo (n 18); Kelemen and Sibbitt (n 18); Merryman, *Comparative Law and Social Change*; Ritttich (n 18).

135 Domingo and Sieder (n 42); Torres (n 42).

136 Murillo (n 43); Graciela Bensusán (n 43).

137 Jean-Frederic Morin and Richard Gold (2013), *An Integrated Model of Legal Transplantation: The Diffusion of Intellectual Property Law in Developing Countries*, 3 October, available at: http://ssrn.com/abstract52335531 (accessed 8 September 2017).

138 Holger Spamann (2009), "Contemporary legal transplants: Legal families and the diffusion of (corporate) law", *BYU L. Rev.*, **6**, 1813–77.

139 *See* D.M. Davis (2003), "Constitutional borrowing: The influence of legal culture and local history in the reconstitution of comparative influence: The South African experience", *Int'l. J. Const. L.*, **1**, 181–95; Lee Epstein and Jack Knight (2003), "Constitutional borrowing and nonborrowing", *Int'l. J. Const. L.*, **1**, 196–223; Yasuo Hasebe (2003), "Constitutional borrowing and political theory", *Int'l.*

presented as an object of study that is not very attractive. The copies never rise to the value of the original source.

The colonial model of legal knowledge is also explained by a description of the law of the Global South as homogeneously formalist. The dominant concept of law in the legal orders of Asia,[140] Africa,[141] Eastern Europe[142] and Latin America[143] is described as one committed to the idea that the legal systems are closed, complete, coherent and univocal. This description, the third explanatory argument, in turn generates a ritualistic practice of law that makes it tremendously inefficient and that does not satisfy the legal needs of its citizens.[144] The relationship between concepts of law, legal education and legal academia complicates things even more. It is argued that the formalist concept of law generates a formalist legal education and legal academia.[145]

Law schools are constructed from legocentrism, encyclopedism and memorization.[146] This legal education is therefore indifferent to the contextual or critical analysis of legal norms and has lectures as its

---

J. Const. L., **1**, 224–43; Wiktor Osiatynski (2003), "Paradoxes of constitutional borrowing", *Int'l. J. Const. L.*, **1**, 244–68; Carlos F. Rosenkrantz (2003), "Against borrowings and other nonauthoritative uses of foreign law", *Int'l. J. Const. L.*, **1**, 269–95; Kim Lane Scheppele (2003), "Aspirational and aversive constitutionalism: The case for studying cross-constitutional influence through negative models, *Int'l. J. Const. L.*, **1**, 296–324.

140 Tom Ginsburg and Albert H.Y. Chen (eds) (2009), *Administrative Law and Governance in Asia* (London: Routledge); Tom Ginsburg (2003), *Judicial Review in New Democracies: Constitutional Courts in Asian Cases* (Cambridge: Cambridge University Press), p. 42.

141 Martin Chanock (2001), *The Making of South African Legal Culture 1902–1936: Fear, Favour and Prejudice* (Cambridge: Cambridge University Press); Samuel C. Nolutshungu (1993), "Constitutionalism in Africa: Some conclusions", in Douglas Greenberg, Stanley N. Katz, Melanie Beth Oliviero and Steven C. Wheatley (eds), *Constitutionalism and Democracy: Transitions in the Contemporary World* (New York: Cambridge University Press).

142 *See, e.g.*, Marcin Matczak (2007), "Judicial formalism and judicial reform: An example of central and Eastern Europe", 25 July (unpublished paper presented at the annual meeting of the Law and Society Association, Berlin, Germany) (describing the persistence of formalist-inflected adjudication in Poland).

143 *See, e.g.*, Merryman and Pérez-Perdomo (n 18), at 66.

144 Merryman and Pérez-Perdomo (n 18), at 66; Atienza (n 56).

145 Daniel Bonilla (2013), "El formalismo jurídico, la educación jurídica y la práctica profesional del derecho en Latinoamérica", in Helena Olea (ed.), *Derecho y pueblo Mapuche* (Santiago: Universidad Diego Portales), at p. 268.

146 *See* Luis Fernando Pérez Hurtado, "Content, structure, and growth of Mexican legal education", *J. Legal Educ.*, **59** (4), 567; Fix Fierro and López (n 57); Montoya Vargas (n 57). *See also*, Duce Julio (n 57).

main teaching tool. The formalist concept of law means that law professors understand that its primary function is that of systematizing legal norms.[147] As such, their paradigmatic academic products are attempts to structure a field of law such that conceptual limits of each category are clear and precise and that the hierarchical or horizontal relationships of the legal norms that form them are clearly established. The weaknesses of this formalist concept and academic practices are deepened if overlaid with the quantitative and qualitative problems of legal academia in the colonies, which are mentioned above.[148] This argument, which constitutes the fourth explanation, makes reference to the weaknesses with respect to the amount and quality of academic production of the colonies,[149] as well as the absences of the conditions that would allow for the creation of a truly original legal knowledge.

Finally, the colonial model of the production of legal knowledge is explained by the supposed self-sufficiency of the metropolis's legal systems.[150] Along with the legal academia that studies them, the legal systems of the metropolis do not need to look beyond their limit, to the Global South, to solve the legal and political problems they face. It is presumed that the Global South has very little to teach the Global North. Hence, as an area of study, comparative law has historically looked fundamentally at the law of the metropolises, not to the law of the colonies. Hence, the legal and academic communities of the Global North are described as self-centered and parochial.

CONCLUSION

The political economy of the production, exchange, and use of legal knowledge has not been explored in depth by legal academia. Yet, its theory and practice determine the ways in which we describe, analyze, and evaluate these processes. The production, exchange, and use of legal knowledge are relevant not only for legal academics but also for politicians, social organizations, and citizens that are active or passive subjects of legal knowledge. Legal knowledge travels constantly through state borders and has important practical consequences for all members of the

---

147 *See generally*, Juny Montoya Vargas (2010), "The current state of legal education reform in Latin America: A critical appraisal", *J. Legal Educ.*, **59**, 545.

148 *See* n 56.

149 *See* Bonilla (n 17).

150 *See* Mattei (n 19).

political community. It is the source of legal norms, theories, and practices that create rights and obligations.

The free market of legal ideas and the colonial models give an account and, at the same time, guide the creation, exchange, and use of legal knowledge. The former, in part because it is part of the conceptual machinery of enlightened liberal modernity that we are already committed to, dominates our normative political and legal imagination. The concepts of subject, time, and space that give structure to this model determine the ways in which we think that the processes of legal knowledge production should be advanced. The free market of legal ideas model also guides some of the dynamics that control these processes in practice. Yet, this model competes for controlling our legal and political imagination with the colonial model.

The colonial model occupies a place in our legal and political imagination as well – even if this place is usually peripheral. It is not common to find an explicit defense of its concepts of subject, time, and space. The colonial model, however, offers a better explanation of the practices that actually determine how legal knowledge is created, exchanged, and used. The colonial model's key categories determine our actions, although we do not recognize it or do it in a shame-faced way. Thus, in order to understand who we are as legal knowledge subjects, we should understand and analyze the theoretical axles that constitute each of these models. Their evaluation and eventual transformation depend on taking this first conceptual step steadily.

3. The geopolitics of constitutionalism in Latin America

Jorge L. Esquirol

I. INTRODUCTION

An increasingly general belief ascribes the waning influence abroad of U.S. constitutionalism to cultural and political idiosyncrasies in the United States. The mythologies of exceptionalism and originalism do not translate well beyond its borders. At the same time, constitutionalism in the global South has exponentially grown in importance. The emergence of "constitutional law powerhouses" among them suggests the inexorable expansion of the field of comparative constitutional law.

In Latin America, this is a particularly pivotal development. The region embraced constitutionalism following independence in the early nineteenth century, and the U.S. constitution has until recently been its pre-eminent model. While standard comparative law accounts confirm the region's indebtedness to continental European private law, they equally emphasize the preponderant influence of the U.S. constitution. Many nineteenth-century Latin American charters closely tracked the 1787 U.S. text. Most Latin American courts did not follow the same example of U.S. constitutional jurisprudence however. With few exceptions, constitutional adjudication in the region did not hew to the same model of constitutional doctrine that is characteristic in the U.S. More recently, though, many constitutional courts in the region have adopted some similar interpretive practices. They have embraced constitutional reasoning techniques reminiscent of strict scrutiny and interest balancing tests, although not always described in these terms. They often cite Anglo-American constitutional theory. And, they appear bolder about relying on decisional precedents.

At the same time, new constitutional texts and reforms in the past 30 years in the region have diverged from the U.S. model. They include robust provisions on social, economic and cultural rights. They recognize much more forcefully the validity of legal pluralism. They include expanded procedural mechanisms for bringing constitutional actions. And, they have expanded review powers for national supreme and constitutional courts. Despite the converging reasoning techniques, it may be said that the United States is simply no longer a good model for Latin American constitutional law. The content of constitutions and constitutional adjudication in the region has taken a different turn, recognizing a broader array of rights and accepting a more active position on the part of judges. This same observation may in fact apply to other countries in the global South that have developed a similarly active constitutional practice. The focus here though is on the Latin American example.

Conversely, from a U.S. perspective, the question has not been definitively settled that U.S. constitutional scholars and courts *should* pay attention to Latin American developments. That side of the debate presumes that a more global constitutional law – including all countries – is in fact desirable. And, there are many known objections to this stance. Some of these include objections to foreign cultural influences, a perceived liberal bias in comparative constitutional law in practice, and the defense of American exceptionalism. In parallel fashion, it may be that the globalization of national practices of constitutional law may not be the best course for newly empowered constitutional courts in Latin America. The reasons for this may be very different however than those typically raised in the United States. It is not simply that the texts of many Latin American constitutions are now too country-specific, or that U.S. constitutionalism is no longer the textual, or sole jurisprudential, model. It also has to do with the broader geopolitics of national constitutionalism.

Indeed, comparative constitutional scholars herald an increasingly global field. They identify phenomena as varied as increased foreign influence on national constitutional adjudication; supranational governing bodies with domestic constitutional effects; and even a transnational culture of constitutionalism.[1] A fuller appraisal of these developments cannot be adequately undertaken in this single chapter. Other contributions in the present volume and elsewhere do address some of these topics. The focus here, more narrowly, is on the potential negative

1 See generally, Rudi Teitel (2003–04), Book Review: "Comparative constitutional law in a global age", *Harvard Law Review*, **117**, 2570; David S. Law and Mila Versteeg (2011), "The evolution and ideology of global constitutionalism", *California Law Review*, **99**, 1163; Anne Peters (2009), "The merits of global constitutionalism", *Indiana Journal of Global Legal Studies*, **16**, 397; Peer Zumbansen (2012), *Comparative, Global and Transnational Constitutionalism: The Emergence of a Transnational Legal-Pluralist Order, in Global Constitutionalism* (Cambridge: Cambridge University Press); and chapters in this volume.

effects of a globalization of national constitutional law on the democratic development of constitutional jurisprudence in countries of Latin America.

Taking a step back to consider the increasing doctrinal production of constitutional courts and scholars in the developing world, it stands to reason that the tide of constitutional influence would begin to change. It would be logical to think that U.S. courts and constitutional scholars – not simply *comparative* constitutional scholars – would be more greatly influenced by, or at least cite, developments in the global South. This has not yet occurred in any routine way, at least not in any way approximating the influence that Anglo-American scholars or the U.S. Supreme Court has had abroad. A marker of the unevenness of influence consists in the quite skewed citation practices of legal scholars in the global North.

Indeed, whether or not the globalization of national constitutionalism is ultimately advisable, it is worthwhile to examine the likely obstacles that stand in the way of its more plural and democratic construction. Some of these obstacles may count as the very reason why such a global constitutional practice might not be desirable in the first place. Within the existing geopolitics of national law, a globalized constitutionalism may unduly hegemonize certain constitutional law doctrines or "best practices". These particular positions portend to impede a more organically expressed evolution of constitutional consciousness within Latin American legal communities. And, this likely translates to less locally representative politics within the realm of constitutional law. Still, assuming global constitutionalism is inexorable despite these potential drawbacks, the discussion here attempts to identify the impediments to its wider representativeness. In doing so, it reveals how global constitutionalism may be a double-edged sword for Latin American courts. The wider debate about globalization is taken up only indirectly. The discussion instead is on the background reasons hindering greater input and influence from Latin America in particular. These reflect the historical and contemporary geopolitics of national constitutionalism.[2]

In short, one may ask why is it that Latin American constitutional precedents and theories carry diminished weight in the United States? There are surely many contributing factors. There would be the usual explanations

---

[2] Of course, there may be some specific projects by states and scholars to address and rectify these imbalances that are better than others. These would need to be assessed individually from this perspective and are beyond the scope of this chapter.

based on: variations in the text of the constitutions themselves; specific national histories; distinct local politics; diverse societies; different political economy; and the like. Rather than discuss these particular differences, this chapter addresses the dominant historical representations of Latin American courts and contemporary accounts of constitutional law, as depicted outside the region. The focus here is principally on comparative and other transnational legal literature produced mostly in the U.S. and other English-language texts. This approach extends and continues some of my past work on the hegemonic external representations of the region's law. It is my contention that these images contribute, in addition to other possible factors, to the skewed citation practices of courts and scholars in the global North.

By way of organization, section II of this chapter addresses historical perceptions in the global North of courts and justice in Latin America. Section III describes more contemporary, comparative constitutional law in the region. Finally, section IV considers the advisability of a globalized constitutional law in this context.

II. DENIAL OF JUSTICE

Latin American judiciaries have long been characterized as dysfunctional. In fact, this view helped justify diplomatic and military intervention in Latin America by the major powers in the nineteenth and early twentieth centuries. It supported "denial of justice" claims in international law. The rationale was a failure of the municipal courts to provide foreigners with judicial redress for alleged harms suffered in the host country. The foreigner's home state had the right to demand a remedy based on notions of state responsibility.[3] This action was pursued through diplomatic and military intervention, including reprisals on the offending state to reverse its decision or to grant compensation.[4] As noted about the era: "The old methods of reprisals were revived in the form of gunboat diplomacy and the continued tendency of the powerful to view the right of protection not as an entitlement to stand before an international tribunal, but as a warrant for the use of unilateral force. The diplomatic component of the

[3] Charles de Visscher (1935), "Le déni de justice en droit international", in *Collected Courses of the Hague Academy of International Law*, vol. 52 (Leiden/Boston: Brill/Nijhoff), pp. 9–11.

[4] Hans W. Spiegel (1938), "Origin and development of denial of justice", *American Journal of International Law*, **32**, 63, 78 ("In earlier times just cause of war and denial of justice were complementary terms.").

expression 'diplomatic protection' was, in such circumstances, an ironic but hardly subtle fiction."[5]

The doctrine of denial of justice also offers a particularly useful vantage point from which to observe the "geopolitics of national law". The latter refers to the hierarchical positioning of the world's national legal systems and the global politics surrounding questions of comity, legal transplants, and the harmonization of laws, among other topics. Along these same lines, the denial of justice doctrine explicitly opens national judicial systems to external scrutiny and stipulates compensation from the state when found lacking. Under its terms, state responsibility is engaged if foreign citizens are wronged in a host country's courts. According to one authority, in the interwar period, "the presumption of (the state's) conformity (with international law) collapses if it is shown, in effect, that because of the insufficiency of the laws, or the faults of those who apply them, foreigners do not receive the treatment that they are due. The denial of justice furnishes this demonstration and gives place to diplomatic protection."[6] As such, the exercise of this doctrine laid bare the relative international standing, and consequent liability, of particular national courts.

In this connection, the scope of such scrutiny-triggering wrongs was the subject of considerable debate. At a minimum, "denial of justice" included foreigners' lack of access to the courts, discriminatory access, or undue delay in proceedings. Beyond that, the claimed wrong could actually extend quite far, as discussed further below. The possibility of making such claims and obtaining redress through the intervention of one's home state placed the interests of foreign investors and foreign residents in relation – one could even say, in tension – with the transnational standing of Latin American legal systems. From the perspective of aggrieved foreigners, as a whole, there was a persistent incentive to serially condemn the operation of national courts. Such characterizations provided the justification for potential extra-national and extra-judicial relief.

Notably, in the latter part of the nineteenth and early twentieth centuries, there was a great influx of European immigration to Latin America. Many of these immigrants retained their original citizenship and allegiance to their home countries and sought their assistance when faced with local disputes, in some cases. More importantly, it was also a period of significant foreign investment from Europe in the region.[7] Disputes

---

[5] Jan Paulsson (2005), *Denial of Justice in International Law* (Cambridge: Cambridge University Press), p. 15.

[6] Visscher (n 3), at 11.

[7] Frank Griffith Dawson (1990), *The First Latin American Debt Crisis* (New Haven: Yale University Press).

in the courts could quickly take on an international dimension depending on the nationalities of the parties. And diplomatic intervention, in legal cases rejected by the courts or decided adversely against the foreign party, depended on making the case that the municipal courts were unable, or unwilling, to judge according to law. Given that European powers and the United States did not much hesitate to intervene in Latin American domestic affairs, it is quite likely such a claim could in fact succeed. As such, the then prevailing geopolitics can be seen to have impacted quite significantly on the general economy of characterizations and standing of national law and courts in the region.

Indeed, this period provides a continuous record of diplomatic and military interventions in Latin America by European powers and the United States.[8] Such interventions were outwardly premised on varied transgressions real and alleged: such as, the non-payment of sovereign debt by Latin American governments; harm occurring within the national territory to citizens and property of a foreign power; and the denial of justice in Latin American courts.[9] According to one commentator in 1944:

> [T]here was no more deplorable page in the relations of Latin America with foreign powers, than that which records the history of diplomatic claims, branded by the Supreme Court of Brazil in one case, as the "terrorism of the indemnities," and by the Supreme Court of Peru, as an "unfortunate history," which shows "naught but the constant display of might over weakness." In this exhibition of international lawlessness, all of the great powers, and some of the small ones, too, joined; and the history of these claims constitutes a most sinister chapter in the relations of the strong toward the weak.[10]

State responsibility for denial of justice claims was a principal basis for these foreign interventions. As a result, Latin American diplomats and officials struggled to narrow its meaning, attempting to limit it to procedural requirements of free access to national courts by foreigners, on a par with the rights of its own citizens.[11]

---

[8] Richard F. Grimmett (2001), *Instances of Use of United States Armed Forces, 1798 to 2001* (Washington, DC: U.S. Congressional Research Service); Ann Van Wynen Thomas and A.J. Thomas Jr (1956), *Non-Intervention: The Law and its Import in the Americas* (Texas: SMU Press); see generally, Jorge L. Esquirol (2012), "Latin America", in Bardo Fassbender and Anne Peters (eds), *The Oxford Handbook of the History of International Law* (Oxford University Press), pp. 566–70.

[9] Id.

[10] J. Irizarry and Y. Puente (1944), "The concept of 'denial of justice' in Latin America", *Michigan Law Review*, **43**, 383, 387.

[11] Spiegel (n 4), at 80 ("It [the definition of "denial of justice"] denotes, according to South American practice, the refusal of access to justice, and, according to the practice of others, every kind of international delict.").

In order to curb additional privileges to foreigners challenging final court decisions, this principle of equal access was raised to the level of constitutional doctrine: "The civil assimilation of the citizen and the alien has long since become current constitutional doctrine in Latin America."[12] Under this limitation, a potential claim by a foreigner could only arise upon a discriminatory bar to the courts or the complete closure of the courts.[13] Indeed, the eminent Argentine publicist Carlos Calvo sought to cabin the international law concept's applicability as part of his much acclaimed Calvo Doctrine.[14] The latter required foreigners to submit exclusively to host state jurisdiction; to submit their disputes with host governments and local individuals to the national courts; to exhaust all local remedies; to abide by the national court's decisions; and to forgo diplomatic recourse.[15] This doctrine came to be promulgated in constitutions, legislation, treaties, and public and private contracts with foreigners.[16] Some versions contained an exception for diplomatic recourse in cases of denial of justice: others attempted to foreclose that possibility all together.[17] In 1936, the U.S. publicist, Oliver Lissitzyn, informs us of treaty efforts to define denial of justice:

> The treaties in which the term "denial of justice" is used are not many, being confined mainly to those with Latin American States. In no treaty is a direct definition of the term to be found. In general, it seems to be used in a rather narrow sense, being frequently supplemented by references to delays of justice, non-execution of sentences, and even identified with negligence in the

---

[12] Irizarry and Puente (n 10), at 387 (citing, J.M. Yepes (1934), "Les problèmes fondamentaux du droit des gens en Amérique", *Acad. de Dr. Int.*, **47**, 91; Hormann Montt (1939), *Derecho Constitucional*, 2nd edn (Santiago: Sociedad Talleres Gráficos), p. 52 et seq.; I. Campillo (1928), *Tratado Elemental de Derecho Constitucional Mexicano* (Jalapa: La Económica), p. 278 et seq.; A. Aragon (1921), *Nociones de Derecho Público Interno*, Sección 153 (Popayán: Imprenta del Departamento), p. 195).

[13] See e.g. Rafael F. Seijas (1884), *El derecho internacional Hispano-americano (público y privado)* (Caracas: El Monitor), p. 518; Guillermo J. Sepúlveda Necoechea (1959), *La denegación de justicia en el derecho internacional: Coneptuación Moderna* (Universidad Nacional Autónoma de México, Escuela de Jurisprudencia (Tesis)), pp. 50–51.

[14] Carlos Calvo (1896), *Le Droit International Théorique et Pratique*, 5th edn (Paris: Arthur Rousseau), vol. 1 at pp. 264–355.

[15] Esquirol (n 8), at 566–70.

[16] M.R. Garcia-Mora (1949–50), "The Calvo clause in Latin American constitutions and international law", *Marquette Law Review*, **33**, 205.

[17] Frank Griffith Dawson, "International law, national tribunals, and the rights of aliens: The experience of Latin America", *Vanderbilt Law Review*, **21**, 712, at 720–25 (1968).

> administration of justice. It is not clear whether the contracting parties wish to distinguish these delinquencies, or merely to render the idea more definite and prevent possible misinterpretation. Nor is it clear whether or not these clauses merely refer to the exhaustion of local remedies as a condition of diplomatic interposition.[18]

The United States never recognized the Calvo Doctrine's validity, claiming the "denial of justice" rights presumably waived by private parties are not properly waivable by them but rather belong to the state.[19] As Frank Griffith Dawson notes, in 1968:

> [T]he Latin American conception of non-intervention also entails denial of diplomatic intervention on behalf of aliens, a broad definition not acceptable to the United States, which defines intervention more restrictively and does not consider itself obliged to avoid intervening on its citizens' behalf, especially where there has been a denial of justice . . . the United States maintains that Calvo Clauses will not prevent interposition otherwise permissible under generally recognized rules of international law.[20]

In general, publicists outside of Latin America cited a broader definition for the concept of denial of justice.[21] It was thought capable of extending to multiple aspects of alleged state failure in judicial actions instituted by foreigners, such as obstacles to making rights effective due to lack of access to the courts; non-existent or inadequate law governing the case; a refusal or delay by the courts to render judgment; a disregard of the law; misapplication of the law to the facts of the case; or a failure of the authorities to carry out the decisions or judgments of its courts. In its broadest acceptation, it could even extend to instances of gross judicial error, described in terms of "manifest" or "notorious" injustice.[22] Lissitzyn notes that in

---

[18] Oliver J. Lissitzyn (1936), "The meaning of denial of justice in international law", *American Journal of International Law*, **30**, 632, at 635–36.

[19] American Law Institute (1987), *Restatement of the Law (Third) of the Foreign Relations of the United States*, Vol. 2 (New York: Thomson Reuters), s. 713, fn g.

[20] Griffith Dawson (n 17), at 721 and 723.

[21] Griffith Dawson (n 17).

[22] Francisco V. García-Amador (1957), "Responsabilidad del Estado por daños causados en su territorio a las personas o bienes de los extranjeros", *Anuario de la Comisión de Derecho Internacional*, **II**, 122 ("En las codificaciones que hemos citado anteriormente, la actuación de los organismos judiciales se califica, expresa o tácitamente, conforme a la 'norma internacional de justicia' (*international standard of justice*), en el sentido de que, aun cuando no se haya infringido el derecho interno, el Estado incurre en responsabilidad si el acto u omisión supone el desconocimiento de una 'norma' generalmente aceptada en

international adjudications, most of them dealing with Latin American states: "Many cases use 'denial of justice' to describe various acts, chiefly of judicial authorities, without attempting to specify its limits. In all these cases, however, its sense is broader than mere failure to grant access to courts, and includes unjust sentences."[23]

In an 1891 international arbitration between France and Venezuela, the arbitrators extended the meaning of judicial error not only to questions of law covered by the treaty between the two states but also to interpretations of Venezuelan law and general legal principles:

> D'un autre côté, la signification du mot "dénégation de justice" veut être précisée. Il convient d'entendre par là toute (sic) acte qui devra être envisagé comme une dénégation de justice, soit d'après les lois du Vénézuéla, soit d'après les principes généraux du droit de gens, soit d'après la convention du 26 novembre 1885, le compromis n'exigeant pas la concordance absolue de ces trois sources juridiques et des différences essentielles, ou même notables, n'existant d'ailleurs pas entre elles sur la matière.[24]

Thus, foreign interposition on the basis of "denial of justice" claims were played out on a broad spectrum from lack of procedural guarantees in the courts, on the one hand, to de facto appeals of alleged judicial errors, on the other. Some jurists of the era did draw a distinction between "denial of

---

materia de organización judicial o del procedimiento. En las codificaciones interamericanas, en cambio, al menos en lo que se refiere a los casos de 'denegación de justicia' y de 'retardo anormal', la calificación del acto u omisión para los efectos de determinar la responsabilidad internacional, depende exclusivamente del derecho interno.") ("In the codifications that we have previously cited, the acts of judicial organs are assessed, expressly or tacitly, according to the 'international standard of justice', in the sense that, even when national law has not been infringed, the state incurs responsibility if the judicial act or omission entails non-compliance with a generally accepted 'norm' in the area of judicial organization and procedure. In the Inter-American codifications, however, at least in cases of 'denial of justice' and 'abnormal delay', the characterization of the act or omission, for the purposes of determining international responsibility, depends exclusively on national law.")

23 Lissitzyn (n 18), at 642.

24 ("Additionally, the meaning of the word 'denial of justice' needs to be specified. It is properly understood by that all acts which must be perceived as a denial of justice, either according to the laws of Venezuela, according to general principles of international law, or according to the treaty of 26 November 1885, the commitment not requiring the absolute concurrence of these three legal sources and essential, or even notable, differences among them not existing, in any case, on the matter.") President of the Swiss Confederation, Arbitrator under the Convention of 1891 between France and Venezuela, in the *Fabiani* case, Moore, *Arbitrations*, **5**, 4878, at 4893–97. Cited in Lissitzyn (n 18).

justice" and "manifest injustice" in the courts. The former, it was argued, required an independent international law wrong: the latter was considered wrongdoing by the courts themselves and therefore not the proper subject of a "denial of justice" claim.[25] Additionally, questions arose as to whether the denial of justice claim was limited to the actions of the judiciary or could include interference from the executive, legislative, or other agency of government.[26] In any case, the only situation which was clearly outside of the purview of the "denial of justice" doctrine was mere harmless error by the local courts. Something more was required, but it was not always clear how much more.

As a result, Latin American courts and commentators struggled to defend the baseline *res judicata* effects of their judicial decisions.[27] The international law doctrine in place and the *realpolitik* of the era undermined the very finality of court decisions throughout the region. In the words of the Venezuelan Supreme Court in 1918, in the matter of the *Claim of Martini & Company*:

> It would be unusual to think that such expressions ("denial of justice") authorize an interpretation which might justify diplomatic intervention every time that an objcction of injustice is made against a judicial decision. Such allegation would be made each time an adverse judgment is given against an alien, the stability of decisions would disappear, and while the natives of the country would be bound by the definitive authority of the thing adjudged, the alien would enjoy the privilege of a final revision of the judgment before an international tribunal.[28]

No doubt, there existed clear cases of frustration of legitimate claims by foreigners in national courts.[29] It is also certain that there were egre-

---

[25] Clyde Eagleton (1928), "Denial of justice in international law", *American Society of International Law*, **22**, 538, 551–54.

[26] Oscar Rabasa (1933), *Responsabilidad internacional del estado con referencia especial a la responsabilidad por denegación de justicia, Imprenta de la Secretaría de Relaciones Exteriores* (México: Imprenta de la Secretaria de Relaciones Exteriores), pp. 16–17 (noting the wide definition of "denial of justice" proposed at the Fourth Pan American Convention of 1910 in Buenos Aires, which included legislative and executive actions, and which was still rejected by the U.S. representative as too narrow).

[27] See e.g. the "Guerrero Report" to the League of Nations. Annexed to Questionnaire No. 4 as adopted in 1926 by the Committee of Experts for the Progressive Codification of International Law, established by the Assembly of the League of Nations in 1924, League of Nations Document C.196.M.70.1927.V.

[28] Venezuela-7 Revista de Derecho y Legislación I43 (Caracas, 1918).

[29] Consider Griffith Dawson (n 17), at 728 (citations omitted) ("Observers of the Latin American scene sometimes incorrectly presume that, due to political

gious instances of judicial corruption, executive and legislative interference in the courts, and the like in relation to specific cases. However, the doctrine of "denial of justice" incentivized the characterization, by the foreign losing party, of the entire national judicial system in question as dysfunctional, corrupt, or incompetent in interpreting its own law.[30]

By the second Pan American conference in 1902, the United States agreed to submit denial of justice claims that could not be resolved diplomatically to international arbitration, either under separate bilateral treaties or referral to the Permanent Court of Justice in the Hague.[31] Some cases were decided by mixed international claims commissions, with a lead arbitrator generally having the last word.[32] Less formally, appeals to the chancelleries and embassies of the relevant foreign power were, in effect, a *realpolitik*-enabled review of judicial decisions.[33] Whether the product of a unilateral major-power determination or the decision of a trusted arbitrator, the background discursive economy had no reason to change. If anything, less direct control by aggrieved states over decisions, now in the hands of arbitrators, could likely contribute to a heightened rhetoric of failed courts.

In any case, judiciaries in Latin America were particularly under scrutiny.[34] Describing several international arbitration cases, one commentator noted in 1959:

---

climates unstable in relation to our own, Latin American courts and judges will be incompetent at best, and corrupt at worst. They fail to realize that typical Latin American disorders, except in the immediate contexts of social revolutions such as swept Mexico and Cuba, do not necessarily disrupt all institutions in a particular society. Thus, members of the judiciary normally remain in office untouched despite military coups.").

[30] Griffith Dawson (n 17), at 720 ("[I]t would seem, in retrospect, as if diplomatic insistence for redress of injuries often depended more on political, than on legal, considerations . . . assertion of international claims was considered to have been used to justify armed invasion and occupation, as in the French expeditions to Mexico in 1838 and 1861, the United States interventions in the Caribbean after 1900, and in the 1902–03 German, British and Italian threat to Venezuela.").

[31] Rabasa (n 26).

[32] Sepúlveda (n 13).

[33] Consider Griffith Dawson, (n 17), at 730–31 ("The manner in which Latin American court proceedings are generally conducted, and the procedural code provisions which govern the course of the proceedings, may seem unfamiliar to alien litigants accustomed to common law jurisdictions. Mere unfamiliarity, however, hardly justifies pleas for denial of justice . . .").

[34] Id.

> [T]he judgments of the supreme courts of the (Latin American) governments complained of were seen with disdain by the complainants; and the international tribunals that took them up rejected their conclusions.[35]

This practice of diplomatic recourse, upheld by the international law doctrines and the practices of the day, stimulated an interest and a textual practice of condemning Latin American courts and legal systems in their entirety. Indeed, assuming local remedies had been exhausted, "the allegation of denial of justice consists of a critique of the conduct of the supreme tribunal of the state".[36] It was to the benefit of an international investment community, and foreign residents in Latin America, to count on a generalized belief that lawlessness reigned throughout the region.[37] Any corroboration of irregularity in any one court proceeding could thus be easily added to this normalized perception of dysfunction and to more easily make out a case for "denial of justice".[38] This very image was generated and recycled by the very incentives created by the doctrine. Indeed, once set in place, it is not difficult to imagine the many financial and other incentives for its overstatement and generalization and, conversely, for the more limited ability to counteract its force with a more balanced counter-narrative.

Again, this is not to say that there were not specific cases of wrongdoing by the courts; periods and places of "lawlessness" in Latin American countries; and all sorts of reproachable situations. It does point to, however, the skewed incentives that would generate a constant and all-purpose narrative of legal failure and lawlessness in Latin America. With respect to the doctrine of denial of justice, this was a particularly active incentive during the nineteenth and early twentieth centuries. And, it goes some way in illuminating the generalized perception of legal breakdown

---

35 Sepúlveda (n 13), at 66.

36 Constantin Th. Eustathiades (1936), "La responsabilité de l'état pour les actes des organes judiciaries et le problème du déni de justice en droit international" (Paris: A. Pedone), p. 311.

37 See e.g. Henri C.R. Lisboa (1906), "Des Réclamations Diplomatiques", *Revue de Droit International et Législation Comparée*, **8**, 237 ("au moindre acte d'autorité du gouvernement vénézuélien, concernant des intérêts étrangers, sa mauvaise réputation suffit pour qu'on s'empresse d'approuver les mesures de répression préparées à la hâte, sans que l'opinion publique soit renseignée sur les motifs et les incidents du conflit et sur les raisons que le Venezuela invoque pour justifier sa conduite").

38 See Procès-Verbaux of the Third Commission for the Codification of Public International Law, cited in Eustathiades (n 36), at 307 ("international responsibility is equally grave because it implies the failure of the state in its international duties, and that one can formulate such an accusation against the state").

in the region, beyond a more evenhanded assessment of what could reasonably be expected of national judiciaries in that period.

More contemporarily, the denial of justice doctrine has experienced a resurgence, especially in the context of international commercial arbitration. Corroborating its extensive historical existence, Jan Paulsson notes: "International law provides standards by which national systems can be judged from the outside."[39] While generally limited to violations of international law, and not national law, in reality the assertion of customary or treaty-based international standards of fairness (and justice) potentially covers any national court decision. Moreover, international remedies are no longer dependent on diplomatic or military intervention: in many cases, individuals and legal persons can pursue their remedies directly in international forums, especially with respect to foreign investor rights.[40]

Furthermore, several other legal doctrines and procedures operate functionally in similar ways, in that they require a judgment "from the outside" of national legal systems. For example, in the arena of U.S. judicial proceedings, *forum non conveniens* motions, political asylum cases, proceedings to enforce foreign judgments, all call for the submission of assessments and diagnostics of the operation of national legal systems. In light of the international legal relations history of Latin America, these procedures generate strong incentives to recycle quite instrumental narratives and reinforce certain types of comparative legal literature about the region. Surely, all of these constructions are subject to the same type of scrutiny suggested in this chapter. And, while the topic requires more specific empirical investigation, the preponderant discursive constructions seem heavily weighted nonetheless toward emphasizing Latin America's perpetual legal dysfunction, often independent of the merits of any particular case.

In sum, the historical perspective presented above supplements more contemporary analyses of Latin American "legal failure" that I have written about elsewhere and briefly examine below in the context of constitutional law. It suggests a hypothesis about the inattention of U.S. scholars and courts to substantive constitutional developments in Latin America during the nineteenth and early twentieth centuries, despite the fact that most Latin American countries shared the model of the U.S.

---

39 Paulsson (n 5), at 4.

40 Laure-Marguerite Hong-Rocca (2012), "Le Déni de Justice Substantiel en Droit Public International", doctoral thesis, Université Panthéon-Assas (Paris II).

constitution. Jeremy Adelman, discussing the state of U.S.-centered Latin American studies in 2001 notes:

> Few subjects elicit more yawns than constitutional and legal history. Yet, with our neglect of the ways in which arrangements among classes, ethnic groups, and genders became encoded into a series of formal and informal rules, the appreciation of how these rules shaped subsequent bargains got lost . . . How, in effect, can we return to a historical study of rule making and institutional life (looking, thereby, at structures that shape the world) without presuming that such structures are immutable, inelastic constraints on agents?[41]

Adelman credits (1) a past over-reliance on structural theories positing Latin America's failures as owing to its wrong institutional legacy, and (2) the subsequent reaction to these overstatements of structure as the reason for the neglect (or rejection) in history studies of institutional topics like Latin American law and constitutions.[42]

Of course, there are additional reasons that could also account for this situation. It may simply be the case that "parent" jurisdictions rarely look to their "offspring" jurisdictions for legal authority or expertise.[43] A parallel could be drawn here to the similar lack of influence of Latin American private law in Europe, its "parent" jurisdiction. Additionally, the political and economic situation in Latin America in the nineteenth century was in many areas quite unstable. This would surely play a role in the perceived non-comparability of their constitutional law. No less, racial and cultural differences appeared quite prominent and pertinent in this era. Latin American states were not regarded as full members of the international community of civilized states until the early part of the twentieth century.[44]

In any case, the generalized negative perception of law and legality in Latin America, as I have been arguing, is also fueled by the geopolitics of national legal systems. In this regard, the financial and political incentives to reproduce "denial of justice" narratives no doubt played a role in

---

[41] Jeremy Adelman (2001), "Institutions, property, and economic development in Latin America", in Miguel Angel Centeno and Fernando Lopez-Alves, *The Other Mirror: Grand Theory through the Lens of Latin America* (Princeton, NJ: Princeton University Press), p. 34.

[42] Adelman (n 41).

[43] See generally, Diego López Medina (2005), *La Teoría Impura del Derecho: La transformación de la cultura jurídica latinoamericana* (Legis Editores, Tercera Re-impresión).

[44] C. DeArmond Davis (1975), *The United States and the Second Hague Peace Conference: American Diplomacy and International Organization, 1899–1945* (Durham, NC: Duke University Press).

characterizing and positioning Latin American jurisdictions as, almost axiomatically, denying of justice. By extension, it is not surprising then that there would be little to no jurisprudential and academic exchange with the United States in the realm of constitutional law. The Latin American texts and courts were likely not perceived as credible sources of real law. The many accounts of denial of justice would have gone far in undermining the credibility of Latin American judicial reasoning and the statements of Latin American courts of their own constitutional and other law. Moreover, the reality that Latin American court judgments – at least in the case of aliens – were not really final and depended on the major foreign powers' chancelleries or diplomatic missions' perceptions would have also significantly de-legitimated their authority.

III. CONSTITUTIONAL FAILURE

Most of the contemporary comparative law scholarship in the United States on constitutional law in Latin America is, in many cases, also quite dismissive. It is noticeably marked by the "law-and-development" paradigm beginning in the 1960s. Indeed, this is the period in which most scholarly attention was paid in the United States to law in Latin America. It stemmed from development era efforts to align law with economic development. This literature is rather indelibly impressed with its original objective of diagnosing Latin American law's inability to produce greater economic growth and political democracy. In fact, this diagnostic approach always already presumes law's failure in the region: its starting point is the insufficiency of economic wealth and orderly democracy.[45] The only question for legal analysts is then: what is it about the law that contributes to making it so?

This framework for thinking about law in Latin America remains paramount in much comparative law on the region. In a nutshell, it is characterized by an idealized image of developed country law, such as U.S. law, contrasted to a hyper legal-realist account of the failings of liberal legalism *in Latin America*. Certainly, there are numerous legal operational failings, instances of clear corruption, incompetence, and a host of other shortcomings in Latin America – as in all societies to some degree. What

---

[45] See e.g. Adelman (n 41), at 27 ("For scholars of Latin America, their subject provided ample evidence of deviation from, and failure to live up to, a norm of change and progress. Latin America thus exemplifies the persistence of some obstacle or hindrance, the inability to adapt or modernize, or compulsive failure, especially when contrasted with other areas of the Atlantic world.").

is unhelpful however, as a clear-eyed comparative account, is juxtaposing the ideology of liberal legalism against the inescapable shortcomings of actual legal systems.[46] This is the case whether liberal myths are depicted in the abstract or projected as if they were the actual operation of developed country law. The picture becomes even more distorted when this idealization of developed country law is contrasted to the operation of actual legal systems *in developing countries*. This is so not only because the same liberal legal myths remain unattainable, but also because those societies generally have fewer resources to support the costly operation of liberal legal systems and, equally important, to sustain the wide-scale production of ideology and apology to legitimate that system, which jurists in resource rich countries are more easily able to do.

Below is a brief overview of the more prominent perspectives on constitutional law in Latin America, viewed from the United States. It is of course incomplete and incapable of capturing the fine nuances of their authors or disciplinary conventions. It is also not meant as an individual critique of the authors cited. Rather, the latter are highlighted as representative of some of the main genres of the field. Other authors and genres could certainly be added to the discussion.

A. Too Many Constitutions

Quite prominent, the law-and-development brand of Latin Americanist scholarship accepts the mythology of the U.S. legal system at face value and contrasts it to Latin America. A 1991 article quite succinctly states its conclusion in the title *The Success of Constitutionalism in the United States and its Failure in Latin America: An Explanation.*[47] In it, the author provides a historical account of the success of U.S. constitutionalism in a highly idealized way.[48] By contrast, he draws on Latin America's past

---

[46] As just one example, supporting the extensive international funding for "adversarial" criminal procedure reform in Latin America, see David Alan Sklansky (2008–09), "Anti-inquisitorialism", *Harvard Law Review*, **122**, 1634, 1687 ("The problem with overblown rhetoric about the advantages of the adversary system is not just that it lumps together questions best considered separately. It can also mix together myth and reality, papering over the notorious gaps between an idealized version of the American adversary system and the system's actual, day-to-day operation.").

[47] Keith Rosenn (1990–91), "The success of constitutionalism in the United States and its failure in Latin America: An explanation", *University of Miami Inter-American Law Review*, **22**, 1.

[48] See generally, Miguel Schor (critiquing Rosenn); cf. Michael Schudson (1998), *The Good Citizen: A History of American Civic Life* (New York: Simon

political and economic difficulties to argue the region's failed constitutionalism. In the end, the point hinges on a comparison between the total numbers of constitutions and constitutional reforms enacted in Latin America versus the United States. The numbers are tabulated for each country. The results show that "since independence the twenty Latin American republics have promulgated some 253 constitutions, an average of 12.65 per country".[49] Thus, for the author, the fact of having two constitutions and twenty-seven amendments over a two-hundred year plus period in the United States marks constitutional success, while an average of thirteen over a similar period indicates failure in Latin America.

Of course, this framing does not count the extensive changes in constitutional law produced by constitutional adjudication in the courts, especially in the United States. It does not take into account the divergent opinions about the constitution not definitively resolved by the high courts. Nor does it take into account the numerous gaps, ambiguities, and contradictions within the U.S. constitution – or other constitutions for that matter – concerning executive powers, states' rights, international treaties, and other anomalies not usually highlighted in uncritical accounts of U.S. law. Moreover, the fact that constitutional change is mostly effectuated through new constitutions and constitutional reforms, instead of as modifications of constitutional precedents, is a distinction that may – or may not – pack much substantive difference. The fact that much constitutional change in Latin America has been implemented through textual revisions is also explainable – at least partially – by the limited role acknowledged to judicial interpretation, at least in the past, within the civilian legal tradition proper to the region.

Still, the political and economic history – and in some cases contemporary accounts – of Latin America seem to suggest the common-sense reality of these assertions of legal failure. Noted Latin Americanists Miguel Centeno and Fernando Lopez-Alves confirm that:

> When Latin America does appear in general discussions of contemporary history or grand theory, it is most often as the negative counterfactual . . . the Black Legend of Latin American failures to develop economic and political institutions is elaborate and deeply ingrained in our disciplinary heritage. Yet little effort is expended in explaining these breakdowns, malfunctions, and disappointments or even analyzing whether they were indeed failures. Why

& Schuster); Peter Charles Hoffer (1998), *Law and People in Colonial America* (Baltimore: Johns Hopkins University Press).

49 Rosenn (n 47), at 6–7.

> not treat Latin America as simply an alternative development, with its own probabilities and variances?[50]

Indeed, if we were to examine more critically the elements sustaining a diagnosis of legal failure, then the Latin American experience cannot be so easily dismissed. Clearly, throughout the history of many countries in the region, there have been irregular transfers of power, military coups, dictatorships, extended periods of emergency rule, etc.[51] However, there is also a significant history of constitutional debate, constitution-making, constitutional adjudication, amendment and reform, and constitutional theory. Even in the context of extended emergency rule, for example, there is valuable, recent academic work on the political "flexibility" that these periods provided within, or in relation to, the constitution.

Indeed, in slightly more detail on this last example, declarations of emergency powers can be seen from a very realist perspective as more than simply power grabs by unscrupulous leaders or the unchecked authoritarianism of pathological rulers. They may also serve to introduce defensible public policies not seemingly implementable, at the time, through the ordinary constitutional order. In a fascinating, recent doctoral dissertation on this question, Jorge González Jácome explains the constitutionally questionable, and seemingly abusive, use of emergency powers within the 1886 Colombian constitution, during the period of emergency rule in the 1930s, as a mechanism through which comprehensive social policy was introduced.[52] According to González Jácome, this approach to emergency rule supports neither of the standard positions regarding emergency powers within liberal constitutions: whether viewed as the original sin which encourages their repeated use or, conversely, as insufficiently explicit emergency provisions which could, if more explicit, forcefully cabin their use. Rather, he positions this emergency constitutional mechanism as an inherent possibility, not so unlike – one could say – a *sua sponte* judicial determination of unconstitutionality, or a re-interpretation by the courts of the constitution. It raises a thought-provoking parallel between

---

[50] Miguel Angel Centeno and Fernando Lopez-Alves (2001), "Introduction", in Centeno and Lopez-Alves (n 41), p. 10.

[51] Centeno and Lopez-Alves (n 41), at 8 ("between 1930 and 1990, the Latin American countries have had 139 extraconstitutional changes in government, an average of 6.95 per country").

[52] Jorge González Jácome, "States of exception and the debate over liberal-democracy in South America: Argentina, Chile and Colombia between 1930 and 1990", doctoral dissertation, Harvard Law School (May 2013) (on file with author).

emergency powers and the power of legal realist critique to chasten the courts into not invalidating popular social legislation in the same era in the United States. In any case, this more comprehensive analysis of what constitutes a "constitutional practice" suggests the need for a wider frame in which to analyze and compare Latin American constitutionalism, broader than mere adherence to the U.S. experience.

B. Constitutions Are Too Easy to Change

A somewhat different perspective on Latin American constitutionalism is provided in a 2006 article provocatively titled "Constitutionalism through the looking glass of Latin America".[53] It presents a thoughtful exploration of the failure of *U.S. constitutionalism* in Latin America. The author is careful to note that: "Law in Latin America did not take a failed path, but, as this Article argues, a different path . . .".[54] In the end, however, his argument "takes up this issue by examining why constitutionalism succeeded in changing the status quo in the United States but failed to do so in Latin America".[55] In this particular piece, the diagnosis is that Latin American constitutions are too malleable and too centralized by design of the elites so that the latter can more easily maneuver once in power. And thus, the author argues, Latin American societies have understandably not committed to the practice of "constitutional politics", whereby constitutional conflict is resolved solely through the institutions and procedures delimited by the constitution itself. Instead, constitutional conflict is resolved through "ordinary politics" which too easily turns to amending or rewriting the constitution, and in some cases to ignoring it all together. According to the author, this realm of constitutional politics remains to be "socially constructed in Latin America", although the newest wave of constitutionalism and democratization bodes promise.[56]

The article's central argument is that Latin American constitutions are not sufficiently "socially moored". As such, these nineteenth and twentieth century charters are understood as merely elite political pacts. At the same time, the author argues, the realm of constitutional politics in Latin America is fused together with ordinary politics, leading to the treatment of constitutions like ordinary legislation. Constitutional politics, by contrast, according to the author, should be higher stakes, require

---

[53] Miguel Schor (2006), "Constitutionalism through the looking glass of Latin America", *Texas International Law Journal*, **41**, 1.
[54] Schor (n 53), at 17.
[55] Schor (n 53), at 24.
[56] Schor (n 53), at 7.

greater social mobilization, demand more consensus, and confront hard-to-change constitutions. However, these two broad assertions may seem somewhat contradictory: advocating both more diffusion and internalization of the constitution socially versus a separate realm of constitutional politics harder to engage. In fact, the observed malleability of Latin American constitutions, and their commonplace role within ordinary politics, seems to suggest the opposite of a lack of social mooring. And, indeed, the author complains that constitutional politics are too much part of the common political process. Under this reasoning, its suggested reform to separate it from ordinary politics may actually lead to social *un*-mooring by limiting constitutional debates to only certain questions and to those who represent them. Conversely, greater social mooring in contexts of deep political conflict may lead to greater politicization of the constitution and to more routine constitutional volatility.

Regardless, the useful distinction identified between constitutional politics and ordinary politics is presumed to stand, however, on some uncontroversial basis. Under the analysis above, that basis is drawn from U.S. history. And, that experience – it is argued by the author – reflects a constitution that is very hard to change and a realm of "constitutional politics" constrained by the procedural and institutional self-restraint of a liberal society. That self-restraint is an extension to the constitutional sphere of pre-existing societal commitments, reinforced by the procedural difficulties in changing that status quo. Indeed, it is precisely this rigidity – the author maintains – which characterizes the U.S. constitution's success "in changing the status quo". While seemingly paradoxical, it is not *necessarily* a contradiction: commitment to constitutional ideology coupled with relatively few changes to the charter may more deeply internalize within society the changes that are actually made. However, relative to this same paradox, Latin American constitutionalism can be argued – if one were so inclined – to be equally successful at changing/maintaining the particular underlying status quo, if not necessarily through the same mechanisms. In the Latin American case, more textual revisions accompany political changes even though most do not change the basic status quo. Notably, that dynamic provides for a different proportion of change to status quo, and both change and status quo look different, than that generated by U.S. constitutional history.

What is more, the whole history of U.S. constitutional politics – while providing a useful account of constitutionalism in the United States – is not operationalizable in mechanical terms elsewhere. The line between constitutional and ordinary politics may not be drawn in the same place, and the elements of constitutional practices may also be different. Indeed, the U.S. model of constitutional politics – as described by the author above – may or may not make sense to political actors in Latin America strategizing about their ultimate ends. While societal commitment to constitutional rule (whether we mean by that commitment to a certain text or to a broader set of practices) seems like a rather uncontroversial goal, not much else is necessarily evident. For example, it may be that more social mooring is desirable in a particular society. But, just as well, as an all-purpose prescription, it may exacerbate an already highly conflictual polity, an overpolitization of the constitution, and an excessive engagement in constitutional reform. Indeed, viewed more realistically, the constitutional politics that has "worked" in the United States is a series of opposing elements, held together by the ideological normalization of their paradoxical co-existence. Simply culling from the very observations in the article cited above, they would include: a broad social mooring of the constitution *and* a practice of constitutional politics separate from ordinary politics; a very hard to change constitution *and* a constitutionalism successful at changing the status quo; the existence of mobilized social movements *and* only social movements limited to goals within the constitution; a politics of constitutional positions *but* not for all political questions all the time; a recognition of the politics of constitutional law and practices *and* a belief in its non-political legal nature especially in terms of judicial reasoning; as well as possibly some other not immediately obvious combinations.

In short, my point here is that a simplified set of characteristics, reduced down from U.S. experience, stands little chance of serving as an effective prescription to entrench constitutionalism in Latin America. In fact, one could not be faulted for thinking that much of this literature has quite a circular feel. The proposed explanations and prescriptions slip back and forth: Latin American constitutions fail because they are too flexible – or too rigid; because the law is too little like society – or too much like it; because constitutions are too centralized – or too little centralized. Thus, without going into more extensive detail as I have elsewhere, these diagnoses appear more reflective of the particular political and economic orientations they serve than any uncontroversial agenda for constitutionalism, whether or not the ends they serve are foregrounded by – or conscious to – any particular diagnostician.

As a result, it may be easy to believe, as does the author above, that "constitutional law in Latin America has an almost surreal quality given that constitutions do not provide accurate maps to how power is distributed . . . Given the magical nature of the formal constitutional rules in Latin America, this Article will peer through the looking glass of constitutionalism in Latin America . . .".[57] Of course, this impression

---

[57] Schor (n 53), at 5–6.

could also describe the surreal and magical quality of seemingly contradictory combinations that characterize U.S. constitutionalism – even if the United States has had many fewer constitutional texts and its history is quite different from Latin America. Yet, marked by the characterization of exceptional contradiction, the seemingly topsy-turvy world of Latin America cannot possibly be taken at face value, much less engaged as sensible legal authority.

Furthermore, the common prescriptions advanced for obtaining the "rule of constitutions", and adduced from idealized or overly simplified versions of U.S. constitutionalism, simply appear to restate its definition, i.e. limiting social conflict to constitutionally contained politics, whose limits are deeply socially internalized but are also distinct from ordinary politics, and which is admittedly politics but also law at the same time. All of these terms and concepts, moreover, are drawn from the perspective of U.S. conceptual history and experience. This may be an overly narrow way to conceive of constitutionalism. And, even if it were universally agreed, the question would then become how to get that to happen in societies where it does not function that same way. Yet the answer – it seems abundantly clear – is not simply any one mechanical blueprint of procedural and institutional components.

C. Constitutional Law is Just Politics

A promising new vein of information about constitutional law in Latin America is the "judicialization of politics" literature.[58] This body of work explores the newest wave of democratization and constitutionalization in the region. It generally develops the thesis that politics in Latin America have become "judicialized". This is the case as new constitutions have introduced new rights and procedural mechanisms which bring political controversies into the courts. It has also accompanied the empowerment of constitutional courts and the expansion of constitutional powers in

---

[58] Linn A. Hammergren (1998), *The Politics of Justice and Justice Reform in Latin America: The Peruvian Case in Comparative Perspective* (Boulder: Westview Press); William C. Prillaman (2000), *The Judiciary and Democratic Decay in Latin America: Declining Confidence in the Rule of Law* (Westport: Praeger); Rachel Sieder, Line Schjolden and Alan Angell (eds) (2005), *The Judicialization of Politics in Latin America* (Basingstoke: Palgrave Macmillan); Javier Couso, Alexandra Huneeus and Rachel Siede (eds) (2010), *Cultures of Legality: Judicialization and Political Activism in Latin America* (Cambridge: Cambridge University Press); Gretchen Helmke and Julio Ríos-Figueroa (2011), *Courts in Latin America* (Cambridge: Cambridge University Press).

existing courts. In this context, the "tutela" and "amparo" proceedings granting individual rights of action to those claiming a violation of their constitutional rights have been an explosive source of constitutional adjudication in the region. Likewise, minimal standing requirements to challenge legislation on constitutional grounds have also opened the courts to substantial constitutional pronouncements. The judicialization of politics literature presents and explains these developments, principally to audiences in the global North.

Indeed, this literature seems to herald the advent in Latin America of the much recommended "constitutional politics" discussed in the section above. It provides for the procedural mechanisms around which social movements may mobilize to seek constitutional remedies and reforms. It also endows individuals in society with easy and direct access to the courts to vindicate their constitutional rights. Moreover, it follows the model recognized as central to U.S. democracy: the legal resolution of some of the most conflictual political questions in society. Thus, scholars of judicialization are quick to point out that questions previously addressed by the political process or other routes are now – and in the process of further becoming – decided by the courts. As such, there has been a renewed emphasis in the operation of courts, the behavior of judges, the structure of the judiciary, and the like.

The judicialization literature is rather heavily weighted to political science analysis. Even legal scholars participating in these studies typically adopt a social science perspective. As such, these studies are rich in analysis of the likely political motivations for certain court decisions; the personal political motivations that may animate certain judges or courts; the strategic behavior of institutional actors operating in a corporate body; and the like. Indeed, this literature is the successor to an earlier era of comparative politics on the independence of Latin American supreme courts. In that body of work, the question of judicial independence was paramount and measured by the number of cases decided by courts against other branches of government. Under this earlier framing, the courts are just one of several powerful political actors within government. The fact that their discretion is supposed to be constrained by legal texts and legal reasoning is considered quite secondary if not all together pre-textual, simply a way of covering over their preferences *post hoc*.

The more recent judicialization literature expands the scope of political and sociological analysis of courts and judges. It examines the multiple possible motivations for court decisions: not just the relationship to the executive and legislative and their related politics but also the micro-politics of the courthouse, long-term career goals, and so on. It significantly omits, however, any earnest consideration of the legal logic that informs court decisions or the doctrines and arguments devised over time in particular courts. Even recent work that recognizes the need for examining the "discursive" dimension of courts in the global South has for the most part limited itself to applying social science models to the verbal utterances of courts.[59]

For example, the appearance of particular legal terms in judicial decisions is tested on a single variable cause-and-effect model, expecting the court's use of formalist interpretations and deference to government policy to coincide with times of economic crisis and, instead, of socially responsive interpretations in times of non-crisis.[60] This framework parallels the comparative politics exercise of testing judicial independence based on the number of court holdings against other branches of government. In this instance, the analysis does not track legal outcomes but rather legal terms. Or, rather, it tracks interpretations of legal terms in relation to an economic crisis variable. According to the author from which this example is taken, formalist interpretations demonstrate the court's submission to government interests while expansive interpretation reflects responsiveness to social interests (although, admittedly, social interests may conflict within society). In the cases examined, the expectations of formalist submission to government policy were, unexpectedly, not borne out by the author's analysis of the court's mode of interpretation.

While quite interesting in some ways, this type of analysis described above does not convey the meaning that the courts themselves are attempting to create in their own decision-making. It does not explain the sense that local lawyers and jurists may make out of these judicial elocutions. As such, this literature does not really engage the legal dimension, or the law-like quality that these judicial decisions may achieve. It may be that political scientists and legal sociologists are reflexively skeptical of all legal reasoning, if it is not immediately linked to political or personal motivations. And, this insight may very well be true. Indeed, it may very well be applicable to all legal confabulations. In the United States, it could equally turn quite a skeptical eye to assertions about the "original intent"

---

[59] See Couso, Huneeus and Sieder (n 58), at 3–4 (citing Diego López Medina for authority, "Our volume explores this landscape of changing legal cultures. Starting with the assumption that formalism is no longer a useful concept for describing Latin American legal cultures – as was in any case always an oversimplification – we explore the repertoires of legal ideas and practices that accompany, cause, and are a consequence of the judicialization of politics.").

[60] See e.g. Pablo Rueda, *Legal Language and Social Change during Colombia's Economic Crisis, in Cultures of Legality* (Cambridge: Cambridge University Press), pp. 25–50.

of the founders as a means to apply the constitution. This same insight would also apply to assertions about any clear, underlying "legal policy" that would prescribe the correct answer when the legal texts are ambiguous or contradictory. It may also ring true for some when confronted with rationalizations about the "living constitution" as a means to decide constitutional cases. Indeed, a hyper-realist critique of all these modes of legal reasoning could immediately discredit any intellectual traction claimed by their proponents.

However, the liberal practice of law requires some faith in a realm of reasoning that is distinctly law-like.[61] From the perspective of its persistent critics, some suspension of disbelief is required to indulge in assertions about, for example, what the framers of the U.S. constitution could have possibly thought about some contemporary legal issue. No less, the living constitution approach may only make sense to those already sharing a particular political bent, and cases may only be convincingly rationalized that way, to a wider audience, in decisions hard for skeptics to openly oppose – such as *de jure* racial equality for example. In sum, the study of constitutionalism in the global South, and in Latin America in particular, tells us little about constitutional law if it does not engage the specific modes of legal meaning-making, reasoning, and conventions of local constitutional discourse in its own terms. Merely tracking the interests motivating particular judges and decisions neglects its most crucial dimensions. The judicialization literature, promisingly, stands poised to engage the other side of the equation as well, that is, constitutionalism's construction as law. Surely, it would be an unjustified presumption to continue to proceed as if no one in Latin America actually accepts any legal reasoning at all, and instead solely engages a political or personal calculus as the judicialization literature seems to suggest.

Total disbelief in legal reasoning across society at all times may possibly be the case, but this would seem like an exaggeration. Paradoxically, in the sphere of legal governance, the projection of law-ness as a convincing decisional discourse is a continually reiterative performance. It requires the continuing legitimation and acquiescence of a significant sector of society, persuaded to go along with some sorts of legal reasoning and conventions. Surely, most types of legal reasoning are easy enough to disbelieve, given our existing set of critical tools. For example, early twentieth-century legal realist critique is credited with thoroughly undermining purely formalist legal argument in the United States. Moreover, one could easily

---

[61] Duncan Kennedy (1997), *A Critique of Adjudication* (New Haven: Harvard University Press), pp. 73–82.

disbelieve the necessary nature of assertions of "original intent" or the "living constitution" in contemporary U.S. constitutional adjudication, as noted above. But, the fact remains that these are debated and discussed on their own terms, as if they could actually deliver the correct constitutional answer.[62] Indeed, it is these debates that constitute the *legal* dimension of constitutionalism. In the absence of this feature, as Latin American law is typically portrayed in the global North, it is no wonder that there is little interest in constitutional law or any other law in the region. It appears that there is no such thing there: it is just politics and personal interest.

By contrast, a fantastic example of scholarly analysis of judicial reasoning in the Colombian context is Diego López Medina's path-breaking, *El derecho de los jueces*.[63] This treatise lays out the jurisprudence of the Colombian constitutional court over a number of doctrinal areas. It argues in favor of recognizing greater precedential value to these judicial constructions. López Medina's analysis has had enormous impact throughout Colombia, including on judges in Colombia's Constitutional Court itself. The reason it is noted here is because it actually does the work of analyzing the Court's and commentators' constructions of legal doctrine, reasoning, and conventions. Moreover, it has had considerable traction within the local epistemic community. Unfortunately, this invaluable contribution to Latin American constitutionalism has not yet been translated into English, and thus this dimension of law in Latin America is less well known in the global North. Regardless, it is a prime example of the legal aspects of constitutionalism that are most relevant locally.

IV. GLOBAL CONSTITUTIONAL AUTHORITY

The discussion above brings us back to the basic question of the desirability of global constitutional law in the first place. To the extent that this means a worldwide epistemic community engaged in common questions of constitutional reasoning, accepted doctrines, theoretical references, and general world view, the answer is not clear. Certainly, basic humanist propositions of intellectual sharing, dialogic intercourse across borders, the benefits of advances developed elsewhere, and other such points are of general value. However, in the arena of national legal systems, not all

---

[62] Hans Vaihinger (2009), *The Philosophy of "As if": A System of the Theoretical, Practical and Religious Fictions of Mankind* (Eastford, CT: Martino Publishing).

[63] Diego López Medina (2000), *El derecho de los Jueces: Obligatoriedad del precedente constitucional. Análisis de sentencias y líneas jurisprudenciales* (Bogotá: Legis).

are equal in the global sphere. There is a recognizable geopolitics of state law. And, these politics are organized around a hierarchical ordering. This hierarchy is likely to influence the dominant practices of a global constitutionalism, including its generally accepted forms, doctrines, and sources of authority. If the current state of geopolitics remains in place, this would no doubt work against the legitimacy of a distinct constitutionalism or constitutionalisms in the global South, or at a minimum significantly limit its role in the wider global order.

The geopolitics of national law noted here are surely related to the relative power of the states from which such legal systems derive. However, there is also a substantial discursive reproduction of hierarchy sustaining the perceived merit of the various national systems. These assessments are constructed in many different ways. They may seek to rank legal systems according to a preferred scale of development or economic policy; degrees of openness to foreign investors and observers; the co-relation between deep capital markets and legal tradition or origins; and the like. It would not be justified to dismiss all of these "indicators" out of hand as mal-intentioned reproducers of unmerited hierarchy: indeed, each of these would have to be analyzed separately. In the Latin American context, however, as I have examined here and in more detail elsewhere, there are long-standing practices of proclaiming the failure of national legal systems. These may be seen by some as simply honest assessments of the realities of the region. However, the structural incentives, say, for example, motivating "denial of justice" claims in the past or the mission to figure out a legal diagnosis for economic underdevelopment, have unduly impressed some of the dominant images and representations. Notably, in both of these particular paradigms just mentioned, the incentive has been to represent the local legal system as failed, either to circumvent it or to transform it. Taken together, such instrumentally produced perceptions, I would contend, contribute to the low standing of Latin America in the geopolitics of national law.

As such, the construction of a global constitutional discourse as a basis for the legitimation of Latin American constitutionalism must confront these *realpolitik* circumstances of influence and power. Engaging in a common mode of constitutional justification may thus be driven – and limited – by the more powerful and influential actors globally. That is, as a practice of legitimation of certain societal positions, the accepted conventions and common modes of reasoning in the global North may more easily predominate. Indeed, they may be the only modes which are generally found credible and convincing, as a matter of law. Thus an orthodoxy of constitutional thought, doctrines, and conventions could easily constrain the more particular meaning-making, constitutional practices, and scope of constitutional law in the global South. It is not hard to imagine that only certain constitutional tests, doctrines, and the like would be seen as legitimate. This may limit the innovation and latitude needed by local courts to more effectively legitimate their constructions of constitutional law and practices.

A quick example of the above is the mandate within the 2009 Bolivian constitution to create a plurinational state, extending to the interpretation and application of the constitution. Operationally, it draws together constitutional court magistrates from both the European and indigenous traditions of the country's citizenry, with the mandate to construct a constitutional discourse that combines the different world views. This exercise of epistemic fusion will surely require a great deal of creativity and innovation in the overall construction of common sources of reference and legitimation. It is one which may be unduly hampered by the imposition of a global constitutional order, at least under its current geopolitics. Under such constraints, this particular project of constitutionalism runs the significant risk of being classified as a quite exceptional and marginal enterprise, never quite believable and endemically failing.

In this same vein, certain quite defensible actions taken by constitutional courts in the global South could be seen – by comparison to accepted conventions in the global North – as simply objectionable judicial activism; improper interference with the legislature or public administration; ultra vires acts of regulation; and other instances of "wrongdoing", inconsistent with a hegemonic constitutional order. Thus, the evolution of constitutional practices suited to local conditions – both material and inter-textual – could be stunted by an inordinate influence and power of a global constitutional field, given the current geopolitics of national law. Despite this, local courts might well continue operating in sync with the ambient legal consciousness of their immediate communities. Yet, a global constitutionalism could potentially undermine a range of options that may be substantially supported locally but rejected by global constitutional authorities. At a minimum, an overemphasis on global authority could simply work to reinforce the hand of particular local interests aligned with the dominant geopolitics. It would reinforce their hand not only as a matter of general international political support but also one of correct or "best practices" law.

Somewhat the same point has been made in different terms by postcolonial scholars. Applied to this setting, the insight suggests that simply advocating for more Latin American inclusion in existing global constitutionalist circuits may not necessarily make way for any distinctive Latin American grounding. A global constitutional order, under its current geopolitics, is near exclusively rooted in the conceptual history of the global North. Simply arguing to be let into this game, in more geographically diverse numbers, does nothing per se to change the existing hierarchy of national law. Indeed, under these same conditions, greater Latin American participation could even more deeply entrench a global North vision of constitutionalism, by simply adding more native adherents to the existing hierarchy and paradigm. A more capacious understanding of constitutionalism would require not merely different geographically situated *interpretations* of a presumed global knowledge, but as Walter Mignolo puts it, different *perspectives* of knowledge.[64] Of course, this type of reasoning presumes one supports the possibility of constructing constitutional law in the global South in greater relation to local political and conceptual histories and not simply wanting to supplant them with some alternative order. As such, resisting an unreflective progression of global constitutionalism would seek alternative roles for national constitutional law, other than the direct transmission of a global hegemonic logic as the supreme law of the land.

Of course, these observations invite consideration of other possible forms that global constitutionalism could potentially take, which may possibly influence a quite different arrangement of geopolitics. In this regard, one could imagine and work toward a more cross-global-South constitutional discourse.[65] Additionally, there is the possibility of the emergence of new hegemonic constitutional powers, potentially arising from a different set of constitutional jurisdictions than simply the United States or Europe. And much new and interesting work is being developed in precisely these areas. Still, the concerns expressed here remain much the same. National constitutional law based on global authority is significantly impacted by the existing hierarchies of national law. This has the potential for further aligning both the form and the substance of the supreme law of different lands to predominant geopolitical interests. As such, in the context of existing legal hierarchies, it threatens to relegate significantly different constitutional practices, and possibly alternative interests they may represent in particular nations, to the status of non-law.

V. CONCLUSION

The relative influence and participation of Latin America within a more robust global community of national constitutional law is subject to the

---

64 Walter D. Mignolo (2005), *The Idea of Latin America*, Blackwell Manifestos (Oxford: Blackwell Publishing), pp. 8–14.

65 See e.g. Gonzalo Aguilar Cavallo (2010), "¿Emergencia de un derecho constitucional común? El caso de los pueblos indígenas (Parte 1)", *Revista Derecho del Estado*, **25**, 41(arguing in favor of *a ius constitutionale comune* in Latin America in the area of indigenous rights).

recognizably existing hierarchy of national legal systems. This legal hierarchy is surely reflective of the disproportionate economic and military power of the world's quite different nations. In the ordering of national law, however, there is also a substantial textual production of assessments, ranks, indicators and the like that presume to sort and classify national law. In Latin America, these have been historically supplemented by international law doctrines, international assistance efforts, and economic development projects which have significantly contributed to the predominant images and perceptions of the national legal systems of the region. Each of these paradigms of assessment can be examined, and potentially criticized, in their own specificity. However, in the main, these transnational narratives have preponderantly worked to classify law in Latin America very marginally. Perceived in this way in the global North, not much interest or influence can be expected to welcome the latest constitutional decisions, doctrines, or theories emanating from the region. Indeed, given these conditions, global constitutionalism is quite likely to continue to minimize and undervalue Latin America's legal production.

Of course, this whole question of relative levels of influence and recognition presumes the advisability, or inevitability, of a worldwide constitutional law community. Such internationalization of constitutional law could mean both greater global legitimation and greater scrutiny of national constitutional practices. Legitimation of national constitutional law, one would presume, would then come to depend more on commonly shared sources of authority, including certain prestigious courts, renowned legal scholars, and ultimately the global society and economy. As a result, the range of acceptable constitutional practices may become more limited to references that are transnationally supported, specifically those endorsed by the dominant geopolitics of national law. In the end, this may unduly limit the alternatives for national constitutionalism and may limit the modes in which constitutionalists can convincingly construct their community's law.

PART II

Latin American Constitutionalism

4. Constitutionalism in the Americas: a comparison between the U.S. and Latin America

Roberto Gargarella

During the last 20 years, I have been studying the development of constitutionalism in the Americas. For that reason, when I was invited to compare the United States and Latin American constitutionalism, I immediately had some ideas about what I wanted to say. Basically, there were two intuitions that I had, and which I wanted to share. According to the first one, the U.S. model of constitutionalism looked more "solid" and coherent than the Latin American one.[1] According to the second, there was something profoundly wrong in the character of the U.S. Constitution, which made me consider that it was profoundly unattractive. After some reflection on the topic, I realized that the different intuitions I had were related to two different criteria, which I was considering in my analysis. The first intuition appeared to be the product of a *formal* criterion of evaluation, basically referred to the (internal) consistency that distinguished the U.S. Constitution – a kind of consistency that I did not find in most

[1] There is at least one crucial clarification that I need to present, at the beginning of this chapter. In what follows, I will be comparing one country – the U.S. – and a complex region – Latin America – which is obviously a problem. I am aware of this serious difficulty but, after so many years studying Latin American constitutionalism, I can claim at least two things in defense of my project. First, I have already been providing detailed information about the development of constitutionalism in the different countries of the region, which makes me confident about what the legal initiatives that these countries adopted and rejected were. *See*, for instance, Roberto Gargarella (2010), *The Legal Foundations of Inequality* (Cambridge: Cambridge University Press), and Roberto Gargarella (2013), *Latin American Constitutionalism, 1810–2010* (Oxford: Oxford University Press). Second, and precisely for this reason, I consider that it is actually possible to talk about a "Latin American approach to constitutionalism": Latin American countries have been enacting and modifying their Constitutions in similar ways, at similar periods. This fact makes it possible to refer to regional constitutionalism as a "unit", even in spite of the differences that separate the different countries.

Latin American Constitutions. Meanwhile, the second intuition seemed to derive from a more *substantive* criterion, related to some of the most cherished values that distinguished the life of American constitutionalism. Pursuing these initial intuitions, in the following pages I shall compare the development of constitutionalism in the U.S. and in Latin America, using both formal and substantive criteria of comparison.

EVALUATING AMERICAN CONSTITUTIONALISM: TWO CRITERIA

In what follows I will develop my evaluative enterprise about constitutionalism in the Americas. I will do so by taking into account two main criteria, one that is *formal* and the other that is *substantive*. The formal or functional criterion shall refer to the (internal) *consistency* of the constitutional model, while the substantive criterion shall be related to the *egalitarian character* of the model. Let me briefly explain and justify the choice of these criteria.

A formal/functional criterion: constitutional consistency. In constitutional matters, it is possible to talk about "consistency" in at least two different ways. Juan Bautista Alberdi, for example, basically made reference to what I shall call *external consistency*. In effect, Alberdi was particularly interested in examining to what extent the existing Constitutions took the surrounding reality seriously: a proper Constitution – he suggested – had to acknowledge the most serious and pressing problems that characterized the particular time in which it was enacted. For him, it was clear that constitutionalism could not solve all the grave existing social problems, but that question was beside the point. What mattered was that the law dedicated all its energies to face and confront the main existing social, political or economic evils of its time. This is why, for him, the "first constitutionalism" of the region, which had dedicated its main energies to the consolidation of independence, had properly fulfilled its job; and so the "second", with which he was involved.[2]

---

[2] The same was the case of the "second" wave of reforms, in which he got deeply involved: these reforms – which took place around the mid-1850s – were mainly dedicated to confront economic backwardness, which represented a crucial problem of the time. In his words, the new Argentinian Constitution had to help overcome the problem of the "desert", this is to say, the fact of having an underpopulated country, full of fertile land but lacking in qualified and unqualified labor force (this is why he tried to promote immigration through the Constitution, for example).

Now, it is obviously difficult to evaluate a Constitution according to the criterion of *external* consistency. To do so requires having a clear understanding of the "external" facts that constitutionalism should ideally take into account; and also a clear understanding concerning the best means appropriate for properly dealing with those external problems. In this chapter, I shall only make some preliminary considerations about this kind of consistency, and instead concentrate my attention on a second type of consistency, namely *internal* consistency.

Internal consistency is easier to recognize than the former one. It appears – I submit – when the different parts of the Constitution work in a coordinated manner, one in favor of the other. In what follows, through my references to internal consistency I will be thinking about the two main parts of the Constitution – that is to say, the section of the Constitution that defines the *organization of powers*, and the one that defines the *structure of rights* – and the way in which they relate to each other.

Let me illustrate what I shall understand (and what I shall not) as cases of internal consistency. For example, one could claim that many of the conservative and liberal Constitutions that prevailed in the Americas were – no matter what we think about their normative attractiveness – internally consistent constitutional models. Hyper-conservative Ecuadorean President Gabriel García Moreno – just to begin mentioning one salient case – claimed that the main objects of his government would be to "put our political institutions and our religious beliefs in harmony". For that reason, he proposed adopting a new Constitution that, on the one hand, created an enormously powerful President (he advocated for a very conservative organization of powers), and, on the other hand, made the entire structure of rights dependent on the importance of Catholic religion (i.e., accept freedom of the press only and as far as the press did not offend the religious dogmas). In that way, both parts of the Constitution were prepared to work together (i.e., most probably, a President endowed with supreme powers would be able to ensure social peace and religion).

The same goes, for instance, with liberal Constitutions, which were mainly directed at protecting basic individual liberties, including private property and liberty of contracts. Liberal Constitutions seemed to be well prepared for the achievement of those goals. On the one hand (we shall come back to this), in those Constitutions, public authorities would be strictly controlled by a system of "checks and balances" (organization of powers); while, on the other, the structure of rights would provide strong protections or ensuring "negative liberties" to the individual members of society.

By contrast – and, for hypothesis – a Constitution that came to ensure "negative liberties" through a long list of individual rights, while at the same time consecrating a super-powerful Executive power, could be deemed internally inconsistent. The same would happen with a Constitution that wanted to dedicate its energies to the imposition of religious values, while establishing, at the same time, a weak Executive authority.

A substantive criterion: egalitarianism. Given the obvious limits of formal and functional analysis, I shall add a second evaluative criterion, which I shall also be using in the following pages. This second criterion will be the (more or less) egalitarian character of the different constitutional projects that appeared in the region, in the last two centuries. Of course, I cannot develop, in this limited space, a broad theory of justice, in order to critically evaluate Latin American constitutionalism. Instead, I shall base my analysis on actual constitutional values and practices, related to the region's constitutional history. In this respect, I shall maintain that the trajectory of American constitutionalism has profoundly been marked by two main ideals, which have been present in the region from the very moment of independence.[3] I am thinking about the values of *collective self-government* and *individual autonomy.* In what follows, I shall call *egalitarian* the Constitution that tries to embrace and put together both these ideals at the same time. By having this regulative ideal in mind, I shall be able to distinguish egalitarian constitutionalism from the other main constitutional models that prevailed in the region in the last two centuries, namely liberalism, conservatism and radicalism (see below). Before saying something more about how to distinguish these models, let me say something about the importance of the values of individual autonomy and collective self-government in the history of constitutionalism in the Americas.

In fact, the choice of these two ideals, namely *individual autonomy* and *collective self-government* is not hazardous. These are two fundamental values that have occupied a crucial place in U.S. political discussions, since the time of independence. Clearly, the main battles that were fought in the region, since independence, were not carried out with the idea of *autonomy* written in the flags of the contenders. However, and just to mention one important example, many relevant military leaders and *caudillos*, in the Americas, did write in their banners expressions such as "religion or death", which in the end clearly referred to the place of individual autonomy in the new nations. In fact, disputes around the power of the Church only summarize and illustrate the many conflicts that appeared in the region concerning individual autonomy. These disputes included, for instance, serious fights concerning the scope of freedom of expression

3 Gargarella (n 1), Ch. 1.

and freedom of conscience; quarrels about the meaning and implication of freedom of the right to privacy; conflicts about freedom of assembly; etc.

In similar terms, it is not difficult to recognize the influence exercised by the ideal of *collective self-government* in the Americas. Just to begin, the same independence revolutions were centrally based on the republican vindication of the right of the locals to govern themselves. Those revolutions were directly based on a claim of self-government, against the domination of foreign countries – England, in the case of the United States; Spain, in the case of most Latin American countries; Portugal, in the case of Brazil. From the early claim of *no taxation without representation,* presented by the early American colonist against England, the demand for self-government always occupied a privileged place in the disputes of the new societies. Perhaps more significantly, that claim continued occupying a central role in the new nations even *after* independence, although in a very peculiar way. In most cases, in effect, those individuals who had been convoked to the war of independence, took part in it, and offered their lives in it, made the ideal of self-government their own. And – as the historian Gordon Wood always emphasized in his study of the American Revolution – they began to use those doctrines against the leaders of the revolution, who had promoted the value of self-government.[4] They demanded a more relevant role for the popular sectors in the decision-making process; they asked for more spaces for political participation; they disputed – in sum – the political organization that emerged after independence.

As anticipated, by having in mind the meaning and importance of these two ideals, we can achieve a better understanding of the main political and legal disputes that took place in the region, during all these years. Moreover, in this way we can better organize our approach to regional constitutionalism and refine our critical analysis of it.

Thus, the most important constitutional models that have been present in regional constitutionalism can be classified according to the way they related with the two main ideals of autonomy and self-government. To summarize, I would distinguish:

- *A conservative approach* which, from the very beginning of the independence revolution, assumed a restrictive view regarding both the ideals of autonomy and self-government. Conservatism tried to organize the entire constitutional system around one particular *conception of the good* – usually, a particular religion – and at the same

---

[4] Gordon S. Wood (1969), *The Creation of the American Republic* (New York: W.W. Norton & Company).

time assumed a restrictive and elitist approach, regarding the role of the majority will in the organization of public affairs.

- *A republican approach*, which was directly opposed to the previous one, particularly in regard to the value of the ideal of self-government; and which at the same time tended to see individual autonomy as subordinated to the needs of the general welfare or the demands of a majoritarian politics.
- *A liberal approach*, which came to reverse the priorities of the republican one. Liberals tended to organize the entire constitutional order around the idea of individual autonomy and respect for individual choices; while at the same time showing a disposition to establish severe restrictions to majority rule in the name of protecting individual autonomy.

In sum, what we find here are three different views, which established a different relationship with the values of autonomy and self-government: one that vindicated the ideal of self-government, even at the risk of undermining the ideal of individual autonomy (republicanism); one that, in contrast to the previous one, appeared to be ready to sacrifice the ideal of collective self-government, in the name of preserving individual autonomy (liberalism); and a third view, that was open to challenge both ideals at the same time, in the name of a comprehensive conception of the good (conservatism).

All the previous considerations would require a more detailed analysis, which I cannot develop at this point, but which I tried to develop in other writings.[5] For the moment, I just want to call attention to the existence of an "empty box" within the main schema of American constitutionalism. In effect – and, as it can be seen in Table 4.1 – low-constitutionalism in the Americas offered, in its more than 200 years of history, very diverse Constitutions: some of them defied both ideals at the same time

Table 4.1 Constitutional models: autonomy and self-government

Conservatism	Radicalism	Liberalism	Egalitarianism
Collective self-government (−) Individual autonomy (−)	Collective self-government (+) Individual autonomy (−) (+)	Collective self-government (−) (+) Individual autonomy (+)	Collective self-government (+) Individual autonomy (+)

[5] *See* n 2 above.

(conservative Constitutions); some others defied one of those values, in the name of the other (liberal and radical Constitutions). However, we do not find Constitutions that, at the same time, showed a strong commitment both to the values of individual autonomy and collective self-government, that is to say, *egalitarian Constitutions*. In what follows, I shall use the term "egalitarianism" to refer to this absent model or "empty box", and also this ideal model as the standpoint from which to provide a substantive evaluation of constitutionalism in the Americas.

Now that I have clarified the content of the two evaluative criteria that I will be using in this work, namely consistency and egalitarianism (meaning individual autonomy and collective self-government), I can proceed with the comparative analysis of constitutionalism in the United States and in Latin America. In order to do so, I will first examine both constitutional orders according to the value of consistency, and only then do the same according to their egalitarian character.

EXAMINING THE (INTERNAL) CONSISTENCY OF U.S. CONSTITUTIONALISM

In general terms, I believe that U.S. constitutionalism still remains closely related to the kind of liberalism that distinguished it from its very origins.[6] The liberalism of the U.S. Constitution manifests itself in diverse clauses of the document, including its defense of individual autonomy, and the limits it establishes to abuses of power. One can recognize these commitments in most of the Constitution's fundamental features, including the central role of its system of "checks and balances"; the model of neutrality – and particularly religious tolerance – that it establishes; its defense of private property and free markets; its hostility towards the State's interference with economic matters; its respect of liberty of conscience, liberty of the press, liberty of association; etc.

Now, let me say something concerning the consistency of the U.S. Constitution, both at its *internal* and *external* level. Concerning the issue of *external* consistency – and assuming the absence of adequate parameters for properly examining it – there is at least one significant issue that reveals the existing tensions between the document that was

---

[6] It is true that the U.S. Constitution establishes a presidentialist system that has become, with the passing of time, still more concentrated, thus threatening the Constitution's internal equilibrium. However, I think that these developments still do not undermine the overall liberal character of the document.

enacted and the actual reality that surrounded it: the issue of slavery, with which the Constitution preferred not to deal even in spite of its crucial and central social importance. When the Framers of the U.S. Constitution minimized and/or hid the problem of slavery, within the original text, they undermined the moral, political and legal value of the Constitution. The unfortunate explosion of the Civil War, some years later, was obviously related to a diversity of factors but, undoubtedly, some of them were related to the nature of the Constitution, which had preferred not to take the question of racial discrimination seriously, and decided to use its energies for other purposes, while denying those radical evils. Undoubtedly, such a constitutional failure represents the main omission – the main internal inconsistency – of the U.S. Constitution.

By contrast, in what concerns its *internal* consistency, the U.S. liberal Constitution can easily pass all the required tests. In fact, the two basic parts of the U.S. Constitution show an almost perfect fit between them, favoring the general well functioning of the legal structure. The main ideal behind the liberal project was the protection and promotion of individual freedom. The main assumption seemed to be that the State, through the use of its coercive powers, represented the most serious threat to personal freedoms. For that reason, liberals proposed using the Constitution to "shield" individuals against potential abuses by the State, and at the same time (the other side of the same coin) to restrict the State's capacities to abuse via its political apparatus.

More specifically, liberals used the Constitution, first, in order to prevent the discretionary use of power and, particularly, to prevent the legislature from becoming a mere instrument in the hands of factious majority groups. Secondly, they tried to prevent the possibility that any government imposed a "moral dictatorship" upon the rest of society (i.e., by establishing an official religion). The constitutional formula for achieving those goals was twofold. It consisted in the establishment of a system of *equilibrium of powers* and a list of basic, inviolable *rights* – particularly rights aimed at the protection of individual freedom, private property, freedom of contract and free markets. Both parts of the Constitutions were thus directed to work together for the promotion of individual freedom and the limitation of power.

To be more specific, the first fundamental feature of the U.S. liberal Constitution consisted of the establishment of basic restrictions concerning the use of power. The idea was to avoid State's abuses and guarantee individual autonomy. In the origins of constitutionalism, and in the face of a particularly serious problem, namely religious imposition, Thomas Jefferson graphically proposed building a "*wall of separation*" that prevented the State from interfering with issues of conscience.[7] Granted, the image of a "wall of separation" was primarily used to refer to the need for preventing the use of State coercion in religious matters. However, that same image helps us understand the liberals' general approach to the issue of the coercive powers of the State. In the end, liberals wanted to build a "wall of separation" that protected each person from the arbitrary imposition of *any* conception of the good; a wall that kept the iron hand of the State away from the people's beliefs.

The second fundamental feature of the U.S. Constitution implied the creation of a system of *checks and balances.* A powerful judiciary, together with bicameralism in Congress, and the powers of veto left in the hands of the Executive, gave shape to the system of "mutual balances". The benefits of this system seem apparent. It forced the legislators to consider their decisions twice, improving the decision-making process; it ensured a special protection to minority groups; it forced each of the different sectors of society to anticipate and evaluate the decisions of the others; it favored the possibility of having "multiple eyes" looking at the same problem; and it made it very difficult for any group of self-interested representatives to simply impose their oppressive decisions upon the others. As James Madison clearly explained in the *Federalist* No. 51 (later known as the *Federalist Papers*), the proposed device provided the members of the different branches of power with the "necessary constitutional means, and personal motives" to resist the oppressive attempts of others. This solution, he argued, was based on a "reflection on human nature":[8] given the impossibility of avoiding or suppressing the people's self-interest as a basic political motivation, the institutional system had to be prepared to counteract its worst consequences. As Madison put it, "ambition must be made to counteract ambition".

---

[7] He wrote: "Believing with you that religion is a matter which lies solely between man and his God, that he owes account to none other for his faith or his worship, that the legislative powers of government reach actions only, and not opinions, I contemplate with sovereign reverence that act of the whole American people which declared that their legislature should 'make no law respecting an establishment of religion, or prohibiting the free exercise thereof; therefore building a wall of separation between church and State." Thomas Jefferson, "Letter to the Danbury Baptist Association in Jan. 1, 1802", in Jefferson (1999), at 397.

[8] "If men were angels" wrote Madison in the *Federalist* No. 51 "no government would be necessary. If angels were to govern men, neither external nor internal controls on government would be necessary. In a government which is to be administered by men over men, the great difficulty lies in this: you must first enable the government to control the governed; and in the next place oblige it to control itself."

The liberal State thus came to ensure that each person adopted and followed his or her ideology and cultivated the talents and ideals he or she preferred. Today, we tend to describe this type of State as "neutral". The *neutrality principle* would basically say that the State should not take sides in favor of any particular conception of the good. In other words, the State should not use its coercive powers in favor of or against any view of the good.[9]

In sum, what we see here is that, according to the liberals' constitutional model, both parts of the Constitution have to be organized so as to work together, in a coherent manner. Both parts are directed at ensuring the prevalence of individual agreements upon majority decisions, thus preserving ample room for free choice and personal autonomy.

One additional note: It is interesting to realize that, in their approach to economic issues, liberals simply extended these initial ideas about the law (or the other way around). Once again, they assumed that State interventionism was the source of most (economic, in this case) evils.

---

[9] In the U.S., many liberals developed a crusade against the establishment of a religion, first at a local and then at a national level. They wanted to prevent the State from using its force and its resources in favor of a particular faith. James Madison was, once again, a key figure in this movement towards neutrality, which recognized a fundamental antecedent in the work of Roger Williams in Rhode Island. Madison in collaboration with George Mason wrote the first "Declaration of Rights", in Virginia, which came to guarantee complete religious freedom to all Virginians. Every person, they argued, had an equal right to follow his conscience in religious matters. However, politicians like Patrick Henry, an important representative of what we describe as radicalism, opposed that Declaration. Henry proposed supporting the different Christian churches through taxation, arguing that the decline of religion would imply a decline of morals. Against his proposal, Madison argued that the State lacked the authority to demand those payments. Moreover, he asserted that the absence of a prevalent and protected religion would not necessarily imply the moral decay of society. This disgraceful situation could come about, for example, because of inadequate and unjust laws, or the lack of a good educational system, but not as the product of a "neutral" State. Trying to give theoretical foundation to his views, Madison also wrote his well-known paper "Memorial and Remonstrance against Religious Assessments". In this document supported by numerous adherents he asserted the importance of blocking Henry's initiative which appeared to be the first step towards the establishment of a religion. As Milton Konvitz asserted, Madison feared that "the removal of some stones from the new wall of separation of church and state in Virginia might lead to the collapse of the wall and to state support of religion in general". Milton Konvitz (1957), *Fundamental Liberties of a Free People: Religion, Speech, Press, Assembly* (Westport, CT: Greenwood Press Publishers), p. 24. Madison's successful campaign contributed, in addition, to the success of Jefferson's Bill for Establishing Religious Freedom in Virginia (ibid., 24). This was probably the first law in the world enacting complete religious freedom.

Then, and in order to respect people's liberties, it was necessary to allow them to choose freely and carry out their economic initiatives. The parallel they established between the moral, the legal and economic order seemed irreproachable: the State – they assumed – had to be neutral regarding the people's different conceptions of the good and their different preferences. It should impose no conception of the good life upon the people as it should impose no economic regulations. For that reason, it was necessary to organize a framework that allowed each person to pursue his own personal initiatives. In sum: *the personal life of each person – they assumed – should depend on autonomous choices as the public life of the community should depend on the particular initiatives and agreements of the people.* Any State intervention against these individual options was then seen as an unacceptable *irruption* into the life of the people, only capable of *distorting* the free will of the citizenry.

EXAMINING THE (INTERNAL) CONSISTENCY OF LATIN AMERICAN CONSTITUTIONALISM

Let me now examine Latin American constitutionalism, in terms of its consistency. We already know that, in what concerns its *external* consistency, Alberdi declared being satisfied with what legal thinkers of his time had managed to achieve. This is, at least, what he said concerning the so-called "first" regional constitutionalism, and also what he assumed was happening concerning the "second" wave of constitutionalism, to which he made a decisive contribution. Of course, we may agree or not with his own evaluation of Latin America's early constitutional history (I already made reference to the difficulties we have for making "external" evaluations). In any case, at this point I want to only make a basic claim regarding *external* consistency. In my opinion, Latin American constitutionalism has not been doing its job properly in this respect, at least with regard to one fundamental "drama" that has been affecting its own existence during long decades: the "drama" of inequality. In my view, there exists no other equivalent problem in Latin American history. If this were true – as I think it is – this omission would point to a serious problem: regional constitutionalism would have dramatically failed to address and dissolve the main "tragedy" it confronted. By failing to do so, Latin American constitutionalism would have become, unfortunately, co-responsible for the grave levels of inequality of exclusion that still affect the region.

Let me now turn to a more detailed analysis about the *internal* consistency of Latin American Constitutions. In this respect, regional constitutionalism presents at least one particularly significant problem, with which I have dealt at length in another work.[10] I am referring to the internal tension that the vast majority of Latin American Constitutions incorporate, between the way in which they have articulated the organization of power, and the way in which they have organized their approach to rights. In other words, Latin American Constitutions have put their robust declarations of rights at risk, by the way in which they organize power. Summarily speaking, the problem would be the following: Latin American constitutionalism has systematically affirmed its commitment to the values of democracy, inclusion and horizontality, in the area of rights. It has done so, for example, by recognizing the most diverse rights of the most diverse minorities; or by showing a serious concern for the legal inclusion of the most disadvantaged groups of society. However, all the important things it promoted with regard to rights have been actually defied and put at risk by its unreasonable insistence on maintaining an organization of powers oriented by opposite goals. In fact, the organization of powers in most Latin American Constitutions is still today – after more than 200 years of existence – characterized by its verticalism and its hostility towards democracy and popular participation in politics. In other words, nowadays, most Latin American Constitutions offer advanced, progressive, twenty-first century style declarations of rights; while they still maintain organizations of powers that seem to belong to the eighteenth and nineteenth centuries, and which can still be properly characterized by their authoritarian profile, and its commitment to political exclusion.

To understand what I am saying, it may be worth examining – at least in brief – the main features of Latin American constitutionalism. More particularly, in the following paragraphs I will try to highlight the way in which the peculiar "mixture character" of regional constitutionalism has affected the internal consistency of the region's main Constitutions. For this purpose, in what follows I will explore the "mixed" content of Latin American Constitutions and, more particularly, the tensions that emerged between the Constitutions that were enacted in the nineteenth century, and the reforms that were incorporated in the following centuries.

Nineteenth-century Latin American constitutionalism was the product of a convergence of ideologies – mainly, liberalism and conservatism. If liberals came to the negotiating table with their initiatives for equilibrium of power and moral neutrality (we have already explored this view), conservatives arrived at those discussions with almost opposite proposals. Conservatives wanted to replace liberal neutrality with moral

[10] Gargarella (n 1).

perfectionism: they wanted to have a State that was active in the enforcement of the Catholic religion. Most significantly perhaps, conservatives despised the system of mutual controls: they preferred to have an unchecked, unaccountable figure, in charge of government, and endowed with the powers necessary for ensuring order, peace and stability.[11]

The consequence of the liberal-conservative constitutional compact was the enactment of Constitutions that, in more or less innovative ways, combined the proposals of both political traditions. In general, and already from this early stage, Latin American constitutionalism preferred to *accumulate* rather than *synthetize* the initiatives of both sectors. The Argentinian 1857 Constitution represented an excellent illustration of what was then achieved. In the section of rights, for example, it included, at the same time, and in the same text, both what liberals wanted, namely religious tolerance (article 14 of the National Constitution), and what conservatives demanded, namely a special status for the Catholic religion (article 2 of the Constitution). And we can recognize the same strategy of "accumulation" in the sphere of the organization of powers – in Argentina's Constitution, as in most regional Constitutions. In effect, since the mid-nineteenth century, what we find in the region are Constitutions that, following the desires of liberals, consecrated a system of "checks and balances" but which, at the same time, and following the demands of conservatives, "unbalanced" that purported equilibrium, by providing additional, special powers to an overtly powerful Executive, thus creating (so-called) hyper-presidentialist regimes.[12] By doing so, as

---

[11] Following the Napoleonic example, the independence leader Simón Bolívar – whose work was enormously influential in the entire region – proposed for Bolivia an Executive appointed for life and with the power to choose his successor. In his message to the Bolivian Congress (May 1826), he stated: "The President of the Republic, in our Constitution, becomes the sun which, fixed in its orbit, imparts life to the universe. This supreme authority must be perpetual, for in non-hierarchical systems, more than in others, a fixed point is needed about which leaders and citizens, men and affairs can revolve" (Bolívar (1976), at 233).

[12] *See* Carlos Santiago Nino (1997), *The Constitution of Deliberative Democracy* (New Haven, CT: Yale University Press). This was, for example, Alberdi's recommended formula for the particular "drama" affecting Latin America during the 1850s. It was necessary to ensure "order and progress" and, for that reason, the system of equilibrium of powers had to allow the President to become "a King" so as to be able to face situations of crisis and maintain peace. For Alberdi, the Chilean Constitution of 1833 had demonstrated that it existed as a good alternative between "the absolute absence of government and a dictatorial government". This was the model of a "constitutional president who can assume the faculties of a King" in situations of "anarchy". Juan Bautista Alberdi (1981/1852), *Bases y*

I shall clarify, Latin Americans incorporated a serious tension within the same institutional system that they were creating.

Let me clarify this point. First, and to repeat, the main result of the liberal-conservative compact, at the level of the organization of powers, was the creation of hyper-presidential political systems, which, in the end, both liberals and conservatives accepted. On some occasions, Latin Americans transferred to the President the power to declare the *state of siege*, and thus limit rights and individual guarantees; in others, they allowed him to militarily "intervene" in the affairs of local States; in most cases they allowed the President to have a decisive participation in the legislative process; etc. The choice of having a super powerful Executive had, as anticipated, a strong impact upon the system of "checks and balances" that, for that reason, was born "unbalanced". What Latin Americans did concerning the organization of powers, represented a significant departure from the original U.S. model of "checks and balances". More radically – one could add – their decision to empower the Executive in such a way implied putting the entire system of "checks and balances" under risk. James Madison would have easily predicted some of the risks that, since those early days, began to menace Latin American constitutional systems: mainly, the "most dangerous branch" – the one that was in control of military powers and growing economic resources – would begin to exercise an undue influence upon the other branches, and thus destroy the desired equilibrium of powers.

Things became still more worrisome in the following century. In fact, since the beginning of the twentieth century, the political, social, economic and legal situation in the entire region suffered dramatic changes. The old scheme of "order and progress" that had prevailed in Latin America since the mid-nineteenth century, and from which Latin America (and particularly its privileged sectors) greatly benefited, was now in crisis. The politically authoritarian regimes that had managed to ensure economic development with peace were finding increasing difficulties in maintaining the old schema intact. Thus, it became necessary to use greater levels of coercion for keeping the old order stable. The serious political, economic, and social crises of those early years – which demanded profound political and economic changes – found immediate translation into the constitutional order.[13] The way in which constitutionalism attempted to dissipate

puntos de partida para la organización política de la República Argentina (Buenos Aires: Plus Ultra).

[13] Tulio Halperín Donghi (2007), *Historia Contemporánea de América Latina* (Buenos Aires: Alianza).

these crises was by incorporating a concern for the "social question", which was typical of more radical/republican or Rousseauean approaches to constitutionalism. These more radical approaches showed a profound concern with issues of social marginalization, and consequently tended to promote an expansion of political rights, popular participation, and economic equality. Those concerns, we should remember, had been marginalized from the 1850s' constitutional discussions. Now, however, the situation was different – a profound social, political and economic crisis was putting at risk the entire model of "order and progress". This is why reformers began to insist on the importance of incorporating those claims and concerns into the old constitutions.[14]

The beginning of this reform took place in Mexico, and was symbolized by the enactment of the Mexican Constitution in 1917. This Constitution, which followed a dramatic revolutionary movement, represented the first and most radical constitutional response to a crisis that was also a legal crisis. In order to respond to it, it decided to incorporate a long and robust list of social, economic and political rights, which – since then – became a crucial feature of the new Latin American constitutionalism.[15]

The Mexican Constitution became thus the emblem of a new approach to constitutionalism, which began to emphasize the importance of social, economic and political rights. Metaphorically speaking, the "working

---

14 *See* n 2 above.

15 For instance, article 27 of the Mexican Constitution maintained: "The Nation shall at all times have the right to impose on private property such limitations as the public interest may demand, as well as the right to regulate the utilization of natural resources which are susceptible of appropriation, in order to conserve them and to ensure a more equitable distribution of public wealth. With this end in view, necessary measures shall be taken to divide up large landed estates; to develop small landed holdings in operation; to create new agricultural centers, with necessary lands and waters; to encourage agriculture in general and to prevent the destruction of natural resources, and to protect property from damage to the detriment of society. Centers of population which at present either have no lands or water or which do not possess them in sufficient quantities for the needs of their inhabitants, shall be entitled to grants thereof, which shall be taken from adjacent properties, the rights of small landed holdings in operation being respected at all times." Another crucial clause was article 123, which included wide protections to workers and recognized the role of trade unions; regulated labor relations reaching very detailed issues, which in a way covered most of the topics that later on would come to distinguish modern labor law. The clause made reference, for example, to the maximum duration of work; the use of labor of minors; the rights of pregnant women; minimum wage; right to vacation; the right to equal wages; comfortable and hygienic conditions of labor; labor accidents; the right to strike and lockout; arbitrations; dismissal without cause; social security; right to association; etc.

class" finally found its place in the new Constitution through the new Bill of Rights. The Mexican example was soon followed by almost all the Latin American countries. We recognize constitutional changes, in similar directions, in the Constitutions of Brazil in 1937, Bolivia in 1938, Cuba in 1940, Ecuador in 1945, and Argentina and Costa Rica in 1949.

So, here we find a new important wave of Latin American constitutionalism (the first wave appeared right after independence, and the second in the mid-nineteenth century, with the liberal-conservative compact). And, still more significantly, here we have the second crucial moment in the life of Latin American constitutionalism.

To summarize: The *first fundamental moment of regional constitutionalism* appeared in the mid-nineteenth century: it was the time when Latin America adopted its basic institutional "matrix", which defined its *organization of powers* since then, and to the present. The *second fundamental moment of regional constitutionalism* began in the early twentieth century and was extended to the entire region after a few decades. At that second moment, Latin America defined its *organization of rights*, which marks its Constitutions since then.

Through these two moments we can recognize the two main characteristics that still distinguish Latin American Constitutions, and that – unfortunately – reveal their significant internal inconsistencies. On the one hand, we have Constitutions that organize power in a centralized way, imperfectly combining a schema of "checks and balances" with a strong presidentialism. So, here we find a first important tension affecting most regional Constitutions: the idea of "institutional equilibrium" (which belongs to the system of "checks and balances") does not fit well with the existence of a hyper-powerful Executive authority (this tension – as we know – had also clear ramifications in the section of rights, which on many occasions included commitments to both liberal tolerance and religious imposition). On the other hand, we find that twentieth-century Constitutions came to organize a renewed system of rights in ways that properly emphasized the importance of social, economic and political rights. By doing so, however, the new Constitutions introduced a new and crucial tension within their corpus: they thus began to combine centralized and vertical organization of powers with "democratic" and socially oriented declarations of rights. As a consequence, the new Constitutions began to reflect the main internal tension/inconsistency that still characterizes Latin American constitutionalism: the tension that emerges between a backward-looking organization of powers, and a progressive or forward-looking organization of rights.

EVALUATING THE EGALITARIAN CHARACTER OF U.S. CONSTITUTIONALISM

Let us now turn to the substantive evaluation of U.S. and Latin American constitutionalism. First, I shall examine the U.S. Constitution, by paying attention to its egalitarian character – namely, its relation to the ideals of individual autonomy and collective self-government. In this respect, we may say that the U.S. document demonstrates results that are less attractive and promising than expected. On the one hand, it seems undeniable that the U.S. Constitution presents an interesting profile, which relates to its concern with the preservation of basic individual freedoms. However, and on the other hand, it seems also clear that an "egalitarian deficit" affects both the main sections of the Constitution, this is to say, both its organization of power and its Bill of Rights.

To begin with: from a substantive viewpoint, the most interesting aspects of the document appear in the Constitution's serious concern with preventing all kinds of abuses of power – both the risk of majority abuses and the risk of minority abuses. As Alexander Hamilton put it, the Constitution had to be prepared for the risks of both majority and minority oppression.[16] The Framers' obsession with the risk of mutual oppressions was clear, and certainly valuable from an egalitarian perspective: a self-governed legal community requires avoiding the risk of oppression. More prominently, the U.S. Constitution shows a salutary concern with the value of individual autonomy, which occupies – and should occupy – a central role in any egalitarian project. We may recognize this concern in its Bill of Rights and the liberties it protected, and also in an organization of power that was modeled accordingly: the system of "checks and balances" seemed to be well prepared to ensure the enforcement of those basic, proclaimed liberties.

Having said that, we can now briefly explore the significant problems that the U.S. Constitution manifests, concerning its egalitarianism. Relating to the way in which it organizes the Bill of Rights, the Constitution can be properly read as a "negative Constitution", this is to say as a Constitution that is essentially committed to the preservation of "negative" liberties – say, preventing harming, injuring, robbing, killing other individuals. At the same time, the Constitution appears to disregard (one could claim it is directly hostile to) "positive" liberties, usually related to social rights.[17]

---

[16] Max Farrand (ed.) (1937), *The Records of the Federal Convention of 1787* (New Haven, CT: Yale University Press).

[17] For instance, Judge Richard Posner stated: "the Constitution is a charter of negative liberties; it tells the state to let people alone; it does not require the federal government or the state to provide services, even so elementary a service

Without going, at this point, deeper about the "negative" or "positive" character of rights, I would assert that, by closing itself so rigidly to any serious consideration about including social rights in its text, the U.S. Constitution strongly undermined its egalitarian content.[18] And this is so, at least, for two reasons. First, the absence of social rights in the Constitution represents an unattractive feature of the U.S. Constitution because the presence of those rights actually contributes to the cause of equality. At minimum, the presence of social rights contributes to strengthening the idea that all members of society share a common moral equality and – consequently – deserve to be so treated. Second, modern constitutionalism (and here, the Latin American example seems particularly interesting) has already demonstrated that it can deal with social rights without, for that reason, destabilizing the rest of the institutional structure or offending basic democratic values, as some could have expected.[19]

In what concerns the relationship between the organization of powers and egalitarianism, I would say that the U.S. Constitution incurs the typical problem of liberal constitutionalism. The problem is the following: obsessed with ensuring its main declared goal, which is the preservation of individual autonomy, liberal constitutionalism incorporates a diversity of "counter-majoritarian" devices that end up seriously undermining its democratic character. This is what political philosopher Roberto Mangabeira Unger called the *dirty little secret* of modern legal life in the United States.[20]

---

as maintaining law and order" (Edelman 1988, 23). Similarly, Judge Scalia has said that "it is impossible to say that our constitution traditions mandate the legal imposition of even so basic a precept of distributive justice as providing food to the destitute" (ibid., 24); and Judge Bork strongly rejected the possibility of "finding" welfare rights in the (U.S.) Constitution.

[18] *See* Jeff King (2012), *Judging Social Rights* (Cambridge: Cambridge University Press); Malcolm Langford (2009), *Social Rights Jurisprudence: Emerging Trends in International and Comparative Law* (Cambridge: Cambridge University Press).

[19] *See* Daniel Bonilla (2013), *Constitutionalism of the Global South: The Activist Tribunals of India, South Africa, and Colombia* (Cambridge: Cambridge University Press); Roberto Gargarella (2010), *The Legal Foundations of Inequality* (Cambridge: Cambridge University Press); Peter M. Hogg, Allison A. Bushell Thornton and Wade K. Wright (2007), "Charter dialogue revisited – or 'Much Ado about Metaphors'", *Osgoode Hall L.J.*, **45**, 1; Conrado Hübner Mendes, *Constitutional Courts and Deliberative Democracy* (2013) (Oxford: Oxford University Press); Cass Sunstein, *The Second Bill of Rights* (2006) (New York: Basic Books); Mark Tushnet (2004), "Weak-form judicial review: Its implications for legislatures", *NZJPIL*, **2**, 7; Mark Tushnet (2008), *Weak Courts, Strong Rights* (Princeton, NJ: Princeton University Press); Mark Tushnet (2009), "Dialogic judicial review", *Ark. L. Rev.*, **61**, 205.

[20] For him, the "secret" consists of a "discomfort with democracy" that "shows up in every area of contemporary legal culture: in the ceaseless identifica-

Initiatives for the inclusion of counter-majoritarian devices in the Constitution began right after the independence period – particularly between the years 1776 and 1786, which was a time of intense political (and particularly legislative) activism at the State level. In the Federalists' view, the prevalent political situation generated very unfair outcomes: most significantly legislative decisions tended to favor just one particular group, namely the group of the debtors, in other words, the majority of society. Madison made direct reference to this situation in one of the most brilliant political analyses of the time, which was published shortly before the Federal Convention. The paper was called "Vices of the Political System", and there the Virginian mentioned the numerous defects that affected the dominant institutional organization.[21] Most of all though, Madison stressed the vices that derived from the "multiplicity", "mutability" and "injustice" of laws approved at the State level.[22] This is to say, in the lucid analysis of one of the most lucid and influential analysts of the time, the activism of State legislatures appeared as the main source of the existing social problems (the threat posed by the existence of "factions"). These assumptions – without doubt – strongly influenced the redesign of the organization of powers, and help explain the decision to undermine and limit the powers of the Legislature. By weakening the Legislature in that way, the U.S. Constitution also weakened its commitment to the value of collective self-government.

The particular institutional "solutions" that were then adopted, for preventing the influence of majority factions in politics, were diverse (we have already mentioned some of them).[23] Let me just highlight two of them, which are particularly important for our analysis of the egalitarian character of the U.S. Constitution.

A strict separation between public officers and the people. At this point, the first distinctive feature that I would mention, concerning the U.S.

---

tion of restraints upon majority rule, rather than of restraints upon the power of dominant minorities, as the overriding responsibility of judges and jurists; in the consequent hypertrophy of countermajoritarian practices and arrangements; in the opposition to all institutional reforms, particularly those designed to heighten the level of popular political engagement, as threats to a regime of rights . . .; in the single-minded focus upon the higher judges and their selection as the most important part of democratic politics". Roberto Mangabeira Unger (1996), *What Should Legal Analysis Become?* (New York: Verso), p. 72.

[21] Among them, he mentioned the States' lack of respect for federal authorities; the absence of norms for preventing political violence; the frequent violations of national laws and international agreements.

[22] Rachal (1975), at 345–58.

[23] However, I have examined many of them in my book (Gargarella, 2010).

Constitution, is what some authors called the "principle of distinction".[24] To state it more clearly: the "Founding Fathers" wanted to avoid the possibility of having political representatives dependent on the will of the people, and thus prey of "factional" or local politics. Their purpose was to ensure a system of "strict separation" between the people and their representatives, under the assumption that the institutional systems that prevailed during the Framing Period, at the local level, failed to avoid that risk. In their opinion, the dominant institutional system, at the State level, allowed the people to exercise intense and undue pressures upon their representatives. The people's representatives tended to become mere "mouthpieces" of their constituency, and were thus forced to represent partial interests, rather than the interests of the whole. This decision, based on a profound distrust about the people's political capacities, implied the acceptance of a particular understanding of political representation, which Edmund Burke had famously presented at Bristol, in 1776, when he defended – through elitist arguments – the "independence" of political representatives. Later on, in the famous *Federalist Papers* No. 10, James Madison presented a similar view for the United States, based on similar assumptions: he did not see political representation as a "second best" or a "necessary evil", but rather as a first desired option. The assumption was that – given their institutional position, social origins and practical experience – representatives would tend to have a better understanding of politics, than the people themselves.[25]

A preference for "internal" rather than "external" controls. The second institutional feature that I want to highlight is closely related to the system of "checks and balances". It refers to the Framers' preference for an "internal", rather than "external", system of controls. Early American politics had experimented with numerous devices for "external" control: from mandatory instructions, to mandatory rotation, to annual elections, to the right to recall, to town meetings, etc. The consolidation of a system of "checks and balances" came together with the reduction of those

---

[24] Bernard Manin (1997), *The Principles of Representative Government* (Cambridge: Cambridge University Press).

[25] In his words, the representative system had to be directed "to refine and enlarge the public views, by passing them through the medium of a chosen body of citizens, whose wisdom may best discern the true interest of their country, and whose patriotism and love of justice will be least likely to sacrifice it to temporary or partial considerations. Under such a regulation, it may well happen that the public voice, pronounced by the representatives of the people, will be more consonant to the public good than if pronounced by the people themselves, convened for the purpose."

external controls to their minimal expression; or their direct suppression (mandatory instructions, the right to recall, etc. were basically eliminated from national politics). The main reason for this was their profound distrust towards majority politics, which was frequently associated with irrationality, passions and excesses.[26] In this context, the only relevant tool for "external" control that remained intact, namely periodic elections, would promptly tend to lose most of its force: without the help of other means of "external" control, periodic elections began to assume an enormous responsibility (expressing the collective viewpoints about politics), which elections cannot properly fulfill by themselves (the people have only one vote to express, perhaps, dozens of claims, demands and rejections). Moreover, and among the "internal" controls that remained intact (basically, the controls exercised by one branch upon the others), those of a more "majoritarian" character were also strongly limited or curtailed: Congress was divided into two Chambers; a Senate (mainly composed of rich property owners) came to control its more "popular" branch; indirect elections became prominent for the election of crucial public officers (the Executive power; the Judiciary; ambassadors; etc.).

As a result, and since the enactment of the 1787 Constitution, "We the people" found severe difficulties in reaching and controlling their representatives, or in influencing the decision-making process, while their representatives in Congress were subjected to the control of large property owners (the Senate), and the strict supervision of the other branches (the House of Representatives' initiatives were thus easily blocked or limited by the other branches, making it very difficult for the majority will to prevail). In sum, the "democratic costs" that liberal constitutionalism accepted paying, in order to preserve basic individual liberties, were undoubtedly excessive from any egalitarian conception that included a serious commitment to the value of collective self-government.

EVALUATING THE EGALITARIAN CHARACTER OF LATIN AMERICAN CONSTITUTIONALISM

Let me now examine the dominant constitutional model in Latin America, namely egalitarianism. The analysis of this issue is, unsurprisingly, difficult and complex. Once again, we can begin this approach by focusing on the two parts of the Constitution, namely the one related to the organization

---

26 Roberto Gargarella (2010), *The Legal Foundations of Inequality* (Cambridge: Cambridge University Press).

of power, and the one related to the organization of rights. With regard to the first part, I have already suggested what I think: an egalitarian project is incompatible with the style of organization of power that still today prevails in most of the region. To put it simply: if an egalitarian project requires the democratization of powers, then it cannot defend an institutional system that is based – as Latin American institutional systems are still based – on the concentration of powers, which represent the negation of that democratization. The point is ingenuous and seems to find strong empirical support.[27] Let me provide some additional support to this point.

To begin with, nineteenth-century Latin American Constitutions "distorted" the U.S. liberal model in a significant way, namely by "adding" a strong and centralized Executive authority to the general schema of "check and balances". Such a move implied at least two things. On the one hand, it put the entire structure of "mutual controls" at risk, by making one of the branches more powerful than the rest: the system of "checks and balances" – we should remember – required that the different branches were basically equal in their relative power. On the other hand, this change modified the liberal schema in a conservative way, by making the decision-making process less sensitive to popular demands. In hyper-presidentialist systems, in fact, the people have fewer "points of access" to the production of general legislation. Of course, one could reply that hyper-presidentialism favors a more "direct" relation between the leader and the masses. In that way – the reply could follow – the people would actually influence the decision-making process. However, this reply seems problematic. First, in political schemes that concentrate the authority in the hands of "one", powerful interest groups have (also) only "one" person to convince, pressure or extort, which in principle promises to make their task easier and less costly (and, as we know, interest groups tend to have privileged access to political authorities). Second, the fact that the "leader" has direct communication with the "masses" does not imply that the "masses" have actually good or better chances to have an impact in the policy-making process.[28]

Unfortunately, a good deal of the political, legal and constitutional

---

27 Carlos Santiago Nino (1992), *Fundamentos de Derecho Constitucional* (Buenos Aires: Astrea); Carlos Santiago Nino (1993), "Transition to democracy, corporatism and presidentialism with special reference to Latin America", in Douglas Greenberg, Stanley Katz, Beth Oliveiro and Steven Wheatley (eds), *Constitutionalism and Democracy, Transitions in the Contemporary World* (Oxford: Oxford University Press); Carlos Santiago Nino (1996), *The Constitution of Deliberative Democracy* (New Haven, CT: Yale University Press).

28 Santiago Nino (1993), id.

doctrine that prevails in the region – even among its most progressive sectors – seems to still be fascinated by the experiences of constitutional authoritarianism, or semi-authoritarianism, which have damaged the region entirely.[29] In defense of this view, there is at least one line of argument that I want to consider. This is the argument that presents hyper-presidentialism as a means for achieving collective self-government.[30] In effect, for some authors, a certain level of concentration of powers seems to represent a necessary condition for confronting and removing the dense web of interests that tend to control the political life of Latin America's unequal societies.[31] For the moment, I would only claim that there are good theoretical reasons and practical experience that work against this view and at the same time in support of an opposite alternative, namely one based on more direct forms of collective self-government. On the one hand, the concentration of power favors abuses of powers; undermines collective deliberation; endangers political stability; and may be perfectly functional to the deepening of social and political inequalities (a review of these arguments appears in Alegre (2006)). On the other hand, the experiences that Latin America had with more direct forms of democracy, have been varied and in no way unsatisfactory: they range from participatory budgets to popular consultation concerning the exploitation of mineral resources, to participatory processes as those defined by the International Labour Organization in case of legislative measures that put the rights of indigenous communities at risk.[32]

To conclude, for the above reasons, it is my opinion that Latin Americans should finally allow their institutions to be more fully connected with democracy, and they could do so by definitely opening the doors of the "engine room" of their Constitutions to popular majorities. Still today, the popular sectors are unfairly prevented from taking control of their political systems. Latin American Constitutions have opened

---

[29] Stephen Levitsky and Kenneth Roberts (2011), *The Resurgence of the Latin American Left* (Baltimore: Johns Hopkins).

[30] Roberto Mangabeira Unger (1987), "El sistema de gobierno que le conviene a Brasil", in John M. Carey, *Presidencialismo vs. Parlamentarismo* (Buenos Aires: Consejo para la Consolidación de la Democracia), pp. 57–68.

[31] Unger, for instance, supports this version of hyper-presidentialism in connection with more or less permanent plebiscitary mechanisms, which would allow the people at large to recover and affirm its own voice. There are things to say in favor of this version of the argument but, regrettably, most of those who defend hyper-presidentialism in Latin America, do so without the nuances and qualifications that Unger offers in support of his view.

[32] *See e.g.* Maristela Svampa and Enrique Viale (2014), *Maldesarrollo* (Buenos Aires: Katz Editores).

their doors to the working class and other disadvantaged groups since the early twentieth century, but only in the area of the Bill of Rights. It seems unacceptable today – at the beginning of the twenty-first century – to still find the doors of the "engine room" of the Constitution closed to those disadvantaged sectors.

And what to say, then, with regard to the way in which Latin American Constitutions came to organize their Bills of Rights? Could at least this aspect of the prevailing Constitutions be considered part of a genuine egalitarian effort, worthy of respect and praise? I shall here concentrate my attention on the most important and attractive novelty offered by the Bills of Rights in most Latin American Constitutions, namely the introduction of social, economic, cultural and multicultural rights. However, I want to mention an initial, perhaps minor caveat, before entering into that analysis. The minor point is as follows. On many occasions – I submit – those valuable social rights were introduced into the new or reformed Constitutions under the influence of forces of traditional origins, such as the Catholic Church (that had been renovating its doctrine, in a more "social" direction, at least since the *Encyclical Rerum Novarum,* from 1891). In that way, the "rights revolution" that came to distinguish the new Latin American Constitutions did not represent – at least frequently – a significant departure from the old legal order. Typically, the new Bills of Rights (which included clear commitments to robust lists of social and economic rights) came together with the introduction of new limits upon personal autonomy – limits that were introduced in the name of traditional values – i.e, a patriarchal understanding of the family; a conservative approach to gender issues; etc. This was typically the case of some extremely influential Constitutions, such as those promoted by Getulio Vargas, in Brazil (1934 and 1937), or Juan Perón, in Argentina (1949). So, even in regard to this interesting aspect of the "new Latin American constitutionalism", namely the introduction of "new social rights", the fate of the egalitarian project seemed seriously affected.

In any case, let us leave that caveat aside, and concentrate the analysis on the more promising aspects related to the constitutionalization of social rights. There are, in fact, a lot of things to be said – from an egalitarian perspective – in favor of the constitutionalization of the new rights. First, there are reasons of principle: it could reasonably be argued that, in order to take individuals and groups as equals, it is necessary to recognize (legally) certain basic social and economic rights, particularly in contexts where those rights are usually challenged or violated. Second, there are also symbolic reasons that support the inclusion of new rights favoring the most disadvantaged members of society. For members of those groups, in fact, the constitutional recognition of their equal status is enormously relevant. In actual practice – one could claim – such recognition has normally had a positive impact in terms of their dignity and their identity (this is what seems to have happened, particularly, with regard to the incorporation of indigenous rights in many of the new regional Constitutions). Third, experience has taught us that the countries that adopted the most austere or "Spartan" Constitution, in what concerns their organization of rights, have become the countries where the (judicial) enforcement of social rights found more difficulties. Think, as a way of illustration, about the cases of Chile or the United States.[33] Fourth, some new constitutional developments – particularly, those related to so-called *dialogic constitutionalism* – help us to recognize that social rights can be enforced without putting in crisis the basic values of democracy and – by contrast – favoring those very values. So, there are many arguments which favor the introduction of social rights into the new Latin American Constitutions. These arguments also help us to recognize the contribution of those legal initiatives to both individual autonomy and collective self-government.

Now, I do not want to deny the importance and force of those arguments, but only add one very important caveat to them, namely that there is a problem when this expansion of the list of rights is not accompanied by consequent changes in the organization of powers. Of course, someone could reply to my claim by saying that the more progressive Latin American constitutional delegates did the best they could, within the difficult circumstances in which they were required to work. They could state: "Progressive delegates began working on the Bill of Rights section of the Constitution, as a first step of a larger project. They succeeded in that job: they completed their mission, with the certainty that their task had to be – and would be – continued and expanded, in the near future, so as to finally achieve the other section of the Constitution (its organization of powers)."

The previous argument confronts at least one important problem (which is not directed at objecting to the incorporation of social rights in the Constitutions, which we have independent reasons to defend). The problem is that the old organization of power – which is, as we

---

33 Bonilla (n 19); Javier Couso, "The politics of judicial review in Chile in the era of domestic transition", in Siri Gloppen, Roberto Gargarella and Elin Skaar (2004), *The Accountability Function of Courts in New Democracies* (London: Frank Cass); César Rodríguez-Garavito (2011), "Beyond the courtroom: The impact of judicial activism on socioeconomic rights in Latin America", *Texas Law Review*, **89** (7), 1669–98; Rodrigo Uprimny (2006), "Legitimidad y conveniencia del control constitucional a la economía", in Rodrigo Uprimny, César Augusto Rodríguez Garavito and Mauricio García Villegas (2006), *¿Justicia para todos? Sistema judicial, derechos sociales y democracia en Colombia* (Bogota: Norma), pp. 147–200.

have seen, distinguished by its liberal-conservative character – does not remain indifferent to the incorporation of a more social and democratic organization of rights. By contrast, such vertical, rather authoritarian organization of the Constitution tends to work against the newly arrived and progressive organization of rights. To state this does not mean to maintain that hyper-presidents, in Latin America, could not or have not, occasionally, promoted relevant social reforms: they can or could do that, and the opposite, basically because they have the power to do almost whatever they want. However, the fact is that the vertical institutional structure that prevails in most Latin American Constitutions tends to become in tension with popular participation and also in tension with the demands of groups fighting for more autonomous power. Not surprisingly, hyper-powerful Presidents tend to read those demands for political participation and control as a direct challenge to their own power and respond accordingly – on many occasions, through the brutal use of the vast coercive powers they have under their control.[34] In this respect, the over-obsession that Latin American doctrinaires have demonstrated towards the expansion of the Bill of Rights – without due attention to the introduction of correlative changes in the organization of powers – cannot but be considered the product of sheer inertia, lack of reflection or, simply, a political mistake, that progressive Latin Americans continue making, without giving much thought to the problem. In sum, Latin American Constitutions seem to have favored self-government through many of their innovations (particularly in the section of rights), while at the same time seemed to help undermine that same value of collective self-government, through the reforms that they decided not to introduce in the old organization of powers.

CONCLUSION

In this chapter, I have critically compared and examined the development of constitutionalism in the U.S. and in Latin America. In order to do so, I have been using one formal criterion, related to the consistency of the different American Constitutions; I have also used a more substantive criterion, related to the egalitarian character of those Constitutions. Summarily speaking, I have first shown the attractiveness of the U.S. Constitution, when compared with most Latin American Constitutions,

[34] Roberto Gargarella (2013), *Latin American Constitutionalism, 1810–2010* (Oxford: Oxford University Press).

in relation to its internal consistency. The U.S. Constitution, which most Latin American countries took as a model or point of reference, seems consistently defined by a liberal philosophy, which is reflected both in a Bill of Rights that is strongly protective of classical rights, and in its organization of powers, which is directed at ensuring political equilibrium. By contrast, most Latin American Constitutions organize an imperfect combination of different, and sometimes opposite, philosophical ideas (which include liberal, conservative and social viewpoints). As a consequence, many of these documents establish controlling mechanisms, which they undermine in the same act, through the adoption of alternative devices that are in tension with the former (i.e., hyper-powerful Executive that does not "fit" within a scheme of "checks and balances"). Similarly, they create a structure of liberal rights, which they immediately challenge with the adoption of other, collective or communal rights that are in tension with the former.

In regard to the second, more substantive analysis, I maintained that most Latin American Constitutions have made significant but imperfect efforts, for becoming more egalitarian. In particular, I claimed that the concentration of powers that most Latin American Constitutions allow, tends to work against the enforcement of the long list of social, economic and cultural rights that these Constitutions properly incorporated. In addition, I also criticized the U.S. Constitution from the perspective of this more substantive criterion. In general terms, I claimed that the U.S. Constitution honors the value of individual autonomy at the cost of sacrificing the value of collective self-government. More specifically, I maintained that the "negative" aspects of the U.S. Constitution, which failed to include any social, economic or cultural right in its Bill of Rights, is unattractive from an egalitarian perspective.

BIBLIOGRAPHY

Abramovich, V. and Courtis, C. (2002), *Los derechos sociales como derechos exigibles* (Barcelona: Trotta).

Alberdi, J.B. [1852] (1981), *Bases y puntos de partida para la organización política de la República Argentina* (Buenos Aires: Plus Ultra).

Alegre, M. (2006), "Democracy without presidents", manuscript (SELA), Yale University, http://www.law.yale.edu/documents/pdf/Democracy_without_Presidents.pdf.

Balkin, J. (1997), "Agreements with hell and other objects of our faith", *Fordham Law Review*, **65**,1703.

Bickel, A. (1962), *The Least Dangerous Branch* (New Haven, CT: Yale University Press).

Bolívar, S. (1976), *Doctrina del Libertador* (Caracas: Biblioteca Ayacucho).
Bonilla, D. (2013), *Constitutionalism of the Global South. The Activist Tribunals of India, South Africa, and Colombia* (Cambridge: Cambridge University Press).
Bonilla, D. and Iturralde, M. (2005), *Hacia un nuevo derecho constitucional* (Bogotá: Universidad de Los Andes).
Cepeda, M. (2004), "Judicial activism in a violent context: The origin, role, and impact of the Colombian Constitutional Court", *Washington University Global Studies Law Review*, **3**, 259.
Edelman, P. (1988), "The next century of our constitution: Rethinking our duty to the poor", *Hastings Law Journal*, **39**, 1.
Farrand, M. (ed.) (1937), *The Records of the Federal Convention of 1787* (New Haven, CT: Yale University Press).
Gargarella, R. (2010), *The Legal Foundations of Inequality. Constitutionalism in the Americas, 1810–1860* (Cambridge: Cambridge University Press).
Gargarella, R. (2013), *Latin American Constitutionalism, 1810–2010* (Oxford: Oxford University Press).
Gargarella, R. (2014), "Deliberative democracy, dialogic justice and the promise of social and economic rights", in H. Alviar, L. Williams and K. Klare (eds), *Social and Economic Rights in Theory and Practice: A Critical Assessment* (London: Routledge).
Gauri, V. and Brinks, D. (eds) (2008), *Courting Social Justice* (Cambridge: Cambridge University Press).
Gaviria Díaz, C. (2002), *Sentencias. Herejías constitucionales* (Bogotá: Fondo de Cultura Económica).
Halperín Donghi, T. (2007), *Historia Contemporánea de América Latina* (Buenos Aires: Alianza).
Hamilton, A., Madison, J. and Jay, J. [1787] (1982), *The Federalist Papers* (New York: Bantam Books).
Hogg, P. and Bushell, A. (1997), "The charter dialogue between courts and legislatures", *Osgoode Hall L.J.*, **35**, 75.
Hogg, P., Bushell, A. and Wright, W. (2007), "Charter dialogue revisited: Or 'much ado about metaphors'", *Osgoode Hall L.J.*, **45**, 1.
Hubner Mendes, C. (2013), *Constitutional Courts and Deliberative Democracy* (Oxford: Oxford University Press).
King, J. (2012), *Judging Social Rights* (Cambridge: Cambridge University Press).
Konvitz, M. (1957), *Fundamental Liberties of a Free People: Religion, Speech, Press, Assembly* (Westport, CT: Greenwood Press Publishers).
Jefferson, T. (1999), *Political Writings* (Cambridge: Cambridge University Press).
Langford, M. (2009), *Social Rights Jurisprudence: Emerging Trends in International and Comparative Law* (Cambridge: Cambridge University Press).
Lemaitre Ripoll, J. (2009), *El derecho como conjuro. Fetichismo legal, violencia y movimientos sociales* (Bogotá: Siglo del Hombre Editores).
Levitsky, S. and Roberts, K. (2011), *The Resurgence of the Latin American Left* (Baltimore: Johns Hopkins).
Liebenberg, S. (2014), "Deepening democratic transformation in South Africa through participatory constitutional remedies", manuscript, University of Stellenbosch Law Faculty.
Manin, B. (1997), *The Principles of Representative Government* (Cambridge: Cambridge University Press).
Nino, C.S. (1992), *Fundamentos de Derecho Constitucional* (Buenos Aires: Astrea).

Nino, C. (1993), "Transition to democracy, corporatism and presidentialism with special reference to Latin America", in D. Greenberg, S. Katz, B. Oliveiro and S. Wheatley (eds), *Constitutionalism and Democracy, Transitions in the Contemporary World* (Oxford: Oxford University Press).
Nino, C.S. (1996), *The Constitution of Deliberative Democracy* (New Haven, CT: Yale University Press).
Rachal, W. (ed.) (1975), *The Papers of James Madison*, Vol. 9 (Chicago: University of Chicago Press).
Roach, K. (2004), "Dialogic judicial review and its critics", *Supreme Court Law Review*, **23**, 49–104.
Rodríguez-Garavito, C. (2011), "Beyond the courtroom: The impact of judicial activism on socioeconomic rights in Latin America", *Texas Law Review*, **89** (7), 1669–98.
Svampa, M. and Viale, E. (2014), *Maldesarrollo* (Buenos Aires: Katz Editores).
Tushnet, M. (2004), "Weak-form judicial review: Its implications for legislatures", *Supreme Court Law Review*, **23**, 213.
Tushnet, M. (2008), *Weak Courts, Strong Rights* (Princeton, NJ: Princeton University Press).
Tushnet, M. (2009), "Dialogic judicial review", *Ark. L. Rev.*, **61**, 205.
Unger, R. (1987), "El sistema de gobierno que le conviene a Brasil", in J.M. Carey, *Presidencialismo vs. Parlamentarismo* (Buenos Aires: Consejo para la Consolidaci ón de la Democracia).
Unger, R. (1996), *What Should Legal Analysis Become?* (London: Verso Press).
Uprimny, R. (2011), "The recent transformation of constitutional law in Latin America: Trends and challenges", *Texas Law Review*, **89** (7), 1587–1610.
Wood, G. (1969), *The Creation of the American Republic* (New York: W.W.Norton & Company).
Young, K. (2012), *Constituting Economic and Social Rights* (Oxford: Oxford University Press).

5. Back to the future? The return of sovereignty and the principle of non-intervention in the internal affairs of the states in Latin America's "radical constitutionalism"

Javier Couso

I. INTRODUCTION

One of the most innovative features of Latin America's constitutional law in the past three decades has been its embrace – at least at the discursive level – of International Human Rights Law, a trend that coincided with the processes of democratic transition and consolidation that took place in most countries of the region, and which has translated into the unprecedented role played by Inter-American Human Rights Law in domestic constitutional law.

That said, in recent years the relationship between the Inter-American Human Rights System and national constitutional law has been under stress in the set of countries that have adopted what in a previous work I call 'Latin America's radical constitutionalism'.[1]

After summarizing the main features of "radical constitutionalism", in this chapter I analyze an important element of the latter which has been ignored by the literature, that is, the recovery by such regimes of the so-called principles of "*self determination of the peoples*" and "*non-interference with the internal affairs of sovereign states*".

In spite of having been introduced to International Law by Latin American jurists, these two principles had been largely forgotten in recent decades, due to the impact of the international human rights movement in the region. The new life brought to the principles of "self-determination"

[1] Javier Couso, Alexandra Huneeus and Rachel Sieder (eds) (2010), *Legal Cultures and Political Activism in Latin America* (Cambridge: Cambridge University Press).

and "non-interference" has – in turn – created significant tensions between Latin America's radical constitutional states and International Human Rights Law, including the Inter-American Human Rights System.

Given this context, I suggest that Venezuela's denunciation of the American Convention on Human Rights (2012) should not be seen as a whimsical act, but instead as a measure coherent with the main features of radical constitutionalism. If this is correct, one should expect that in the future other "Bolivarian" states (such as Ecuador or Bolivia) could follow Venezuela's path.

Finally, I argue that the illiberal turn taken by the United States' constitutional law since 11 September 2001,[2] expressed in the toleration of the systematic violations of human rights perpetrated by the government (such as the denial of habeas corpus to the prisoners at Guantanamo Bay, the practice of torture, and the "target killings" of citizens without judicial oversight) has been used by the radical democracies of Latin America as an excuse to attack the Inter-American Human Rights System.[3]

II. THE END OF THE HEGEMONY OF LIBERAL CONSTITUTIONALISM IN LATIN AMERICA

Halfway through the 1990s, the panorama of constitutionalism in Latin America was relatively simple, at least from a theoretical point of view. With the inauguration (or recovery) of democracy, and the consolidation of human rights discourse, liberal constitutionalism appeared to be "*the only game in town*". In fact, both the right and the left in Latin America seemed to agree that democracy and constitutional rule of law were inseparable.[4] This regional consensus on liberal constitutionalism was part of a global one around what Alec Stone Sweet has called "*higher-law constitutionalism*".[5]

---

[2] Jeremy Waldron (2010), *Torture, Terror, and Trade-Offs: Philosophy for the White House* (Oxford: Oxford University Press).

[3] David Cole, "Must counterterrorism cancel democracy?", in *The New York Review of Books*. Accessed 28 December 2015 at http://www.nybooks.com/articles/2015/01/08/must-counterterrorism-cancel-democracy/.

[4] *See* Pilar Domingo (2012), "El estado de derecho, la reforma judicial y la justicia de transición en América Latina", in Vesselin Popovski and Monica Serrano, *Justicia transicional y consolidación democrática: la comparación de la eficacia de los mecanismos de rendición de cuentas en Europa del Este y América Latina* (Tokyo: United Nations University).

[5] According to Stone Sweet, this approach to constitutional law assumes the notion of constitutional supremacy and of justiciable rights. *See* Alec Stone Sweet

Another phenomenon that aroused a great deal of consensus in Latin America was the relevance of International Human Rights Law in the domestic sphere, including the notion that national sovereignty should defer to the decisions of international tribunals created by human rights treaties.[6]

The combination of the two trends just noted generated a remarkable convergence in that part of the Latin American constitutions that recognize fundamental rights (as opposed to what Roberto Gargarella calls the "*engine room of the Constitution*", where no such convergence exists).[7]

An example of the influence achieved by International Human Rights Law in Latin American constitutionalism is the fact that – in many states of the region – high courts closely follow the decisions of international human rights courts, especially those of the Inter-American Court of Human Rights.[8]

All the above has led to significant changes in the legal culture of jurists, judges, and even ordinary people,[9] a process which has weakened the separation between the different "legal traditions" of the continent,[10] particularly in the field of public law. This explains the fact that in many Latin American countries "rights talk" is as prevalent as it is in the United States.[11]

(2000), *Governing with Judges: Constitutional Politics in Europe* (Oxford: Oxford University Press), p. 7.

6 *See* Daphne Barak-Erez (2004), "The international law of human rights and constitutional law: A case study of an expanding dialogue", *International Journal of Constitutional Law*, **2** (4), 611–32, and Jean Cohen (2012), *Globalization and Sovereignty: Rethinking Legality, Legitimacy and Constitutionalism* (Cambridge: Cambridge University Press).

7 *See* Roberto Gargarella (2014), *La sala de máquinas de la Constitución: dos siglos de constitucionalismo en América Latina (1810–2010)* (Buenos Aires: Katz).

8 *See* Humberto Nogueira Alcalá (2012), "El uso del derecho convencional internacional de los derechos humanos en la jurisprudencia del Tribunal Constitucional chileno en el periodo 2006–2010", *Revista Chilena de Derecho*, **39** (1), 149–97.

9 *See* Diego López Medina (2004), *Teoría impura del derecho: la transformación de la cultura jurídica latinoamericana* (Bogotá: Legis-Universidad de los Andes and Universidad Nacional de Colombia); Javier Couso (2014), "Las democracias radicales y el 'nuevo constitucionalismo latinoamericano'", *Seminario en Latinoamérica de Teoría Constitucional y Política*, Yale Law School; and Huneeus y Sieder (2010).

10 *See* John Henry Merryman (2007), *The Civil Law Tradition: An Introduction to the Legal Systems of Europe and Latin America*, 3rd edn (Redwood City, CA: Stanford University Press).

11 *See* Catalina Smulovitz (2010), "Judicialization in Argentina: Legal culture or opportunities and support structures?", in Couso, Huneeus and Sieder (n 1), at 234–53.

III. THE CHALLENGE OF "RADICAL CONSTITUTIONALISM"

Even though the legitimacy of liberal constitutionalism, judicial review and the role of International Human Rights Law in domestic constitutional law remains strong in most of Latin America, the consensus on liberal constitutionalism has lost momentum since the introduction of radical constitutionalism in Venezuela, Ecuador, Bolivia and Nicaragua.[12]

This approach to constitutional law seeks to unify state power, in order to confront multinational corporations and other forms of private power which radical constitutionalism blames for the persistency of socio-economic inequality in the region. According to this perspective, the influence of transnational capital in Latin America is so strong that only a united front of the executive, legislative and judicial branches can effectively challenge the former.

From a structural point of view, the new constitutions of the so-called "Bolivarian Republics" include the following features: (a) the weakening of the principle of separation of powers; (b) the strengthening of the power of the executive branch; and, (c) the elimination of bicameralism and its replacement by a single legislative body, which has facilitated the control of the executive and legislative branches by the same party.

In addition to the above-mentioned features, in recent years Bolivarian constitutionalism has introduced the indefinite re-election of the President of the Republic, with the explicit goal of ensuring the continuity of the "revolutionary process". Thus, for example, in March 2014 the President of Ecuador, Rafael Correa, defended the indefinite re-election of the head of the executive branch on the grounds that "*I have a responsibility to ensure that this process is irreversible*".[13] A few months later, in May 2014, Correa insisted on this point, asserting that "*we must continue to adjust our institutions to reality, and not give way to the return of the elites*".[14]

---

[12] Roberto Viciano and Rubén Martínez Dalmau (2010), "Aspectos generales del nuevo constitucionalismo latinoamericano", in *El nuevo constitucionalismo en América Latina* (Quito: Corte Constitucional del Ecuador).

[13] The full quote is: "*Personally, I think it my duty to review the decision of banning reelection, because I have a responsibility to ensure that this process is irreversible.*" The media outlet that reported these statements quoted Correa as saying that "*the country should start a serious debate on the prohibition established by the Constitution of the Republic of the indefinite reelection of elected dignitaries*". *El Universo* (2014), "Rafael Correa medita una posible reelección presidencial". Accessed 9 September 2017 at http://www.eluniverso.com/noticias/2014/03/02/nota/2266336/rafael-medita-posible-reeleccion-presidencial.

[14] *El Universo* (2014), "Rafael Correa apoya enmienda de la Constitución para la

The emphasis on making sure that the processes of radical change underway are "irreversible" is, in my view, the key to understanding the nature of Latin America's radical constitutionalism. Indeed, the introduction of the indefinite re-election of the President to guarantee the continuity of the revolutionary process suggests that, instead of providing an institutional framework aimed at allowing different ideological sectors to compete for the control of government, radical constitutionalism seeks to perpetuate the control of the latter by a specific political sector. In this conception, the Constitution is not conceived as a limit on the power of the state, but as a means of strengthening a specific ideological project, in a manner analogous to how the dictatorship of Augusto Pinochet used the Chilean Constitution of 1980 to try to perpetuate a – very different – political, social and economic model.

Even though the use of the Constitution to make a revolutionary process irreversible suggests a deeply flawed way to understand the role of constitutional law, such a position has an internal logic. For those who truly believe that the processes currently underway in Venezuela, Ecuador, Bolivia and Nicaragua represent an unprecedented emancipatory experience, the notion of allowing "counter-revolutionary" parties to gain access to the Executive branch is simply absurd.

IV. RADICAL CONSTITUTIONALISM AND THE INTER-AMERICAN HUMAN RIGHTS SYSTEM

While the characteristics of Latin America's radical constitutionalism outlined in the previous sections are relatively well known to observers of constitutionalism in the region, the tension between the former and International Human Rights Law has received almost no scholarly attention.

Of course, most analysts of Latin American constitutional politics know about the decision of Venezuela to denounce the American Convention on Human Rights (in September of 2012) but, what is less known, is that that action was not a whimsical one, but instead one that was aligned with the particular way in which radical constitutionalism conceptualizes its relationship with International Human Rights Law.

This is apparent in the official memorandum through which Venezuela notified the denunciation of the American Convention on Human Rights.

---

reelección indefinida". Accessed 9 September 2017 at http://www.eluniverso.com/noticias/2014/05/24/nota/3005426/rafael-correa-apoya-iniciativa-legislativa-reeleccion.

The document, signed by the then Minister of Foreign Affairs of Venezuela, Nicolás Maduro, includes this significant passage:

> (. . .) In recent years, the practice of the organs governed by the Pact of San José, both the Inter-American Commission and the Inter-American Court of Human Rights have moved away from the sacred principles that they are called to protect, instead becoming a political weapon aimed at undermining the stability of certain governments, especially that of our country, adopting a line of action openly interfering with the internal affairs of our government, thus violating and ignoring basic and essential principles widely recognized in International Law, such as the principle of respect for state sovereignty and the principle of self-determination of peoples (. . .).[15]

Notice how the main reason given by Venezuela to denounce the American Convention on Human Rights was the alleged violation by the organs of the Inter-American Human Rights System of three principles of International Law that – until a few decades ago – were extremely important to the Latin American states, but that had been forgotten in recent times: the respect for state sovereignty, the self-determination of sovereign peoples, and the non-interference with the internal affairs of states.[16]

Furthermore, Venezuela's official memorandum exhibits a strong rejection of the notion of the subordination of domestic constitutional law to International Human Rights Law:

> The (Inter-American Human Rights System) can not seek to exclude, ignore, or replace the constitutional order of the Party-States, as the international protection that derives from it is adjunct or complementary to that provided by the domestic law of the American States. However, repeated decisions by the Inter-American Commission and the Court have violated the clauses and principles of the Constitution of the Bolivarian Republic of Venezuela, as stated by the Constitutional Chamber of the Supreme Court of our State (. . .).[17]

The reader will note the distance that this passage exhibits from the way most Latin American constitutional scholars currently understand the relationship between domestic constitutional law and International

---

[15] Bolivarian Republic of Venezuela, Ministry of Popular Power for Foreign Relations (2012), "Carta de denuncia a la Convención Americana sobre Derechos Humanos por parte de Venezuela ante la OEA". Accessed 9 September 2017 at http://es.scribd.com/doc/105813775/Carta-de-denuncia-a-la-Convencion-Americana-sobre-Derechos-Humanos-por-parte-de-Venezuela-ante-la-OEA.

[16] "*The Bolivarian Republic of Venezuela will continue to promote respect for the most sacred principles of International Law, such as independence, non-interference in internal affairs, sovereignty and the self-determination of peoples* (. . .)". Ibid., at 9.

[17] Ibid., at 2–3.

Human Rights Law. Indeed, at a time when most of the constitutionalists of the region adhere to the notion that there is a "*block of constitutionality*"[18] composed of a combination of national constitutional law and International Human Rights Law, Bolivarian constitutionalism asserts the pre-eminence of national constitutional law.

Given the importance of the principle of non-interference in the internal affairs of states in Venezuela's decision to abandon the Inter-American Human Rights System, in the next section I discuss the crucial role that the former had during much of the twentieth century in Latin America.

V. THE ORIGIN AND USES OF THE PRINCIPLE OF NON-INTERFERENCE IN THE INTERNAL AFFAIRS OF SOVEREIGN STATES

In the last section, we saw how Venezuela invoked the principles of respect for national sovereignty, of the self-determination of peoples, and of the non-interference with the internal affairs of states to justify its denunciation of the American Convention on Human Rights. Venezuela's emphasis on these traditional principles of International Law had a very specific purpose: to blame the United States for its abandonment of the Inter-American System.

This accusation, which had already been hinted by Hugo Chavez in 2010,[19] was explicitly affirmed by the then President Nicolás Maduro, once Venezuela materialized its denunciation of the American Human Rights Convention (in September 2013). According to press reports:

> The President of Venezuela, Nicolás Maduro, affirmed that the Inter-American Human Rights System was "captured" by the United States as a way [to] justify the withdrawal of his country (from the Inter-American Human Rights

---

[18] Rodrigo Uprimny (2001), "El bloque de constitucionalidad en Colombia: un análisis jurisprudencial y un ensayo de sistematización doctrinal", in Daniel O'Donnell, Inés Margarita Uprimny and Alejandro Villa (eds), *Compilación de jurisprudencia y doctrina nacional e internacional* (Bogotá: Oficina del Alto Comisionado de Naciones Unidas para los Derechos Humanos).

[19] Hugo Chavez said on that occasion of the Inter-American Human Rights System the following: "*It's a mafia (. . .) Institutions like this nefarious Inter-American Commission on Human Rights do not defend human rights. It is a politicized body, used by the Empire to attack governments like Venezuela's.*" *See El País* (2012), "Venezuela abandona el sistema de derechos humanos interamericano". Accessed 9 September at http://internacional.elpais.com/internacional/2013/09/10/actualidad/1378780644_769381.html.

> System). "Time has run out for the Inter-American Commission of Human Rights Committee (. . .); is captured by the interests of the State Department of the United States" Maduro said. He said the Inter-American System of Human Rights, including the Commission and the Court, "drifted into an instrument of persecution against the progressive governments that started" with the arrival of Hugo Chavez to power in Venezuela, in 1999.[20]

The link established by Venezuela between, on the one hand, the importance of national sovereignty and the principle of non-interference in the internal affairs of states and, on the other, the hostile action against his government supposedly perpetrated by the United States, appealed to a long history of disagreements between various Latin American states and their northern neighbor, a history which was in fact very present in the origins of the consecration of the principle of non-interference in the internal affairs of states. Indeed, even though this principle was eventually enshrined in the UN Charter (1945),[21] it had been promoted and adopted earlier by the Latin American states, in order to contain what was considered to be the "imperial" tendencies of the United States.

The notion that the introduction of the principle of non-intervention with the internal affairs of sovereign states was in fact a Latin American response to a long "tradition" of both peaceful and violent interventions by the United States in the region appeared first in a text published in 1962 by Alejandro Alvarez, one of the most influential International Law scholars of the first half of the twentieth century. According to this Chilean jurist:

> In classical International Law, a state, especially a great power, can intervene, in certain cases, in the affairs of another state not only by peaceful means, but even by violent means. (. . .) The Latin American states, from their independence, have formally outlawed and condemned this kind of intervention in the Pan American Conferences, which proclaimed the principle of non-intervention, in order to condemn the policy pursued by the United States on its continent's neighbors.[22]

---

20 "*Today the withdrawal from the American Convention on Human Rights takes shape. Venezuela accuses the Commission of being an appendix of the United States.*" *La Nación* (2013), "Venezuela acusa a la CIDH de ser apéndice de Estados Unidos". Accessed 9 September at http://www.nacion.com/mundo/latinoamerica/Venezuela-CIDH-apendice-EE-UU_0_1365263467.html.

21 Article 2, para 7, states: "Nothing in the present Charter shall authorize the United Nations to intervene in matters within the domestic jurisdiction of any state." Quoted by Carpizo (2003), at 251.

22 Alejandro Álvarez (1962), *El nuevo derecho internacional en sus relaciones con la vida real de los pueblos* (Santiago: Editorial Jurídica de Chile).

Notice how Alvarez, a liberal jurist, explicitly links the interest expressed by the Latin American states to introduce the principle of non-intervention with the internal affairs of other states as a way to end the traditional United States' policy of intervention in its southern neighbors.

In another passage of the work under review, Alvarez recalled how (at the Seventh Pan American Conference), the United States finally acquiesced to support international condemnation of intervention in the affairs of other states. In his words:

> The head of the delegation of the United States stated that there had been a radical change in the policy of the new administration of his country, President Roosevelt; they pointed to the latter's message, in which he opposed any attempt of hegemony (by his country) and supported instead the policy of the "good neighbor". This statement, welcomed with joy by the Latin American states, has reinforced the sense of continental solidarity, until then hindered by the political hegemony of the United States (. . .).[23]

The principle of non-intervention with the internal affairs of states would be eventually "rescued" from oblivion forty years after Álvarez's defense of it by another prominent Latin American jurist, the Mexican Jorge Carpizo who, reacting to the unwarranted military intervention perpetrated by the United States in Iraq (in 2003) "resuscitated" the principle of non-interference with the internal affairs of sovereign states, noting in passing that the latter had been a key contribution to International Law by Latin America.[24] In his words:

> The intervention is a non-consensual interference of one or more States in the domestic or external affairs of others, violating the sovereignty and independence of the state affected. The procedure can be performed by using force or through non-violent means; it can be carried out directly or indirectly (through a third country), openly or clandestinely, through espionage services, within the territory of the state or by trying to interfere with the help of its diplomats. The intervening state is more powerful than the one suffering interference, which it is unable, in turn, to meddle in the affairs of the aggressor (. . .). It is then clear that intervention is a symptom of the inequality of the international order, and constitutes an illegitimate act of force, . . . [25]

After this conceptual and critical analysis of the intervention of strong states on weak states, and after the emphasis he makes of intervention

---

[23] Ibid., at 252.

[24] Carpizo recalls with satisfaction: "*This principle is a Latin American contribution to International Law. These ideas were incorporated in various articles of the UN Charter.*" Ibid., at 253.

[25] Ibid., at 250.

in the internal affairs of the states as a "symptom" of the inequality of the international order, Carpizo adopts a more direct tone, affirming that the region where he comes from (Latin America) has always been a strong advocate of the principle of non-intervention in internal affairs *precisely because it has been the victim of a history of interventions.* In his words:

> Latin America, especially Mexico, the Caribbean and Central America, who have suffered military invasions and all kinds of other forms of interventions, developed the principle of non-intervention and then worked to obtain the legal recognition of the concept in (international) treaties.[26]

That said, Carpizo recounts how the United States initially refused to accept the legal recognition of the principle of non-interference in the internal affairs of sovereign states. According to him, the United States blocked the legal adoption of this principle at the Havana Conference of 1928, but eventually it was forced to accept it five years later (in the Montevideo Conference of 1933), due to the explosive situation prompted by the emergence of the Nazi and Fascist regimes in Europe, which made it imperative for the U.S. to cement a close unity with the Latin American states.

The new position adopted by the United States was later ratified and deepened at the Ninth Inter-American Conference of Bogotá, in 1948 (which created the Organization of the American States). At this international meeting, a treaty was introduced which included the following norm: "No State or group of States has the right to intervene, directly or indirectly, for any reason whatever, in the internal or external affairs of any other."

Later in the piece we are analyzing, Carpizo enthusiastically defends the virtues of sovereignty, self-determination and non-interference in the internal affairs of other states, even in the era of globalization, stating that, in his opinion:

> Sovereignty is and remains an essential feature of national and International Law, both at the service of human beings, their dignity and their fundamental rights, and peace among nations (. . .) From the notion of sovereignty (. . .) and the fact that all states have equal rights, derives the concept of self-determination (. . .) The anti-colonial self-determination is primarily a legal and political instrument, which makes direct reference to the right of independence of peoples previously living under a colonial state.[27]

---

[26] Ibid., at 252.
[27] Ibid., at 256.

At this point, it is useful to remember that neither Alejandro Álvarez nor Jorge Carpizo were radical jurists, but, on the contrary, convinced liberals. It is also important to note that, although Álvarez wrote up until the mid-twentieth century, while Carpizo did so until the twenty-first century, both based their defense of the principles of self-determination and non-interference in internal affairs of states in light of the experience of intervention by the United States which many Latin American countries had suffered in the past.

At any rate, precisely because of the strong commitment to the values of the rule of law and liberal constitutionalism, both Álvarez and Carpizo acknowledged that their appreciation of the principle of non-intervention in the internal affairs of the states must be balanced with the principle of respect for the human rights of individuals. In the words of Carpizo:

> . . . A government cannot invoke the idea of sovereignty to massacre its people (. . .) International Law cannot be complicit with massive human rights violations committed by the state; but to use humanitarian intervention as an excuse to interference (represents) a flagrant violation of International Law. You cannot attack the commission of a crime by committing another crimes. You cannot allow humanitarian assistance to result in the imposition of your power to other countries. It is not legally possible to let (humanitarian concerns) to become a new form of imperialism (. . .) It is not possible that humanitarian assistance destroy the principles of self-determination and non-intervention. It is not permissible for a few countries to decide, by themselves, that it is time to support a state and, under this pretext, invade it . . . [28]

VI. THE USE OF THE PRINCIPLE OF NON-INTERVENTION BY LATIN AMERICA'S RADICAL CONSTITUTIONALISM IN ITS ATTACK ON THE LEGITIMACY OF THE INTER-AMERICAN HUMAN RIGHTS SYSTEM

The brief summary of the origins of the principles of self-determination of the peoples and of non-intervention in the internal affairs of states provided above reveals that they represent something of a Latin American "tradition". After going into oblivion for some decades (during the period of transition to democracy, between 1980 to 2010) they were rediscovered by the Bolivarian states in order to attack what they perceived as an abuse of the Inter-American Human Rights System by the United States (in order to destabilize their revolutionary projects).

---

[28] Ibid., at 14.

The problem with this move is that – in doing so – the Bolivarian leaders violated one of the pillars of contemporary constitutionalism: the notion that the principle of non-intervention in the internal affairs of sovereign states cannot be invoked in cases of gross human rights violations.

The recovery of the principle of non-intervention with the internal affairs of states we have described in this chapter can thus be explained both by the emphasis on popular sovereignty which characterizes the Bolivarian states and by the fact that the principle was originally introduced to oppose the history of illegitimate interventions perpetrated by the United States in various Latin American countries.

Additionally, there are two other elements that in my view have contributed to expose the Inter-American Human Rights System to the – no doubt, exaggerated – accusation that it has been used by the United States to attack the radical Latin American states, due to the former's ideological hostility to them.

The first element is the peculiar fact that precisely one of the few countries in the American continents which has yet to grant jurisdiction to the Inter-American Court of Human Rights (the United States) has nonetheless been allowed to appoint judges in the very body it does not recognize as having jurisdiction over it.[29] The second element is that the city where a key entity of the Inter-American Human Rights System sits (the Commission), is Washington, DC.

Looked at from a comparative perspective and, in fact, from a purely logical point of view, it is incomprehensible that a country that has consistently refused to give jurisdiction to the Inter-American Human Rights Court can, however, appoint judges and commissioners to the organs of the System, while also serving as the headquarters of one of the key actors.

While these last elements are problematic only from a symbolic point of view, it is undeniable that they have a neocolonial air, thus giving plausibility in the eyes of large segments of the Latin American region to the accusation raised by the Bolivarian leaders that the Inter-American Human Rights System has an ideological bias against the Bolivarian republics.

Given the above, it would be healthy for the Inter-American System of Human Rights that, until the United States finally grants jurisdiction to the Inter-American Human Rights Court, they stop nominating judges or commissioners to the System. Also, the latter would gain in legitimacy if it relocated the headquarters of the Inter-American Human Rights

---

[29] Such was the case of Thomas Buergenthal, who was President of the Inter-American Court of Human Rights in the period 1985–1987.

Commission to San José (Costa Rica) or to the capital of any of the countries of the region who are fully committed to the System from a legal standpoint.

VII. CONCLUSION

Any discussion of Latin American constitutionalism has to bear in mind that – due to the difficulties that most liberal democracies of the region continue to experience in trying to reduce gross socio-economic inequalities – liberal constitutional democracy is permanently threatened in its legitimacy. In fact, the consensus that prevailed in the 1990s on the "inevitability" of liberal constitutionalism was eventually challenged by the emergence of radical-democratic experiments which, in turn, have been accompanied by a constitutional discourse that directly conflicts with some key elements of liberal constitutionalism (such as the separation of powers, or the prohibition of indefinite re-election in presidential regimes).

In this chapter, I have analyzed a – still unexplored – feature of Latin America's radical constitutionalism, namely its recovery of the so-called "*principle of non-interference with the internal affairs of sovereign states*", a concept introduced into international law by the Latin American states in the first decades of the twentieth century, in an attempt to stop what – even liberal – jurists of the region considered to be the "imperial" tendencies of the United States.

The principle of non-interference with the internal affairs of sovereign states has been used in recent years by the Bolivarian Republics to attack what they perceive as a "neocolonial" use of the Inter-American Human Rights System by the United States, a country which, despite not having granted jurisdiction to the Inter-American Human Rights Court is, however, an important actor in the System, not just because the headquarters of the Inter-American Human Rights Commission are in Washington, DC, but because it has consistently managed to place judges and commissioners in the System.

These last facts, coupled with the illiberal turn that constitutionalism has taken in United States since 11 September 2001 (which is expressed in the constitutional indifference toward gross human rights violations, such as the lack of due process in Guantanamo Bay, the practice of torture, and the "target killings"), have offered Latin America's radical democracies the perfect excuse to gradually walk away from the Inter-American Human Rights System.

BIBLIOGRAPHY

Álvarez, Alejandro (1962), *El nuevo derecho internacional En sus Relaciones con la vida real de los Pueblos* (Santiago: Editorial Jurídica de Chile).

Barak-Erez, Daphne (2004), "The international law of human rights and constitutional law: A case study of an expanding dialogue", *International Journal of Constitutional Law*, **2** (4), 611–32.

Carpizo, Jorge (2003), "Autodeterminación, no intervención y justicia internacional", lecture given on the occasion of the opening ceremony of the Ibero-American Congress of Constitutional Law, Sevilla, 3 December, in *Pensamiento Constitucional*, **X**, 245–60.

Cohen, Jean (2012), *Globalization and Sovereignty: Rethinking Legality, Legitimacy and Constitutionalism* (Cambridge: Cambridge University Press).

Cole, David (2015), "Must counterterrorism cancel democracy?", *New York Review of Books*, 8 January. Accessed 9 September 2017 at http://www.nybooks.com/articles/archives/2015/jan/08/must-counterterrorism-cancel-democracy/.

Couso, Javier (2014), "Las democracias radicales y el 'Nuevo Constitucionalismo Latinoamericano'", in *El Seminario de Teoría Política y Constitucional en Latinoamérica* (SELA, Yale University Law School).

Couso, Javier, Huneeus, Alexandra and Sieder, Rachel (eds) (2010), *Legal Cultures and Political Activism in Latin America* (Cambridge: Cambridge University Press).

Domingo, Pilar (2012), "El estado de derecho, la reforma judicial y la justicia de transición en América Latina", in Vesselin Popovski and Monica Serrano (eds) *Justicia Transicional y Consolidación Democrática: La comparación de la eficacia de los mecanismos de rendición de cuentas en Europa del Este y América Latina* (Tokyo: UNU Press).

Gargarella, Roberto (2014), *La sala de máquinas de la Constitución: dos siglos de constitucionalismo en América Latina (1810–2010)* (Buenos Aires: Katz).

Garretón, Manuel Antonio (1994), "Procesos de derechos humanos y de la democratización", *Revista de Estudios Latinoamericanos*, **26** (I), February.

López Medina, Diego (2004), *Teoría Impura del Derecho. La Transformación de la cultura jurídica latinoamericana* (Bogotá: Legis-Universidad de Los Andes-Universidad Nacional de Colombia).

Merryman, John Henry (2007), *The Civil Law Tradition: An Introduction to the Legal Systems of Europe and Latin America*, 3rd edn (Redwood City, CA: Stanford University Press).

Noguiera, Humberto (2012), "El uso del derecho convencional internacional de los derechos humanos en la jurisprudencia del Tribunal Constitucional chileno en el period 2006–2010", *Revista Chilena de Derecho*, **39** (1), 149–87.

O'Donnell, Guillermo (1998), *Poliarquías y la (des) Estado de Derecho en América Latina* (Notre Dame, IN: Helen Kellogg Institute for International Studies).

Smulovitz, Catalina (2010), "Judicialization in Argentina: Legal culture or opportunities and support structures?", in Javier Couso, Alexandra Huneeus and Rachel Sieder (eds), *Legal Cultures and Political Activism in Latin America* (Cambridge: Cambridge University Press).

Stone Sweet, Alec (2000), *Governing with Judges: Constitutional Politics in Europe* (Oxford: Oxford University Press).

Uprimny, Rodrigo (2001), "El bloque de constitucionalidad en Colombia: un

análisis jurisprudencial y un ensayo de sistematización doctrinal", in Daniel O'Donnell, Inés Margarita Uprimny and Alejandro Villa (eds), *Compilación de jurisprudencia y doctrina nacional e internacional* (Bogotá: Oficina del Alto Comisionado de Naciones Unidas para los Derechos Humanos).
Viciano, Roberto and Martínez Dalmau, Rubén (2010), "Aspectos Generales del Nuevo Constitucionalismo Latinoamericano", in *El nuevo constitucionalismo en América Latina* (Quito: Corte Constitucional del Ecuador).
Waldron, Jeremy (2010), *Torture, Terror, and Trade-Offs: Philosophy for the White House* (Oxford: Oxford University Press).

6. Constitutionalism old, new and unbound: the case of Mexico

Francisca Pou Giménez

I. INTRODUCTION

Mexico shares many of the features that characterize other Latin American contemporary countries, but its pattern of constitutional change is non-standard. In the 1980s and 90s, the countries of the region operated a collective return to democracy that included the summoning of constitutional assemblies and the enactment of new constitutional texts.[1] By contrast, Mexico underwent in the same period a long concatenation of changes – some of them piecemeal, others more robust, yet profoundly altering, taken as a whole, the political and legal scene – while keeping all along its 1917 constitutional text. It is unclear however, how much of the iconic revolutionary document remains after more than 500 constitutional amendments that find new additions every month.[2] Reformism, therefore, is a badge of Mexican constitutional life: it speaks of the deep

[1] For general chartings of Latin American constitutions enacted over the last wave of democratization in the region, *see* Rodrigo Uprimny (2015), "The recent transformations of constitutional law in Latin America: trends and challenges", in César Rodríguez Garavito (ed.), in *Law and Society in Latin America: A New Map* (London: Routledge); Gabriel L. Negretto (2012), "Replacing and amending constitutions: The logic of constitutional change in Latin America", *Law & Soc'Y. Rev.*, **46**, 749; Gabriel L. Negretto (2013), *Making Constitutions: Presidents, Parties, and Institutional Choice in Latin America* (New York: Cambridge University Press).

[2] *See* Jorge Carpizo (2011), *La reforma constitucional en México: Procedimiento y realidad, Boletín Mexicano de Derecho Comparado*, **131**, 543 (reporting reforms in 533 constitutional Sections – some of the 136 Sections of the Constitution having been amended several times) and Hector Fix-Fierro (2014), "Engordando la Constitución", *Nexos* (February) (also taking "an amendment" to be a modification to a constitutional Section and counting 573 of them by mid-January 2015). *See also* M. Amparo Casar and Ignacio Marván (2014), *Reformar sin mayorías: La dinámica del cambio constitucional en México: 1997–2012* (Mexico City: Taurus) (organizing their analysis around "constitutional decrees", each one containing amendments to one or several Sections enacted in a particular moment in time,

bonds the Mexican legal system retains with the past, but it should equally convey the idea of permanent, never-ending adjustment of basic rules and institutions.

In this chapter I will explore Mexican contemporary constitutionalism from both a static and dynamic viewpoint, while emphasizing the salience of the latter and suggesting that a focus on the dynamics of permanent constitutional change is critical to understand core features of the country's constitutional democracy. The analysis will be organized around constitutional text, which is clearly a limitation – there is always more to political and legal life than text. This way of proceeding, however, allows us, in an orderly fashion, to present traits of the Mexican constitutional system that are important under any reading, facilitates comparative analysis, and sets foundations for more comprehensive ulterior evaluations. Moreover, since it has been a distinctive feature of Mexican politics to center on the Constitution, as opposed to statutes or policy, to such a great extent – this being one of the features of Mexican democracy that deserves analysis – this methodological choice delivers in our case more than an average reward.

Section II will start by providing a cursory description of the contents of the Mexican Constitution (as it stands by mid-2014) by substantive area: the separation of powers, federalism, the judiciary, the electoral system, fundamental rights and the "economic constitution". Although occasional references to the distant past will be made to render the narrative meaningful, the focus will be on events over the last 20–25 years – the time span in which the other regional countries operated their return to democratic life. An effort of general mapping – even if a bit cramped, unable to capture all nuances and destined to be adjusted as amendments ensue – can be useful in a context in which, precisely because of the frequency of change, it is rarely attempted, and it may help insert Mexican constitutionalism into regional debates.

In the remainder of the chapter, the analysis will proceed by distinguishing three kinds of evaluations one can undertake regarding a constitution: content-based evaluations, which focus on the sort of institutions, substantive standards and rules it includes; process-based evaluations, which ponder what sort of decision-making process it emerges from; and frequency-based evaluations, which assess the effects of living under profuse and frequent (versus rare) constitutional change – independently of the content of the Constitution that results from change and the quality of the processes by

---

and counting 206 decrees between 1920 and 2012, 69 of them passed over the last 15 years).

which change is attained. Sections III, IV and V will respectively examine the Mexican case from each of these dimensions, trying to discern general patterns, and will draw disquieting conclusions from all three.

All in all, the chapter will emphasize traits of the Mexican constitutional scenario that are more troubling than thrilling. It will ponder the advantages but also the significant costs of Mexican gradualism, and it will identify traits that are arguably problematic from the perspective of what a more inclusive democratic scenario would look like in the context of a country currently ridden by dreadful problems. To be sure, as other contributors in this volume compellingly argue, it is critically important not to subscribe and inadvertently help fortify narratives of "constitutional failure" that are often based on asymmetric assumptions about the value of rules and institutions in some parts of the world versus others, reflecting a non-neutral political economy of legal knowledge in whose context the constitutionalism of the South is portrayed as "naturally" defective and poor.[3] An analysis captured by biases of this kind could, moreover, render invisible (or hinder the development of) valuable rules, institutions and practices in our societies.

That granted, I believe that constitutional structures and rules in post-authoritarian Mexico have reached a point where they will probably succeed only to the extent they are finally replaced by something qualitatively different. In a scenario marked by rule-of-law fragility and political and social exclusion, Mexico's dynamics of non-stop, elite-driven constitutional amendment has planted the seeds for a profound transformation while holding up their potential. It may finally occur that the Mexican Constitution, whose contents and patterns of change this chapter will present, will be taken more seriously by both people and public authorities, and more extensively used from now on. If that happens, however, it will probably be along a course of events that could lead to its ultimate replacement – if done peacefully, maybe a story of "constitutional success" after all.

II. THE MEXICAN CONSTITUTION IN THE TWENTY-FIRST CENTURY

Though at the beginning of independent political life Mexico experienced pervasive political instability and the first half of the twenty-first

---

[3] *See* Bonilla and Esquirol in this volume. *See also* Mauricio García Villegas (2010), "Sociología y crítica del derecho", *Doctrina Jurídica Contemporánea*, **51**, 65.

century saw the rapid succession of several constitutional texts (Cádiz, 1824, 1836, 1843 and 1848), the country then spent several decades under the long-lasting liberal 1857 Constitution. The document was, however, only intermittently in force, and under its umbrella – when not dealing with foreign invasions or interventions and episodes of civil strife – very different political projects were advanced, from social and political liberalization and state secularization under the lead of Benito Juárez to the highly exclusory, "modernizing" policies of Porfirio Díaz, based on foreign investment, oligarchic exploitation of natural resources and control of social unrest within an ever more authoritarian political frame.

At the beginning of the twentieth century the Mexican Revolution – unleashed by extreme land concentration and political repression – led to summoning the Queretaro constitutional assembly and the subsequent approval of the 1917 text, still in force. The political dynamics in the country were afterwards marked by the progressive consolidation in power of the *Partido Revolucionario Institucional* (PRI), which would stay in power for seven decades.[4] The gradual advent of political pluralism from the 1980s onwards – contrary to the natural expectation in a country with a pretty demanding amendment formula – was accompanied by a steady increment in the amount of amendments effectuated on the foundational document. As Fix-Fierro documents, almost two-thirds of the total number of amendments are post-1982 – a fifth of the total having been passed during the Calderon sexennial period;[5] and in only one year of presidency, Peña Nieto propelled six major reforms in the areas of education, telecommunications, energy, anti-trust, transparency and the electoral system which touched, to a smaller or greater degree, around 60 percent of the total number of constitutional sections, besides adding to the Constitution an extremely long and detailed body of transitory provisions. The following sections succinctly survey the main traits of the Constitution that have resulted from such a long process.

---

[4] Casar and Marván (n 2), describe constitutional evolution under PRI rule by distinguishing five periods, named after salient changes in the general shape of the political system: factionalism without parliamentarian discipline (1917–28); emergence and consolidation of a single party and of legislative discipline (1928–46); the hegemonic party years (1946–63); dominant party and moderate pluralism (1964–78); and evolution from dominant to majoritarian party (1979–97).

[5] *See* Fix-Fierro (n 2).

The Separation of Powers

Following the rule in America, Mexico set out from the beginning a presidential system that it has retained to date. The long decades of PRI political hegemony gave the impression that the country lived under an all mighty federal president, armed with a panoply of constitutional and meta-constitutional powers.[6] When the advent of political plurality made institutional design relevant, however, it turned out that – on the books and viewed from a comparative perspective – the Mexican presidency was in fact rather weak.[7]

The President is elected for six years with no chance of re-election: after Porfirio Díaz's long decades of power retention, "effective suffrage and no re-election" was a core motto of the 1917 foundational moment.[8] Distinctively in a region characterized by widespread resort to the institution,[9] the Mexican President lacks the power to rule by decree.[10]

---

6 *See* M. Amparo Casar (1996), "Las bases político-institucionales del poder presidencial en México", *Política y Gobierno*, **1**, 61 (emphasizing that Mexican presidentialism did not traditionally exhibit the expected consequences of this form of government and analyzing the factors that operated as political-institutional sources of presidential power in the country); and Fernando Serrano Migallón (2007), "Facultades metaconstitucionales del Poder Ejecutivo en México", in Roberto Saba (ed.), *Poder Ejecutivo: SELA 2006* (Buenos Aires: Editorial Del Puerto) (elaborating on the meta-constitutional powers of the Mexican President).

7 Eric Magar (2014), "Los contados cambios al equilibrio de poderes", in Casar and Marván (n 2), at 281. *See also* Tom Ginsburg, Jose Antonio Cheibub and Zachary Elkins (2012), "Still the land of presidentialism? Executives and the Latin American constitution", in Detlef Nolte and Almut Schilling-Vacaflor (eds), *New Constitutionalism in Latin America: Promises and Practices* (Farnham: Ashgate) (charting the powers and attributions of presidents in contemporary Latin American countries).

8 A distinctive feature of the Mexican model is the absence of a vice-president, and the Constitution sets forth a complex list of instructions – somehow simplified after a 2013 constitutional amendment – clarifying what to do to designate a substitute when one is lacking.

9 Ginsburg et al. (n 7).

10 But there was widespread Executive legislation under two figures: "state of emergency" and the "extraordinary delegation of faculties" bestowed often by Congress on presidents in the nineteenth century. Codes and other important pieces of legislation were issued by the Executive. *See* Stephen Zamora et al. (2005), *Mexican Law* (Oxford: Oxford University Press), p. 150, fn 79 (citing Jorge Carpizo (1991), "El Presidencialismo mexicano", at 102, and Jesús Orozco Henríquez (1988), "El sistema presidencial en el constituyente de Querétaro y su evolución posterior", at 49, in *El Sistema Presidencial Mexicano (Algunas Reflexiones)* (Mexico: Instituto de Investigaciones Jurídicas, Universidad Nacional Autónoma de México). The Executive has unilateral ruling powers in an additional narrow

They may present bills (which they do profusely), veto legislation (which they do rarely) and hold emergency powers – extensively used in the past,[11] not resorted to in recent times and set under tight constraints after the 2011 human rights reform.[12]

Presidential powers are articulated with those of Congress through a pretty standard system of checks and balances. The President directs the army and foreign policy, shares treaty-making powers with the Senate and must cooperate with it to make a number of important appointments – the General Prosecutor, the Supreme Court Justices and higher diplomats among them.

The Legislative branch is organized along the lines of a pretty symmetrical bicameral system in which context the Chamber of Deputies and the Senate collaborate as equals in the production of legislation, with slight pre-eminence of the Senate in some matters and slight pre-eminence of the Deputies in others (typically purse-related). The Chamber of Deputies is composed of 500 representatives elected for only three years and the Senate is composed of 128 individuals – elected under rules intending to be sensitive to geographical representation – elected for six.

As commentators have underlined, the Mexican Congress was also designed to be weak.[13] At the 1917 constituent moment, it was thought that one of the reasons Porfirio Díaz had so extensively resorted to exception powers was the strong position of the Legislative branch under the 1857 Constitution: that would have "forced" him to resort to informal, illegal powers.[14] The 1917 Constitution therefore set a Congress sitting only for five months a year and following an internal protocol that forces the two chambers to engage in an endless ping-pong game to issue any

---

case: an inter-secretarial commission headed by the President (the *Consejo de Salubridad General*) can issue general regulations when facing a serious health crisis (Section 73-XVI of the Mexican Constitution).

[11] On the massive resort to emergency powers amidst the instability of the second half of the nineteenth century, *see* José A. Aguilar Rivera (2001), *El manto liberal. Los poderes de emergencia en México, 1821–1876* (Mexico City: Instituto de Investigaciones Jurídicas, Universidad Nacional Autónoma de México); Carlos Bravo Regidor (2012), "De la épica de la victoria a la política de la derrota: Juárez, la Constitución y la Convocatoria de 1967", in Adriana Luna, Pablo Mijangos and Rafael Rojas (eds), *De Cádiz al siglo XXI: Dos siglos de constitucionalismo en México e Hispanoamérica 1812–2012* (Mexico City: CIDE), pp. 203–67.

[12] *See* Section 29 of the Constitution, setting a scheme that requires the concurrence of the President, Congress and the Supreme Court.

[13] Zamora et al. (n 10), at 180–86.

[14] The argument along these lines developed by Emilio Rabasa is said to have influenced the choice. *See* Emilio Rabasa (1956 [1912]), *La Constitución y la Dictadura* (Mexico City: Porrua).

piece of legislation. The integration of the legislative chambers by perpetual freshmen (since re-election was forbidden until the 2013 reform), aided by an ever-changing pool of variably skilled "advisors" – not permanent officials – has compounded the situation.

In his survey of amendments in this area, Eric Magar underlines that the horizontal separation of powers has been an area of the Constitution not extensively altered over the last 15–20 years.[15] In view of unending reform along so many other dimensions, this is surprising and could be associated with the Mexican "political class" endorsement of a self-preservationist dynamics of change.[16] Most of the changes that have occurred are associated with the transparency and accountability agenda.[17] But they have not been far-reaching and have not eased, in any case, the Mexican Congress's extremely poor public image. In relation to this, it had been repeatedly suggested that non re-election was among the main causes of generalized non-professionalism among legislators and that it has shielded them from all forms of relevant accountability. The 2013 amendments finally changed the system: starting in 2018, it will be possible to re-elect Senators for one more period (12 years in total) and Deputies for three more (12 years in total).[18]

A feature that sets Mexico apart from the majority of its Latin American neighbors is the weakness of direct or participatory democracy instruments. After total inactivity in this area in recent decades, the 2013 constitutional reform recognized two channels: popular legislative initiative and

---

[15] Magar (n 7), at 260–61.

[16] As I will later suggest, the dynamics of permanent constitutional reform in some areas, particularly in the domain of fundamental rights, could be interpreted as a way of gaining short-term legitimacy – while avoiding modifications that could alter the privileges that "to be in politics" continues to represent in Mexico. *See* n 25 below.

[17] Magar counts 37 Sections amended in this domain, but remarks that only 11 of the changes altered in a substantive fashion the pre-existing equilibrium. Among them he stresses the changes on the schedule for the Executive to present the Budget and the Public Account and the creation of a supervision body (*Auditoría Superior de la Federación*) at the service of the Deputies Chamber – all of which increased the power of the Deputies over the Executive in financial matters – and the clarification of the mechanics of the Presidential veto on legislation, which reinforced Congress. In his view, globally seen the amendments left the Executive as relatively weak as it was before, reinforced the Deputies, left the Senate in the same position, and reinforced the Supreme Court over the other two branches (given, for instance, its new powers of appointment in the Judiciary Council and its attributions regarding popular consultation). Magar (n 7), at 266–79.

[18] The reform makes it mandatory for states to allow re-election of state representatives and municipal presidents in state constitutions.

popular consultation. Both are conceived, however, in highly restrictive terms – this is particularly true of consultation, which is barred in a long list of subject matters and must pass previous constitutional muster in the Supreme Court.[19] No possibilities of recall have been allowed. In the same amendment package, also with the idea of heightening the political profile of citizens, the possibility of leading independent candidacies (i.e. candidacies non-sponsored by a political party) to federal elections was approved.[20]

A description of the contours of the separation of powers in contemporary Mexico must finally underline the multiplication of independent agencies in recent times. From the 1980s and 90s, bodies as different as the National Human Rights Commission, the National Institute of Statistics and Geography (INEGI), the Bank of Mexico (Banxico) or the Federal Electoral Institute (IFE) were given the status of "independent constitutional organisms" – and regulated, basically, by the Constitution itself. The 2013 reforms have given independent status to additional bodies that had formally remained under the Executive umbrella: the Federal Institute of Telecommunications (IFETEL), the Federal Economic Competence Commission (COFECE), the National Commission of Evaluation (CONEVAL) and the Federal Institute of Information Accessing (IFAI). Amendments conferred independent status even to the Federal Prosecutor Office (PGR) and to the newly created National Institute for the Evaluation of Education (INEE).[21] These developments evince to what extent the "independent agency kit" has been considered an unquestioned institutional solution, almost automatically resorted to by politicians when seeking to bestow a patina of "efficacy" and "impartiality" on troubled policy areas. The institutional design of these bodies – in terms of appointment rules, jurisdiction (many of them combine management, regulation and adjudication) and mechanisms of external control – are remarkably varied. The fact they now manage huge areas of public policy previously under control of the traditional branches makes their careful analysis mandatory.

---

19 Sections 35.VII and VIII, and 71.4 of the Mexican Constitution.

20 Section 55.II of the Mexican Constitution.

21 The Federal Prosecutor's Office is among the least well-regarded institutions in the country; its performance as head of federal criminal investigations has been outrageous. The reform seeks to fortify its independence vis-à-vis the Executive and creates two specialized prosecutors (on electoral matters and corruption). The Institute of Education Evaluation, for its part, was created in 2012 within the "education reform" package, after a long conflict with the teaching unions; inexplicably, the reform focuses exclusively on teachers' evaluation and discipline, instead of tackling the structural determinants of the profound deficiencies remaining in this crucial policy area.

Federalism

The Mexican Constitution adopted a federal system following in its origins the "dual" logic found in so many other American texts: the Constitution lists the areas of jurisdiction attributed to the Federation and the rest remains in the state's hands.[22]

Contrary to what this choice of constitutional design suggests, however, Mexican federalism was not built from below. It was not the sort of arrangement necessary to maintain the unity of the country in view of strong regional political identities that we find in Germany, Canada or the United States. In the process of state reconstruction which followed the Revolution after the instability of the nineteenth century, federalism was sacrificed.[23] As Casar remarks, this can be partly explained by the process of building institutions in a country with feudal pockets, poor communications, meager economic development, salience of the army, etc., but it was also a core effect of a political project in whose context the leader of the party acquired, first, the possibility of defining the composition of the federal system – controlling access to the post of governor – and afterwards, its behavior, in the context of a system of a hegemonic party.[24]

In consonance with this, at the constitutional level the original dual logic progressively eroded. Continuous one-by-one amendments have given extensive attributions to the Federation and have organized very important matters as areas of shared jurisdiction, coordinated or managed by the Federation. As scholars underline, many features would now be closer to cooperative federalism than to traditional dualism,[25] if all coated in an unambiguous centralizing fingerprint. To this we must add the use of mechanisms to subordinate states via funding: tax revenues are collected mostly by the Federation, which then manages them in the "system of fiscal coordination" making large use of conditional cash transfers. State

---

22 The Constitution provides the Federation with an "implied powers" clause (Section 73.XXX) that has been rarely resorted to, since direct enlargement of federal powers through constitutional amendment has made it unnecessary.

23 Casar (n 6), at 89.

24 Id.

25 *See* José M. Serna de la Garza (2009), *El sistema federal mexicano: Un análisis jurídico* (Mexico City: UNAM, Instituto de Investigaciones Jurídicas), and Jose Maria Serna de la Garza "Las reformas al federalismo mexicano" (2014), in Casar and Marván (n 2) (analyzing constitutional amendments in the area over the last 15 years). *See also* Martín Díaz Díaz (1996), "México en la vía del federalismo cooperativo. Un análisis de los problemas en torno a la distribución de competencias", in Barra Mexicana-Colegio de Abogados, *Homenaje a Fernando Alejandro Vázquez Pando* (Mexico City: Ed. Themis), 129–73.

constitutions, for their part, offer a most varied collection of scenarios we cannot describe in any detail here. The federal Constitution sets a minimum content they must include, but it is all referred to the structuring of the power branches. Beyond that, we find great heterogeneity: some of them have extensive bills of rights, others skinny ones; some have constitutional review, others don't; some develop federal provisions on the recognition of cultural diversity, others don't. And so on.

The Federal District was long under the Federation's control. In 1993, a process began that gave the city a status close to the states, with an elected Chief of Government, a unicameral Legislative Assembly, a Superior Tribunal of Justice and its own electoral branch. Political life in the city is lively and the fact the leftist party has always won has created an interesting counterpoint to politics at the federal level. Mexico City, however, is still out of the constitutional amending process, and calls for a "political reform" in the Federal District are periodically made.

Municipalities, finally, were for long strongly subordinated to the states – particularly governors – and lacked independent rule-making powers. In 1999, the Constitution granted them exclusive areas of jurisdiction and several Supreme Court rulings reinforced in the years that followed the position of municipal sources of normativity and revenue. Their performance remains, however, mortgaged by excessive political rotation – up to the 2013 reform, municipal presidents' terms have been for three years with no chance of re-election – and – with the exception of a few, highly populated, urban municipalities – municipalities are characterized by precarious infrastructure, poor regulation and insufficient funding. Absent true commitment on the part of national authorities, the development of indigenous local authority – prefigured in Section 2 of the Constitution – remains incipient.

Although successful Supreme Court performance in the area of jurisdictional conflicts has given some oxygen to political decentralization, the legal framework of Mexican federalism is, on the whole, ambiguous and weak. Discussion about the constitutional role of state constitutions, or about how state legal systems are supposed to fit into the new architecture emerging from recent reforms in the human rights and economic areas is still pending. States get regularly mentioned as instances of the sort of corruption and inefficacy the country has failed to eradicate. The reinforcement of federalism seems to be definitely outside the political agenda.

The Judiciary

As in most federal countries, two judicial strands coexist. Criminal and civil matters fall under state jurisdiction (though there have always been federal crimes and they are being enlarged all the time) and labor and commercial ones under federal jurisdiction. The country combines procedures and codes characteristic of the Civil Law tradition with a judicial structure similar to the one found in the United States, with district judges, circuit courts and a Supreme Court at the top. In Mexico, however, the federal judiciary has operated as general supervisor of state rulings through the writ of *amparo*, which allows citizens to question them before federal judges. This has greatly reinforced, of course, the centralizing flavor that impregnates the country.

Over the last 25 years the most consequential reforms in the area have touched three rubrics: judicial review, judicial governance and the regulation of criminal trials.

As regards judicial review, these last decades have transformed a system based for very long on the exclusive, hegemonic figure of the *amparo* writ into a hybrid, multiple-tiered system that offers many channels of constitutional review, before different judicial authorities, through different procedures and with different effects.

On proclaiming independence, Mexico did not develop a U.S.-like diffuse system of review but a French-like system of political-legislative review, replaced by the mid-nineteenth century with a judicial one grounded exclusively on the writ of *amparo*.[26] The *amparo* is a writ citizens can file to denounce before a federal judge the violation of their constitutional rights at the hands of a public authority. The notion of public authority is unqualified, so the writ protects as much against a police arbitrary seizure, as against a statute, a judicial ruling or an administrative decree. When filed against a norm, *amparo* protection has *inter partes* effects. Powerful as it may seem on paper, over the years the *amparo* transmuted into an exceedingly complex channel, largely denaturalized from its original rights-protecting function. Its centrality within the legal system caused it to progressively acquire more and more functions. At an early state, in the nineteenth century, it became a tool of legality review – and this ended up damaging its edge as a tool of constitutionality review. The extremely baroque quality of its procedural regulation has rendered it usable only with the aid of specialized lawyers, and the perception is that it has largely allowed the most powerful – many of them companies, not citizens – secure exceptions to the application of general rules.[27]

---

[26] J. Ramón Cossío (2013), *Sistemas y modelos de control de constitucionalidad en México* (Mexico City: UNAM, Instituto de Investigaciones Jurídicas) (presenting the complete historic evolution of the system).

[27] Francisca Pou Giménez (2014), "El nuevo amparo mexicano y la protección de los derechos: ¿ni tan nuevo ni tan protector?", *Anuario de Derechos Humanos*, **14**, 91, 93.

Recent times have importantly supplemented this panorama. First, in 1994, the system added two review channels designed after the Kelsenian, centralized model: the action of unconstitutionality – allowing for the abstract review of general norms which can produce their *erga omnes* invalidation – and the constitutional controversy – a refurbishing of an institution Mexico had kept dormant from the previous century, now redesigned after the Kelsenian model to channel conflicts of jurisdiction between federation, states and municipalities. This same year, the Supreme Court was reformed, but no Constitutional Court or Chamber was added: it remained the exclusive apex court, though an effort was made to release it from areas of jurisdiction unrelated to constitutional matters. Second, in 2011, the Supreme Court changed the interpretation of a constitutional provision and recognized diffuse powers of review to all Mexican judges. This great architectural change removed from federal judges the privilege of being the sole owners of the Constitution. Mexico now consequently has a hybrid model of review, as most other Latin American countries,[28] though it combines three strands, not two: centralized, semi-centralized (*amparo*) and diffuse. Moreover, after the 2011 human rights reform, the Supreme Court said Mexican judges must effectuate both constitutionality and conventionality review. Lastly, we must mention the *amparo* constitutional and legal reform of 2011–13. It was intended to simplify *amparo* to make it effective for rights protection, but the result was moderate. Although it allows for collective claims and defines more broadly under what conditions a rights violation can be denounced, judges will have to provide via interpretation that extra dose of access to justice that an insufficient statutory streamlining does not assure.[29]

A second strand of evolution that brings Mexico in line with the standard Latin American path was the setting in 1994 of a system of autonomous judicial self-governance with the creation of the *Consejo de la Judicatura Federal* (Federal Judicial Council) and analogous bodies at the state level.[30] Distinctive in Mexico is the strong hold the Supreme Court

---

[28] *See* Uprimny (n 1); Justin Frosini and Lucio Pegoraro (2008), "Constitutional courts in Latin America: A testing ground for new parameters of classification?", *J. Comp. Law*, **2**, 39 (underlining the hybrid nature of judicial review systems in Latin America, the latter emphasizing how contemporary developments in the region create ground and demand the crafting of new forms of theoretical classification to adequately describe them).

[29] Pou Giménez (n 27).

[30] The creation of institutions, controlled by judges or a combination of judges and political appointees to manage access, adscription, promotion and discipline within the judiciary was seen as instrumental to reinforcing (or gaining for the first time) judicial independence. International donors and institutions promoted

retains over the Council – presided over by the president of the Court.[31] The Mexican judiciary has retained most of its old, strongly hierarchical style and the Supreme Court concentrates a wide range of functions that in other countries are performed by two or three different institutions.[32]

To the preservation of traditional hierarchical fingerprints, we must add the retention of very formalistic styles of adjudication that, until recently, have done little in terms of effective rights protection for the majority of the population. While over the last 20 years the Supreme Court did quite well as arbiter of inter-branch conflict, the performance of the whole Mexican judiciary in terms of rights protection has been poor.[33] Things have clearly started to notably change, however; these few last years the Supreme Court has gone public in deliberations, it has issued important rulings that have substantially changed rights and case law in a number of fields, and it has become an active participant in the debate about the relations between national and inter-American law, even if ferocious disagreement between justices leaves undetermined the direction the Court will take in the coming years.[34]

The third strand of changes is presided upon by the turn from an

---

them as a part of a rule of law-reinforcing agenda. *See* Linn Hammergren (2007), *Envisioning Reform: Conceptual and Practical Obstacles to Improving Judicial Performance in Latin America* (Pennsylvania: Penn State University Press); Pilar Domingo and Rachel Sieder (2001), *Rule of Law in Latin America: The International Promotion of Judicial Reform* (London: Institute of Latin American Studies).

[31] *See* Andrea Pozas-Loyo and Julio Ríos-Figueroa (2011), "The politics of amendment processes: Supreme Court influence in the design of judicial councils", *Texas Law Rev.*, **89**, 1807, 1807–33.

[32] Julio Ríos-Figueroa (2011), "El sistema de administración de justicia", in Gabriel L. Negretto (ed.), *Debatiendo la reforma política: Claves del cambio institucional en México* (Mexico City: CIDE), 164.

[33] Julio Ríos-Figueroa and Gretchen Helmke (2011), "Introduction", in Julio Ríos-Figueroa and Gretchen Helmke (eds), *Courts in Latin America* (Cambridge: Cambridge University Press), 5. The country did not participate in the wave of new developments in rights adjudication that has singularized the courts of Colombia, Costa Rica or Argentina.

[34] On the system of TV broadcast of deliberations in the Plenary Chamber of the Court, *see* Francisca Pou Giménez (2017), "Changing the channel: Broadcasting deliberations in the Mexican Supreme Court", in Richard Davis and David Taras (eds), *Justices and Journalists: The Global Perspective* (Cambridge: Cambridge University Press); for a quick identification of new Supreme Court doctrines in the domain of rights (and in other constitutional areas), *see* José Ramón Cossío, Jimena Ruiz Cabañas, Julio Martínez Rivas and Santiago Oñate Yáñez (2017), *Constitución Política de los Estados Unidos Mexicanos Comentada* (Valencia: Tirant lo Blanch).

inquisitorial system in criminal trials to an adversarial one – a tendency shared in all Latin America. The reform was designed in 2008 to be gradually implemented at the state level (where most criminal trials proceed) and reinforced in 2013 by the issuance of a code of common procedural rules applying nationally. Improving the performance of the criminal system is one of the major challenges the country faces – it now works poorly in every possible respect.

The consolidation of democracy in Mexico, to sum up, has come hand in hand with a clear reinforcement of the judiciary within the constitutional system. But Mexican judges have started to release only very slowly their bonds with the past, and the system carries a heavy burden in terms of inherited institutions and procedures that match poorly with the recent, far-reaching reforms in the bill of rights. What the judiciary will do with the new constitutional tools in the rights area, will surely be, in any case, among the most dynamic developments in the constitutional system in the years to come.

Electoral Management

The Mexican transition to democracy – not surprisingly after decades of iron-handedly PRI-controlled periodical "elections" – started with an accent on electoral matters. In the 1980s a long series of intermittent amendments that found their last episode in the 2014 "political reform" started.[35] Changes in the electoral system were gradual and led to a country with a system that – besides an Executive elected under majoritarian principles – elects Congresses through a combination of majoritarian and proportional representation – both at the federal and the state level.

A main feature of the model is the existence of a huge and well-funded electoral branch with probably no peer elsewhere. Its first tier is administrative: it was headed from 1990 to 2014 by the *Instituto Federal Electoral* (now replaced by the *Instituto Nacional Electoral*, INE). The IFE/INE not only organizes elections, but also enforces a large body of rules governing the finances and activity of the political parties on a permanent basis (and not only in election time). The second tier is jurisdictional: it is formed by the Electoral Federal Tribunal (TEPJF), with a superior chamber

---

[35] *See* José Woldenberg et al. (2007), *El cambio político en México* (Mexico City: Cal y Arena) and Lorenzo Córdova Vianello (2014), "Sistema electoral y sistema de partidos. Pluralismo político en las reformas constitucionales en materia electoral", in Casar and Marván (n 2) (mapping the numerous episodes of electoral reform from the 1980s on). On the 2014 reform, *see* the materials available at http://pac.ife.org.mx/reforma2014 (accessed 28 November 2014).

sitting at Mexico City and five regional chambers spread across Mexico. It is formally part of the federal judiciary though has autonomous operation, has both legality and constitutionality review attributions (though abstract review of electoral statutes is retained by the Supreme Court). What's amazing is that these institutions are only for federal electoral law: every state (and Mexico City) has its own two-tiered electoral branch, employing buildings and personnel that work on a permanent basis.

The amount of resources employed by the Mexican electoral branch has been justified as being necessary to set the foundations of democracy in a country with decades of polluted elections. For two decades, the IFE piled up prestige and reliability, until recently the branches in charge of appointing its councilors let the institution decay in some measure. The 2014 reform, in what was interpreted as a questionable "package" negotiation among political parties, unexpectedly replaced the IFE with the INE and packed their *consejeros*. The plan was having the institution absorb the functions of state electoral branches and eliminate the latter – thus saving resources and reinforcing electoral authorities before pressures of state governors. In the end, the elimination did not occur, but the resulting system is clearly more centralized.[36]

Fundamental Rights

The rights' area has experienced deep changes in recent years, but they have come late, compared to those affecting other parts of the Constitution. Three rubrics must be referred to: the catalogue of protected rights, the principles about identification, interpretation and application of rights, and the regulation of rights guarantees.

Although the 1917 Constitution was a world pioneer in its enshrinement of social rights, the catalogue of protected rights was updated only very slowly. Over the last 15 years, there were continuous piecemeal additions: the rights of indigenous peoples – declared to be foundational to the nation and holders of both autonomy and accommodation rights; the right to information and access to governmental data – the basis of the strong transparency agenda advanced in the country; the reinforcement of equality guarantees – though short of including a "material equality" clause; the strengthening of due process and the recognition of victim

[36] State institutes remain, but now organize state elections in coordination (and supervised) by the INE, which appoints their councilors. The INE has lost disciplinary attributions (transferred to the TEPJF) and the latter can now attract jurisdiction to supervise the regularity of state elections in some cases.

rights; the right to health, food, water, healthy environment, culture or the practice of sports; the recognition of special rights for children, a reform of educational rights, among others.[37]

Notwithstanding this large catalogue on paper, the constitution of rights remained dormant these last decades. There was almost total absence of rights-based litigation as late as 2005. There was no use of international human rights law; there was no public interest litigation; on the contrary, it was companies which took advantage of the *amparo* to protect economic claims; there were no collective suits (not even after a 2010 amendment succinctly named them in the Constitution); human rights commissions – created in 1988 – failed to make a difference; abstract review was not used in defense of rights, and so on. The feebly organized and demobilized Mexican civil society was not using the Constitution to vindicate, in or outside courts, decent levels of rights' enjoyment.

A big step forward arrived in 2011, when a Section 1 amendment conferred constitutional status to all human rights enshrined in treaties while prompting all authorities to promote, respect, protect and guarantee rights, properly remedying their violations and having the obligation to interpret them *pro personae*. As has been noted, this amendment signals a "change of paradigm",[38] the evolution from "retail" to "wholesale" change in the domain of rights.[39] The reform was accompanied, as we have mentioned, with a too shy *amparo* amendment that lessens some of the traditional barriers but fails to engage in the sort of radical remodeling capable of assuring a real change in terms of access to justice.[40]

---

[37] *See* Pou Giménez (2014), "Las reformas en materia de derechos fundamentals", in Casar and Marván (n 2), for a mapping of all rights-related constitutional amendments in the 1997–2012 period, and Miguel Carbonell, id., for a detailed account of three major ones in the areas of human rights, transparency and criminal procedure.

[38] Miguel Carbonell and Pedro Salazar (2011), *La reforma constitucional en materia de derechos humanos: un nuevo paradigma* (Mexico City: IIJ – UNAM).

[39] Pou Giménez (n 37), at 112.

[40] The reform relaxes standing requirements, allows for collective claims, admits *amparo* against certain private agents displaying public functions, redefines relevant rights affectations and opens the door to *erga omnes* invalidation of unconstitutional statutes under some conditions. But the regulation of procedure and, in general, the language and the structure employed by the *Amparo Act*, continue to be confusing and incomprehensible by an average citizen. *See* Eduardo Ferrer Mac-Gregor and Rubén Sánchez Gil (2014), *El nuevo juicio de amparo. Guía de la reforma constitucional y la nueva Ley de Amparo* (Mexico City: Porrúa-IMDPC-UNAM) (providing an exhaustive general view of the novelties) and Pou Giménez (n 27) (emphasizing the modesty of the changes from the viewpoint of effective rights protection).

Together with the concurrent admission of diffuse control on the part of all Mexican judges and the Supreme Court criteria on the relations between national and international human rights law – recently redefined, however, to curtail the *pro personae* principle[41] – no doubt the Mexican Constitution of rights will start to move differently. Today, the Constitution includes leading-edge argumentation tools – including acknowledgment of international human rights categories more explicitly than the average regional text. Events these past two or three years evince the dynamizing potential of the new provisions. We should, however, not overlook the fact that, as I will refer to below, the Constitution retains provisions in complete tension with the new features.

The Economic Constitution

At the beginnings of 2013, during the first year of the Peña Nieto presidency, a group of amendments importantly changed, after being unaltered for many years, the Mexican economic constitution. The reform affected three main areas: energy, telecommunications and anti-trust.

As is known, the original 1917 text was characterized by a strong statist imprint in the conception of economic activity and the treatment of property rights. Section 27 stated in its original terms that all property was originally held by the nation and recognized peasant communities' (*ejidos*) collective title to land – the Mexican Revolution having been fought to a great extent after land redistribution. The strong prevalence of the state over the market was confirmed by two crucial episodes: the petroleum expropriation decreed in the 1940s and the nationalization of the banking sector in 1981.[42]

The first alterations to this state of affairs came with the presidency of Miguel de la Madrid and, far more consequentially, that Carlos Salinas de Gortari. De la Madrid sought to give predictability and definition to the boundaries of state involvement in the economy and amended Sections 25, 26, 27, 28 and 73 to that effect, though the idea of "state guidance of the economy" remained firmly in the books. Salinas's changes were more radical and affected core tenets of the original constitutional pact. His reforms withdrew the banking sector from those reserved to the state, conferred autonomy on the Bank of Mexico and, more consequentially,

---

[41] *See* Supreme Court, CT 293/2011.

[42] *See* Carlos Elizondo Mayer-Serra (2014), "¿Una nueva constitución en el 2013? El capítulo económico", *Cuestiones constitucionales*, **31**, X. In this section I broadly follow this author's narrative of the evolution of market-state relations in the Mexican Constitution.

created agrarian courts, stopped land distribution and recognized property title to *ejido* peasants, who could now alienate land, exploit it with others or transfer it as corporate capital. He also championed free trade and signed the North American Free Trade Agreement (NAFTA – but without touching the Constitution).

After this, even during the years that followed the 1994 financial crisis (the "tequila effect" crisis) – except for a small Zedillo reform eliminating state exclusivity over railway and satellite sectors – the economic constitution remained unaltered. There was much talk, however, about the need to tackle "structural reforms" to secure competitiveness in the global scenario. For all the constitutional modifications politicians had been eager to agree on, they were resistant to face others that clearly affected deep vested economic interests. Peña Nieto seemingly assumed office with that priority in mind and sought an elite negotiation with the main political party leaders, in the context of the so-called *Pacto por México*, and produced an extremely long list of scheduled reforms. Passed in only one year, the 2013–14 reforms are far-reaching, but it is not entirely clear what message they give concerning state–market relationships. The energy reform, by far the most controversial because it concerns the exploitation of Mexico's petroleum resources – which provide a gigantic percentage of the budget – allows the participation of private capital in exploration and exploitation tasks, through contracts that are intended to assure the state a fair rent. The telecommunications and anti-trust reforms, by contrast, are directed to contain, at least in part, the excessive standing of private economic power. As Elizondo underlines, the fact these reforms were the product of deep transactions in the context of the *Pacto por México* (discussed in a package with the electoral, transparency and political reforms) have rendered their contours exceedingly fuzzy. Tricky provisions and notions were left to be pinned down in the developing statutes, now under hasty discussion in Congress.

III. A CONTENT-BASED APPRAISAL

The overview in the previous section, though quick and necessarily cursory, gives preliminary ground to address some of the content-related questions that frequently articulate collective discussions on Latin American constitutionalism. After its long, reformist path, how does Mexican constitutionalism look? Does it share the traits that scholars have identified as common features of contemporary Latin American constitutionalism? Where does Mexico stand if we distinguish liberal and radical strands?

What are the most salient traits of the current Mexican Constitution as a framework for common political and social life?

On a preliminary analysis, Mexico proves to share most Latin American constitutionalism's core common traits.[43] Thus, the country now enjoys an extensive rights catalogue, including last-generation rights, and an explicit acknowledgment of bonds with international human rights law. The substantive part of the Constitution includes the recognition of cultural diversity as a core definitional element of the polis. There are specific channels for the guarantee of rights, both extrajudicial (human rights commissions) and judicial, including an *amparo* writ – not sufficiently redesigned, however, to ensure effective protection. On the top of a federal scheme, the country has a particularly well-assorted, three-tiered system of judicial review – another Latin American staple – and a system of judiciary self-governance under the lead of a Judiciary Council, as do most of its neighbors. It also participates in the regional trend towards "judicial reform", which has led to the adoption of an adversarial system in the criminal domain. A presidential system has been retained, as in all Latin America, in whose context the Executive interacts with a bi-cameral federal parliament through a U.S.-style system of checks and balances. The Executive is not particularly powerful, but neither is Congress, designed to act with parsimony – though it has had enough incentives to quickly and continuously amend the Constitution.

Mechanisms of direct democracy are, however, distinctively timid: a very restrictive version of popular consultation and legislative initiation has been recently established. There is also an emphasis on electoral matters we do not find elsewhere, with a huge and expensive administrative and judicial structure devoted to give reliability to elections and control political parties. In the economic chapter, the fingerprint of the Mexican Revolution is still textually detectable, but the message of the 2013–14 reforms is that of a country centrally concerned with assuring the conditions for fluid capitalist market transactions. The multiplication of constitutionally independent agencies has detracted from majoritarian politics extensive policy areas, touching not only on the economic domain but also on areas associated with fundamental rights – education, freedom of speech and right to information – and even to more atypical state functions such as criminal investigation.

In view of this, Mexican contemporary constitutionalism seems therefore to be clearly associated with what we call the liberal model, in contrast

[43] I rely on Uprimny's proposed catalogue of shared regional constitutional features (n 1).

with the novel experiences in Bolivia or Ecuador: there are no innovations in the design of the division of powers to respond to more diverse sources of political legitimacy; there exists an explicit, strong recognition of the nation's cultural plurality but development is left to lower norms and does not reshape the design of national institutions; instruments of participatory democracy are particularly weak; transparency has an important place in the bill of rights and has led to the establishment of a specialized institution, which is innovative. But overall, the Mexican Constitution contains simply a recognizable evolution of what Gargarella calls the traditional "liberal-conservative" Latin American model[44] in whose context, in the balance between majoritarian components and anti-majoritarian ones, there is an undisputable emphasis on the latter – given the reinforcement of the judiciary, the enlargement of the bill of rights, the integration of the country into the inter-American system, the multiplication of independent agencies, or the application of tight schemes of checks and balances in extensive areas (popular consultation, state of emergency, etc.).

We could deepen this preliminary appraisal in a number of directions, refining the description of certain constitutional junctures or evaluating them from one or another normative stance.[45] Much of the singularity of the Mexican Constitution is not captured, however, by a preliminary inventory of content: it is largely independent of the regulation it makes of particular institutions because it is associated with the style, structure, textual organization, language and substantive import of the text when examined as a whole. The Mexican Constitution is at this point a pretty untidy collection of provisions: it is a long and extremely detailed text, it is not well structured, it is very heterogeneous – sometimes contradictory – and it is exceedingly complex on a number of counts. These features have, in my view, prominent effects on the sort of normative framework for social and political life it provides – they are the most salient edges in terms

---

[44] Roberto Gargarella (2005), "Una maquinaria exhausta. Constitucionalismo y alienación legal en América", *Isonomía*, **33**, 7, 19; Roberto Gargarella (2008), *Los fundamentos legales de la desigualdad. El constitucionalismo en América: 1776–1870* (Madrid: Siglo XXI Editores).

[45] In his contribution to this volume, for instance, Gargarella evaluates American constitutionalism using criteria of two main sorts: functional and substantive. The functional dimension of his analysis assesses the degree of constitutional congruence of American constitutions – both internal congruence (the degree to which their internal sections, elements or parts work coherently, reinforcing and not undermining their mutual efficacy) and external congruence (the extent to which these constitutions take responsibility for the problems and realities that are really salient in the society in point). The substantive dimension of his analysis assesses how egalitarian these constitutions arguably are.

of "constitutional content". I will therefore devote the remaining section to identify and briefly discuss them.

First, the Mexican Constitution is very long and regulates many aspects with all possible detail, in the style of a legal code, shaping in profuse detail the contours of many domains of public policy and the institutions it regulates.[46] This creates a structural necessity to keep on amending – because rules become more easily outmoded – and burdens interpretive tasks. It is true that many contemporary constitutions are long – Latin American ones among them – and not everything in a Constitution of detail is a problem, since detail can be instrumental to enforcement and can make control of judicial decisions easier. The combination of length, detail, and other traits we will immediately identify, however, render the Mexican Constitution overweight and a bit oppressive as a directly enforceable charter, and makes it difficult for citizens to "appropriate" it.

The effects of detail are compounded by the fact that the structural organization of the text has been severely eroded and the provisions one would expect to find grouped – rights, federalism, the separation of powers – are spread out and mixed all along the text. Moreover, the 2013–14 amendments came accompanied with an assortment of lengthy transitory provisions that regulate in every detail how things are to proceed regarding institutions and policy plans in the areas of energy, telecommunications, electoral administration, education supervision, transparency and competition. The normative status of this extensive, codified, transitory constitution is elusive and reinforces the impression that we are left with a document that is puzzling in many respects.

The Mexican Constitution is also stylistically very heterogeneous: it evinces the fingerprint of several layers of constitutional script coming from very different moments in time, reflecting different constitutional logics and different ideas about how to write a constitution. In the rights area, for instance, some provisions are exceedingly detailed, as we noted, while others are abstract; some rights are enshrined in negative terms (i.e. the Constitution specifies what public authorities cannot do) and others positively (by means of a direct reference to the underlying value that justifies the enshrinement of a specially protected claim); some rights find a counterpart in the federalist division of power (i.e. they are treated as areas of jurisdiction and the Constitution specifies who may regulate the right) and others don't. This creates difficulties to reconstruct constitutional

---

46 The Constitution has grown from around 22 000 words in 1917 to almost 70 000 in February 2014 – not counting the transitory clauses. *See* Elizondo (n 42), and Fix-Fierro (n 2).

meaning and to articulate sound theories of constitutional interpretation – especially in the domain of rights.

More importantly, the Mexican Constitution is also very heterogeneous at the level of content, because amendments have not been done in view of their impact on the pre-existing constitutional body. For sure, substantive heterogeneity obtains always to some extent in constitutions, which are typically the result of political transaction, negotiation. As has been noted, producing a constitution *ex novo* does not ensure coherence either.[47] Fundamental rights and values, moreover, are by their intrinsic nature prone to enter into conflict with one another in the context of specific cases: to a certain extent, as we know, the Constitution of a pluralistic society is designed to include a wide range of values and principles whose ultimate reconduction to unity remains to be seen. But in Mexico, the pattern of unending, fragmentary change, stirred by political conjuncture, and led by politicians who ostensibly see gains only in what they add to the text – not in struggles to synthesize additions, suppressions and extant clauses – in the context of a constitution of detail that decides many things by itself, has produced a set of blatant contradictions within the Constitution that cause a lot of trouble.

Thus, the Mexican Constitution contains at the moment several anti-conventional provisions, such as the one denying political rights to persons under criminal proceedings – contrary to Section 23 of the American Convention on Human Rights (ACHR) and the right to the presumption of innocence enshrined in Section 20.B.I of the Constitution[48] – the ones allowing prosecutorial detention for as much as 80 days in some cases,[49] the imposition of liberty-restraining penalties by administrative authorities,[50]

---

[47] *See* Tom Ginsburg (2012), *Comparative Constitutional Design* (Cambridge: Cambridge University Press), 2 and Justin Blount, Zachary Elkins and Tom Ginsburg, "Does the process of constitution-making matter?", in that volume, at 50 (stressing that, for all contemporary emphasis on constitutional design, quite a few factors remain operative in actual constitution making, propitiating heterogeneity).

[48] Section 23 of the ACHR refers to the limitation (not denial) of the right to vote (not the range of political rights referred to in Section 38.II of the Mexican Constitution) and only for persons convicted (not those simply charged with certain counts, which may well have been charged with no merit or even with the direct intention of eliminating them from an electoral race (for instance).

[49] *See* the regulation of the so-called *arraigo* (house arrest) in Section 16 of the Mexican Constitution.

[50] *See* Section 21 of the Mexican Constitution, contrary to Sections 1 and 2 of the ILO Covenant 29, Section 8 of the ACHR and Section 8.3 of the International Covenant on Civil and Political Rights (exempting community work from being "forced labor" wherever it is dictated by a *judge* after due proceedings).

or the regulation of the rights of foreign people.[51] As the Supreme Court's internal battles illustrate,[52] these pathologies have greatly complicated the task of clarifying the articulation between internal and external sources of law – declared to be of the same hierarchy in the domain of rights by Section 1 of the Constitution – and have obstructed the progression towards more substantive constitutional reasoning – one of the core goals of the 2011 human rights reform. The first years of life of the Mexican new "rights constitution" have been mortgaged by the amount of technical talk produced to try to make sense of the problems caused by internal inconsistency.[53]

A too complex, frequently obscure and sometimes incoherent constitution is a constitution that sets obstacles to its own enforcement. If constitutions are to operate to some extent as coordinating devices capable of generating a fair degree of self-enforcement,[54] the Mexican document is then problematic. A bona fide reader, including those familiar with legal terminology, is soon puzzled when trying to sort out what the Constitution is about. In the case of politicians and public officials genuinely interested in its enforcement, the same difficulties will arise. It is true that the endurance of the 1917 Constitution, in its changing versions, cannot be explained without presupposing a loyalty to a set of identifiable agreements – in this sense the Constitution has been "self-enforcing", from the perspective of the range of political and social groups that could have forced its replacement. But this was so, I believe, because the Constitution that was enforced in this sense was not the Constitution in

---

[51] *See* Sections 8, 9, 11, 31, 32 and 33 of the Mexican Constitution. It is difficult to articulate many of these provisions – and the provisions on naturalized citizens, who have some rights severely limited in comparison to natural-born citizens – with the relevant treaty provisions and even with the apparent "spirit" of other provisions of the Constitution.

[52] *See* Fernando Silva García (2014), "Derechos humanos y restricciones constitucionales: ¿reforma constitucional del futuro vs. interpretación constitucional del pasado? (Comentario a la CT 293/2011del pleno de la SCJN)", *Cuestiones Constitucionales*, **30**, 251; Rubén Sánchez Gil (2014), "Notas sobre la Contradicción de tesis 293/2011", *Revista Iberoamericana de Derecho procesal constitucional*, **21**, 333.

[53] The Mexican Constitution would then be inconsistent in Gargarella's sense (*see* his contribution in this volume) since there are open problems of practical articulation between the substantive part of the Constitution and the way it regulates the "engine room", and in the stronger sense of containing internal contradictions within each structural part of the Constitution.

[54] *See*, for instance, Russell Hardin (1989), "Why a constitution?", in Bernard Groffman and Donald Wittman (eds), *The Federalist Papers and the New Institutionalism* (New York: Agathon Press).

all its actual detail. Once a passage is made from a political conception of the Constitution to a normative conception destined to be daily enforced and to discipline the relations between citizens and authorities – not only the relations among the latter – content matters, and the complexity of content matters increasingly.

A further consequence of these content features concerns the role of judges in the daily administration of the Constitution. The judiciary, particularly the Supreme Court, will be the single actor repeatedly summoned to try to confer some coherence to the complex constitutional "whole". It will then be particularly important to assure that constitutional adjudication proceeds within an institutional and procedural architecture that properly equilibrates the role of the constitutional judge within the system.[55] At any rate, it is important to see that the internal complexity of the Constitution makes it more difficult to meaningfully supervise the exercises of adjudication advanced within such wide margins. The Constitution now provides citizens with new tools to argue almost all that they could wish and, as I mentioned, they can trigger promising dynamics that had been, indeed, unduly weak in Mexico over the last decades. By the same token, however, it may be difficult to sustain that the response citizens receive from judges is arbitrary or unfounded: the variety and disparity of constitutional provisions allows for a good measure of comfy judicial cherry-picking.

IV. A PROCESS-BASED APPRAISAL

A second source of evaluation focuses on the genesis of constitutions, i.e., on the sort of process (composition of the deciding body, deliberation dynamics, voting rules, etcetera) they derive from, in terms of political and social inclusion and procedural adequacy. Some scholars have suggested that the actual content of a constitutional text is less relevant for middle and long-term constitutional "success" than it being the product of a constituent moment allowing citizens and salient political and social groups perceive the Constitution as "their own": as a collective venture they feel participants of, delivering a set of foundational rules they can meaningfully feel co-authors of.[56] In the Mexican case, we would have to evaluate

---

55 *See* Roberto Gargarella (2014), *Por una justicia dialógica: el poder judicial como promotor de la deliberación democrática* (Madrid: Siglo XXI Editores).

56 *See* Oscar Vilhena Vieira et al., *Resiliência Constitucional. Compromisso maximizador, consensualismo político e desenvolvimento gradual* (on file with author) (arguing that the negotiated and inclusive genesis of the Brazilian

therefore what kind of constitutional moment the Constitution emerges from and the sort of process through which amendments have come to life.

Things look from this stance, again, sub-optimal. On the one hand, the original constituent assembly is now far back in the past. There is little in common between the political community represented in Querétaro in 1917 and Mexican contemporary society. Although the 1917 assembly – initially convened to reform the 1857 Constitution – was articulated around most important social claims, many others that are now central were obviously unaddressed, and the representative texture of the constituent body – which consisted of 219 males[57] – is of course utterly defective when viewed from current standards. And although school curricula ensure the tireless socialization of Mexican children into the national myths, the sense of political continuity that might remain is not grounded on what the Constitution actually says – among other things because it has changed too much and people are not aware of its content; at a maximum it invokes a text that, as I have mentioned, has been historically important in a sense different from the one in which we would say today a constitution matters – as a *binding* and directly enforceable document.

On the other hand, as implied by the fact so great an amount of amendments have been passed, constitutional reform in Mexico is just another incidence of ordinary politics. This may come as a surprise in view of the amendment formula, which requires support of two-thirds of attending members in each Chamber of Congress and ratification by half of the 31 state legislatures.[58] As noted by scholars, however, to account for actual

---

Constitution has been key to its success as a general framework capable of containing a succession of pretty different political projects); Blount, Elkins and Ginsburg (n 47), at 31–59 (recommending caution, noting that many hypotheses on the relations between processes and outcomes remain to be authoritatively tested and reviewing existing literature on – among other factors – the alleged effects of popular participation in constitution-making). For further exploration, *see* Stefan Voigt (2003), "The consequences of popular participation in constitutional choice: Towards a comparative analysis", in Anne van Aaken et al. (eds), *Deliberation and Decision* (Aldershot: Ashgate) and Justin Blount (2011), "Participation in constitutional design", in Tom Ginsburg and Rosalind Dixon (eds), *Comparative Constitutional Law* (Cheltenham: Edward Elgar), 112–14.

[57] Salomón Díaz Alfaro (1998), "La composición del congreso constituyente de Querétaro de 1917", in *El constitucionalismo en las postrimerías del siglo XX. La constitución mexicana 70 años después*, 219.

[58] Section 135 of the Mexican Constitution. The Mexican formula is "one-size-fits-all" (it does not set forth different procedures for core versus more routine alterations) and it is laconic, leaving unregulated questions such as who can present amendment bills, which sort of parliamentary discussion must be held before the 2/3 vote, or what lies in state legislatures. As we have noted, Mexico City – not

rigidity one must take into account not only the number of institutional players involved and the size of the majorities required, but an assortment of additional elements: the temporal organization of the process (e.g. whether intervening institutions must act at specific points in time or not, or whether voting rounds must be multiple); the need to call for a popular referendum or not; the shape of the party system. To this we can add the range of structural incentives to engage in change.[59] In Mexico, even if the size of the requisite majorities is not trivial, amendments need not obtain approval in consecutive terms, there are neither players outside ordinary political actors nor a need to call directly upon the people. The formula therefore makes constitutional law-making extremely close to ordinary law-making – all the more so because Section 135 leaves internal procedural steps unregulated and the practice has been to analogically apply what is done in the ordinary legislative process.

The pattern of amendment is very distant, in short, from "higher law-making" in an Ackermanian sense – a distinctive process singled out in terms of inclusion, participation, deliberation and high-spiritedness.[60] Amending the Constitution is legislating by (barely) other means. Constitutional reforms, for instance, are as easily lobbied for as ordinary legislation; sometimes public opinion finds out about an amendment after it has already been passed; occasionally, certain changes gain higher profile – but just in the way some statutory bills generate more debate from time to time. To be sure, we could see it all as a democratic advantage: present generations in Mexico would have the Constitution in their hands far more than usual and there would be, therefore, less tyranny of the past over the present. By the same token, however, the present whose decisions constrain (to some degree) the future does not do so on the basis

---

being technically "a state" – does not participate in the ratification process. The Constitution does not contain unamendable provisions.

[59] *See* Donald Lutz (1995), "Toward a theory of constitutional amendment", in Sanford Levinson (ed.), *Responding to Imperfection* (Princeton: Princeton University Press) (charting possible variations in amendment design and crafts an "index of rigidity" and giving Mexico a score of 2.55 – the highest being 5.6 for the ex-Yugoslavia and the lowest 0.80 for Austria). *See also* Víctor Ferreres Comella (2000), "Una defensa de la rigidez constitucional", *Doxa*, **23**, 29 (noting that actual rigidity emerges from the combination of six factors: federalism, the kind of majority or supermajority that is called for, the presence or absence of referendum, the system of political parties (and the degree of party discipline), the presence or absence of historical factors that can make the alteration of certain constitutional decisions a "taboo", and the degree of conservatism of prevailing political culture).

[60] *See* Bruce Ackerman (1993), *We the People* (Cambridge, MA: Harvard University Press).

of particularly valuable reasons or procedures. There seem to be weak grounds, in short, to recognize special democratic credentials to amendments on the basis of their pedigree. There is perhaps nothing intrinsically wrong in having constitution-making by ordinary means, but if the ordinary political system operates less than acceptably – as it arguably occurs in Mexico – then one must abandon of course any special hopes about the democratic texture of the Constitution.

Fast-track dynamics in the domain of constitutional change is further reinforced by the fact the judicial review of constitutional amendments has been progressively foreclosed by the Supreme Court. Perhaps paradoxically in a country that lives under hectic constitutional change, the Supreme Court has closed the door both to substantive and to procedural analysis of regularity in all channels of review.[61] Again, it is not that judicial review of constitutional amendments is unproblematic from a democratic viewpoint – particularly where the Constitution does not contain clauses written in stone and does not explicitly grant this power to the corresponding most powerful Court. The point is simply to note that the absence of the more complex interaction between courts and legislators this review would probably produce, reinforces a dynamics of unbounded constitutionalism.

V. A FREQUENCY-BASED APPRAISAL

As Elkins, Melton and Ginsburg emphasize in their work on constitutional endurance, a fruitful way of analyzing constitutionalism focuses on whether the constitution has changed a lot, very little, insufficiently, excessively or – could it ever be assessed – just in the optimal degree. From this perspective, one ponders the effects of change or non-change per se,

[61] In a 2002 case (CC 82/2001, filed by an Oaxaca municipality) the Court said that in resolving *constitutional controversies* it could review neither the substantive nor the procedural regularity of constitutional amendments. As regards *actions of unconstitutionality* (abstract review) the Court said in AAII 168/2007 and 169/2007 (resolved in 2008) that the procedural regularity of constitutional amendments could not be reviewed in that channel. As regards *amparo*, the Court had said in the "Camacho" cases (AARR 2996/96 and 1334/98) that the procedural regularity could be checked, even if it detected no procedural flaws in the instant case. But in addressing the so-called "Intellectuals" saga (where a group of opinion formers were arguing that constitutional provisions on campaign financing violated free speech) changed the law: while at first (AARR 186/2008, 552/2008) the Court said denunciations of procedural and substantive flaws were not "evidently" inadmissible in *amparo*, it eventually held they cannot be examined (AR 488/2010).

beyond what is to be said of the merits of the resulting text in terms of content or in terms of the procedure used to enact it.

As these authors remark, constitutional endurance, stability or permanence – i.e. constitutional actual rigidity – can be associated with positive elements such as the development of habits of obedience to the constitution; the reinforcement of the effects of pre-commitment on public authorities (who come to be effectively constrained by the rules set to bind them); the possibility of more orderly managing of the times and processes of legal-political life; the development of auxiliary institutions which help fulfill constitutional mandates (something impossible if the constitution is changing all the time); the progressive development of a sense of political *demos* around the constitutional text; an increase in predictability which may boost economic development; or the benefits associated with having a "division of labor" scheme that empowers current political majorities in liberating them from the need to address certain matters.[62] Constitutional stability, however, can also be associated with drawbacks such as a weaker representation of present-day citizens' concerns, fewer possibilities for intense political participation, or fewer possibilities of getting rid of sub-optimal institutions which may remain in the system only because of inertia.

What are we to say, from this analytical stance, about Mexican constitutional *reformismo*? Should we emphasize the passive, conservationist side of a Constitution that has been massively amended but not disappeared, and the benefits of constitutional stability and permanence? Should we praise a text that has given some ground to political life for a century and has accompanied/conducted for 25 years a process of increasing democratization? Or should we rather emphasize the innovative dimension of amending and note that the Mexican text has only survived through permanent amendment, stressing therefore the drawbacks associated with instability? Does the Mexican scenario suggest an optimum combination of change and permanence? What relation is there between *reformismo* and Mexican political and social realities?

In my view, and setting aside a core problematic effect of permanent change I have already referred to – i.e., that it has resulted in a complex and often incoherent text in terms of content – the Mexican pattern of gradual, fragmentary and ceaseless constitutional change does not provide

---

[62] *See* Zachary Elkins, Tom Ginsburg and James Melton (2009), *The Endurance of National Constitutions* (Cambridge: Cambridge University Press), 12–35; Tom Ginsburg, "Constitutional endurance", in Ginsburg and Dixon (n 56), 112–14.

many grounds for praise. To be sure, we cannot rely on counterfactuals – perhaps things would have been worse had the country undergone frequent replacements instead of frequent amendments – and nothing in this chapter could methodologically provide something close to a set of causal explanations. Within the limits of that disclaimer, there are several features in today's Mexican scenario whose degree of connection with patterns of constitutional instability should be, in my view, further explored.

First, endless change could be not unrelated to the widespread unfamiliarity with the content of the Constitution that now prevails among citizens and even specialized audiences. I find it impossible to count today the Constitution among the elements that bind Mexicans together, but if any sense of identification remains, it is certainly not with its actual contents. And the impossibility of keeping track of what is under way at any moment, in terms of constitutional law-making, prevents deliberation and public criticism both before amendments are passed and after them – since by that time, professors, media and people are already distracted by the new amendments already under consideration. The non-interruption of the reform dynamics thus effectively contributes to shield political action from criticism. It also weakens, in my view, the effectiveness and quality of judicial review, since judges have little incentive or energy to develop strong doctrines on the meaning of one or another particular provision if they assume it will not remain in the books for long – or if they know the "whole" they should make it cohere with will suffer continuous alteration. For the same reasons, academic analysis gets thinner or lighter than usual: there is no point in focusing on particular points of the law if one believes they will soon be replaced by other rules and institutions, rendering less attractive the publication and discussion of research done on their basis.

Second, the constitutional pattern has weakened, in my view, the logic of pre-commitment and has done little to help install the rule of law and the logic of constitutionalism, understood as a system of limited government. In Mexico, it has been just too easy for authorities to avoid the application of the normative framework designed to constrain their political action. The vast amount of reforms in the area of fundamental rights accomplished in recent times illustrates, I believe, to what extent politicians have operated on the assumption of a toothless, unfrightening constitution. Thus, in a period that will be sadly remembered by the appalling amount of people killed or who have disappeared at the hands of private and state agents, politicians have added a large amount of human rights to the Constitution, seemingly to proclaim that they were doing "something nice" for the people. This way of proceeding has provided them immediate legitimacy gains, while the costs – in terms of having those rights enforced by judges against them – have been (rightly) calculated as being low and transferred to future incumbents. Whenever one or another constitutional provision has episodically proved actually menacing – as happened when the Supreme Court declared long-term unsupervised home detentions unconstitutional in 2008 – party cupules have found ways to gather the majorities necessary to amend the Constitution and preventively get rid of them.

The Mexican amendment dynamic seems to illustrate, in this regard, a phenomenon that sociologists consider distinctive of Latin American legal fields, associating patterns of legal production with patterns of inefficacy. García Villegas and Rodríguez Garavito argue that the precarious social embeddedness of the political system and its lack of hegemony over others (the space of production, the domestic sphere, etc.) complicates the management of social problems through ordinary political channels and favors the over-production of norms: "The deficit of legitimacy derived and caused by the instrumental inefficacy of the state", they remark, "is sought to be compensated by the production of legal discourse and norms in response to the social demands of security, social justice and participation".[63] The legal system gets overburdened with tasks that the political system cannot handle, and reforms are designed to legitimate state action in areas ridden by deep social claims: the efficacy of the norms that get produced is less important than its communicative and symbolic function.[64]

Third, Mexico has seemingly forgone the advantages of the division of labor ingrained in the logic of rigid constitutionalism. Because at every point everything is up for grabs, legislators have not attempted the careful and detailed legal craft necessary to make constitutional mandates permeate to the levels of statutes and regulations. The heavy readjustments among upper and lower norms necessary in a country undergoing massive redesign has not been done, in part because the process has not been advanced by politicians with a view of the global architecture they were trying to build.

Lastly, in the last decades *reformismo* has constrained, in my view, the opportunities of Mexicans to express themselves as a political com-

---

[63] García Villegas (n 3), at 284–85 (with internal citation to José Eduardo Faria (1988), *Eficacia juridica e violencia simbólica: O direito como instrumento de transformacao social* (São Paulo: Editora da Universidade de São Paulo)).

[64] Id., at 287. As these authors remark, this does not mean that legal reform produced for symbolic motivations will be always instrumentally ineffective: it means it is unlikely that they will produce the material effects that are contemplated in the norms and that were mentioned by politicians as the reason justifying their enactment. Id., at 288.

munity. The distance from the foundational moment hinders people's identification with the constitutional project and their self-perception as citizens living under a common frame of values and rules. People have not been involved for long in the sort of more intense republican exercise necessary to give oneself a new constitution and have thus forgone the benefits that come from a "spirited return to the basics". This state of affairs may be illustrated by the first fissures that occurred at the end of 2014, as people reacted massively in the streets to outrageous killings and disappearances in the state of Guerrero under the joint action of state agents and drug cartels. President Peña's response – a ten-point plan to "restore the rule of law", eight points of which consisted of enacting legal and constitutional amendments[65] – confirms, in any case, the aim or direction of traditional automatisms: politicians using amendment proposals to (try to) prevent citizens from engaging in (much-feared) high-voltage political action.

VI. CONCLUDING THOUGHTS: MEXICAN CONSTITUTIONALISM AND THE SHAPE OF DEMOCRATIC LIFE

The scenario I have pictured in this chapter is not heartening. The function of the analysis is not, however, to make a contribution to a hypercritical global narrative of (customarily biased) "Latin American miseries" but to present a view of the law at a time in which Mexico is undergoing a particularly acute crisis on a number of fronts. The magnitude of the challenges currently faced by the country – in terms of eradicating public and private violence, diminishing dramatic levels of inequality, improving education and health, eradicating corruption or making political life more inclusive – seem to be mirrored in the challenges raised by its constitutional system. The problems we have identified along the way could well be therefore epiphenomenal: the features of Mexican constitutionalism we have pictured could be not causes, but reflections or effects of troubled social and political dynamics. In this regard, a merciless description of the Constitution can be considered part of a merciless self-critical description of social and political realities that seems apposite to create conditions instrumental to their transformation.

Viewed from the regional stance, the Mexican Constitution evinces a

[65] *See* www.animalpolitico.com/2014/11/pena-nieto-acuerdo-seguridad-comision-anuncio-mensaje-palacio-nacional (accessed 2 December 2014).

clear inclination for the solutions characteristic of the liberal model of constitutionalism, not to the post-liberal, radical experiences that are under way in some parts of the Americas.[66] But as I have sought to emphasize, the Mexican Constitution stands out by being a text that contains at this point "a bit of everything", embodying a "whole" largely produced by superimposition: adding elements of new constitutionalism without getting rid of many of the old structures and norms.

Mexico's constitutional updating has been extremely gradual, but also hectic and unremitting. This has bestowed a sensation of volatility to the Constitution and our analysis has suggested how this could be linked to difficulties in developing habits of obedience – installing in the mind of politicians the idea they can change at any moment the framework rules intending to limit their behavior – and patterns of political identification. Judicial enforcement of basic rules is further compounded by the fact the resulting text is often incoherent and invariably complex to make sense of.

Mexican constitutionalism embodies, in addition, and in a pattern of unquestionably top-down change, a context in which it is political elites who have determined what to do in response to urgent political issues. While changes in the last 25 years have created a frame for democracy, day-to-day Mexican democratic life remains low-voltage when viewed substantively, from the perspective of the citizen. The frenzy of politicians to keep on amending the basic law – even if partially explained by the need to update an old system – seems to have given them for a long time a comfortable pretext to avoid the costs of to start enforcing it. Hyper-reformism has prevented the development of a national-wide political debate based on shared values, while seriously encumbering the development of the sort of accountability dynamics that are peculiar to democracy.

Unquestionably, Mexican constitutionalism now includes tools that may empower the citizenry to an extent hard to imagine a decade ago. The new rights' Constitution can trigger new forms of interaction – of citizens among themselves and among citizens and judges or other authorities – that could unleash collective social and political energies. As of today, however, whether the Mexican Constitution will finally become the vessel of a more fulfilling democratic life in the decades to come – or whether

66 *See* Javier Couso Salas (2014), "Las democracias radicales y el 'nuevo constitucionalismo latinoamericano'", in Marisa Iglesias et al., *Derechos humanos: posibilidades teóricas y desafíos prácticos: SELA 2013* (Buenos Aires: Libraria Ediciones) (reconstructing and critically appraising their main features).

citizens, as in the Jeffersonian image, will conclude that they have outgrown their constitutional coat[67] – is something that remains to be seen.

[67] Thomas Jefferson (1930), "Letter to Samuel Kercheval [1816]", in Lester J. Cappon (ed.) (1988), *The Adams–Jefferson Letters: The Complete Correspondence between Thomas Jefferson and Abigail and John Adams* (Chapel Hill, NC: University of North Carolina Press), cited in Elkins, Ginsburg and Melton (n 62), at 16, 25 ("When a society has grown out of sync with its constitutional arrangements, pressure to renegotiate may become severe. Jefferson's metaphor of a grown man wearing his boyhood coat is apt here: when a constitution no longer fits its polity, it is altogether appropriate that the constitution be shed, lest it stunt the growth of the nation inside it.").

7. Socioeconomic rights and majoritarian courts in Latin America

David Landau

During the past several decades, many courts in Latin America have been active in enforcing socioeconomic rights. While traditional theorists tended to argue that they raise intractable problems of democratic legitimacy and judicial capacity, and thus should either be left out of constitutions entirely or should be left judicially unenforced, recent trends in international human rights and comparative constitutional law have attacked these conclusions. In particular, recent trends in Latin American constitutionalism have put significant pressure on the traditional view that socioeconomic rights should be non-justiciable.

I argue here that their enforcement in the region raises an important paradox: courts have often found ways to make socioeconomic rights justiciable, but in some common patterns of enforcement they have had relatively little transformative impact. One important idea for understanding this paradox, tied to the theme of this chapter, stems from recent themes in U.S. constitutional theory: courts often behave as majoritarian rather than counter-majoritarian institutions. Thus, they sometimes favor patterns of jurisprudence that tend to bolster their own support among politically powerful actors. For example, courts have often favored individualized models of enforcement, where aggrieved (often relatively affluent) litigants can go to the court and seek an individual remedy giving them a treatment or other benefit, and "negative injunctions", where courts strike down efforts by the political branches to use austerity measures to reduce existing welfare packages, often enjoyed by civil servants and others who are relatively privileged. To be clear, the claim is not that social rights jurisprudence reaching the most marginalized members of society is impossible or does not occur. Recent scholarship suggests that certain modes of enforcement, especially structural remedies forcing the state to construct or improve social welfare programs, have success at reaching the very poor.[1] The claim here is instead that under common conditions, courts both inside and outside of Latin America utilize, and have incentives to utilize, modes of enforcement with impacts that are skewed towards less marginalized groups.

These majoritarian patterns of jurisprudence, when they materialize, carry out functions that are different from those hypothesized in most of the existing literature. For example, in enforcing socioeconomic rights, courts often substitute for bureaucratic organs that fail broad swaths of the public (a service-provision function).[2] Further, courts enforcing socioeconomic rights sometimes block measures that are unpopular but nonetheless pass the political branches because of international or domestic pressure (a principal–agent function).[3] Finally, courts enforcing socioeconomic rights can help to build up constitutional culture by making the constitution directly relevant to people's lives (a constitutional culture-building function).[4] The majoritarian model of judicial review explored in this chapter has important implications for the enforcement of socioeconomic rights and beyond. Most obviously, it suggests that those relying on courts to carry out projects of social transformation may be overstating the case. On the other hand, it also suggests that judicial enforcement of social rights is potentially useful for a broader range of reasons than is often recognized.

I. SOCIOECONOMIC RIGHTS AND THE NEW CONSTITUTIONALISM: TOWARDS JUSTICIABILITY

Much classic theory on socioeconomic rights focused on problematizing their nature and especially their enforceability. According to these theorists, socioeconomic rights are different from traditional negative rights in several ways. First, they are thought to suffer from a "radical indeterminacy" because they can require fulfillment in any number of different ways.[5] The

---

1 *See, e.g.*, Cesar Rodriguez-Garavito and Diana Rodriguez-Franco (2015), *Radical Deprivation on Trial: The Impact of Judicial Activism on Socioeconomic Rights in Latin America* (Cambridge: Cambridge University Press); Daniel M. Brinks and Varun Gauri (2014), "The law's majestic equality? The distributive impact of litigating social and economic rights", *Perspectives on Pol.*, **12**, 375; David Landau (2012), "The reality of social rights enforcement", *Harv. Int'l L. J.*, **53**, 189.

2 *See* Section III.A (below).

3 *See* Section III.B (below).

4 *See* Section III.C (below).

5 Frank Michelman (2003), "The constitution, social rights, and liberal political justification", *Int'l J. Const. L.*, **1**, 13, 31 (referring to the term without

right to housing, for example, is indeterminate in the sense that it is unclear what kind of house is required, what amenities the house must include, the time frame under which the house must be delivered, etc. Second, they were uniquely thought to involve courts in the setting of budgetary priorities, the spending of money, and the creation of social programs.[6] In short, socioeconomic rights were thought to involve challenges to judicial legitimacy and capacity that were fundamentally different in kind from those involved with negative rights.

This traditional view inculcated Latin American constitutionalism in important ways. In Mexico's 1917 Constitution, for example, which was one of the oldest constitutions in the world to contain social rights, the provisions have long been thought to be non-justiciable.[7] The rights were seen as central to the ideology of Mexican constitutionalism, but meant to bind the political branches and not the courts. Similar devices were employed in other Latin American countries, either textually or non-textually. In Chile, socioeconomic rights were included, but were excluded from the scope of the constitutional individual complaint mechanism.[8]

Shifts both inside and outside the region have put pressure on this conception. In international human rights law, the default position has shifted, with scholars and policymakers increasingly likely to see positive rights as justiciable.[9] They have pointed out, for example, that many negative rights (like the right to a fair trial) also involve the spending of money, and that negative rights as well as positive rights can involve

---

endorsing the argument that it makes socioeconomic rights non-justiciable); *see also* Frank Cross (2001), "The error of positive rights", *UCLA L. Rev.*, **48**, 857 (noting that one reason for non-enforcement of socioeconomic rights is that "such rights, by their nature, are highly indeterminate").

6 *See, e.g.*, Cross (n 5), at 889–90 (discussing the problem within the context of the United States).

7 *See, e.g.*, Jorge R. Ordoñez, "La justiciabilidad de los derechos sociales en México: 90 años de carrera con obstáculos", *Suprema Corte de Justicia de la Nación, Publicaciones Becarios de la Corte*, **1**, 183, available at: http://207.249.17.176/Transparencia/Lists/Becarios/Attachments/299/Becarios_183.pdf (accessed 19 September 2017); Miguel Carbonell (2008), "Eficacia de la constitución y derechos sociales: esbozo de algunos problemas", *Estudios Constitucionales*, **6**, 43, 65 (noting that the *amparo* has proven insufficient to protect socioeconomic rights because of its narrow standing rules).

8 *See* Chile Constitution (1980), Art. 20 (defining the rights that the *recurso de protección* can be used to protect).

9 *See, e.g.*, Malcolm Langford (2009), "The justiciability of social rights: From practice to theory", in Malcolm Langford (ed.), *Social Rights Jurisprudence: Emerging Trends in International and Comparative Law* (Cambridge: Cambridge University Press), pp. 3, 31.

problems of indeterminacy.[10] Within the region, "new constitutionalist" currents of thought have put pressure on the non-justiciability position.

The term new constitutionalism has been widely used in Latin America, but not always precisely defined. In general within the region, the concept connotes a series of shifts in the importance and meaning of constitutional laws, but these shifts are difficult to pin down because they vary significantly from place to place.[11] They are linked to broader shifts in international human rights law and comparative constitutional law but also rooted in Latin American legal history. One important shift is that the structural part of the constitution, historically dominant in Latin American constitutionalism, has become subordinate to the "dogmatic" or rights portion of the constitution.[12] A dominant story in Latin American history is one in which constitutions had long been ignored; and the new constitutional movement was an attempt to make them "real". The new constitutionalists sought to activate rights provisions, such as socioeconomic rights, that had been found in constitutions for a long time but had not been given much content by courts.[13] They further sought to prevent systemic violations of human rights that had been carried out in the region in the recent past.[14]

Further, the new constitutionalism has suggested new methods of constitutional interpretation. Constitutional rights are now interpreted in light of higher-order principles like human dignity, and thus constitutional interpretation becomes a more heavily value-laden enterprise.[15] Techniques like proportionality, and particularly the influential work of Robert Alexy and his Latin American disciples, allow courts to adjudicate carefully between conflicting rights or principles.[16] These techniques are

---

[10] *See* id., at 30.

[11] For an overview of some of these shifts, *see* Javier Couso (2010), "The transformation of constitutional discourse and the judicialization of politics in Latin America, in Javier Couso, Alexandra Huneeus and Rachel Sieder (eds), *Cultures of Legality: Judicialization and Political Activism in Latin America* (Cambridge: Cambridge University Press), p. 141.

[12] *See, e.g.*, Roberto Gargarella (2013), "Dramas, conflictos, y promesas del nuevo constitucionalismo latinoamericano", *Anacronismo y Irrupción*, **3**, 245, 253.

[13] *See* Rodrigo Uprimny (2011), "The recent transformation of constitutional law in Latin America: Trends and challenges", *Tex. L. Rev.*, **89**, 1587, 1600 (noting that the "transformative" constitutions of recent Latin American history have generally taken two tracks: extending rights and increasing popular political participation).

[14] *See* id., at 1599.

[15] *See, e.g.*, Miguel Carbonell (2010), "Desafíos de nuevo constitucionalismo en América Latina", *Precedente*, **2010**, 207, 214.

[16] *See generally* Carlos Bernal Pulido (2007), *El Principio de proporcionalidad y los derechos humanos: El principio de proporcionalidad como criterio para*

important because they provide courts with the ammunition needed to enforce constitutional rights, such as socioeconomic rights, that have long lain dormant.

Finally, the movement suggests a new role for the judge within the legal order. Judges become more central figures as they are tasked with interpreting and applying newly active constitutional rights within their jurisdictions. Charged with applying proportionality tests and applying rights in light of higher-order principles, constitutional judges are seen as more creative and proactive figures.[17] Socioeconomic rights are in many ways close to the core of this project, because they involve rights that have been historically under-enforced (indeed in many places ignored), and they may operate for the benefit of groups that have historically been marginalized.[18] Thus, currents of new constitutionalist thought have put pressure on the non-justiciability position. And indeed, socioeconomic rights are now enforced to a degree in most of the major Latin American countries, including Brazil, Argentina, Colombia, Costa Rica, and Venezuela.[19]

The Colombian example is perhaps a useful case study. Major political forces at the constituent assembly of 1991 were in agreement that socioeconomic rights should be included in the Colombian Constitution. However, they took differing positions about the justiciability of these rights. In particular, the national president Cesar Gaviria argued that the rights should be included but not rendered justiciable (at least by individual complaint).[20] He laid out the classic position in favor of directive principles: inclusion of the rights would help to validate the importance of socioeconomic issues and would allow political parties, civil society groups, and citizens to focus the state's attention on them, but should

---

determinar el contenido de los derechos fundamentales vinculante para el legislador, 3rd edn (Madrid: Centro de Estudios Políticos y Constitucionales).

[17] *See* Uprimny (n 13), at 1607.

[18] *See* Gargarella (n 12), at 246 (noting that these rights were historically under-enforced).

[19] *See, e.g.*, Daniel Brinks and William Forbath (2011), "Commentary: Social and economic rights in Latin America: Constitutional courts and the prospects for pro-poor interventions", *Tex. L. Rev.*, **89**, 1943, 1944 ("[T]he courts of the region are well past discussing whether they should enforce [socioeconomic rights], and are now fully engaged in exploring how and to what effect they can and should enforce them.").

[20] *See, e.g.*, Intervention of Cesar Gaviria at the Opening of the Constituent Assembly, 5 February 1991, in Manuel Jose Cepeda (1992), *Introducción a la Constitución de 1991* (Bogatá: Presidencia de la República), at pp. 329, 340–41 ("As is obvious, these socioeconomic and collective rights cannot be directly enforced by an individual before a judge.").

not allow the courts to get involved.[21] The final constitutional product reflected a compromise position: the key provision listed certain rights as being "of immediate application" but excluded the socioeconomic rights from this list.[22] The Constitution also allowed constitutional complaints (*tutelas*) to be taken in order to protect "fundamental rights", but it did not define this term.[23]

The new Colombian Constitutional Court, in some of its first decisions, found ways to make socioeconomic rights justiciable. It rejected a rigid classification between first generation rights and socioeconomic rights, holding that the classification of a right as fundamental had to be made case by case and in the generally pro-guarantee spirit of the Constitution.[24] It also drew on German precedent to create a right to a vital minimum, which was synthesized from explicit constitutional rights and principles and the right of citizens to have at least a minimum level of economic subsistence.[25] This construct allowed the Court to link socioeconomic rights to the right to life and the principle of human dignity; the connectivity doctrine in turn allowed the Court to enforce socioeconomic rights via *tutela* whenever they were linked to these other rights.[26] In recent jurisprudence, the Court has held that socioeconomic rights, in and of themselves, can be fundamental rights in some aspects and some circumstances.[27] Thus the Court has moved towards a position that makes socioeconomic rights directly justiciable, even without regard to the connectivity doctrine.

A consideration of the outlier countries which have resisted making socioeconomic rights justiciable is again useful in mapping the outer reaches of the influence of the new constitutionalism. Mexico, as already noted, has a long history of both including socioeconomic rights and

---

[21] *See* id.

[22] *See* Colombia Constitution (1991), Art. 85.

[23] *See* Colombia Constitution (1991), Art. 86. Note that the Constitution did contain a division of rights provisions into different categories, including "fundamental rights" and "economic, social, and cultural rights". The former contained mostly negative rights, while the socioeconomic rights were generally put in the latter category. This division was done by the Codification Committee before the second and final floor debate, not by the Assembly itself. The Court, in its early socioeconomic rights decisions, declined to give the labeling much weight. *See, e.g.*, Decision T-406 of 5 June1992, § 14.

[24] *See, e.g.*, id., § 15.

[25] *See* Decision T-426 of 24 June 1992, § 5 (synthesizing the right from explicit rights and guarantees in the constitutional text).

[26] *See, e.g.*, Decision T-491 of 13 August 1992, § 2.

[27] *See, e.g.*, Decision T-760 of 31 July 2008, § 3 (affirming that the right to health is a fundamental right in its basic aspects without regard to the connectivity doctrine).

refusing to render them justiciable;[28] the Chilean Constitution included socioeconomic rights but has the same tradition of non-justiciability and made most of them textually non-enforceable by at least the individual complaint.[29] Both countries are also on the margins of the new constitutionalism discourse, rather than close to the center as in Colombia. But in both countries, there are now at least debates about the justiciability question. In Mexico, for example, Supreme Court magistrate and well-known jurist Jose Ramon Cossio has argued that these rights, properly understood, should be rendered justiciable, although he has also lamented the fact that citizens and civil society are not bringing socioeconomic rights cases to the Court.[30] He argues that the objections to socioeconomic rights involve pragmatic objections to the ways in which these rights would be enforced, and not arguments against justiciability.[31] More broadly, some scholarship has considered the impact of recent reforms to the Mexican system of constitutional protection which strengthened the individual complaint and increased the relevance of international law for constitutional interpretation on the socioeconomic rights questions.[32] The main argument is that by incorporating elements of international human rights law, the reforms have rendered socioeconomic rights justiciable.[33]

In Chile, similarly, the domestic context around socioeconomic rights centers largely on a well-known failure: claimants in dire situations who sought coverage for HIV/AIDS medications lost their cases, even though they at a key point tried to frame their cases around the right to life rather than health.[34] Nonetheless, recent scholarly debate on this issue centers around a

---

28 *See* n 7.

29 *See* n 8.

30 *See* Jose Ramon Cossio, "Problemas para la exigibilidad de los derechos sociales y económicos en México", available at: biblio.juridicas.unam.mx/libros/6/2873/8.pdf (accessed 15 September 2017).

31 *See* id.

32 *See*, *e.g.*, Omar Gomez Trejo (2014), "Estánderes internacionales en material de derechos económicos, sociales, y culturales", in Magdalena Cervantes Alcayde et al. (eds), *Hay justicia para los derechos económicos, sociales, y culturales?* (Mexico City: Suprema Corte de Justicia de la Nación), pp. 159, 159–60; Rodrigo Guitérrez Rivas (2014), *La justiciabilidad de los derechos económicos, sociales, culturales, y ambientales en el marco de las recientes reformas constitucionales en material de derechos humanos*, in id., at 92, 97–98.

33 Other scholarship has noted that at least some Mexican decisions seem to recognize socioeconomic rights – like the right to health – in at least some contexts. *See* Maria del Rosario Huerta Lara (2009), "Expansion y justiciabilidad de los derechos sociales en Mexico", *Letras Jurídicas*, **20**, 1.

34 *See*, *e.g.*, Jorge Contesse and Domingo Lovera Parmo (2008), "Access to medical treatment for people living with HIV/AIDS: Success without victory in

2008 decision in which the Constitutional Court held that private health insurers (largely serving the middle and upper classes) which charged different prices to consumers based on gender and age violated the constitutional right to health.[35] While much of the debate has centered around whether the decision was in fact a real application of socioeconomic rights, the literature does show an emerging debate on socioeconomic rights enforcement even in a legal culture that has been hostile to that enforcement.[36]

The justiciability debate in Latin America is not over, but it does seem to be moving towards a consensus position that favors enforcement.[37] As the next section will show, the way that socioeconomic rights are enforced in Latin America demonstrates a tension between different aspects of the new constitutionalism. While courts increasingly embrace justiciability, in many cases they enforce socioeconomic rights in ways that are relatively unlikely to be transformative. This is not an aberration: it reflects the fact that courts are often majoritarian rather than counter-majoritarian actors.[38]

II. THE HOW AND WHY OF SOCIOECONOMIC RIGHTS ENFORCEMENT IN LATIN AMERICA

This section describes the key modes of enforcement in the region and seeks to give an explanation as to why those modes are important. A few

Chile", *Sur: International Journal on Human Rights*, **8**, 142 (noting that the litigants achieved their political goals even though the courts declined to intervene, rejecting the argument that the case really involved the right to life and not the right to health).

[35] Rol 1710-10-INC, 6 August 2010.

[36] For a sampling of that debate, *see* Santiago Montt and Jose Luis Cardenas (2011), "La declaración de inconstitucionalidad del artículo 38 TER de la ley de ISAPRES: Mitos y realidades de un fallo histórico", in Javier Couso (ed.), *Anuario de Derecho Publico Universidad Diego Portales 2011* (Santiago: Universidad Diego Portales), p. 17 (arguing that the decision "enters a new stage of [Chilean] economic constitutional law" but that its ultimate effect is unclear); Luis Cordero Vega (2011), "Comentario a la sentencia de inconstitucionalidad de la tabla de factores de ISAPRES: un aparente triunfo de los derechos sociales", *Anuario de Derechos Humanos*, **7**, 151, 158 (arguing that the decision is an application of the right to health in a sense, although one that may have a "regressive effect" because it leaves out users of the public health system who cannot afford private health care).

[37] *See* Brinks and Forbath (n 19), at 1944 (summarizing a series of symposium contributions as showing that Latin American courts have moved beyond the question of whether socioeconomic rights are justiciable and on to the question of how to enforce them).

[38] *See* Section III (below).

courts in the region, especially the Colombian Constitutional Court, have experimented with structural remedies where the court seeks to pressure the state to create, build up, or improve the performance of social welfare bureaucracies.[39] These rights have received significant scholarly attention and debate regarding their effectiveness at changing state practices and at aiding marginalized groups.[40] However, Latin American courts often enforce socioeconomic rights through two other models: an individualized model of enforcement, where a single petitioner goes to a court to get a single remedy, and a negative injunction model, where a court strikes down legislative attempts to alter the status quo by reducing the existing social welfare net.[41] The advantage of both models is that they fit easily into traditional models of rights enforcement; the trouble with both is that they are often not particularly transformative. Neither requires the state to construct new programs, and the primary beneficiaries are likely to be more affluent groups like civil servants, rather than the very poor.

The reasons why these two models have been common are of course more speculative, but one can ascertain two broad groups of explanations. A first emphasizes ideological restrictions on judicial role – judges gravitate towards traditionalist methods of enforcement because they are more comfortable with those methods.[42] Without dismissing the obvious importance of that factor, I suggest that political restrictions and incentives have also played a role. Recent constitutional theory from the United States is helpful as a guidepost: much recent work on the U.S. Supreme Court finds that it often behaves as a majoritarian rather than counter-majoritarian actor. The insights from that theory, I suggest, are helpful in understanding patterns of social rights enforcement in the region.[43]

A. Two Major Models of Enforcement

In a range of countries including Brazil, Colombia, and Costa Rica, a major model of enforcement is individualized: citizens come to the court for an individual remedy, whether a readjustment of a pension or access to a treatment.[44] This model bears some logic to the traditional theory of

---

39 *See* n 1, and sources cited therein.

40 *See* id.

41 For a fuller description of both models, *see* Landau (n 1).

42 *See* Section III.B (below).

43 *See* Section III.C (below).

44 *See, e.g.*, Florian F. Hoffmann and Fernando R.N.M. Bentes (2008), "Accountability for social and economic rights in Brazil", in Varun Gauri and Daniel M. Brinks (eds), *Courting Social Justice: Judicial Enforcement of*

the *amparo*: those who sue get access to a right or privilege, but the right is not automatically generalized to the broader society. For example, several countries have a robust right to health jurisprudence where individual petitioners can file claims to get access to medicines or treatments that they need to survive or to live a dignified life.[45]

This model is perhaps the purest at fitting the judicial review of socioeconomic rights into traditional patterns of judicial review within Latin America. Benefits can be targeted or given out selectively only to those who actually bring the lawsuit. Further, because constitutional instruments are often (although not always) very complex, the need to bring an individual complaint before receiving the remedy will screen out litigants that lack the resources or knowledge needed to bring the suit.[46]

In a second model (which I have elsewhere called "negative injunction"), courts use socioeconomic rights as a way to block policy changes (such as austerity measures) that weaken the economic position of an individual or group.[47] Whereas in the first model, socioeconomic rights are turned into individual entitlements to social goods, in the second model they are modeled as negative rights to stop governmental invasion of pre-existing entitlements. Thus, courts in Brazil have prevented austerity measures imposing cuts in civil servant pensions;[48] courts in Colombia have stopped the state from using austerity to reduce the real value of civil

---

Social and Economic Rights in the Developing World (Cambridge: Cambridge University Press) (finding that in Brazil, judges heard a large number of individual cases on the right to health and tended to grant relief, but that they shied away from granting relief in system-wide cases); Defensoría del Pueblo, La tutela y el derecho a la salud 2012, at 226 tbl. 8 (showing that the percentage of all individual complaint or *tutela* cases in Colombia involving the right to health has hovered between 23 and 40 percent of all individual complaints filed in the country in the last decade); Varun Gauri, Jeffrey K. Staton and Jorge Vargas Cullell (2015), "Transparency and compliance: The Costa Rican Supreme Court's monitoring system" (2015), *J. Pol.*, **77**, 774 (describing and critiquing the Costa Rican Court's individualistic model of enforcement), available at: http://www.law.uchicago.edu/files/files/staton_transparency_compliance.pdf (accessed 2 October 2017).

[45] *See* n 44.

[46] *See* Hoffmann and Bentes (n 44) (noting the complexity of the Brazilian individual complaint instruments needed to bring an individual suit).

[47] *See* Landau (n 1), at 444–47.

[48] *See, e.g.*, Daniel Brinks (2011), "'Faithful servants of the regime': The Brazilian Constitutional Court's role under the 1988 Constitution", in Gretchen Helmke and Julio Rios-Figueroa (eds), *Courts in Latin America* (New York: Cambridge University Press), p. 128 (describing some of these cases and noting that the Brazilian STF is most likely to step in in cases that combine corporatist interests of fellow judges with the interests of the general public).

servant salaries.[49] An interesting combination of both the individualized and negative injunction models is the *corralito* litigation in Argentina, where the courts never flatly struck down an austerity policy freezing bank accounts but did issue a myriad of individualized injunctions granting relief to individual petitioners, generally well after the fact.[50] The negative injunction model offers a second interesting way of squaring the judicial review of socioeconomic rights with traditional theories of judicial role. Courts issuing such a remedy are not required to create social programs, but merely exercise a veto over government attempts to make cuts.

A full assessment of these models of litigation is beyond the scope of this chapter; their effects at any rate are highly complex and contingent on institutional conditions.[51] For our purposes it is sufficient to see some of their limits in terms of social transformation. The individualized model works by giving individual petitioners the resources and knowledge to sue for access to a social good that they are entitled to under existing systems; the negative injunction model stops the state from constricting existing programs. Neither model aims to build programs that do not yet exist, and therefore to expand the social safety net. The logic of both is to regulate existing social welfare programs (which are often quite under-inclusive in Latin America), rather than to draw the marginalized into those programs.[52] It thus may be the case in some countries that there is a robust

---

[49] *See* Decision C-1433 of 23 October 2000 (holding that all public sector workers have a right not to have the real value of their salaries decrease from year to year); C-1064 of 10 October 2011 (modifying that holding so that only poorer workers making less than twice the minimum wage would receive absolute protection for the real value of their salaries, and allowing reductions in salaries for wealthier workers during some conditions).

[50] For a description of the cases, *see* Catalina Smulovitz (2006), "Judicialization of protest in Argentina: The case of corralito", in Enrique Peruzzotti and Catalina Smulovitz (eds), *Enforcing the Rule of Law: Social Accountability in the New Latin American Democracies* (Pittsburgh: University of Pittsburgh Press), p. 55.

[51] *See, e.g.*, Brinks and Forbath (n 19), at 1951 (noting that a comprehensive evaluation of the impact of socioeconomic rights litigation may be "beyond the reach of empirical research altogether" because of the complexity of the question, and pointing out that individualized litigation that directly reaches the affluent may nonetheless have indirect effects on the poor).

[52] For similar arguments on the impact of individual litigation on the poor because of selection in terms of which actors bring lawsuits, *see* Octavio Luis Motta Ferraz, "Harming the poor through social rights litigation: Lessons from Brazil", *Tex. L. Rev.*, **89**, 1643 (arguing that the Brazilian right to health litigation distributes resources towards the relatively affluent by providing those with the resources to sue with a virtually unqualified right to health); Landau (n 1) (arguing that the same effect obtained even with the relatively easy to use Colombian *tutela*).

socioeconomic rights jurisprudence, but that jurisprudence has relatively little transformative effect.

B. Limitations on Judicial Role and Judicial Capacity

One way to understand the pattern of enforcement in Latin America is to note that making socioeconomic rights justiciable does not cause the legitimacy and capacity worries that animated the enforcement dilemma to disappear. Instead, it forces courts to face those dilemmas, with the risk that courts will be insufficiently bold. In short, one perspective on the limitations on judicial review of socioeconomic rights is that they stem from courts that are unduly traditionalist and take a limited view of the separation of powers.

Mark Tushnet, for example, notes that while the proponents of socioeconomic rights review properly point out that socioeconomic rights cases do not raise difficulties that are different in kind from negative rights, they do often raise problems that are different in degree.[53] Both positive rights like healthcare and negative rights like due process may involve the spending of money and the setting of priorities, for example, but positive rights require a bigger set of alterations to the status quo and therefore involve courts in these issues to a greater extent.[54]

From this perspective, the individualized remedy and negative injunction strategies may be attractive to judges because they do not place courts in a difficult position from the standpoint of judicial role or capacity. Both remedies look like the kinds of orders that courts have long been accustomed to issuing, and which are relatively easy to enforce. Neither requires some act that would require the court to gain an unusual amount of information or which would be unusually difficult to carry out.

To a degree, these constraints on judicial role and capacity are malleable. The Colombian Constitutional Court, for example, has adopted a celebrated approach with its two major structural interventions in 2004 and 2008. In the first case, the Court used its doctrine of a "state of unconstitutional conditions" to undertake a structural intervention in the public policy on Colombia's roughly 3 million internally displaced persons.[55] The doctrine allows the Court to offer broader structural remedies, rather than those merely resolving the individual case at issue, when it identifies a large number of potential claimants and systematic failures at the policy

---

53 *See* Mark Tushnet (2006), *Weak Courts, Strong Rights* (Princeton: Princeton University Press), p. 234.

54 *See* id.

55 *See* Decision T-025 of 22 January 2004.

level.[56] The Court held that although a legal framework existed, national and local authorities in fact were not implementing a coherent set of policies, due to failures in both capacity and will.[57] In the second (healthcare) case, the Court avoided using the language of a state of unconstitutional conditions but nonetheless undertook a series of structural remedies in order to repair systematic problems within the healthcare system.[58] These included problems with the definition of the standard package of benefits, the benefits received by poorer households in the subsidized system versus those held by households in the contributory system, and problems with the flow of financial resources within the system.[59]

As several scholars have noted, these structural cases (both of which are still ongoing) are innovative. They have adopted a model that requires that state to report on its progress at certain intervals, both through written report and regular public hearings.[60] The Court then refines its orders in response to these reports. Further, the Court has drafted in civil society in interesting ways. In the displaced persons case, for example, the Court has relied heavily on a Monitoring Commission made up of elements of civil society to monitor the state and feed policy information to the Court.[61] These cases build off of the structural injunctions found in the United States and several other contexts, but tailor that model to the Colombian context.[62]

---

56 *See* id., § 7 (laying out a five-factor test for declaring a state of unconstitutional conditions, including the "(i) massive and generalized violation of various constitutional rights affecting a significant number of people, (ii) the prolonged omission of the authorities to comply with their obligations to guarantee rights, (iii) the failure to produce legislative, budgetary, or administrative measures necessary to avoid the violation of rights, (iv) the existence of a social problem whose solution requires the intervention of various entities, requires the adoption of a complex and coordinated grouping of actions and demands a level of resources that requires an important additional budgetary effort, (v) if all the people affected by the same problem were to accede to the tutela to protect their rights, greater judicial congestion would be produced").

57 *See* id., § 6.3.

58 *See* Decision T-760 of 31 July 2008, § III (listing the individual and structural orders of the Court).

59 *See* id., § 6.

60 *See* Cesar Rodriguez-Garavito (2011), "Beyond the courtroom: The impact of judicial activism on socioeconomic rights in Latin America", *Tex. L. Rev.*, **89**, 1669, 1693–94 (describing the Court's process of enforcement in T-025).

61 *See* Cesar Rodriguez-Garavito and Diana Rodriguez-Franco (2010), *Cortes y cambio social: Como la corte constitucional transform el desplazamiento forzado en Colombia* (Bogotá: DeJusticia), p. 85 (giving an overview of the composition of the Commission and its work).

62 On U.S. structural injunctions, *see*, for example, Malcolm Feeley and

The Colombian structural decisions are therefore justly celebrated within the region, and useful to spark a debate on judicial role. They help to focus attention on a set of questions that remain underexplored, and focus more attention than is typical in the new constitutionalism to questions of remedy. The healthcare case is a good example: the Court adopted a structural approach after years in which it had issued individual remedies, and in the face of concern about the equity effects of those remedies.[63] The case in turn has allowed the Court to achieve broader goals for more marginalized groups, such as the equalization of benefits for those citizens in the subsidized regime. The decisions also highlight ways in which courts may be able to overcome deficits in judicial capacity. The Court's skillful using of public hearings and the media may be helpful in achieving compliance in complex cases, and its reliance on civil society commissions and other devices might help to ameliorate some of the weaknesses in the Court's monitoring and information-gathering capabilities.[64]

At the same time, limitations on socioeconomic rights enforcement appear in part to be political, rather than just being based on judicial role conception or a lack of judicial capacity.[65] The Colombian Court's dramatic structural interventions have coexisted with a very large number of individualized judgments on health, pensions, and other social rights.[66] As I explain in the next section, part of the answer to this puzzle is that

---

Edward Rubin (2000), *Judicial Policy Making and the Modern State: How the Courts Reformed America's Prisons* (Cambridge: Cambridge University Press).

63 *See* Alicia Ely Yamin and Oscar Parra Vera (2010), "Judicial protection of the right to health in Colombia: From social demands to individual claims to public debates", *Hastings Int'l & Comp. L. Rev.*, **33**, 431, 444–45.

64 For a more in-depth discussion of these points, *see* David Landau (2013), "Aggressive weak-form remedies", *Const. Ct. Rev.*, **5**, 244 (South Africa) (examining ways in which aspects of the Colombian model of structural review could be useful in the South African context).

65 *See, e.g.*, Paola Bergallo (2011), "Courts and social change: Lessons from the struggle to universalize access to HIV/AIDS treatment in Argentina", *Tex. L. Rev.*, **89**, 1611 (finding that the Argentine courts began treating the HIV/AIDS issue with structural remedies, but later turned to more targeted litigation that affected only discrete individuals and groups).

66 Furthermore, some of the Court's structural jurisprudence has been targeted at relatively affluent groups. An example is the UPAC litigation discussed below, where the Court attempted to use a large-scale remedy to bail out mostly middle-class homeowners in the formal housing system. *See* text below accompanying nn 76–81. And it is notable that the health case combined orders designed to aid the poor directly (e.g., requiring an equalization in benefit packages) with those designed to repair the system for the public more broadly (e.g., requiring that the package of benefits be clarified and updated to take account of the Court's *tutela* jurisprudence). *See* T-760, § III.

theorists still overlook the extent to which judicial review can be a majoritarian rather than counter-majoritarian exercise. Social rights enforcement is an area where an undue emphasis on counter-majoritarian courts may overemphasize the degree to which courts will carry out projects of social change for the most marginalized.

C. The Majoritarian Court

The postulate that courts are basically counter-majoritarian institutions has long infused U.S. constitutional theory, forming the core concern of theorists for several generations. The central challenge, from a counter-majoritarian perspective, is how to justify unelected judges seizing the power of constitutional interpretation away from political actors. The most famous set of responses revolve around the political process theory school of John Hart Ely: courts wield power legitimately when they work to correct defects in the political process, and in particular to unblock channels that have prevented discrete and insular minorities from exercising political power or from being represented.[67] Ely's core set of concerns were the civil rights movement in the United States, but his theory works well as an underpinning of the transformative project of new constitutionalism: courts have a mandate to transform the political system for the benefit of traditionally marginalized groups.[68] Scholars of comparative constitutional law have gravitated towards this conception, arguing, for example, that courts are perhaps more likely than other branches of government to be a voice for the poor.[69]

Both recent and older work has shown that the theory of the counter-majoritarian court (as a descriptive reality, rather than a normative goal) is unlikely to hold. Recent work suggests that the Supreme Court gained power by being useful to prevailing political coalitions, rather than being

---

[67] *See* John Hart Ely (1981), *Democracy and Distrust: A Theory of Judicial Review* (Cambridge, MA: Harvard University Press).

[68] For an example of the appropriation of the political process theory in comparative constitutional law, *see* Theunis Roux (2013), *The Politics of Principle: The First South African Constitutional Court* (Cambridge: Cambridge University Press), p. 334 (exploring the puzzle of the South African Constitutional Court's weakness in enforcing political rights, which would seem to be the most justified exercises of judicial review under Ely's theory).

[69] *See, e.g.*, Siri Gloppen (2006), "Courts and social transformation: An analytical framework", in Roberto Gargarella et al. (eds), *Courts and Social Transformation in New Democracies: An Institutional Voice for the Poor?* (London: Routledge), p. 35 (mapping the conditions under which courts may be receptive to pro-poor claims).

independent of those coalitions.[70] In other words, the Supreme Court has rarely departed from the will of the prevailing coalition for very long, because of the selection of justices and because of pressure that can be put on the Court.[71] More strongly, some recent work finds that the Court's decisions have rarely gone against public opinion. Finally, an older line of work argues that the Court has generally been unable to spark significant social change unless it has substantial political support. The myth of the heroic court in cases like *Brown v. Board of Education*[72] has been undercut by research showing that real progress was limited until the Court gained the support of Congress.[73] Put together, these two lines of work have cast doubt on the idea that courts in the United States are likely to be the voice of the marginalized in the face of a hostile or indifferent political system.

Both dominant models of socioeconomic rights enforcement in Latin America can fruitfully be seen from the perspective of a majoritarian rather than counter-majoritarian judiciary. The individualized model of enforcement allows courts to issue relief to give benefits, like a treatment or a pension, directly to a claimant, and to do so at low risk.[74] It also allows courts to offer relief in individual cases without having to deal directly with the collective consequences or costs of a policy change. It essentially allows the court to give benefits to individual litigants without having to pick up the tab. Finally, it allows the court to look like the good face of government, in contrast to the service provider which failed to do its job properly and is characterized as the dysfunctional face. The negative injunction model allows courts to restore civil service or other benefits which are being threatened by the political branches.[75] These cases thus

---

[70] *See* Keith Whittington (2008), *The Political Foundations of Judicial Supremacy* (Princeton: Princeton University Press) (arguing that political leaders gave power to the Court because it served their interests to do so); Mark Graber (1993), "The non-majoritarian difficulty: Legislative deference to the judiciary", *Studs. Am. Pol. Dev.*, **7**, 35 (arguing that many of the Court's major cases were the result of Congress inviting the judiciary to decide in order to take pressure off of intra-party splits).

[71] For the classic statement of this position, *see* Robert A. Dahl (1957), "Decision-making in a democracy: The Supreme Court as a national policy-maker", *J. Pub. L.*, **6**, 279 (arguing that the Court is unlikely to be a protector of minority interests against the majority for very long).

[72] 347 U.S. 483 (1954).

[73] *See, e.g.*, Gerald Rosenberg (2008), *The Hollow Hope: Can Courts Bring About Social Change?*, 2nd edn (Chicago: University of Chicago Press).

[74] *See* text accompanying nn 44–46.

[75] *See* text accompanying nn 47–49.

again allow the court to play the benevolent face of government in contrast to the threats being made by other state institutions. These cases are much riskier for the court than individualized cases, since they involve a far more significant range of state interests (often, macroeconomic policy management or fiscal stability). But the potential rewards for a court, in term of popularity, are also significant because of the salience of these cases.

Majoritarianism raises a set of concerns that run beyond traditionalist conceptions of judicial role or limitations on capacity, because it suggests that in many contexts, courts have political incentives to favor the interests of groups that are relatively affluent, such as what one might call in certain contexts the "middle class". A striking example is the famous Colombian case involving UPAC, the national housing system. When a deep economic crisis threatened that system in the late 1990s, the Constitutional Court stepped in within a context where the other branches of government essentially took little action.[76] It struck down key elements of the existing system and forced the government to provide bailouts and more buyer-friendly loans to several hundred thousand debtors, who were generally not poor (because the formal housing sector was composed of relatively wealthy groups).[77] The Court's actions were highly creative and showed little restraint based on traditional conceptions of judicial role: it held a widely covered public hearing on the issue to which it invited a number of different social groups.[78] Further, after striking down the entire system but deferring the order so as to give the state only a few months to rewrite the entire law,[79] it essentially rewrote key parts of the new law by declaring them only conditionally constitutional. For example, it held that interest rates charged within the system must be below those charged in other parts of the economy because of the constitutionally protected nature of housing.[80] The justice who wrote several of the key opinions was dubbed the "housing justice". He soon

---

[76] *See* Rodrigo Uprimny Yepes (2006), "The enforcement of social rights by the Colombian Constitutional Court: Cases and debates", in Gargarella (n 69), at 127, 136 (describing the context of the UPAC crisis).

[77] In the two key decisions, the Court first struck down the entire existing UPAC system on the grounds that it had been improperly promulgated, *see* Decision C-700 of 16 September 1999, and then upheld the new version of the law passed by the Congress but used the power of conditional constitutionality to effectively rewrite significant portions of the law, *see* Decision C-955 of 26 July 2000.

[78] *See* Decision C-700, id., § VI (describing the hearing).

[79] *See* id., § VII.5 (deferring the effect of the judgment of unconstitutionality until the end of the current legislative term in 2000).

[80] *See* Decision C-955 of 26 July 2000, § V.B.4.

ended his term in the Court and was named on the Liberal party ticket as the unsuccessful vice-presidential candidate.[81]

The political pressures placed on courts in this context vary from system to system in ways that are still not fully understood. In contexts where parties are very strong, like Chile and Mexico, justices' main incentives are likely to be to the parties themselves, and they have relatively little incentive to generate direct public support.[82] This may be one reason why socioeconomic rights jurisprudence continues to be extremely limited in both countries.[83] Where parties are weaker, however, as in Brazil and Colombia, or where the political system is widely held in disrepute (as in many Latin American countries), justices may indeed have a strong incentive to generate the support of the general public. Within Latin America, this incentive sometimes appears to manifest itself in a robust socioeconomic rights jurisprudence that nonetheless benefits relatively affluent groups rather than the most marginalized members of society.

III. THE MANY FUNCTIONS OF SOCIOECONOMIC RIGHTS ENFORCEMENT IN LATIN AMERICA: BEYOND TRANSFORMATION

This section follows on the last one by seeking to give an account of the functions that socioeconomic rights play in Latin American systems. It builds on the key insight developed in the previous sections: many of the patterns of socioeconomic rights enforcement found in the region are essentially majoritarian. Majoritarian exercises of judicial review, like counter-majoritarian exercises, raise a problem of justification, but the nature of the problem is at least partially distinct. While those defending counter-majoritarian exercises must explain why courts should be able to second-guess the decisions of the political branches, those defending

---

81 *See, e.g.*, "El Efecto 'Vice'", Semana, 8 April 2002, available at: http://www.semana.com/noticias-nacion/efecto-vice/20354.aspx (accessed 15 September 2017).

82 South Africa offers an interesting example. Roux notes that the Constitutional Court works in the context of a very strong dominant party, the ANC, and is not well known or particularly popular with the general public. *See* Theunis Roux (2009), "Principle and pragmatism on the Constitutional Court of South Africa", *Int'l J. Const. L.*, **7**, 106, 111. Unlike the Mexican and Chilean courts, the South African court has attempted to enforce socioeconomic rights, but has done so in a highly cautious way, preferring to prod government institutions slowly rather than to appeal directly to the people. *See* id., at 133–36.

83 *See* text accompanying nn 28–36.

majoritarian exercises must explain why courts are useful at all.[84] This section gives a partial account of that utility, at least within the Latin American context. In so doing, it points out that the functions of socio-economic rights enforcement are more diverse than often recognized in the literature: social transformation and poverty-alleviation are of course important aspirations, but social rights enforcement also carries out a range of other functions.

A. Service Provision and Dysfunctional States

Courts providing a high volume of individualized remedies may be working within bureaucratic systems that are dysfunctional. This appears to be the problem in the healthcare systems of both Brazil and Colombia. In both countries, the systems themselves have pervasive problems. The Colombian system uses private healthcare insurers to provide services, under the supervision of the state. But there are important failures at the regulatory, service-provision, and supervisory levels. The state regulators do a poor job defining the standard package of benefits to which patients are entitled; private service providers routinely deny care for items that should be included in that package; and state entities charged with supervision in fact have exercised very little.[85] In Brazil, the system is state run but also plagued with improper denials of care and could move extremely slowly.[86] In systems like these, courts can become almost a part of the bureaucracy, correcting faults within the system and allowing petitioners to get relief. Petitioners have applied to the courts in both countries in large numbers because they know that the courts will get them surer relief, and often quicker relief, than they can get in the ordinary bureaucracy.

The overall effect of this model of courts as service providers is extremely complex, and is an area where more work is needed. There are some cases where a large number of court decisions have induced the bureaucracy to alter their broader policies. This happened with HIV/AIDs medications in both Brazil and Colombia, where bureaucracies began covering the

---

[84] *See*, *e.g.*, Michael C. Dorf (2010), "The majoritarian difficulty and theories of constitutional decision-making", *J. Const. L.*, **13**, 283, 284–85 (the majoritarian nature of judicial review "mostly dissolves [the counter-majoritarian] problem, but it raises a distinct one: Are courts that roughly follow public opinion capable of performing what is generally understood as their core counter-majoritarian function – protecting minority rights against majoritarian excesses? Do American courts, in other words, have a majoritarian difficulty?").

[85] *See* Yamin and Parra Vera (n 63), at 433–39.

[86] *See* Hoffmann and Bentes (n 44).

treatment in response to judicial pressure.[87] There is less evidence that courts using this model can construct improvement in the quality of the bureaucracy. The basic flaws in the Brazilian and Colombian healthcare systems have not been corrected. Indeed, by granting targeted relief to patients who choose to sue – and who are likely among the more vocal and politically powerful – courts may actually reduce the political pressure for reform, allowing a bad model to persist.

Further, judicial intervention in these cases can sometimes exacerbate problems or create new ones. In Brazil, commentators have noted that the jurisprudence creates a "queue-jumping" phenomenon: it allows those who sue to jump to the front of the line, ahead of those waiting for normal bureaucratic channels to operate, which in turn encourages more litigation even for those treatments that would have been covered as a matter of course.[88] In Colombia, the Court created a similar but more complex problem by holding that some treatments outside of the normal package of benefits could be covered if needed and ordered by a court, but would be paid for by the state rather than the private insurer because of their extraordinary nature.[89] This led the private insurers to actually encourage litigation in some cases as a way to get a holding that they could provide an extraordinary service (perhaps invented or unnecessary) and be reimbursed by the state.[90] In turn, the private insurers' behavior led to a flood of judicial orders for state-covered reimbursements, straining the flow of resources within the system.

At the same time, it would be a mistake to view judicial interventions in

---

[87] *See* Ana Cristina Gonzalez and Juanita Duran (2011), "Impact of court rulings on health care coverage: The case of HIV/AIDs in Colombia", *Medicc Rev.*, **13**, 54 (noting that regulators responded to court decisions by adding treatments to the standard package of benefits, but arguing that this was done without adequately considering the fiscal sustainability of the system); Octavio Luis Motta Ferraz (2009), "The right to health in the courts of Brazil: Worsening health inequities", *Health & Hum. Rts. J.*, **11**, 33, 35 (finding that the Congress may have responded in part to an initial wave of litigation on HIV/AIDS by passing a law in 1996 requiring coverage of these medications).

[88] *See* Hoffman and Bentes (n 44), at 143 (arguing that queue-jumping harms the rest of the members of the system, many of whom are "likely indigent").

[89] *See* Katharine G. Young and Julieta Lemaitre (2013), "The comparative fortunes of the right to health: Two tales of justiciability in Colombia and South Africa", *Harv. Hum. Rts. J.*, **26**, 179, 189.

[90] *See* id., at 190 (arguing that the Court's reimbursement rule for non-standard packages of benefit treatments encouraged substantial corruption). The same rule led them often to deny coverage for included treatments in an effort to get a judicial order holding the treatment to be outside the standard package and thus reimbursable. *See* id.

these cases as pathological. They have a powerful political logic because these interventions allow courts to position themselves as defenders of the public against an indifferent or incompetent bureaucracy. Citizens favor these interventions because they provide at least some avenue through which they can get redress for situations in which they are being treated shabbily by private or state actors providing essential services. And the state itself may not mind a model that provides relief to a group of petitioners while reducing the pressure to reform or improve the overall architecture of the system. Finally, the service-provision model at least gives a substantial group of petitioners access to services that would have been denied to them otherwise. In this sense, it serves as a kind of institutional second-best for a world in which bureaucracies function poorly and there is little prospect of improvement.

B. Democracy-Promotion and Principal–Agent Problems

The second broad pattern of enforcement – the negative injunction – is generated by a related political logic. Scheppele has noted that in some situations, courts may have a plausible claim to be a better representative of the public than the political branches themselves.[91] She uses the Hungarian austerity decision of 1995 to make this point. Under significant pressure from international financial institutions, the government agreed to huge cuts in social welfare programs. Particularly because Hungary was transitioning from a communist state, these cuts affected a broad swath of society and focused on the middle class rather than the poor.[92] For example, they cut social security benefits and programs of support for new parents. The Constitutional Court struck many of the cuts down because they did not adequately protect vested property interests and settled expectations. The Court's decision was immediately very popular with the public and led to further negotiations between the state and the international institutions, which softened the impact of the austerity measures in the final version.[93]

Scheppele's story fits nicely within a majoritarian, principal–agent model of review. Rather than defending the interests of marginalized

---

[91] *See* Kim Lane Scheppele (2004), "A realpolitik defense of social rights", *Tex. L. Rev.*, **82**, 1821.

[92] *See, e.g.*, Andras Sajo (2006), "Social rights as middle class entitlements in Hungary", in Roberto Gargarella et al. (n 69), p. 83 (arguing that the Hungarian decision largely protected the economic interests of the middle class from cuts in the communist-era welfare state).

[93] *See* Scheppele (n 91), at 1947 (according to opinion polls, "overwhelming majorities" of between 80 and 90 percent of the Hungarian population approved of the Court's decision in its immediate aftermath).

groups against the majority, the court defends the public against its representatives in cases where these representatives are not adequately carrying out popular will. The court acts as a "fire alarm" mechanism to alert the people that something has gone wrong in the relationship between the governors and the governed.[94] In the case of Hungary, one might argue that the extreme pressure applied by international financial institutions coupled with problems in the developing party system created a representation problem.[95] The Court's decision flagged the problem and restarted the negotiation process.

Austerity measures may represent one example of the kind of situation in which the principal–agent model is likely to work well. Domestic institutions may be under significant pressure from international institutions, and may be more responsive to those institutions than to domestic political actors. Further, the crisis itself may lead political institutions to overestimate the need to undertake structural reforms and to underestimate the damage done to the affected population.

An example is the Colombian economic crisis of the late 1990s, already alluded to above, and during which the country was in active negotiation to receive funding from international financial institutions in return for sweeping structural reforms.[96] A crisis in the system of interest rates for the formal housing sector placed hundreds of thousands of middle-class debtors in danger of default, but the political branches did not design any effective response.[97] Civil society groups made up of diffuse debtors tried to form but claimed that they had trouble reaching the political branches, perhaps because they were not a pre-existing pressure group with access to the levers of power.[98] The Court stepped in and forced attention to the

---

94 *See* David Law (2009), "A theory of judicial review and judicial power", *Geo. L.J.*, **97**, 723, 731 (arguing for a principal–agent theory of judicial review in which the courts act as a fire alarm against government that exceeds its bounds and mobilizes the populace against those excesses).

95 *See* Scheppele (n 91), at 1929 ("At that point, theories of democratic accountability go silent, and in fact, it is hard to see just how countries whose policies are being micromanaged by outsiders can meet the basic test of democratic politics – that public policy is accountable to the preferences of voters.").

96 *See* Sebastian Edwards and Roberto Steiner (2000), "On the crisis hypothesis of economic reform: Colombia 1989–91", *Cuadernos de Economia*, **112**, 445–493, (describing the "extended facility agreement" Colombia entered into with the IMF, for the first time in its history, in June 1999, to carry out sharp spending cuts, labor reforms, and other measures).

97 *See* Uprimny (n 76), at 136.

98 *See*, *e.g.*, (1998), "Usuarios piden acabar con el UPAC", *El Tiempo*, 18 November, available at: http://www.eltiempo.com/archivo/documento/MAM-853292 (accessed 18 September 2017).

issue by holding an extraordinarily broad public hearing at which politicians, experts, and civil society groups testified; it then forced legislative action by entirely striking down the existing system but deferring that decision for a few months in order to give the president and the Congress time to remake the law.[99] The justice who wrote some of these major decisions (and who later ran for vice-president) defended them in the press by paraphrasing the great populist leader Jorge Eliécer Gaitán: "The people are more intelligent than their leaders."[100] The argument of the Court seemed to be that it was correcting a majoritarian democratic failure; a failure noted even by the dissenters.[101] The Court also struck down reductions to the budget that reduced real public sector salaries, although it later gave the state more flexibility in implementing these reforms and gave reinforced protection only to lower income workers.[102] A variant of the same basic story may explain anti-austerity decisions in Brazil and Argentina, and the post-economic crisis in Europe.[103]

A major problem with the principal–agent model is that the line between democracy-enhancing interventions and populism is quite thin, and perhaps impossible to draw. There may indeed be moments where courts represent democratic popular will better than the political branches. But courts may also claim this mantle in cases where political institutions make an informed, although painful, choice for austerity in response to a full

---

[99] *See* Decision C-700 of 16 September 1999, § VI; (1999), "UPAC: se midieron las fuerzas", *El Tiempo*, 28 July, available at: http://www.eltiempo.com/archivo/documento/MAM-894490 (accessed 18 September 2017).

[100] *See* Interview with José Gregorio Hernández (200), *La República*, 12 November ("[I]f you are talking about the criticisms, there is no need for the Court to discuss them because they have already been defeated, and in what a fashion, by public opinion . . . [T]he work of the Constitutional Court has been well received by the people. Because the people are much more intelligent, as Gaitán says, than their leaders.").

[101] *See* Decision C-700 of of 16 September 1999 (Eduardo Cifuentes Munoz and Vladimiro Naranjo Mesa, dissenting) ("The absence of leadership in a country that does not confront its great conflicts and concerns, for the moment hides the impropriety of the actions of the Court and leads one to look with indulgence on its evident extra-limiting of powers. But the enormous cost of this kind of intervention, although momentarily popular, will gravitate negatively on the constitutional jurisdiction that, in the end, will not resist this great disfigurement.").

[102] *See* Decision C-1433 of 23 October 2000; Decision C-1064 of 10 October 2001.

[103] *See, e.g.*, Roberto Cisotta and Danielle Gallo (2014), "The Portuguese Constitutional Court case law on austerity measures: A reappraisal", LUISS Guido Carli Working Paper 4/2014 (describing key decisions of the Portuguese Constitutional Court), available at: http://eprints.luiss.it/1298/1/WPG_04-14_Cisotta_Gallo.pdf (accessed 18 September 2017).

range of political input, and courts overturn this choice because they can reap the benefits of a popular decision without having to pay any costs. They may falsely, in other words, tell the public that it can have its cake and eat it too. Much may depend on the exact model of review used by the court, and in particular whether the decision leaves room for negotiation or instead shuts down political options.[104]

The aim here, at any rate, is not to make a normative evaluation of a complex form of judicial review, but merely to point out that the phenomenon – like the service provision model explored above – has a political logic. While courts face significant risks in striking down major pieces of austerity legislation, they can also position themselves as the guardians of popular input against distorted or poorly functioning political institutions.

C. Constructing Constitutional Culture

Finally, it may be that a majoritarian enforcement of socioeconomic rights – particularly through the individualized model – is helpful in constructing a constitutional culture, or a culture where actors outside the judiciary have taken constitutional values seriously. This is an area in which far more research must be done, since we know almost nothing about how constitutional cultures are constructed in different contexts. Nonetheless, it may be plausible that a broadly majoritarian model of socioeconomic rights enforcement, which targets the middle class or general public rather than the marginalized, would be helpful to the construction of a constitutional culture. The service provision model explained above may demonstrate why: citizens who receive direct relief from the courts in the face of a recalcitrant bureaucracy will see a constitution that works materially in their favor. Under this theory, citizens may become attached to constitutions because of the material benefits they receive from them, rather than symbolic or abstract decisions.

The Colombian case provides some evidence that this pathway is a potential one. Since the economic crisis of the late 1990s, a very high percentage of individual complaints (or *tutelas*) filed in the country have been based on socioeconomic rights (chiefly rights related to healthcare or

---

[104] An example is the comparison of the two salary decisions issued by the Colombian Constitutional Court. The first required salary increases for all public sector workers equal to the rate of inflation; the second created more flexibility by requiring such increases in all circumstances only for poorer workers making less than twice the minimum wage, and allowing real decreases for other workers if adequately justified by the state. *See* n 101.

pensions). The percentage of all individual *tutelas* on the right to health alone has hovered between 20 and 40 percent since 1999, reaching a high of 40 percent in 2008.[105] The Court has maintained this jurisprudence despite a series of critiques by important legal actors. In an important 1997 decision, Justice Eduardo Cifuentes Munoz (the creator of the Colombian "vital minimum" doctrine) argued that the flood of individual *tutelas* was distorting the healthcare system and having problematic equity effects, and tried to order changes in the judicial approach.[106] This decision did not stem the sharp increase in healthcare *tutelas*. Moreover, the 2008 structural healthcare decision (written by Manuel Jose Cepeda, a designer of the court and later one of its most influential justices) was driven partly by concerns about the equity and distortions caused by individual relief.[107] This decision may have reduced the volume of healthcare *tutelas* somewhat (down from 40 percent of dockets in 2008 to just over 20 percent two years later), but it has not caused the Court to eliminate this line of cases.[108]

We do not know why this is. It does seem likely, though, that the Court's individualized socioeconomic rights jurisprudence played some role in protecting the Court against backlash. Two presidents – Ernesto Samper and Alvaro Uribe – as well as the Supreme Court launched attacks against the Court between 1996 and 2002.[109] In each case, the Court and its allies took the same approach: they framed proposals that at times were rather narrow changes to the Court's powers, and at other times sweeping attacks on a number of aspects of judicial power, as grave threats to the *tutela* itself. During the discussion of the Supreme Court's relatively technical proposal to disallow *tutelas* from being taken against ordinary judicial decisions, the then president of the Constitutional Court stated that the measure would "deal a mortal blow to the *tutela*".[110] Similarly, during discussion of then-President Uribe's much more sweeping propos-

105 *See* Defensoria del Pueblo (n 44), at 226 tbl. 8.

106 *See* Decision SU-111 of 9 August 1997.

107 *See* Yamin and Parra Vera (n 63), at 444–45.

108 *See* Defensoria del Pueblo (n 44), at 226 tbl. 8.

109 *See* Year V, 329 Gaceta del Congreso, 15 August 1996 (Samper proposal); Year VI, 59 Gaceta del Congreso, 19 March 1997 (Supreme Court and Council of State proposal); Year XI, Gaceta del Congreso 484, 12 November 2002 (Uribe proposal).

110 Year VI, 451 Gaceta del Congreso, 31 October 1997, at 20 (statement of Antonio Barrera). The president of the Supreme Court, after the effort had failed, would claim that the Constitutional Court and its supporters had "incited the population" by framing the reforms as a "conspiracy against the tutela". *See* John Gutierrez (1997), "Congreso no dio la Talla en Reforma de Tutela", *El Tiempo*,

als, which would have disallowed the *tutela* from being taken against socioeconomic rights or judicial decisions, required a super-majority to strike down constitutional amendments and laws, and closed off judicial review of declarations of emergency and states of internal commotion, the Court quickly met in special session and unanimously approved a statement that the reforms, while ostensibly technical, "would in reality eliminate the efficacy of the *tutela*".[111] During all of these periods, key allies of the Court in civil society and academia made similar statements. The approach seems to have worked: political actors feared to attack the *tutela* and none of these court-curbing measures were passed. Statements from key political actors make it clear that they were unwilling to go after such a popular instrument, even when prodded by a popular president like Uribe.[112]

What is clear, then, is that the Court managed to construct the *tutela* in a way that made it hard to attack, and the linchpin of *tutela* jurisprudence is individualized socioeconomic rights cases. What remains unclear is the extent to which the constitutional culture around the *tutela* is due to other factors and the extent to which the model can be generalized to other places.

IV. CONCLUSION: CONCEPTUALIZING A MAJORITARIAN COURT IN LATIN AMERICA

This chapter has argued that the purposes of socioeconomic rights jurisprudence in Latin America, have been, in part, misperceived: courts have often assimilated these rights not so they work for the benefit of the marginalized in order to transform society, but so that they bolster the fortunes of more affluent groups. The political incentives and constraints on courts, explained in recent strands of U.S. constitutional theory, make this outcome unsurprising. Courts are largely majoritarian rather than counter-majoritarian actors.

---

28 November, available at: http://www.eltiempo.com/archivo/documento/MAM-680262 (accessed 18 September 2017).

111 *See* (2003), "La Corte se va Lanza en Ristre Contra la Reforma", *El Tiempo*, 31 July, available at: http://www.eltiempo.com/archivo/documento/MAM-991678 (accessed 18 September 2017).

112 *See* (2003), "Reforma Agita Congreso", *El Tiempo*, 1 August (discussing criticism of the proposal in Congress, including both those ostensibly allied with Uribe), available at: http://www.eltiempo.com/archivo/documento/MAM-1034549 (accessed 18 September 2017).

The normative implications of this argument – for socioeconomic rights and other fields of comparative constitutional law – are complex and require further exploration. On the one hand, it seems to dampen the promise of courts to carry out transformative projects, and reminds scholars and policymakers that vigorous or robust patterns of socioeconomic rights enforcement are not necessarily equated with social transformation. On the other hand, the findings here suggest that courts perform a wider range of functions than is often recognized in the literature. Instead of viewing courts as counter-majoritarian actors standing outside of politics, we may continue to gain a more fruitful understanding of judicial politics by viewing judiciaries as integral parts of their own political regimes.

PART III

U.S. Constitutionalism in the 21st Century

8. Constitutional drafting in Latin America: a quantitative perspective*

David S. Law and Tom Ginsburg

I. INTRODUCTION

Generalizations about the practice of constitutional drafting within a region as diverse as Latin America are bound to be inherently imprecise. A single region can be home to considerable constitutional heterogeneity.[1] It is also clear, however, that there exist geographical and regional patterns in the adoption of formal legal rules.[2] Distinctive regional characteristics can endure in the face of globalization for a multitude of reasons. In the case of Latin America, for example, they may be borne of historical, religious, linguistic, and geographical ties, or they may reflect the existence of shared concerns and experiences, such as American hegemony or a legacy of strongman rule.

This chapter offers an empirical overview of constitutional drafting patterns and trends in Latin America over the last 60 years. We use various quantitative measures and indices of constitutional content to contrast Latin America with other regions and shed light on whether and in what ways constitutional drafters in Latin America have responded to frequent concerns such as excessive American influence, overconcentration of executive power, and human rights abuses.

* Our thanks to James Melton and deepest gratitude to Mila Versteeg for generously sharing updated data and similarity scores.

1 *See, e.g.*, Tom Ginsburg (2014), "East Asian constitutionalism in comparative perspective", in Albert H.Y. Chen (ed.), *Constitutionalism in Asia in the Early Twenty-First Century*, pp. 32, 41 (noting the existence of "three broad types of constitutional system" within Asia: "liberal-democratic, hybrid, and socialist-Leninist").

2 *See, e.g.*, Everett M. Rogers (2003), *Diffusion of Innovations*, 5th edn (New York: Free Press), pp. 276–77, 320–21 (discussing the diffusion of policy innovations among neighboring American states and within regions); Zachary Elkins and Beth Simmons (2005), "On waves, clusters, and diffusion: A conceptual framework", *Annals Amer. Academy Pol. & Soc. Sci.*, **538**, 33, 34 (noting that diffusion research seeks to explain the existence of "temporal and spatial clusters of policy reform").

Section II examines the extent to which Latin American countries continue to use the U.S. Constitution as a model for their own constitutions. In both scope and substance, Latin American constitutions are becoming increasingly dissimilar to the U.S. Constitution over time. Indeed, not only has Latin America become increasingly divergent from the model of the U.S. Constitution, but it has become more divergent than the rest of the world.

Section III compares constitutions in Latin America with those of other regions along a number of substantive dimensions. Relative to other regions, constitutional drafting in Latin America is characterized by a stingy approach to executive power and a generous approach to the protection of rights. Latin America's combination of extensive de jure rights, on the one hand, and a long history of autocratic leaders and human rights abuses, on the other, is a reminder that governments do not always deliver in practice what they promise on paper. Prior work suggests that levels of actual respect for rights have improved over the last two decades, with the result that the gap between the promise and the reality of Latin American constitutionalism may be narrowing.[3] As interesting as that line of research happens to be, however, this chapter focuses exclusively on how constitutions are drafted, rather than how they are interpreted or implemented. Accordingly, we deliberately limit our analysis to the text of the constitutions themselves. Our findings suggest that constitutional drafting is characterized to some degree by variation along regional lines, and that there is at least some substance to the notion of a Latin American approach to constitutional drafting.

II. AMERICA ANXIETY: LATIN AMERICA'S ESCAPE FROM THE SHADOW OF THE U.S. CONSTITUTION

As Latin American countries gained their independence and embarked upon drafting a slew of constitutions over the course of the nineteenth century, their constitutional drafters looked routinely to the U.S. Constitution as a model – perhaps too much so in some cases.[4] The earliest

---

[3] David S. Law and Mila Versteeg (2013), "Sham constitutions", *California Law Review*, **863**, 907–11.

[4] George Athan Billias (2011), *American Constitutionalism Heard Round the World, 1776–1989: A Global Perspective* (New York: NYU Press), pp. 129–40; Zachary Elkins, Tom Ginsburg and James Melton (2009), *The Endurance of National Constitutions* (New York: Cambridge University Press 2009), p. 26;

constitutions of Mexico and Venezuela, adopted in 1824 and 1811 respectively, borrowed heavily from the American model, while portions of Argentina's 1853 Constitution and Brazil's 1891 Constitution were copied verbatim from the U.S. Constitution.[5]

It is clear, however, that Latin America's days of using the U.S. Constitution as a model are long over. Different methods of measuring constitutional similarity yield the same conclusion: similarity to the U.S. Constitution among Latin American constitutions declined precipitously over the twentieth century. This trend is evident whether we consider Latin America as a whole or individual countries within the region. Of course, Latin America is not unique in turning away from the U.S. Constitution as a model for constitutional drafting. The declining similarity of new constitutions to the U.S. Constitution is a global trend that holds true of common law and civil law countries, U.S. military allies and non-allies alike.[6] However, the decline in Latin America has outpaced the decline in the rest of the world.

Latin American constitutions exhibit growing dissimilarity to the U.S. Constitution in both their scope and their substantive content. Elkins, Ginsberg and Melton employ a measure of constitutional similarity that focuses on the extent to which constitutions are similar in scope, meaning that they address or omit the same topics.[7] The underlying data from the Comparative Constitutions Project (CCP) encompasses provisions relating to structural matters (such as federalism, presidentialism, and separation of powers) as well as provisions relating to the content and enforcement of rights. The similarity in scope between any two constitutions is calculated by adding up the number of topics that the two constitutions both address or omit, then dividing by the total number of possible topics. The resulting score ranges between 0 and 1: a score of 0 means that two constitutions cover precisely the opposite topics from one another, while a score of 1 means that two constitutions both address and omit exactly the same topics. As Figure 8.1 illustrates, newer Latin American constitutions have over time become increasingly dissimilar to the U.S. Constitution in terms of scope.

Carlos F. Rosenkrantz (2003), "Against borrowings and other nonauthoritative uses of foreign law", *International Journal of Constitutional Law*, **1**, 269; Roberto Gargarella (2013), *Latin American Constitutionalism 1810–2010: The Engine Room of the Constitution* (New York: Oxford University Press).

[5] Billias (n 4), at 105, 124–40.

[6] David S. Law and Mila Versteeg (2012, "The declining influence of the United States Constitution", *New York University Law Review*, **87**, 762–858.

[7] Elkins, Ginsberg and Melton (n 4), at 24–26.

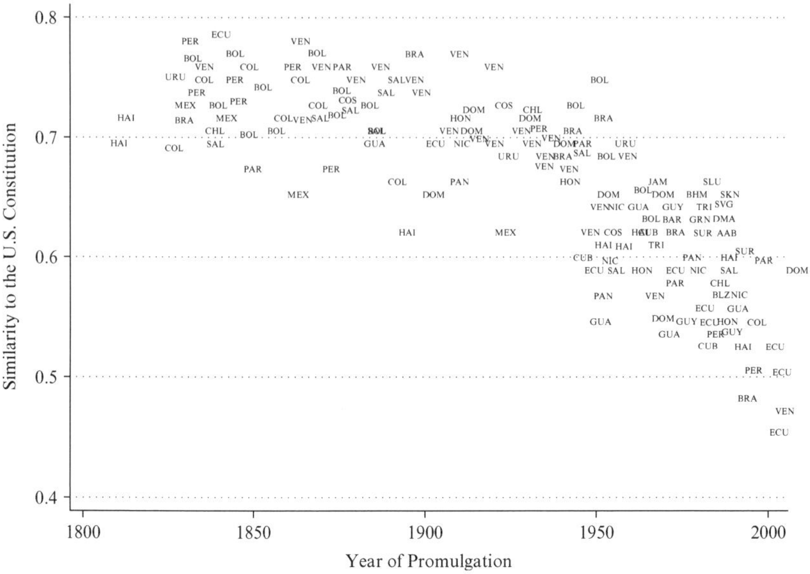

Figure 8.1 Similarity between Latin American constitutions and the U.S. Constitution over time

Another approach to measuring constitutional similarity is to compare the substance of common constitutional elements. This is the approach followed by Law and Versteeg,[8] who employ a constitutional similarity index consisting of 60 rights-related provisions: the more of these 60 provisions that two constitutions share in common, the higher their similarity score. We use an updated version of the data used by Law and Versteeg[9] that captures the presence or absence of these 60 index provisions in every national constitution from 1946 through 2012.[10] Over this period,

[8] Law and Versteeg (n 6).

[9] David S. Law and Mila Versteeg (2011), "The evolution and ideology of global constitutionalism", *California Law Review*, **99**, 1163; Law and Versteeg (n 6).

[10] The approach of focusing only on constitutional rights, and omitting structural provisions from the analysis, somewhat ameliorates the problem of how to weight highly dissimilar provisions for purposes of arriving at a single numerical measure of substantive constitutional similarity. It is one thing to say, for example, that provisions guaranteeing a right to asylum and freedom of expression should count equally for purposes of measuring constitutional similarity between two countries; it is another thing to say that the existence of presidentialism should count the same as the existence of a right to asylum.

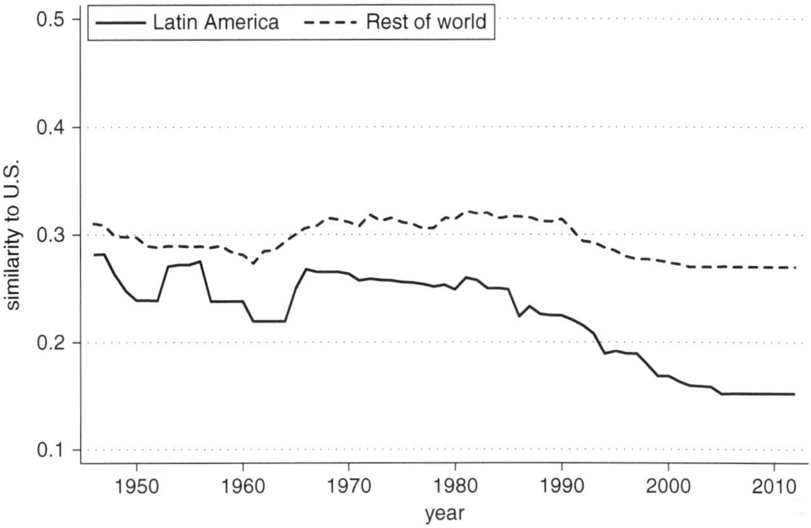

Figure 8.2 Constitutional similarity to the United States in Latin America and the rest of the world

average levels of similarity to the U.S. Constitution declined not only in Latin America, but also in the rest of the world. However, as Figure 8.2. shows, the decline has been much more marked in Latin America: the average level of similarity to the U.S. Constitution started at a lower level and has subsequently declined more precipitously in Latin America than elsewhere. Nor does this decline in similarity appear to be limited to the post-World War II period: analysis of the CCP data, which covers an overlapping set of rights dating all the way back to 1789, suggests that the decline has been underway for well over a century.[11]

The overall trend for Latin America as a region holds true for every individual Latin American country as well. Not a single country traditionally identified as part of Latin America exhibits greater constitutional similarity to the United States now than immediately following World

Consistent with Law and Versteeg ((n 8), at 799 fn 75), "Latin America" is defined as consisting of Argentina, Belize, Bolivia, Brazil, Chile, Colombia, Costa Rica, Ecuador, El Salvador, Guatemala, Guyana, Honduras, Mexico, Nicaragua, Panama, Paraguay, Peru, Suriname, Uruguay, and Venezuela.

[11] Zachary Elkins, Tom Ginsburg and James Melton (2012), "Comments on Law and Versteeg's *The Declining Influence of the United States Constitution*", *New York University Law Review Online*, **87** (11), 15.

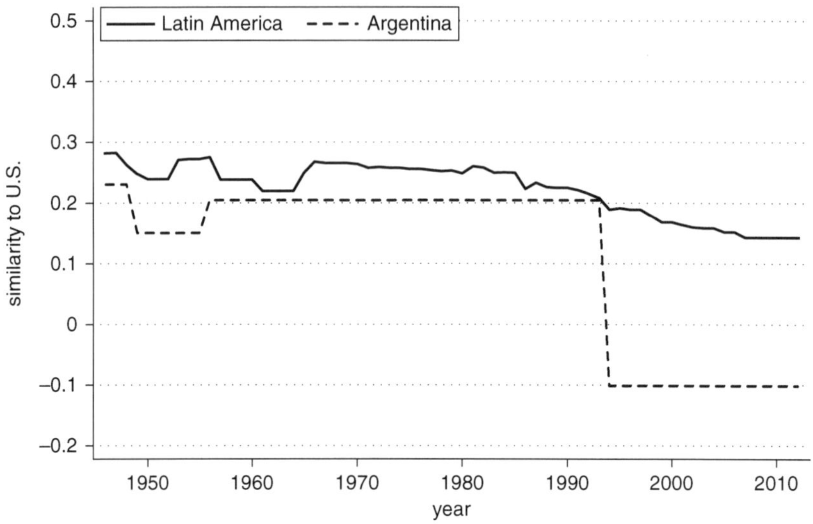

Figure 8.3 Constitutional similarity between Argentina and the United States

War II.[12] A stark example of this turn away from the American model is Argentina, which has swung from slavish imitation to the opposite extreme. Nowhere was the influence of the U.S. Constitution greater than in nineteenth-century Argentina, where U.S. Supreme Court cases were treated as having precedential value.[13] Since Argentina's constitutional amendments of 1994, however, the similarity score between Argentina and the United States has turned negative (see Figure 8.3), which means that the constitutional dissimilarities between the two countries now outnumber the similarities (as measured by their rights-related provisions). Within

---

[12] Suriname's constitutional similarity to the United States is marginally higher now than in 1975, the year that it gained independence from the Netherlands. However, although Suriname is included in the data used to calculate the trend in Latin America as a whole, there are at least two reasons not to include Suriname in generalizations about post-war constitutional patterns in Latin America. First, although Suriname is located on the South American continent, it is Dutch-speaking and often identified as a part of the Caribbean rather than Latin America. Second, the fact that Suriname did not gain independence or possess its own constitution until 1975 prevents comparisons over the entire post-war period.

[13] Jonathan Miller (1997), "The constitutional authority of a foreign talisman: A study of U.S. practice as authority in 19th century Argentina and the Argentine elite's leap of faith", *American University Law Review*, **46**, 1483.

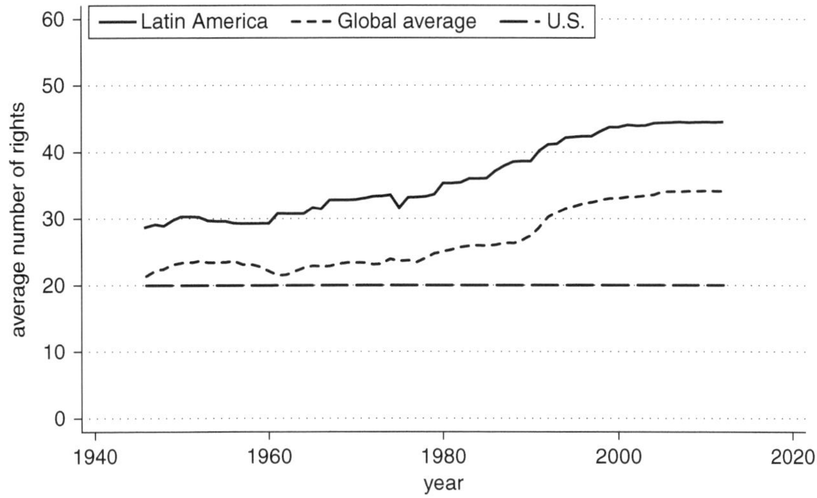

Figure 8.4 Growth in the average number of index rights

Latin America, only the Venezuelan constitution is more dissimilar to the U.S. Constitution than the Argentinian Constitution.

At least part of the explanation for why constitutions around the world, and especially in Latin America, exhibit declining similarity to the U.S. Constitution lies in the fact that the number of rights in the U.S. Constitution has remained fixed at a relatively low level rather than expanding in tandem pace with global trends. One of the most conspicuous global trends in constitutional drafting has been "rights creep", or the tendency of constitutions to incorporate a growing number of rights over time.[14] In 1946, constitutions contained an average of 21 out of the 60 rights-related provisions that make up the Law–Versteeg index of substantive constitutional similarity. With 20 out of 60 rights, the U.S. Constitution was squarely in the global mainstream at that time, at least in terms of the sheer number of rights that it contained. By 2012, however, the global average had grown to 34, while the U.S. Constitution's tally remained fixed at 20.

In sharp contrast to the United States, Latin America has been at the forefront of the global trend of adding new rights. Figure 8.4 contrasts the degree of rights creep in Latin America and the rest of the world, measured in terms of the average number of index provisions found in a given region's constitutions. At present, Latin American constitutions contain

[14] Law and Versteeg (n 9), at 1194–98.

Table 8.1 Latin America's rank in each category among all eight regions

Category	Rank
Endurance	5
Rights	1
Political	1
Economic	2
Criminal	1
Executive Power	5
Legislative Power	5
Scope	3
Detail	2

an average of 45 of the 60 rights-related provisions in the Law–Versteeg similarity index.[15] As noted in Table 8.1, Latin American constitutions lead the world in terms of the number of civil, political, and criminal procedure rights that they boast and are second only to Central and Eastern European constitutions in the number of economic rights.

Declining similarity among Latin Amcrican constitutions to the U.S. Constitution is at least partly a by-product of this expansion in the number of rights that they contain. The sharp drop in Argentina's similarity score seen in Figure 8.3 illustrates how rights creep can cause dissimilarity to the U.S. Constitution. Its 1994 constitutional amendments made explicit a variety of guarantees on matters ranging from consumer rights and gender discrimination to voting rights. As a result, the number of index provisions found in the Argentinian Constitution jumped sharply from 26 to 41, or double the number of index rights found in the U.S. Constitution.

Not all Latin American countries have turned away from the parsimonious American model to the same extent. Chile, in particular, stands out within Latin America for a relatively high level of constitutional similarity to the United States, behind only Guyana and Belize (see Figure 8.5). It is also distinguished by a noticeable rebound in similarity to the U.S. Constitution following the Pinochet regime's adoption of a new constitution in 1980. Even with this rebound, however, constitutional similarity to the United States failed to regain its 1946 levels, and it is now declining again.

Like Chile, Venezuela has experienced fluctuations in constitutional similarity to the United States. Its constitution-making processes of 1946, 1953, and 1961 marked a period of peaks and valleys. Unlike Chile,

---

15 The exact mean for Latin America is 44.5.

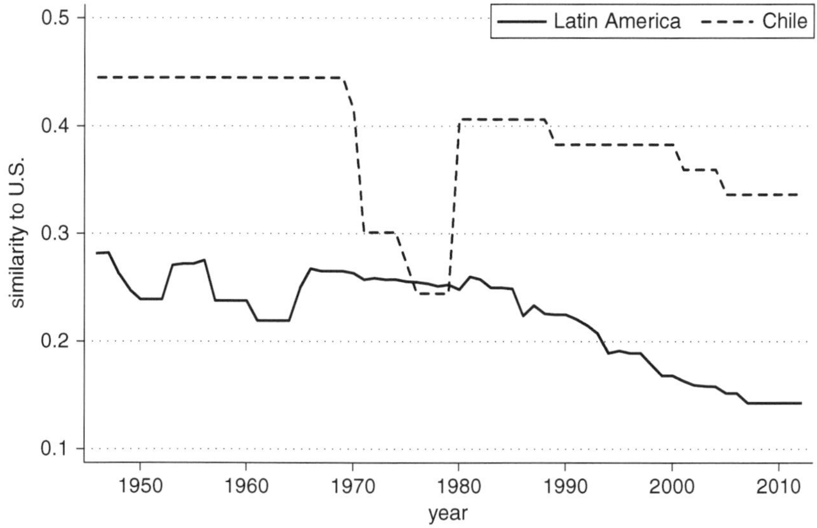

Figure 8.5 Constitutional similarity between Chile and the United States

however, Venezuela did not veer back in the direction of the United States. Instead, it has narrowly edged out Argentina to lay claim to the lowest level of constitutional similarity to the United States in all of Latin America (see Figure 8.6). As is also true of the Argentinian Constitution, the dissimilarities between Venezuela's 1999 Constitution and the U.S. Constitution outnumber the similarities, at least in the area of rights.

The trends in Brazil and Colombia have been less erratic and more typical of the region as a whole. In Brazil, constitutional similarity to the United States fell sharply with the adoption of the 1989 Constitution but recovered slightly with the amendments of 2005, which brought the country more in line with the regional average (see Figure 8.7). Colombia, meanwhile, has acted as a kind of constitutional bellwether for Latin America. One could say that it has tracked the overall regional trend more closely than any other individual country, but it might be more accurate to say that Colombia has instead *anticipated* regional trends. For decades, it held constant at a level slightly below the regional average until the rest of the region drifted down to the same level (see Figure 8.8). It then fell below the regional average again with its adoption of a new constitution in 1991, but the overall trend in the region once again followed suit.

A ranking of all Latin American constitutions in descending order of similarity to the U.S. Constitution as of 2012 reveals an intriguing coincidence. As seen in Table 8.2, Guyana and Belize top the list, but they also

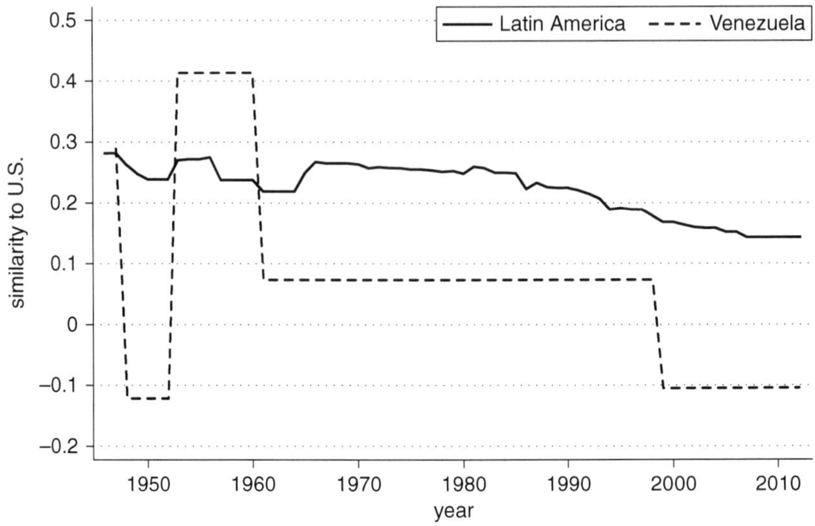

Figure 8.6 Constitutional similarity between Venezuela and the United States

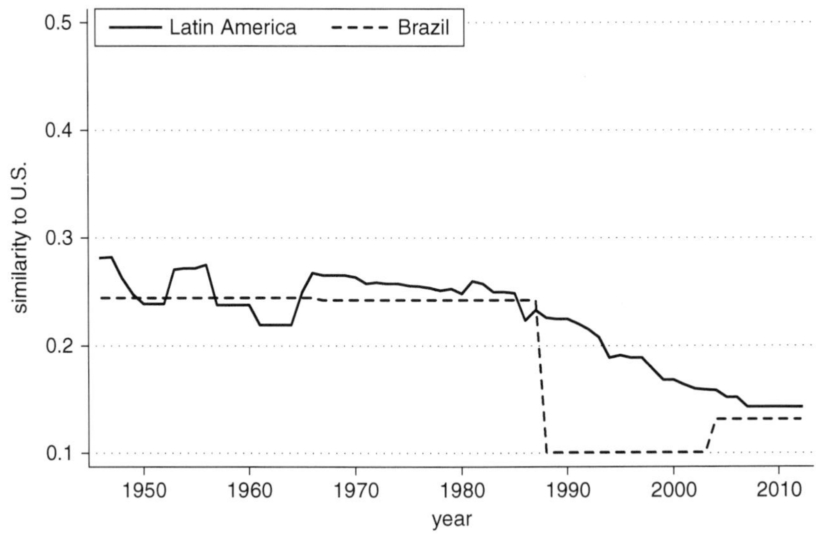

Figure 8.7 Constitutional similarity between Brazil and the United States

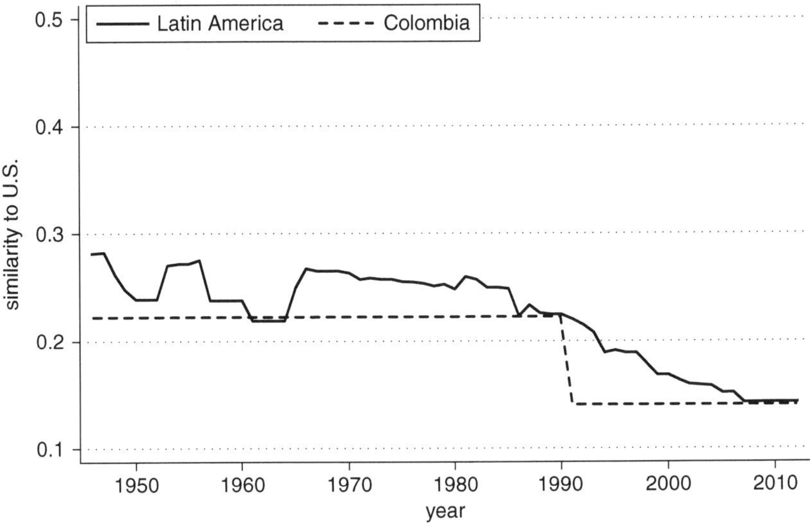

Figure 8.8 *Constitutional similarity between Colombia and the United States*

Table 8.2 *Latin American constitutions ranked by similarity of rights provisions to the U.S. Constitution as of 2012*

Country	Similarity to U.S.
Guyana	0.4348
Belize	0.3852
Chile	0.3367
Mexico	0.3222
Suriname	0.2891
Bolivia	0.2288
Honduras	0.2054
Costa Rica	0.1958
Uruguay	0.1721
Nicaragua	0.1578
Colombia	0.1406
Panama	0.1315
Brazil	0.1315
Paraguay	0.0822
El Salvador	0.0466
Guatemala	0.0175
Ecuador	0.0116
Peru	–0.0469
Argentina	–0.1014
Venezuela	–0.1048

happen to share the distinction of being the only two English-speaking countries in the region. Whether linguistic ties play a role in fostering constitutional similarity or are merely a proxy for the actual causes of the similarity, it may be more than a coincidence that the two countries with the greatest constitutional similarity to the United States also happen to be the only two countries that speak the same language as the United States. At the opposite end of the rankings, Argentina and Venezuela compete for the title of having the most dissimilar constitution to the U.S. Constitution. Although Venezuela edges out Argentina, Argentina's negative score suggests that its repudiation of the American model is complete.

III. A COMPARISON OF LATIN AMERICA WITH OTHER REGIONS

This section offers a descriptive account of how Latin American constitutions as a whole rank globally along a number of substantive dimensions, such as the extent to which they purport to protect various kinds of rights and the degree of executive power that they contemplate. The measures and rankings reported here rely on the wide-ranging data collected by the Comparative Constitutions Project (CCP). Table 8.3 presents the global comparisons for all of the substantive indices, divided further by region to facilitate comparison with Latin America. Each index is described further below.

A. Scope and Detail

We use quantitative measures of the scope and detail of national constitutions developed by Elkins, Ginsberg and Melton,[16] where *scope* refers to the sheer number of topics addressed by the text of the constitution (out of a total of 92 possible topics) and *detail* refers to the number of words per addressed topic. The results, shown in Figure 8.9, reveal that Latin American constitutions have historically exhibited a relatively high level of scope and detail relative to constitutions in other regions. In terms of scope, Latin America led the world along these dimensions in the immediate post-World War II period but was edged out by Eastern Europe and South Asia around the turn of the twenty-first century. In terms of detail, Latin America is second only to South Asia, but the gap is more conspicuous. Middle Eastern and North African constitutions have, on the whole, exhibited the least breadth and detail.

16 Elkins, Ginsberg and Melton (n 4).

Table 8.3 Regional differences in constitutional content

Region	n	Mean Age	Rights Indices				Powers Indices		Specificity	
			Overall	Political	Economic	Criminal	Executive	Legislative	Scope	Detail
Latin America	**33**	**28**	**0.51**	**0.66**	**0.45**	**0.5**	**0.33**	**0.26**	**0.59**	**0.23**
W. Europe/North America	24	79	0.34	0.50	0.30	0.34	0.42	0.27	0.53	0.11
East Europe/ post-Soviet	32	15	0.51	0.72	0.49	0.44	0.47	0.34	0.61	0.08
Sub-Saharan Africa	47	16	0.41	0.64	0.36	0.37	0.41	0.29	0.59	0.16
Middle East/N. Africa	19	33	0.25	0.43	0.22	0.16	0.46	0.23	0.51	0.07
South Asia	7	19	0.42	0.52	0.41	0.41	0.29	0.22	0.62	0.30
Oceania	14	56	0.27	0.42	0.07	0.41	0.18	0.18	0.42	0.19
East Asia	17	34	0.34	0.51	0.33	0.26	0.30	0.32	0.55	0.14
Global Average	*193*	*32*	*0.40*	*0.59*	*0.36*	*0.38*	*0.38*	*0.28*	*0.57*	*0.15*

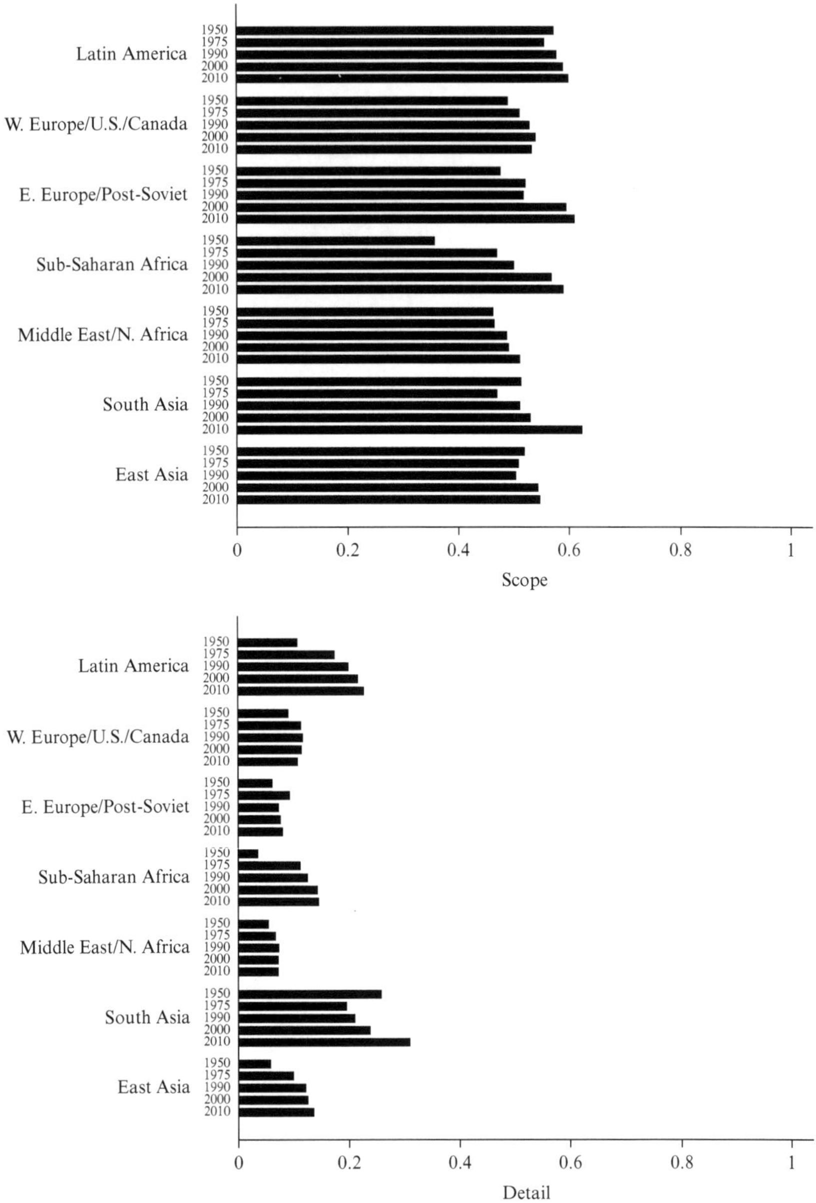

Figure 8.9 Constitutional scope and detail, by region and over time

B. Executive and Legislative Power

Latin America's history of political authoritarianism renders the formal constitutional allocation of powers among government institutions a topic of particular interest. Accordingly, we consider the degree of *executive power* and *legislative power* conferred by Latin American constitutions. Following the approach of Ginsburg,[17] we employ an index of executive power that captures such factors as the maximum number of years that the executive can remain in office and the level of constitutional detail surrounding the selection and removal of the head of state. Our index of legislative power, meanwhile, consists of 32 binary indicators drawn from the CCP data set that correspond to the components of Fish and Kroenig's[18] additive index of de facto legislative power. Figures 8.10 and 8.11 depict the

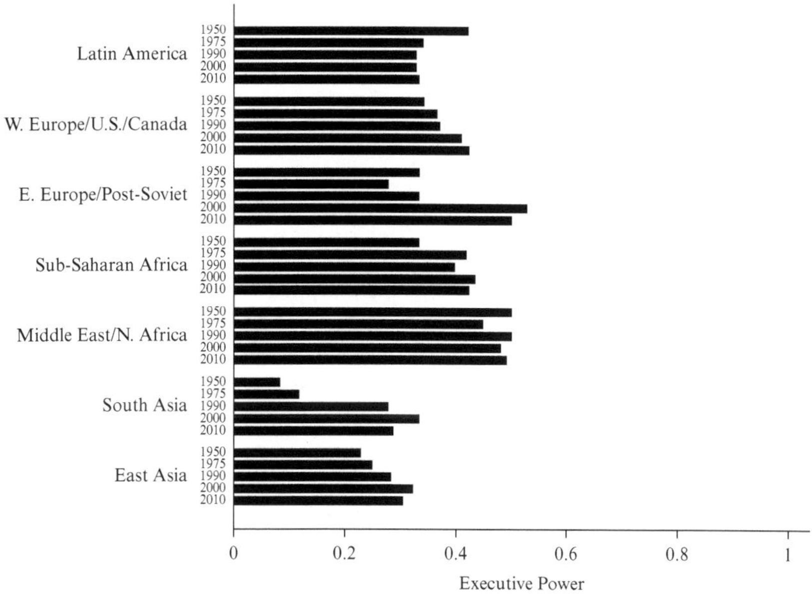

Figure 8.10 *Extent of executive power found in constitutions, by region and over time*

[17] Tom Ginsburg (2009), "The Constitutional Court and the judicialization of Korean politics", in Andrew Harding and Penelope Nicholson (eds), *New Courts in Asia* (London: Routledge).

[18] M. Steven Fish and Mathew Kroenig (2009), *The Handbook of National Legislatures: A Global Survey* (New York: Cambridge University Press).

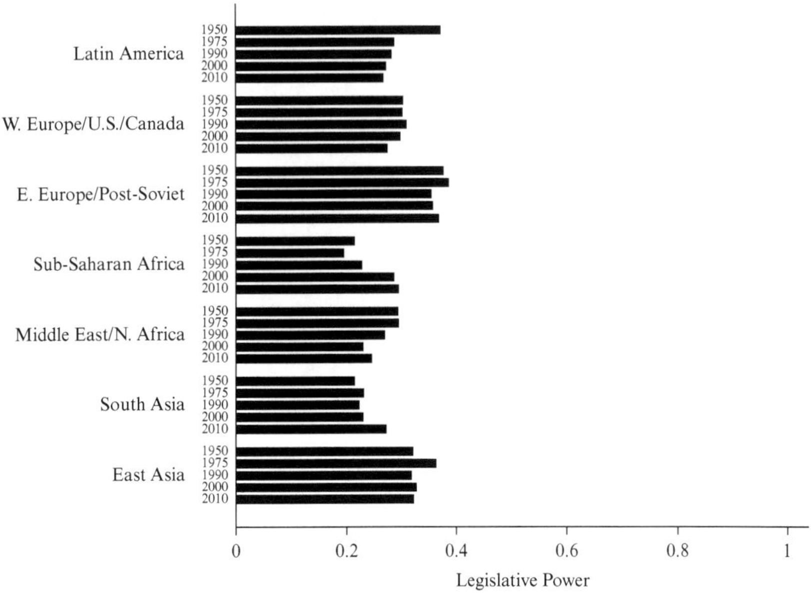

Figure 8.11 Extent of legislative power found in constitutions, by region and over time

levels of executive and legislative power found over time in Latin American constitutions as well as constitutions elsewhere.

The level of formal executive power found in Latin American constitutions declined sharply between 1950 and 1975 as constitutional drafters reacted to a long and problematic history of strong presidentialism and *caudillismo*. In 1950, Latin American constitutions were second only to Middle Eastern constitutions along the dimension of formal executive power; now, Latin America ranks a mere fifth out of eight regions. The relatively stingy de jure rules governing executive power belie the relatively high degree of de facto executive power that continues to be exercised in Latin American countries such as Bolivia, Colombia, and Venezuela, among others. But efforts to constrain power have resulted in shorter formal tenure of leaders (see Figure 8.12), and modestly higher detail on how executives are selected (see Figure 8.13).

Middling levels of de jure executive power in Latin America are matched by middling levels of de jure legislative power. Latin American constitutions are thus unlike either Middle Eastern constitutions, which favor legislative power over executive power, or East Asian constitutions, which exhibit the opposite bias in favor of executive power.

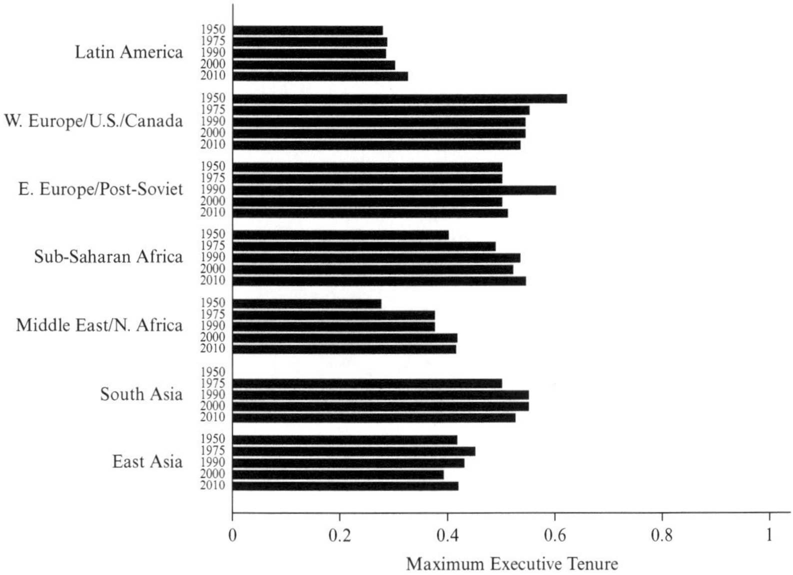

Figure 8.12 Details of executive tenure, by region and over time

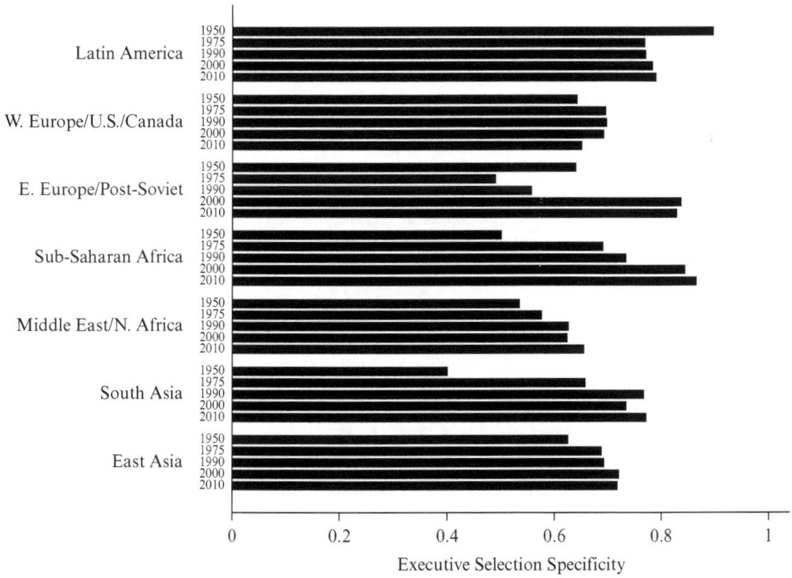

Figure 8.13 Details of executive selection specifity, by region and over time

C. Rights

To measure the degree to which constitutions purport to protect rights, we employ several different indices that correspond to different categories of rights. The first, captured in Figure 8.14a, is an overall rights index, which is simply the percentage of rights included in the constitution, out of a total of 81 rights covered by the CCP data set. (This index overlaps with, but is distinct from, the Law–Versteeg index employed above.) We also created sub-indices for criminal procedure rights, economic rights, and civil and political rights (see Figures 8.14b, c and d). The sub-indices cover a total of 19 civil and political rights, 25 criminal procedure rights, and 19 economic rights. For each type of right, the corresponding sub-index indicates the percentage of that type of right in a given constitution. Thus, for example, a constitution that contains 5 of the 25 rights in the criminal procedure category would receive a score of 0.2, or 20 percent, in that category.

On paper, Latin America boasts the highest levels of protection for civil and political rights as well as the rights of criminal defendants. In the area of economic rights, Latin America ranks second only to Eastern Europe, where protection for economic rights surged dramatically in the 1990s as one country after another sought to repudiate the legacy of communism

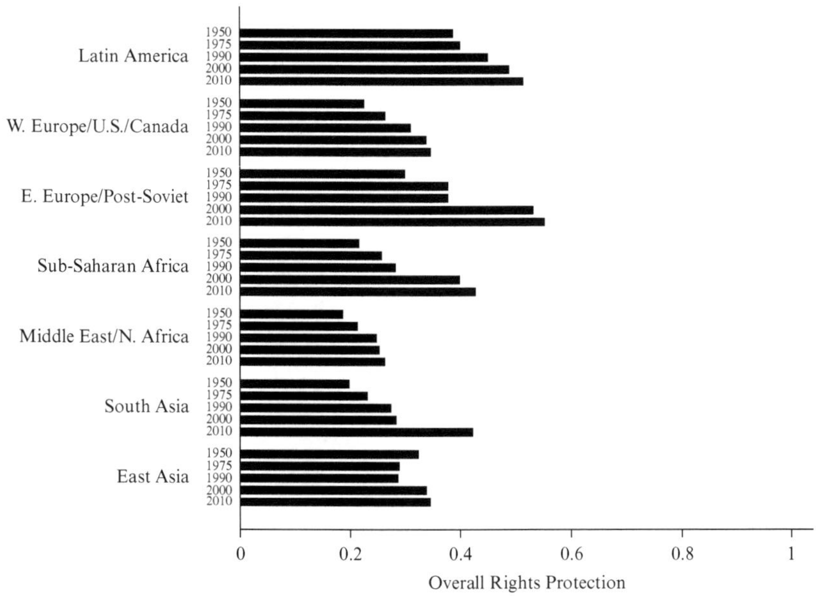

Figure 8.14a Overall level of rights protection, by region and over time

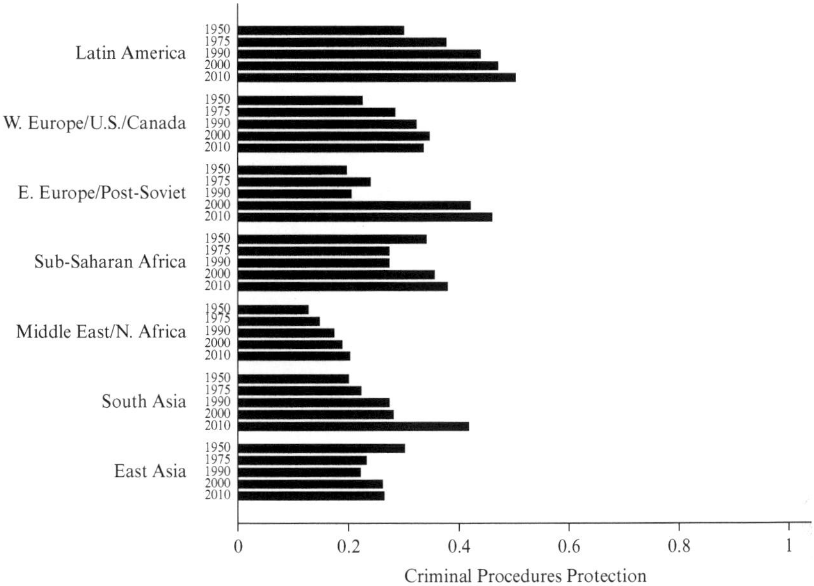

Figure 8.14b Criminal procedure rights, by region and over time

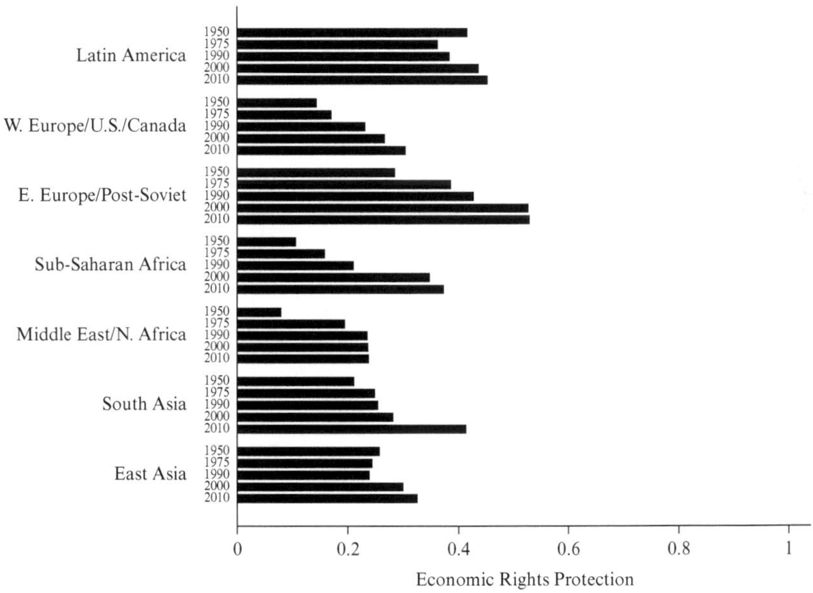

Figure 8.14c Economic rights, by region and over time

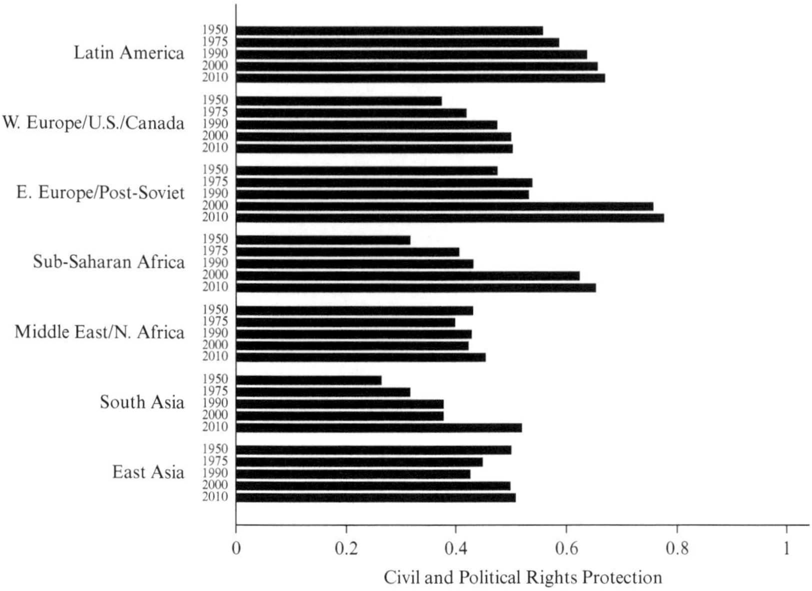

Figure 8.14d Civil and political rights, by region and over time

following the collapse of the Soviet Union. By contrast, Latin American constitutions started from a relatively high baseline and experienced steady and moderate growth in the formal protection of rights over the postwar period.

In practice, of course, respect for human rights has not always been a strong suit of Latin American regimes. This does not necessarily mean, however, that the growing number of rights found in Latin American constitutions are merely hollow promises. The various measures of constitutional compliance used by Law and Versteeg[19] suggest that actual respect for civil, political, socioeconomic, and group rights has improved in Latin America since the early 1990s. Law and Versteeg further find that these real-world performance improvements have outpaced the addition of new constitutional rights over time. The result is a trend in Latin America away from ineffective or sham constitutions toward relatively strong constitutions that boast growing protection for rights in both theory and practice. Compared to other regions, Latin America ranks slightly above average at fulfilling constitutional rights guarantees. It trails Western Europe, North

[19] Law and Versteeg (n 3), at 907–11.

America, East Asia, and the Pacific region but ranks ahead of Central and Eastern Europe and Central Asia, which in turn fare better than Africa and the Middle East. The largest gap between what rights are promised on paper and what rights are upheld in practice is found in South Asia.[20]

D. Stability

Latin America's history of constitutional instability matches its history of political upheaval and regime instability. Frequent constitutional replacement in the region has followed no set pattern but instead involved a combination of "churn", "cycling",[21] and "evolution". Not surprisingly, Latin American constitutions continue to rank below average in terms of their longevity. Constitutional longevity in Latin America has, however, improved somewhat in recent decades, with the result that the gap is not enormous. By global standards, constitutional longevity in Latin America is better described as middling than poor. As reported in Table 8.3, the average age of constitutions in Latin America is currently 28, while the global average is 32. This places Latin America near the middle of the pack: it ranks fifth out of eight regions and is ahead of South Asia, sub-Saharan Africa, or Eastern Europe, which brings up the rear with an average constitutional lifespan of just 15 years.

IV. CONCLUSION

Latin American constitutionalism is rich with opportunities for comparative inquiry thanks to the region's long tradition of adopting formal constitutional texts. Scholars have examined these texts using a variety of methods,[22] but as the other chapters in this volume illustrate, the existing literature has barely begun to exhaust the possibilities. This chapter has taken the still relatively novel approach of identifying and examining textual patterns over time on the basis of quantitative or "large-n" data.[23] Quantitative research of this type does not purport to capture all

---

20 Ibid.

21 Elkins, Ginsberg and Melton (n 4), at 25.

22 Gargarella (n 4); Gabriel Negretto (2013), *Making Constitutions: Presidents, Parties and Institutional Choice in Latin America* (New York: Cambridge University Press).

23 David S. Law (2010), "Constitutions", in Peter Cane and Herbert M. Kritzer (eds), *Oxford Handbook of Empirical Legal Studies* (Oxford: Oxford University Press), p. 379.

the details of formal constitutional texts, but it does offer a clear, systematic, and transparent basis for challenging stereotypes and preconceived notions about constitutional drafting patterns.

In the case of Latin America, quantitative analysis suggests that, at least in the aggregate and on average, the following constitutional stereotypes may now be outdated: (1) Latin American constitutions tend to emulate the model of the U.S. Constitution; (2) Latin American constitutions contemplate excessive executive power; and (3) the rights provisions found in Latin American constitutions are essentially hollow promises. Relative to constitutions in other regions of the world, Latin American constitutions tend to be relatively detailed and to contemplate levels of formal executive power that are both relatively moderate and declining over time. Moreover, while they also tend to contain an extensive catalog of rights; the actual implementation of these rights is improving in the region, on average.

Our findings also highlight the need for comparative constitutional scholarship that adopts a regional as opposed to a national or global focus. With the obvious and predictable exception of Europe – where regional integration has generated a complex and widely studied body of regional constitutional law – studies that adopt a regional perspective are considerably less common in the literature than studies that focus on individual countries or even, for that matter, on global patterns. Scholars are certainly justified in taking a cautious approach to generalizing about geographical regions as vast and diverse as Latin America, Africa, and Asia. Too much caution, however, means that we run the risk of overlooking or failing to investigate genuinely regional phenomena. And empirical research increasingly suggests that regional phenomena do exist. Our conclusions with respect to Latin America are consistent with previous findings to the effect that geographic regions exhibit distinctive patterns of constitutional drafting.[24] This persistent finding of regional constitutional patterns, notwithstanding either the homogenizing effects of globalization or the heterogeneity that can exist even among neighboring countries, merits further inquiry and explanation.

---

[24] For example, Tom Ginsburg (2013), "East Asian constitutionalism in comparative perspective", in Albert H.Y. Chen (ed.), *Constitutionalism in Asia in the Early Twenty-First Century* (Cambridge: Cambridge University Press); Law and Versteeg (n 3).

BIBLIOGRAPHY

Billias, George Athan (2011), *American Constitutionalism Heard Round the World, 1776–1989: A Global Perspective* (New York: NYU Press).

Chen, Albert H.Y. (2010), "Pathways of Western liberal constitutional development in Asia: A comparative study of five major nations", *International Journal of Constitutional Law*, **8** (1), 849–84.

Chen, Albert H.Y. (2013), "Introduction: Constitutionalism and constitutional change in East and Southeast Asia – An historical and comparative overview", in Albert H.Y. Chen and Tom Ginsburg (eds), *Public Law in Asia* (Farnham: Ashgate).

Elkins, Zachary, Tom Ginsburg and James Melton (2009), *The Endurance of National Constitutions* (New York: Cambridge University Press).

Elkins, Zachary, Tom Ginsburg and James Melton (2012), "Comments on Law and Versteeg's *The Declining Influence of the United States Constitution*", *New York University Law Review Online*, **87**, 11–24.

Fish, M. Steven and Mathew Kroenig (2009), *The Handbook of National Legislatures: A Global Survey* (New York: Cambridge University Press).

Gargarella, Roberto (2013), *Latin American Constitutionalism 1810–2010: The Engine Room of the Constitution* (New York: Oxford University Press).

Ginsburg, Tom (2014), "East Asian constitutionalism in comparative perspective", in Albert H.Y. Chen (ed.), *Constitutionalism in Asia in the Early Twenty-First Century* (Cambridge: Cambridge University Press).

Ginsburg, Tom (2009), "The Constitutional Court and the judicialization of Korean politics", in Andrew Harding and Penelope Nicholson (eds), *New Courts in Asia* (London: Routledge).

Hirschl, Ran (2004), *Toward Juristocracy* (Cambridge, MA: Harvard University Press).

Law, David S. (2010), "Constitutions", in Peter Cane and Herbert M. Kritzer (eds), *Oxford Handbook of Empirical Legal Studies* (Oxford: Oxford University Press).

Law, David S. and Mila Versteeg (2013), "Sham constitutions", *California Law Review*, **101**, 863–952.

Law, David S. and Mila Versteeg (2011), "The evolution and ideology of global constitutionalism", *California Law Review*, **99**, 1163–257.

Miller, Jonathan (1997), "The constitutional authority of a foreign talisman: A study of U.S. practice as authority in 19th century Argentina and the Argentine elite's leap of faith", *American University Law Review*, 46, 1483.

Negretto, Gabriel (2013), *Making Constitutions: Presidents, Parties and Institutional Choice in Latin America* (New York: Cambridge University Press).

Rosenkrantz, Carlos F. (2003), "Against borrowings and other nonauthoritative uses of foreign law", *International Journal of Constitutional Law*, **1** (2), 269–95.

9. The global diffusion of U.S. legal thought: changing influence, national security and legal education in crisis

Fernanda Nicola

> Law is spread as much by literature as by legislation. Commerce, education and religion may be as important conduits as governmental action in bringing about legal change.[1]

I. LEGAL DIFFUSION AND MULTIDIRECTIONAL WINDS

During the twentieth century, the center of production of legal ideas shifted from France to Germany and then to the United States. Here, the dominant legal reasoning framed the law as a phenomenon of social organization that was not confined to a specific legal system.[2] There were both external and internal factors influencing U.S. legal thought which explain this change of wind from continental Europe to the United States. Externally, after World War II the United States garnered influence by positioning itself for political and economic global leadership. Internally, the critique of social purpose functionalism articulated by the legal realists provided new problem-solving approaches integrated in a reconstructive and pragmatic understanding of law called positive-sociology functionalism.[3] Finally, legal diffusion occurred through public law disciplines based on U.S. constitutional law theories of rights, neo-formalism, and balancing conflicting policy analysis.[4]

---

[1] *See* William Twining (2006), "Diffusion of law: A global perspective", *J. Comp. L.*, **1**, 237, 238.

[2] *See* Ugo Mattei (1993), "Why the wind changed: Intellectual leadership in Western law", *Am. J. Comp. L.*, **42**, 195, 195–96.

[3] *See* Fernanda Nicola (2010), "Family law exceptionalism in comparative law", *Am. J. Comp. L.*, **58**, 777, 795.

[4] *See* Duncan Kennedy (2006), *The Globalizations of Law and Legal Thought*, in David Trubek and Alvaro Santos (eds), *The New Law and Economic Development:*

The diffusion of legal education takes place through law schools, non-governmental organizations (NGOs), international financial institutions (IFIs) and other avenues. Legal diffusion has different political agendas, often in conjunction, for instance, with law and development reforms or more broadly due to the prestige of U.S. legal training and academia.[5] U.S. legal thought reached Latin America, Asia, Europe and Africa through the transplant of legal institutions. The diffusion of U.S. legal styles often changed the process rather than the content of legal education, which resulted in local curriculum reforms that reflected the more pragmatic U.S. education style.[6] Some scholars have harshly criticized the export of U.S. legal thought for its distinct adversarial judicial process that decentralizes power and privatizes disputes while creating advantages for the powerful and wealthy, expanding inequality and social stratification.[7] Others have instead claimed that the diffusion of teaching methods geared to the adoption of U.S.-based clinical legal education aims at informing, adapting, and promoting social justice in a way that addresses the contextual realities of the importing country.[8]

A. Legal Diffusion through Legal Education

Since the beginning of the twentieth century the United States has been a successful recipient of European legal ideas.[9] However, by the end of World War II, the direction changed as the United States became a major center of production of the global legal consciousness, or the *langue*, used by transnational legal elites.[10] In the post-war era, law schools played an important role in the diffusion of U.S. legal thought around the world often driven by law and development goals.[11] Cosmopolitan law schools

---

A Critical Appraisal, pp. 19, 57 (Cambridge/New York: Cambridge University Press).

5 *See* Michele Graziadei (2009), "Legal transplants and the frontiers of legal knowledge", *Theoretical Inquiries in Law*, **10**, 723, 724.

6 *See* William Twining (2005), "Social science and diffusion of law", *J.L. Soc'y*, **32**, 203, 204; John H. Merryman (2000), "Law and development memoirs: The Chile Law Program", *Am. J. Comp. Law*, **48**, 481, 484.

7 *See* Ugo Mattei and Laura Nader (2008), *Plunder: When the Rule of Law Is Illegal* (Chichester: John Wiley & Sons).

8 *See* Richard Wilson (2012), "Clinical legal education in Latin America", symposium hosted by the *Drexel Law Review*, 12 October.

9 *See* Mattei (n 2), at 195–96.

10 *See* Kennedy (n 4), at 57.

11 *See* Mark Galantier and David Trubek (1974), "Scholars in self-estrangement: Some reflections on the crisis in law and development studies", *Wis. L. Rev.*, **4**, 1062, 1067.

in North America received many Jewish *émigré* law professors who maintained their European ties after the war. U.S. law schools developed graduate programs initially influenced by European doctoral models, but later on switched gears to influence legal elites around the globe.[12] In past decades, graduate programs in North America educated lawyers who became part of global legal and political elites working in transnational firms or international organizations.[13] U.S.-based academics increasingly served as legal advisors to draft, interpret, and reform the constitutions of countries in transition, or to lead neoliberal market reforms legitimized by the Washington consensus ideology in allegedly corrupt governments in need of constant legal reform.[14] In either case, U.S. law schools and their professors became important agents of legal change exporting either the mainstream or the critiques to U.S. legal thought to the rest of the world.[15]

Even though the diffusion of U.S. legal education has been studied more systematically by social scientists than lawyers, lawyers remain central agents of legal change.[16] Positivists' accounts of law and development have addressed the reforms in legal institutions rather than the change in legal reasoning and culture of the receiving groups. Critical scholars, however, have shown resistance to legal transplants when the transfer of foreign legal doctrines might create irritation in the receiving system, when the transfer only partially penetrates depending on the commitment to its adoption by legal and political elites,[17] or when the transfer is accepted, albeit with continuous suspicion, by post-colonial elites shifting from the reception of European to U.S. legal thought.[18]

The difficulty in mapping the diffusion of U.S. legal thought, rather than the reception of a particular institution or a judicial/legislative rule, is

---

[12] *See* Gail Hupper (2007), "The rise of an academic doctorate in law: Origins through World War II", *Am. J. Legal Hist.*, **49** (1), 1.

[13] *See* Yvez Dezalay and Bryant G. Garth (2012), *Lawyers and the Construction of Transnational Justice* (Abingdon/New York: Routledge).

[14] *See* Jorge Esquirol (2008), "The failed law in Latin America", *Am. J. Comp. L.*, **56**, 75; Noah Feldman (2005), "Imposed constitutionalism", *Conn. L. Rev.*, **37**, 857, 860.

[15] *See* Wendy Brown and Janet Halley (eds) (2002), *Left Legalism/Left Critique* (Durham: Duke University Press), p. 10.

[16] *See* Twining (n 6), at 204.

[17] Daniel Berkowitz, Katharina Pistor and Jean-Francois Richard (2003), "The transplant effect", *Am. J. Comp. L.*, **51**, 163–203.

[18] *See* Sylvia Wairimu Kang'ara (2012), "Beyond bed and bread: Making the African state through marriage reform – constitutive and transformative influences of Anglo-American legal thought", *Hastings Race & Poverty L.J.*, **9**, 353; Gunther Teubner (1998), "Legal irritants: Good faith in British law or how unifying law ends up in new differences", *Mod. L. Rev.*, **61** (1), 11.

how to measure the influence of U.S. legal ideas in another country's legal reasoning style. Legal education is an excellent starting point because law schools provide the necessary training which every lawyer must undertake. Since the 1990s, U.S. law schools have developed graduate programs including masters or doctorates in law that have educated professors in Canada, Israel, Korea, Colombia, and Taiwan.[19]

The prestige of U.S. legal education went hand in hand with the predominance of Western legal ideas such as the promotion of democracy and the rule of law. For instance, China's increasing geopolitical power and economic performance in the last twenty years led to dramatic changes in its traditional and post-communist legal system slowly committing to introduce Western rule of law principles.[20] The prestige of being involved in institutions such as the World Trade Organization (WTO), as well as maintaining the prized most favored nation trade status, nudged China towards reforming its legal system in a way that was more in line with Western principles, at least on the surface.[21] Legal change in China was prompted also by the dramatic expansion of its legal education. Universities in the United States are the sites where many Chinese legal scholars regularly visit through U.S. legal assistance programs and funds for cooperation.[22] U.S. law literature is ample in law libraries of Chinese universities and the highest numbers of citations of foreign literature are directed to American scholarly works, cases and legislation. Chinese scholars are familiar with many law terms which originated from or were affected by U.S. law, such as: administrative regulations and deregulation, public choice and game theory, disclosure of government information and certainly the due process principle and hearings.[23] Increasingly, China's lower court judges are experimenting with plea bargaining, using informal precedent, and hearing an increasing number of rights-based claims.[24]

---

[19] *See* Gail Hupper (2008), "The academic doctorate in law: A vehicle for legal transplants?", *J. L. Educ.*, **58**, 413, 415.

[20] *See* William Alford (2000), "Exporting "the Pursuit of Happiness" Aiding Democracy Abroad: The Learning Curve by Thomas Carothers (book review)", *Harv. L. Rev.*, **113**, 1677, 1683.

[21] *See* Donald S. Clarke (2003), "China's legal system and the WTO: Prospects for compliance", *Wash. U. Global Stud. L. Rev.*, **2**, 97.

[22] *See* Jacques DeLisle (1999), "Lex Americana? United States legal assistance, American legal models, and legal change in the post-communist world and beyond", *U Pa. J. Int. L.*, **20**, 179, 180.

[23] *See* Haibo He (2008), "The dawn of the due process principle in China", *Colum. J. Asian L.*, **22**, 57.

[24] *See* Benjamin L. Liebman (2008), "China's courts: Restricted reform", *Colum. J. Asian L.*, **21**, 1.

By focusing on the legal diffusion of U.S. legal thought through legal education, this chapter aims to go beyond the binary interaction between borrower and lender in a fixed direction. Rather than a wind going in a unilateral direction replacing another one, legal diffusion should be understood as a multidirectional change in winds pointing to an overlap of legal practices in which one becomes predominant at a certain point and time in legal education without substituting the other.[25]

B. Signs of the Waning Influence of U.S. Legal Thought

The emerging influence of BRICS (Brazil, Russia, India, China and South Africa) over international trade and their convergence on governance models has created resistance and counter-harmonization processes to U.S. foreign trade hegemony.[26] The erratic trade policy in the Trump era continues to weaken the U.S. foreign trade agenda. In testing the limits of the diffusion of U.S. legal thought around the world – from public to private law – U.S. legal doctrines, ideas, and policies appear as retro rather than avant-garde compared to emerging global models. For instance, South African transformative constitutional law principles embedded in its Constitution of 1996 have allowed the South African Constitutional Court to engage in a comparative constitutional discourse that has become a model in a diverse number of legal subjects, from socio-economic rights to same sex marriage.[27] In a similar way Brazilian trade strategies within the multilateral forum of the WTO have carved their own policy autonomy in order to challenge issues such as exchange rate misalignments through antidumping measures.[28]

The successful advancement of U.S. legal ideas after World War II

---

25 *See* Twining (n 1), at 238.

26 *See* Lucia Scaffardi (2013), "BRICS a multi-centre 'legal network'?", *Beijing L. Rev.*, 5, 140–48; Amy Kapczynski (2009), "Harmonization and its discontents: A case study of TRIPS implementation in India's pharmaceutical sector", *Calif. L. Rev.*, **97**, 1571, 1576.

27 *See* Macarena Saez (2015), "Transforming family law through same-sex marriage: Lessons from (and to) the western world", *Duke J. Comp. & Intl. L.*, **25**, 125; Karl E. Klare (1998), "Legal culture and transformative constitutionalism", *SALJ on Human Rights*, **14**, 146.

28 *See* Alvaro Santos (2012), "Carving out policy autonomy for developing countries in the World Trade Organization: The experience of Brazil and Mexico", *Va. J. Int'l L.*, **52**, 551, 553; *see also* Vera Thorstensen, Emerson Marçal and Lucas Ferraz (2012), "Exchange rate misalignments and international trade policy: Impacts on tariffs", *J. World Trade*, **46**, 597.

went hand in hand with neoliberal policies that were promoted globally by the Washington Consensus in the 1990s. From the mid-1990s until 2005, neoliberalism was waning as a result of disappointment with the neoliberal market shock therapy in Russia and Latin American and opposition to structural adjustment policies across the Global South. This changed law and development strategies to include civil society as well as human and social goals in the post-neoliberal development agenda.[29] The rising legal and political elites from the peripheries and semi-peripheries of China, Africa, and Latin America were moving from straightforward neoliberal economic recipes and rights-based approaches to a more selective reception of U.S. legal thought.

The gap created by the demise of the Washington Consensus allowed both Left and Right to experiment with their approaches to economic development. Both approaches, recently revamped by the populist agendas of Maduro, Orban and even Trump, include attention to localism, paying respect to differing capabilities, and tailoring reforms to the context in which they take place depending on local elites and social recipients.[30] Although legal realism, legal process, and rights neo-formalist insights of U.S. legal thought were successfully globalized elsewhere, these no longer satisfied the needs of rising legal elites from the Global South, the semi-peripheries of China, Africa and Latin America who were seeking to integrate global and native styles, and even more recently Brexit and Trump supporters who felt left out from economic globalization and the rise of neoliberalism.[31]

C. The Decline of One Kind of U.S. Constitutionalism

During the 1980s, the diffusion of U.S. legal thought went hand in hand with neoliberal policies not only in law and development circles, but also in private and regulatory law circles in the European Union (EU). The diffusion of U.S. mainstream law and economics was central to the engineers of the internal market in Europe reforming product liability law.[32]

---

29 *See* David Kennedy (2006), "The 'Rule of Law', political choices, and development common sense", in Trubek and Santos (n 4).

30 *See* Amartya Sen (2009), *The Idea of Justice* (Cambridge, MA: Belknap Press of Harvard University Press).

31 Duncan Kennedy (2017), "A left of liberal interpretation of Trump's 'big' win, Part One: Neoliberalism", *Nev. L.J. Forum*, **1**, 98.

32 *See* Daniela Caruso and Roberto Pardolesi (2012), "Per una storia della direttiva sulla responsibilitia da prodotto difettoso", *Danno e Responsabilta*, **9** (Special Issue on product liability).

U.S. law and economics was appealing to European elites for its combination of rights neo-formalist approaches and analytics borrowed from neoliberal economics. The idea of Kaldor–Hicks efficiency provided a target not only for legislatures, but also for judges driven by economic efficiency rationales.[33] With the increasing political and legal divide across the Atlantic marked by the Iraq war and other regulatory conflicts over privacy protection, Right v. Left approaches to U.S. law and economics were no longer taken at face value. Instead, for European private lawyers, the selective reception of U.S. law and economics became part of their strategies in relation to European integration.[34]

Praise for U.S. constitutional law by its liberal and cosmopolitan elites appears in decline. For example, sounding almost defeated, Anne-Marie Slaughter stated that "[o]ne of our great exports used to be constitutional law."[35] According to Harold Hongju Koh, today foreign courts in well-established democracies prefer to cite the case law of the European Court of Human Rights in cases concerning equality, liberty and prohibitions against cruel treatment, rather than U.S. case law. This downturn in U.S. dominance is often explained as a result of the increasing sophistication of transnational elites all over the world. Additionally, these courts appear more liberal than their U.S. counterparts. As journalist Adam Liptak noted, "American ideas are for export, and there's very little effort in the U.S. legal system to import ideas." In this respect, the Scalia–Breyer debate in the United States illustrates the difficulty in importing liberal legal ideas into U.S. constitutional law when justices are profoundly divided over the use of comparative law in constitutional adjudication.[36] Perhaps more important to the lessening impact of U.S. jurisprudence is "the adamant opposition of some Supreme Court justices to the citation of

---

[33] Duncan Kennedy (1998), "Law and economics from a critical legal studies perspective", in Peter Newman (ed.), *The New Palgrave Dictionary of Economics and the Law* (London/New York: Palgrave Macmillan/Stockton Press).

[34] *See* Fernanda Nicola (2008), "Transatlanticisms: Constitutional asymmetry and selective reception of U.S. law and economics in the formation of European private law", *Cardozo J. Int'l & Comp. L.*, **16**, 101; James Q. Whitman (2004), "Two western cultures of privacy: Dignity versus liberty", *Yale L.J.*, **113**, 1151, 1156.

[35] *See* Adam Liptak (2008), "U.S. Court is now guiding fewer nations", *The New York Times*, 17 September, available at: http://www.nytimes.com/2008/09/18/us/18legal.html? r=0 (accessed 14 September 2017).

[36] *See* Sujit Choudry (2006), "Migration as a new metaphor in comparative constitutional law", in Sujit Choudry (ed.), *The Migration of Constitutional Ideas* (Cambridge/New York: Cambridge University Press).

foreign law in their own opinions".[37] For example, Israeli Supreme Court Chief Justice Aharon Barak has publically stated that the U.S. Supreme Court "is losing the central role it once had among courts in modern democracies".[38] Meanwhile, only a few U.S. Supreme Court justices have noticed the chilling effect that isolationist judicial thought can create. For example, Justice Ginsburg noted, "the failure to engage foreign decisions had resulted in diminished influence for the United States Supreme Court". The Canadian Supreme Court, she said, is "probably cited more widely abroad than the U.S. Supreme Court". There is one reason for that, she said: "You will not be listened to if you don't listen to others."[39] Foreign Constitutional and Supreme Courts could be looking less at U.S. courts due to the reputation of their government abroad and the over-judicialization of federal judges at home. In a similar vein, other constitutional courts will position themselves at the opposite side of the legal spectrum than the U.S. Supreme Court in an attempt to broadly reject a Western individualist notion of rights, like in the case of the Plurinational Constitutional Court in Bolivia.[40]

The aforementioned attitudes can be found in a David S. Law and Mila Versteeg article showing how in the last couple of decades a large number of countries explicitly refused to borrow or transplant from the U.S. constitutional arrangement and its rights-related provisions.[41] Through 60 years of comprehensive data on the content of the world's constitutions, the authors reveal that there is a generic component to global constitutionalism characterized by rights and institutional arrangements that appear in nearly all formal constitutions. Their general thesis, however, is that such a global constitutional toolkit is no longer influenced by U.S. constitutionalism and we are witnessing the end of an American hegemony. In recognizing that the U.S. constitution might have lost its appeal as a model to inspire constitutions in other countries, the authors go even further. They explain that the study of U.S legal culture aims to avoid mistakes like the ones incurred in American jurisprudence. At times, U.S. law can become the anti-model. For instance, India's Constitution drafters

---

37 *See* Liptak (n 35).

38 *See* Aharon Barak (2002), "A judge on judging: The role of a supreme court in a democracy", *Harv. L. Rev.*, **116**, 19.

39 *See* Liptak (n 35).

40 *See* Diego Eduardo Lopez-Medina (2013), "Rights discourse and theory in the new plurinational constitutional court of Bolivia" at Harvard Law School in the IGLP program on comparative law (June).

41 *See* David S. Law and Mila Versteeg (2012), "The declining influence of the American Constitution", *N. Y. U L. Rev.*, **87**, 762, 767.

specifically rejected importing American due process jurisprudence to avoid the consequences of the *Lochner* case.[42] In a similar way, the drafters of the South African abortion legislation were indirectly influenced by the U.S. experience in the aftermath of *Roe v. Wade*.[43] On the other hand, the fact that the negative model is something that scholars and lawyers would want to study and understand, but not necessarily adopt, shows that the U.S. remains an influential cultural model.[44]

II. LEGAL DIFFUSION UNDER NEW CLOTHES

Legal scholars have suggested that the global diffusion of U.S. constitutional law and the discipline of comparative constitutional law appear in decline.[45] This chapter posits that what is changing is not the preeminence of U.S. legal thought around the globe but its means of diffusion. Rather than under the guise of comparative constitutional law, legal scholars have engaged in the diffusion of U.S. national security law post 9/11.[46] National security lawyers have carved an independent doctrinal canon and an analytical skillset for global professionals that are readily exportable. Rather than promoting global justice and critical thinking, under the attacks of legal reformers U.S. legal academia is turning inwards to training lawyers for Bar passage and local business transactions.

A. The Rise of National Security Law

The declining influence of comparative constitutional law (CCL) in U.S. legal academia has provided the opportunity for national security law

---

42 *Lochner v. New York*, 198 U.S. 45 (1905). *See* Heinz Klug (2000), "Model and anti-model: The United States Constitution and the 'rise of world constitutionalism'", *Wis. L. Rev.*, **3**, 597, 606.

43 *Roe v. Wade*, 410 U.S. 113. *See* Rachel Rebouche (2011), "The limits of reproductive rights in improving women's health", *Ala. L. Rev.*, **63**, 1.

44 *See* Kim Lane Scheppele (2003), "Aspirational and aversive constitutionalism: The case for studying cross-constitutional influence through negative models", *Int'l J. Const. L.*, **1**, 296, 297.

45 *See* David Fontana (2011), "The rise and fall of comparative constitutional law in the post-war era", *Yale J. Int'l L.*, **36**, 1.

46 *See* Kim Lane Scheppelle (2006), "The migration of anti-constitutional ideas: the post-9/11 globalization of public law and the international state of emergency", in Sujit Choudry (ed.), *The Migration of Constitutional Ideas* (Cambridge/New York: Cambridge University Press).

(NSL) to play a leading role in U.S. law schools' curriculums.[47] In the past decades, many American law schools have replaced CCL and international law classes with courses on NSL and U.S. foreign relations.[48]

The internal mode of diffusion of CCL was grounded in two dimensions based on U.S. constitutional thinking: a formalist and a functionalist one. The formalist dimension relied on a universalist and rights-based approach to fundamental rights, whereas the functionalist dimension addressed the structure of government, which reflected on how federalism should deal with social tensions in balancing individual freedoms and socio-economic benefits.[49]

In contrast, the mode of diffusion of NSL has a formalist dimension based on habeas corpus rights and the distinction between citizens and aliens as well as civilian law versus laws of war. In its functionalist dimension, NSL scholarship balances state security with the privacy and civil liberties of targeted individuals.[50]

Despite the structural parallels between the CCL and NSL, there are some differences due to the formation and the politics of the different legal elites. U.S. lawyers and academics involved in NSL are no longer part of a cosmopolitan liberal elite, but they are criminal lawyers, immigration lawyers, or international and foreign relations lawyers committed to studying counter-terrorism and military commissions. The mode of diffusion is no longer a discourse among constitutional or supranational courts from different countries or regions of the world, but the study of national executives and their relation to federal/military courts.[51]

B. From Crisis to the Changes in U.S. Legal Education

U.S. legal education is in the midst of a "crisis", for lack of a better term, based on the financial crisis: skyrocketing student debt, in part financed by the government, the downturn in law school applications, and the

---

47 *See* William C. Banks (2005), "Teaching and learning about terrorism", *J. Legal Educ.*, 55, 35.

48 *See* Michael J. Glennon (2005), "Teaching national security law", *J. Legal Educ.*, **55**, 49.

49 *See* Kennedy (n 4), at 57.

50 *See* Mathew C. Waxman (2012), "National security federalism in the age of terror", *Stan. L. Rev.*, **64**, 289, 290.

51 *See* Richard H. Fallon Jr and Daniel J. Meltzer (2007), "Habeas corpus jurisdiction, substantive rights, and the War on Terror", *Harv. L. Rev.*, **120**, 2029, 2037; Anne-Marie Slaughter (2005), *A New World Order* (Princeton: Princeton University Press); James E. Pfander (2004), "Article I tribunals, Article III courts, and the judicial power of the United States", *Harv. L. Rev.*, 118, 643, 644.

high unemployment rates for lawyers. One approach to solving the crisis, which is supported by scholars and practitioners, aims at transforming U.S. law schools from intellectual global hubs into localized training schools for lawyers proposing to shift from a three- to two-year JD (Juris Doctor) program and to open pro bono practice firms in law schools. Due to a sharp decrease in student enrollment, U.S. law schools are cutting resources for their international programs to strengthen local practice and Bar exam passage. Many predict a long-term crisis for law schools spurred in part by the global financial crisis, the availability of cheap online legal services, and the high cost of legal education. It is too early, however, to determine the real consequences of the current crisis in legal education ranging from structural changes in the employment market for lawyers to the lavish expenditures of law schools in fancy buildings and high faculty salaries.[52] Yet this second more simplistic narrative appears to have more traction by severely impacting law schools' reputations and allowing quick-fix solutions that might have a disastrous impact on the long-term intellectual output of law schools.

The reformist approach to the crisis in legal education aims at transforming U.S. law schools from intellectual global hubs into localized, low-cost training schools for transactional lawyers driven by Bar passage.[53] Reformists promote the privatization of legal education, transforming the nature of U.S. law schools with changes such as: deregulating law schools, eliminating expensive clinical or outward-looking legal training, and favoring the ongoing attempts by the American Bar Association to eliminate professorial tenure.[54] As a result, the diffusion of U.S. legal consciousness will increasingly take place beyond U.S. law schools, often under the auspices of U.S. legal education abroad. What changes is the vehicle of legal diffusion rather than its message.

Legal reformers attacking U.S. legal education are pushing for privatization through the emergency of student debt and a critique of interdisciplinary and theoretical scholarship not geared to form local lawyers.[55] In offering such an inward-looking solution to the legal education curriculum, legal reformers are missing the point for many reasons.

Foremost, it is not clear that the recipe offered by legal reformers to transform the legal curriculum through privatizing law schools will

---

[52] Brian Z. Tamanaha (2012), *Failing Law Schools* (Chicago/London: University of Chicago Press).

[53] Paul Campos (2012), "The crisis of the American law school", *University of Michigan Journal of Law Reform*, **46** (1), 177–224.

[54] Tamanaha (n 52).

[55] Tamanaha (n 52).

improve the job opportunities of their students.[56] On the contrary, empirical studies have shown that after obtaining law degrees, students have a median increase of income earnings that varies according to various historical factors.[57] In addition, empirical studies have disproven the so-called "buyers' remorse" among law graduates, which reformers connect to student debt from law school.[58]

Additionally, the actual crisis of legal education ought to be understood in its historical perspective and narrowed to the job crisis of an elite Bar while many legal services to the poor or the middle class are still in demand and overpriced. Through a historical analysis of various legal crises over time, scholars have shown how the legal profession tends to adapt to new market needs.[59]

Lastly, legal reformers claim that law students are failed by law schools that use their resources to advance legal scholarship rather than to teach legal skills, and propose to shorten the time of law school education from three to two years.[60] Not only have many studies shown that the correlation between failing law students and theoretical or critical approaches to legal education is largely flawed and unproven, but its result would dramatically alter the nature of U.S. law schools at home and abroad as sites offering critical thinking and social justice visions to young lawyers.[61] An example at the local level is what Jamie Raskin has undertaken at the Washington College of Law, and law schools around the country, with the Marshall Brennan Constitutional Literacy Project. This bottom-up and outward-looking training strategy aims to engage law students to raise the consciousness of young students in local public high schools as a form of "popular constitutionalism in action".[62] At the global level, U.S. law

---

56 *See* Jennifer S. Bard ((2012), "Failing law schools", *J. Legal Educ.*, **33**, 417, 420.

57 Michael Simkovic, and Frank McIntyre (2013), "The economic value of a law degree", American law and economics conference, 18 May. *See also* Frank McIntyre and Michael Simkovic (2014), "The economic value of a law degree", *J. Legal Stud.*, **43**, 249.

58 *See* Ronit Dinovitzer, Bryant G. Garth, and Joyce Sterling (2013), "Buyers' remorse? An empirical assessment of the desirability of a legal career", *J. Legal Educ.*, **63**, 211, 212.

59 *See* Bryant Garth (2013), "Crises, crisis rhetoric, and competition in legal education: A sociological perspective on the (latest) crisis of the legal profession and legal education", *Stan. L & Pol'y Rev.*, 24, 503, 504.

60 *See* Brian Z. Tamanaha (2006), *Failing Law School* (Chicago/London: University of Chicago Press).

61 *See* Bard (n 56), at 420, and Robin West and Danielle Citron, "On legal scholarship", available at https://aals.org.

62 *See* Jamie B. Raskin (2013), "The Marshall-Brennan constitutional project:

schools have emerged as sites in which legal elites have the resources to monitor the democratic failures even in Western countries,[63] or they can train the students and the future elites committed to advancement of the Inter-American Human Rights System.[64]

Beyond the current debate spurred by the crisis in U.S. legal education, the consequences on law schools are severe and the curricular changes or the lack of funding have impacted primarily the interdisciplinary and global approach promoted by legal academia. With the increasing competition from Europe, China, Brazil and India offering competitive and often less costly legal education, U.S. law schools are challenged to reform and rethink their curriculum for global elites.[65] For instance, the EU was spurred by economic and legal integration to rethink and reform; various EU soft and hard law initiatives are creating dynamic and competitive law schools aiming at creating a transnational legal elite of lawyers.[66]

C. U.S. Legal Education Reproducing Legal Elites Abroad

It is no longer clear whether the production of transnational legal elites will continue taking place in U.S. law schools through their pricy graduate programs offering skills tailored to local rather than global legal practice. For instance, the average cost of a graduate EU degree is $16 000 for an LL.M. degree, against the $50 000 average in the U.S., and there are at the moment 173 EU programs offering such degrees. Since 2003, in Europe there have been at least 36 new international LL.M. programs established in 27 different law schools in Europe.[67] In addition, issues of prestige are at stake when the perception of the Parisian Bar is that those who skipped the *École du Barreau* and circumvented the local exam to pass the New York Bar took

American legal education's ambitious experiment in democratic constitutionalism", *Denv. U. L. Rev.*, **90**, 834, 838.

63 Kim Lane Scheppele (2016), "Enforcing the basic principles of EU law through systemic infringement procedures", in Carlos Closa and Dimitry Kochenov (eds), *Reinforcing the Rule of Law Oversight in the European Union* (Cambridge: Cambridge University Press).

64 See Claudio Grossman (2009), "The inter-American system and its evolution", *Inter-Am. and Eur. Human Rts. J.*, **2**, 49.

65 *See* Claudio Grossman (2010), "Raising the bar: US legal education in an international setting", *Harv. Int'l L. J.*, **32**, 16, 17.

66 *See* Julian Lonbay (2012), "The changing regulatory environment affecting the education and training of Europe's lawyers", *J. Legal Educ.*, **64**, 479, 481.

67 *See* Memorandum from the Office of Global Opportunities for Rachel Gordon to the faculty of Am. Univ. Wash. Coll. of Law Eur. LL.M Programs (11 February 2013) (on file with the author).

a shortcut trying to circumvent the more demanding French Bar passage regime. Before taking the allegedly "easier" route of finishing an undergraduate law degree in Europe or in Asia, and then getting an American LL.M., students should consider that the New York Bar is viewed as a shorter and less difficult route than the arduous one of going to Bar School and passing the Bar back at home. In both Asia and Europe, studying for the Bar or practicing before taking the Bar exams requires several years' preparation and has a much lower pass rate than the New York Bar.

The shift in influence of U.S. legal education, as a means of diffusion, has therefore affected law schools in the U.S. rather than abroad. In the United States, law schools are turning inwards, cutting the funding to teach international law courses for JD students in favor of "real" courses, i.e. private and transactional law, rather than public international law which is perceived as impractical for obtaining a "real legal job" and as nurturing "unrealistic expectations".[68] The mode of diffusion of U.S. legal education is therefore changing. Law schools that shape the consciousness of the students committed to social justice at home or abroad through a mix of pragmatic, analytical, and interdisciplinary training skills are being replaced by problem-solving programs narrowly committed to local transactional practice. With respect to the subject's thoughts rather than comparative constitutional and global human rights classes, the external focus of U.S. legal education happens increasingly through the lens of NSL and U.S. foreign policy or foreign relations.

Even though it might become unattractive or too expensive to pursue legal education in the United States, the prestige of its pedagogy does not appear undermined. On the contrary, the use of the Socratic method in the classroom, the adoption of the Bluebook Law Review style and the shift from treatise to case method, are spreading throughout the Europe, Asia, and Latin America. Another example of the spreading of American style in judicial deliberations is the increasing use of dissenting and concurring opinions introduced by the European Court of Human Rights.[69] The academic push towards introducing U.S. style dissenting and concurring opinions in the Court of Justice of the EU is justified to address a stifling and cryptic judicial reasoning, or to create more visibility in its human rights jurisprudence.[70] Finally, the transplant of U.S. legal education

---

[68] *See* Eric A. Posner and Jack L. Goldsmith (2005), *The Limits of International Law* (Oxford/New York: Oxford University Press).

[69] Ugo Mattei (1993), "Why the wind changed: Intellectual leadership in western law", *American Journal of Comparative Law*, **42** (1), 195–219.

[70] *See* Grainne de Burca (2013), "After the EU Charter of Fundamental Rights: The Court of Justice as a human rights adjudicator?", *Maastricht J. Eur. &*

abroad is facilitated by the fact that its legal elites speak the language that in turn contributes to the global norm-production of legal regimes.[71]

Questions remain as to which legal elites and which ends are served by the push towards U.S. style legal education. The increasing emergence of U.S.-style law schools created by non-U.S. academic institutions has become part of the U.S. legal discourse. However, there is little research on how U.S. legal education and legal style are advanced by non-U.S. academics or institutions that are located beyond U.S. borders. Americanization is not necessarily a neocolonial and imperial strategy, but it might serve local elites different purposes, often departing from the U.S. underlying goal.[72]

Yet the diffusion of U.S. legal education continues by other complex and indirect means, especially abroad where U.S. law schools in Asia, Europe, and Latin America are engaged in spreading legal education that is often underexplored.[73] For instance, U.S. law schools have committed to transitional and global legal education with summer or semester programs abroad, trying to modernize and make more attractive their curriculum to law students. However, once explored more closely, such attempts come at a high cost because they consolidate a model that reproduces the power structures of the global political economy.[74] Finally, the unintended consequences that academic globalization of U.S. education abroad encounters when going to authoritarian and non-democratic regimes can be seen in the case of Yale University's establishment of an undergraduate college in Singapore. There, limits on campus free expression, freedom of assembly, and other civil and political rights affect Yale's ability to deliver U.S.-style education.[75] Similar issues were raised in the New York University Abu Dhabi campus in relation to discrimination by sexual orientation and the overall dilution of human rights standards.[76]

Comp. L., **20**, 168, 169; Vlad Perju (2009), "Reason and authority in the European Court of Justice", *Va. J. Int'l L.*, **49**, 307, 308.

71 *See* Graziadei (n 5), at 724.

72 *See* Bret Stancil and Larry Catá Backer (2013), "Beyond colonization: globalization and the establishment of programs of U.S. legal education abroad by indigenous institutions", *Drexel L. Rev.*, **5**, 317, 318.

73 *See* Anil Kalhan (2013), "Thinking critically about international and transnational legal education", *Drexel L. Rev.*, **5**, 285.

74 *See* Vasuki Nesiah (2013), "A flat earth for lawyers without borders? Rethinking current approaches to the globalization of legal education", *Drexel L. Rev.*, **5**, 371, 372.

75 *See* Martin S. Flaherty (2013), "'But for Wuhan?': Do law schools operating in authoritarian regimes have human rights obligations?", *Drexel L. Rev.*, *5*, 296, 297.

76 *See* Zvika Krieger (2013), "The Emir of NYU: John Sexton's Abu Dhabi debacle", *The Atlantic*, 13 March.

The shift in modes of diffusion of U.S. legal education, namely the inward-looking business practice coupled by an understanding of international and comparative law through the national security lens will impact the consciousness of future transnational legal elites. The change in consciousness that U.S. law schools are witnessing is elucidated by two graduation speeches delivered at different times at American University, Washington College of Law. These two speeches reflect the change in the way our young graduates should perceive their future role as transnational legal elites distributing legal services.

In his graduation address at the Washington College of Law in 1986, Professor Duncan Kennedy began his commencement speech saying:

> Try your best, oh graduating students of the WCL, to avoid doing harm with your lawyer skills. [. . .] If you — if most lawyers — took the choice of clients seriously according to the vacuous piety that you should avoid doing harm with your lawyer skills, it seems likely that some clients would have to pay more for less legal service, and other people would get more service for less money. Your moral intuitions would influence the distribution of legal talent, through the market, along with the buying power of clients. Would that be better or worse than the current situation? I think it would be better.[77]

Addressing the Washington College of Law in 2013, Harold Hongju Koh gave his graduation speech starting with his family story and in particular how his father was an ambassador for Korea in the U.S. Later in his life Koh found himself representing the U.S. at the UN and when an ambassador from another country sits beside him and hears his story, he says these words that Koh proudly echoes:

> So your father was an ambassador to the U.S. and in one generation you are an ambassador from the U.S. America is the only country where that could happen, that is why you are the greatest nation. It is not your weapons, it is not your money, he said, it is your openness, your diversity, your commitment to law and Human Rights that is the source of your leadership [. . .] A first distinctive feature global [. . .] (Y)ou must understand international law because you belong to the first genuinely global generation, unlike your parents, the defining image of your era is not a world divided by the Berlin Wall, it is a world connected by the world wide web [. . .].[78]

---

[77] *See* Duncan Kennedy (1987), "The responsibility of lawyers for the justice of their causes", *Tex. Tech L. Rev.*, **18**, 1157, 1160.

[78] *See* Harold Hongju Koh (2013), Address at the Am. Univ. Wash. Coll. of Law commencement, 19 May, available at: http://media.wcl.american.edu/Mediasite/Play/c6b0c0f75d8a4bb48d6e8aab280edf451d (accessed 14 September 2017).

The moral position presented by Kennedy at the 1986 graduation was based on the premise that, even in an adversarial situation, when you are asked to represent a client you disapprove of, as a lawyer, you can make a choice based on your moral belief and the commitment you took towards yourself and the entire society. As a young lawyer, you do not have to take your client's case when he is "*using*" his legal rights in a bad case.[79] The idea is that lawyers have a conscience based on different political or moral beliefs and they can make bad or good choices to distribute legal privileges accordingly.

Almost twenty years later, Koh praises two important features of the Washington College of Law, namely its public interest commitment and how international law and human rights courses are a fundamental part of the law school's curriculum. Today protecting our sovereignty, according to Koh, means engaging with the world through a framework of international law to promote the global public interest. Like Kennedy, Koh addressed the fact that a good lawyer is not just a counselor but they have a moral conscience that will prevent her from making bad choices based on her sense of justice. However, he goes further, explaining how in his career he has condemned torture as a human rights advocate but he has also legitimized the use of drones in war as a government lawyer, for which he has been harshly criticized.[80] On this note he finished his speech with "you are entitled to speak your mind [and] so is everyone else[.] [A]ll you can do is work your hardest, do your best [. . .] all you can do is live your life with integrity[.] [I]f you do they should judge you fairly."[81]

In both speeches there is the sense that the skills law schools impart to young lawyers should not take over their moral conscience when making their professional choices. In this respect, there is not much change in the message that U.S. legal education offers to its young practitioners. Both speakers address the notion of public interest that changes from housing and poverty law to human rights and NSL according to the historical period of their legal education. While Kennedy's speech is geared toward incorporating social justice into professional choices for everyday lawyers, in Koh's speech the global public interest is advanced through the practice of human rights and NSL. By comparing these graduation speeches, almost twenty years apart, we can appreciate how U.S. legal education has influenced and at the same time is becoming an integral part of a

---

79 *See* Kennedy (n 77), at 1160.

80 David Cole (2013), "How we made killing easy", *The New York Review of Books* blog, 6 February, available at: http://www.nybooks.com/blogs/nyrblog/2013/feb/06/drones-killing-made-easy/ (accessed 14 September 2017).

81 Koh (n 78), at 1.

global legal consciousness in which ethical choices made by U.S. lawyers bear consequences both for national and international settings. Yet the discourse on how U.S. legal thought is reproduced through these graduating lawyers has somehow changed in focusing on a different type of legal practice, from tort law addressing social injustice, to NSL posing very hard questions for lawyers that will inevitably affect a global audience.

10. The limits of U.S. racial equality without a Latin American constitutional "right to work" – a thought experiment

Tanya Katerí Hernández

While some might dispute the premise that the United States constitutional model is in theoretical decline, there is very little dispute that its racial equality jurisprudence has significantly narrowed over the last three decades.[1] Anti-discrimination jurisprudence has demonstrated a decided shift to color-blindness and a progression from a desire to narrow the examination of the political meaning of race to a complete disavowal of the social significance of race.[2] Volumes have been expended in theorizing the reasons for the retrenchment in racial equality law that narrowly focuses on intentional discrimination rather than discriminatory impact or cultural meaning,[3] all in the pursuit of a color-blindness that prizes formal equality over substantive equality.[4] For instance, a number of commenta-

[1] *See, e.g.*, Stephen Steinberg (1995), *Turning Back: The Retreat from Racial Justice in American Thought and Policy* (Boston: Beacon Press), p. 213 (noting the law's intensifying dissociation from racial justice); Kevin M. Clermont and Stewart J. Schwab (2009), "Employment discrimination plaintiffs in federal court: From bad to worse?", *Harv. L. & Pol'y Rev.*, **3**, 103, 104 (stating that empirical review of employment discrimination cases demonstrates that plaintiffs are disfavored in federal courts).

[2] *See* Tanya Katerí Hernández (1998), "'Multiracial' discourse: Racial classifications in an era of color-blind jurisprudence", *Md. L. Rev.*, **57**, 97, 140 (discussing Supreme Court cases that exemplify the salient jurisprudential move towards color-blindness in educational admissions, voting rights, government business contracting, and the capital sentencing process).

[3] Charles R. Lawrence III (1987), "The id, the ego, and equal protection: Reckoning with unconscious racism", *Stan. L. Rev.*, **39**, 317.

[4] T. Alexander Aleinikoff (1991), "A case for race-consciousness", *Colum. L. Rev.*, **91**, 1060, 1115 (maintaining that color-blind theory has been transformed into serving the ultimate goal of color-blindness as a formality rather than as a means of ending material inequality).

tors view the retrenchment in anti-discrimination law as the result of the 1980s' Reagan-led white backlash against institutions perceived as sympathetic to black interests.[5] Some commentators even view the conservative Supreme Court's majority's seeming hostility to racial equality claims brought by non-whites as emblematic of racism itself[6] and "intentional blindness".[7] The jurisprudential imbalance in deference to white claims of inequality as compared to the suspicion of most non-white claims of inequality[8] is particularly evident in the employment discrimination context.[9]

Yet a comparative law perspective may offer an additional explanation for the constrained U.S. equality jurisprudence that has thus far not been fully considered. Specifically, a comparative assessment of Latin American constitutional frameworks suggests that the lack of a constitutional "Right to Work" as exists in many Latin American contexts (as a worker protection distinct from the U.S. use of the term to refer to the right to be free of compelled union membership), may adversely impact U.S. race jurisprudence. This chapter submits that without a constitutional Right to Work in the U.S., courts may not be adequately focused on the realities of the workplace context with its prevalent racial bias. Indeed, substantive racial equality is not possible without fully considering the vulnerabilities of workers that both exacerbate racial discrimination and impede the ability to make claims of discrimination. The workplace is thus pivotal in actualizing racial equality.[10]

---

[5] *See, e.g.*, Kimberlé Williams Crenshaw (1988), "Race, reform, and retrenchment: Transformation and legitimation in antidiscrimination law", *Harv. L. Rev.*, **101**, 1331, 1362.

[6] *See, e.g.*, David Kairys (1996), "Unexplainable on grounds other than race", *Am. U. L. Rev.*, **45**, 729, 735.

[7] *See* Ian Haney-López (2012), "Intentional blindness", *N. Y. U. L. Rev.*, **87**, 1779, 1861 ("Intentional blindness, not intentional ignorance, more aptly characterizes the racial jurisprudence of the Supreme Court's conservatives. They seem to understand that racism is a pervasive problem, yet oppose the courts and the Constitution to contribute to the solution.").

[8] Vincent Martin Bonventre (2014), "(Part 4–Scalia's Voting) The Supremes' record in racial discrimination cases: Decisional & voting figures for the Roberts Court", New York Court Watcher Blog, 16 March, available at: http://www.newyorkcourtwatcher.com/2014/03/part-4-scalias-voting-supremes-record.html (accessed 20 September 2017) (tracking the Supreme Court conservative majority voting record that demonstrates that only White "reverse discrimination" plaintiffs garner any success in the current application of equality jurisprudence).

[9] Cheryl I. Harris and Kimberly West-Faulcon (2010), "Reading Ricci: Whitening discrimination, racing test fairness", *UCLA L. Rev.*, **58**, 73, 80 (noting that "the paradigmatic victim of race discrimination is now White").

[10] *See* Cynthia Estlund (2003), *Working Together: How Workplace Bonds Strengthen a Diverse Democracy* (Oxford: Oxford University Press).

Moreover, constitutional frameworks often profoundly influence the judicial assessment of employment discrimination contexts.[11] This dynamic has been observed in the United States, and this chapter considers a particular constitutional influence in Latin America – that of the Right to Work.

Specifically, this chapter conducts a thought experiment to consider both the potential benefits of a Right to Work and what its absence may implicate for the United States. To be clear, this inquiry is by no means intended to present empirical proof of the benefits of a Right to Work. Indeed, it would be quite challenging to assert any definitive causality between the textual provision of a Right to Work and its potential for beneficial effects upon jurisprudential analysis or race discrimination claims. However, there is much to be gained from exploring what even the possible influence of the Right to Work provides from a transnational comparison. While many different factors may co-exist, this chapter focuses on the possible role of a Right to Work. Like all thought experiments, the value is not in a definitive "QED" proof of causality, but rather in how constrained contexts can be reconsidered, minds opened, and fresh perspectives contemplated.[12]

This thought experiment is particularly relevant in the context of comparing jurisdictions with similar communities of judges drawn from white elite social spheres which would otherwise suggest a similar cautious reception to claims of racial discrimination. A vast literature confirms that the social status of judges influences their perception of legal claims. It is thus a worthy endeavor to consider what sort of interventions may help to mitigate the adverse effects of white elite social status on the judicial evaluation of discrimination claims.

The chapter proceeds in the following manner. Section I introduces the parameters of the Right to Work set forth in international human rights treaties and Latin American constitutions. Section II explores the potential value of an aspirational constitutional "Right to Work" to racial equality jurisprudence as it exists in Latin America. Section III then examines the U.S. context and the possible harms to racial equality caused by the absence of a constitutional "Right to Work". Section IV considers that without a constitutional Right to Work in the United States, to serve

---

[11] George Rutherglen (2010), *Employment Discrimination Law: Visions of Equality in Theory and Doctrine*, 3rd edn (New York: Foundation Press), pp. 4–5.

[12] QED stands for the Latin phrase *quod erat demonstrandum*, meaning "what was to be demonstrated", or, less formally, "thus it has been demonstrated" and is a notation often placed at the end of a mathematical proof to indicate its completion. *See Cambridge Dictionary* at http://dictionary.cambridge.org/us/dictionary/english/qed (accessed 20 September 2017).

as an external judicial prompt about the salience of workplace realities, racial jurisprudence will be adversely subjected to the assessments of many jurists with no personal experience with worker vulnerabilities in racially hierarchical workplaces.

I. THE RIGHT TO WORK

The origins of the Right to Work emanate from the International Human Rights context. Article 23 of the Universal Declaration of Human Rights ("UDHR"), which was enacted in 1948, protects the Right to Work. It states, "Everyone has the Right to Work, to free choice of employment, to just and favourable conditions of work and to protection against unemployment."[13] Stemming from this right, the International Labor Organization ("ILO") protects the Right to Work in the Convention Concerning Employment Policy (No. 122), enacted in 1964. "With a view to stimulating economic growth and development, raising levels of living, meeting manpower requirements and overcoming unemployment and underemployment, each Member shall declare and pursue, as a major goal, an active policy designed to promote full, productive and freely chosen employment."[14] The policy ensures that "there is work for all who are available for and seeking work; such work is as productive as possible; [and] there is freedom of choice of employment and the fullest possible opportunity for each worker to qualify for, and to use his skills and endowments in, a job for which he is well suited, irrespective of race, colour, sex, religion, political opinion, national extraction or social origin".[15]

The ILO further protects the Right to Work in the Employment Policy Recommendation No. 169, enacted in 1984. The recommendation recalls the International Covenant on Economic, Social and Cultural Rights ("ICESCR"), adopted by the United Nations General Assembly in 1966, which "provides for the recognition of inter alia the Right to Work, which includes the right of everyone to the opportunity to gain his living by work which he freely chooses or accepts, and for the taking of appropriate steps to achieve progressively the full realisation of, and to safeguard, this right . . . Noting the deterioration of employment opportunities in most

---

13 Universal Declaration of Human Rights, G.A. Res. 217A (III), U.N. Doc. A/810 at 71 (1948).

14 International Labour Organization, Convention concerning Employment Policy (ILO No. 122), 569 UNTS 65, preamble, entered into force 15 July 1966.

15 Id., at Art. 1(2).

industrialised and developing countries and expressing the conviction that poverty, unemployment and inequality of opportunity are unacceptable in terms of humanity and social justice, can provoke social tension and thus create conditions which can endanger peace and prejudice the exercise of the Right to Work, which includes free choice of employment, just and favourable conditions of work and protection against unemployment . . .".[16] Among the General Principles of Employment Policy outlined in the Recommendation is "[t]he promotion of full, productive and freely chosen employment provided for in the Employment Policy Convention".[17] This promotion "should be regarded as the means of achieving in practice the realisation of the Right to Work".[18] The ILO further recommends that "[f]ull recognition by Members of the Right to Work should be linked with the implementation of economic and social policies, the purpose of which is the promotion of full, productive and freely chosen employment."[19]

In summary, the UDHR, ILO Convention 122 and Recommendation 169, and the ICESCR all provide for the Right to Work, free choice of employment, and protection against unemployment. Encompassed in those rights is the right to just and favorable working conditions. "Equitable conditions of work also include the provision of adequate remuneration."[20] "Fair remuneration involves the principle of equal pay for equal work."[21]

These international documents have been influential on employment and labor protections in Latin America.[22] Most Latin American countries have been members of the ILO since it was created in 1919, and as a whole the Latin American region is second only to Western Europe in the record of ratification of ILO conventions.[23] It follows that ILO standards are extensively used in the making of Latin American labor law.[24] Moreover, ratified international treaties and covenants, including ILO conventions, are integrated into the national legal system, and prevail over national

---

16 International Labour Organization, Employment Policy (Supplementary Provisions) Recommendation, R169, Preamble (1984).

17 Id., at Art. 1.

18 Id.

19 Id., at Art. 2.

20 James Avery Joyce (ed.) (1978), *Human Rights: International Documents*, Vol. 1 (Leiden: Sijthoff & Noordhoff), at p. 584.

21 Id., at 585.

22 Arturo S. Bronstein (2010), "Labour law in Latin America: Some recent (and not so recent) trends", *Int'l J. Comp. Lab. L. & Indus. Rel.*, **26**, 17, 19.

23 Id.

24 Id., at 20.

laws and regulations whenever a conflict arises between national and international law.[25] "[I]t is not uncommon for national judges to set aside national law and decide on the basis of ratified ILO standards if they hold that the former is in breach of obligations arising out of ratification of these standards."[26] It is also most noteworthy that most if not all Latin American governments are now keen supporters of the ILO Decent Work Agenda.[27]

The U.S. employment-at-will context thus contrasts greatly with the Right to Work constitutions of many Latin American countries.[28] Indeed, within the United States the term "Right to Work" instead refers to protecting "the right of every American to work for a living without being compelled to belong to a union".[29] In the United States, a Right to Work law is one that prohibits the traditional union security devices of the closed shop and union shop. It may be enacted in the form of a constitutional amendment, a statute, or both, and by its terms such a law usually forbids discrimination with respect to employment or continuation of employment on account of membership or non-membership in a labor organization. In addition, it generally contains a clause forbidding contracts between employers and labor unions requiring membership in the union

---

25 Id., at 21.

26 Id.

27 Id., at 40. "Putting the Decent Work Agenda into practice is achieved through the implementation of the ILO's four strategic objectives, with gender equality as a crosscutting objective: Creating Jobs – an economy that generates opportunities for investment, entrepreneurship, skills development, job creation and sustainable livelihoods. Guaranteeing rights at work – to obtain recognition and respect for the rights of workers. All workers, and in particular disadvantaged or poor workers, need representation, participation, and laws that work for their interests. Extending social protection – to promote both inclusion and productivity by ensuring that women and men enjoy working conditions that are safe, allow adequate free time and rest, take into account family and social values, provide for adequate compensation in case of lost or reduced income and permit access to adequate healthcare. Promoting social dialogue – Involving strong and independent workers' and employers' organizations is central to increasing productivity, avoiding disputes at work, and building cohesive societies." ILO (2006), "Decent Work for All: UN moves to strengthen global efforts and sustainable development to promote Decent Work for poverty reduction", *World of Work*, **57** (September), at 4, 5, available at: http://www.ilo.org/wcmsp5/groups/public/---dgreports/---dcomm/documents/publication/dwcms_080598.pdf (accessed 2 October 2017).

28 *See* n 39.

29 National Right to Work Legal Defense and Education Foundation, Inc., "Right to work frequently-asked questions", available at: http://www.nrtw.org/b/rtw_faq.htm (accessed 20 September 2017).

as a condition of employment.[30] States that have enacted Right to Work statutes and constitutional amendments[31] view compulsory unionism in any form – "union", "closed", or "agency" shop – as a contradiction of the Right to Work principle and the fundamental human right that the principle represents.[32] This chapter will not discuss the U.S. refracted version of a Right to Work, but will instead focus upon the international human rights understanding of a Right to Work.

II. THE POTENTIAL VALUE OF AN ASPIRATIONAL CONSTITUTIONAL "RIGHT TO WORK" TO RACIAL EQUALITY JURISPRUDENCE

In drawing the contrast between the United States and Latin America, I do not mean to suggest that the material equality of non-whites is starkly different across the two regions. In fact, many socioeconomic indicators suggest that both regions continue to struggle with large-scale material racial inequality.[33] Rather, the importance in the contrast to the Latin American Right to Work context lies in how the existence of a constitutional Right to Work may prime judges to consider the realities of the workplace when evaluating labor law claims given the constitutional mandate for the state to ensure just and favorable conditions of work and protection against unemployment. Operating under the constitutional

---

30 Michael F. Alberti (2003), "Validity, construction, and application of state right-to-work provisions", *A.L.R.5th 243*, **105**, 11.

31 *See* Ala. Code § 25-7-1; Ariz. Const. art. XXV; Ark. Stat. Ann. §§ 11-3-301 through 11-3-304; Fla. Stat. Ann. § 447.01; G.A. Code Ann. § 34-6-6 to 28; Idaho Code §§ 44-2001 through 44-2011; Iowa Code Ann. §§ 20.8, 20.10 and 731.1 through 731.8; Kan. Stat. Ann. § 44-831; La. Rev. Stat. Ann. §§ 23:881 through 889; Miss. Code Ann. § 71-1-47; Mich. Act No. 349; Neb. Rev. Stat. §§ 48-217 through 219, 824; Nev. Rev. Stat. §§ 613.130, 613.230, 613.250 through 613.300; N.C. Gen. Stat. §§ 95-78 to 84; N.D. Cent. Code §§ 34.01.14 – 14.1; Okla. Code § 51-208; S.C. Code Ann. §§ 41-7-10 through 90; S.D. Codified Laws §§ 60-8-3 through 8-8; Tenn. Code Ann. §§ 50-1-201 through 204; Texas Codes Ann. Title 3 §§ 101.003, 004, 052, 053, 102, 111, 121, 122, 123, 124; Utah Code Ann. §§ 34-34-1 through 34-17; Va. Code Ann. §§ 40.1-58 through 40.1-69; Wyo. Stat. Ann. §§ 27-7-108 through 115.

32 National Right to Work Legal Defense and Education Foundation, Inc. (n 29).

33 *See, e.g.*, Tanya Katerí Hernández (2013), *Racial Subordination: The Role of the State, Customary Law, and the New Civil Rights Response* (Cambridge: Cambridge University Press); Tanya Katerí Hernández (2013), *La Subordinación racial en Latinoamérica* (Bogotá: Siglo del Hombre).

mandate of a Right to Work, signals the salience of workplace realities. Thus, while the "Right to Work" does not literally guarantee every citizen a job let alone a job free of any uncomfortable circumstances, the constitutional articulation of the aspiration for equitable workplaces has value.

Indeed, Mauricio Garcia-Villegas notes that "aspirational constitutions keep alive a political conscience of social change".[34] While such constitutions cannot insure that social change will result, they provide the fertile soil with which social movements can try to effectuate change.[35] Julieta Lemaitre also suggests that aspirational constitutions are part of a "legal fetishism" that provides psychic sustenance to law reformers committed to pursuing social change in the midst of massive inequality.[36] Moreover, Roberto Gargarella notes that the U.S. constitution's absence of a detailed delineation of aspirational social rights "often works against their materialization".[37]

It should of course be noted from the outset that to speak of a "Latin American" Right to Work, is an over-broad term. The region is far from a legal monolith despite the shared Spanish colonial experience and formations as civil law jurisdictions.[38] Indeed, while a large number of the countries contain constitutional rights to work, it is not the case that all do.[39] Indeed, Chile is an example of a Latin American country that not

---

[34] Mauricio Garcia-Villegas (2003), "Law as hope: Constitutions, courts, and social change in Latin America", *Fla. J. Int'l L.*, **16**, 133, 140.

[35] Id., at 140–41 (stating that "it would seem that, at least in some cases, aspirational constitutions create a strong symbolic connection between the constitutional text and at least some grass-roots leaders, who find in the constitution a political banner that inspires them to use legal strategies to vindicate rights"). *See also* Rodrigo Uprimny (2011), "Las Transformaciones constitucionales recientes en América Latina: tendencias y desafíos", in César R. Garavito (ed.), *El Derecho en América Latina: Un Mapa para el pensamiento jurídico de siglo XXI* (Buenos Aires: Siglo Veintiuno Editores), pp. 109, 123 (arguing that aspirational constitutional processes seek to deepen democracy and combat social, ethnic, and gender exclusion and inequality).

[36] Julieta Lemaitre (2008), "Legal fetishism: Law, violence, and social movements in Colombia", *Rev. Jur. U.P.R.*, **77**, 331, 343.

[37] Roberto Gargarella (2012), "Latin American constitutionalism then and now: Promises and questions", in Detlef Nolte and Almut Schilling-Vacaflor (eds), *New Constitutionalism in Latin America* (London: Routledge), pp. 143, 153.

[38] Rogelio Pérez Perdomo (1991), "Notas para una historia social del derecho en América Latina: La relación de las prácticas y los principios jurídicos", *Rev. Colegio de Abogados P.R.*, **52**, 1.

[39] *See* Constitución Nacional [Const. Nac.] (Arg.), Art. 14; Const. Nac. Arg., Art. 14bis.; Const. Nac. Arg., Art. 75.23; Constituição Federal [C.F.] [Constitution], Art. 5 (XIII and XX) (Braz.); Constitución Política del Estado Plurinacional de Bolivia, Art. 46–48; Constitución Política de la República

only does not have a constitutional Right to Work, it also is distinctive in how bare it is of social rights.[40] Yet it is the variety of constitutional frameworks in the region itself that supports the thesis that an explicit Right to Work yields benefits. For instance, in Roberto Gargarella's comparison with the extreme spartan nature of the Chilean Constitution he notes:

> Typically when judges do not find a written basis for these new rights (when the constitution contains no mention of the right to health or indigenous rights, say), they tend to act as if such rights do not exist at all. In other words, there seems to be a link between the "non-inclusion of new rights" and "judicial non-recognition of new rights". This is not to imply that inclusion of new rights in a constitution magically makes them real; rather, the point is that the absence of these rights works against their materialization.[41]

In contrast to Chile, Brazil exemplifies the opposite constitutional extreme with its long delineation of numerous social rights including the Right to Work. For that reason, it serves as a useful case example. At the same time there has been a longstanding critique of the difficulty Afro-Brazilian Plaintiffs encounter with a judiciary that has been traditionally resistant to recognizing general claims of racial discrimination based on the presump-

de Chile [C.P.], Art. 19(16); Constitución Política de Colombia [C.P.], Arts 13, 25–27, 43; Constitución Política de la República de Costa Rica, Art. 56; Constitución Política de la República de Cuba, Arts 9(b), 44, 45; Constitución de la República Dominicana, Art. 8; Constitución de la República de Ecuador, Arts 33, 66(2), 325; Constitución de la República de El Salvador, Arts 2, 37; Constitución de la República de Guatemala, Art. 101; Constitución de la República de Honduras, Arts 60, 127; Constitución Política de los Estados Unidos Mexicanos [C.P.], as amended, Diario Oficial de la Federación, 5 February 1917 (Mex.), Art. 123; Constitución de la República de Nicaragua [Cn.], as amended by Ley No. 330, Reforma Parcial a la Constitución de la República de Nicaragua, 13 January 2005, Arts 27, 57, 80; Constitución de la República de Panama, Arts 19, 64; Constitución de la República de Paraguay, Arts 86, 88, 89; Constitución Política de la República de Peru, Arts 2, 22; Constitución de la República Bolivariana de Venezuela, Arts 21, 87, 89.

[40] Constitución Política de la República de Chile [C.P.], Art. 19(16) ("Every individual has the right to freely enter employment contracts and to freely choose his/her occupation with a just pay."). *See also* Roberto Gargarella (2013), *Latin American Constitutionalism, 1810–2010: The Engine Room of the Constitution* (Oxford: Oxford University Press), p. 145 ("The countries that appear to fall the farthest behind in this slow march toward public recognition of social rights appear to be those that, for one reason or another, more strongly resisted the incorporation of those social demands into the bodies of their constitutions. Examples that stand out include the austere Chilean Constitution.").

[41] Gargarella (n 37), at 153.

tion that all Brazilians are racially mixed.[42] The Brazilian labor cases thus provide a useful context to explore whether the contrast to the labor law courts where the anti-discrimination principle is complemented by a co-existing Right to Work, yields a more hospitable venue for proving claims of discrimination.

In addition, Brazil is a country in which Afro-descended social justice movements have garnered a great deal of traction in advancing their anti-discrimination laws in ways that somewhat approximate the panoply of laws that exist in the United States for purposes of a transnational comparison.[43] It is also a jurisdiction where employment contracts can be terminated at any time by either party without cause in ways that somewhat approximate the U.S. employment-at-will context.[44] The primary distinction with the U.S. employment-at-will context is that the Brazilian Right to Work context justifies the right to receive a termination payment and prior notice in the event of dismissal, but other than granting prior notice there are no formal procedural requirements which employers must comply with prior to dismissals without cause (except for a few designated job categories).[45] In short, while the Brazilian case example cannot stand in as the embodiment of a singular "Latin American" Right to Work experience, its particularities do situate it as a useful exploration of the possible salutary benefits of a Right to Work in the anti-discrimination context, and in turn how it compares to the U.S. absence of such a Right to Work.

Indeed, a concrete example of the osmotic influence of aspirational constitutions in the operation of racial equality claims can be located in an examination of Brazilian workplace discrimination claims. Despite the fact that Brazilian racial discrimination law in general has been critiqued for its pro-defendant demand of direct evidence of racial bias rather than indirect

---

42 Seth Racusen (2002), "A mulato cannot be prejudiced: The legal construction of racial discrimination in contemporary Brazil", PhD dissertation, Massachusetts Institute of Technology.

43 Mala Htun (2004), "From 'racial democracy' to affirmative action: Changing state policy on race in Brazil", *Lat. Am. Res. Rev.*, **39**, 60; Hernández (n 33), at 118–29 and 151–64.

44 Lex Mundi Labor and Employment Practice Group (2012), *Labor and Employment Desk Book*, available at: www.lexmundi.com/Document.asp?DocID=3903 (accessed 20 September 2017), at pp. 31–32.

45 Id. Female employees who are pregnant are protected against dismissal without cause for the length of their pregnancy and for the five months following the birth of their child. Such protection against dismissal without cause also applies to trade union officials and employees who serve in the company's Internal Commission for Accident Prevention. The applicable collective bargaining agreement may also establish other protections against dismissal. Id.

evidence with statistical showings of patterns of racial disparity,[46] an empirical tabulation of published Labor Court decisions from 2008–2014, shows a very strong win rate for plaintiffs alleging racial discrimination that contrasts starkly with the plaintiff struggle to win race claims outside of the Labor Court context.[47] Indeed, this chapter purposefully focuses on the recent time frame in order to draw the contrast between the success rate in Labor Court decisions since the Labor Code's 1999 inclusion of color discrimination claims,[48] with the fortification of constitutional anti-discrimination in 1995,[49] and the anti-discrimination penal law in 1997.[50]

In the Brazilian legal system the specialized labor courts operate parallel to the general jurisdiction civil and criminal justice courts. The first instance level Trial Labor Courts (Varas do Trabalho) can be appealed to Regional Labor Courts (Tribunais do Trabalho – TRT). The highest Court of Appeal for labor cases is the Superior Labor Court (Tribunal Superior do Trabalho – TST).[51] Finally, the Federal Supreme Court (Supremo Tribunal Federal – STF) can exercise jurisdiction for extraordinary appeals in cases where the judgments below concern the Constitution.[52]

In my empirical review of Labor Court appeals, plaintiffs were successful 70 percent of the time in 68 national Superior Labor Court cases available online (TST/Tribunal Superior do Trabalho – the highest Labor Court). In addition, in a sample of 18 regional Labor Court cases (TRT/Tribunal Regional do Trabalho – appellate Labor cases) from the same time period, plaintiffs were successful 72 percent of the time. Despite the fact that the judicial opinions issued in civil law jurisdictions such as Latin America tend to be concise and parsimonious in the theoretical discussion of laws, the potential influence of the Right to Work can be traced nonetheless.[53]

---

46 Justice Studies Center of the Americas (JSCA) (2004), *The Judicial System and Racism against People of African Descent: The Cases of Brazil, Colombia, the Dominican Republic and Peru* (Santiago: JSCA).

47 I tabulated the cases by searching for "racial discrimination/discriminação racial" in the website of the national Superior Labor Court, Tribunal Superior do Trabalho at http://www.tst.jus.br/en/home, along with the same search in the sampling of the 24 Regional Labor Courts, Tribunais Regional do Trabalho at http://www.lexml.gov.br/.

48 Lei No. 9.799 de 26.5.1999 (Braz.) (adding section 373-A to the C.L.T. Consolidação das Leis do Trabalho).

49 Lei No. 9.029 de 13.4.1995 (Braz.).

50 Lei No. 9.459 de 13.5.1997 (Braz.).

51 Constituição Federal [C.F.] [Constitution], Art. 111 (Braz.).

52 Constituição Federal [C.F.] [Constitution], Art. 102 (Braz.).

53 Alejandro M. Garro (1995), "On some practical implications of the diversity of legal cultures for lawyering in the Americas", *Rev. Jur. U.P.R.*, **64**, 461, 474–75 (observing that there are significant differences in the style of writing civil

A useful example is the 2014 TST (Superior Labor Court) case of Ricardo Fagundes Nunes, an Afro-Brazilian man whose denial of various promotions by the Porto Alegre Institute of the Methodist Church (an educational institution), was prompted by a supervisor who explicitly stated "it depends on me whether that black man moves forward or not".[54] In the Court's assessment of the problematic work structures that allowed racial discrimination to affect the promotion process (such as a lack of formal parameters for evaluating candidates and the lack of transparency in how promotion decisions were made), the Court did not restrict itself to the mechanical application of the specific law that prohibits discrimination in the workplace.[55] The Court instead went on to elaborate how the protection of workers from discrimination is an international human right mandated by the Constitution including Article 7's Right to Work "aim to improve the . . . social condition" of workers. With this aim, the Court noted that simply because other black workers were employed by the defendant did not mean that the employer was not capable of the discriminatory treatment alleged by the plaintiff.

Moreover, once the plaintiff-worker presented his witness testimony regarding the racialized perspective of the supervisor and the lack of a formal evaluation process, the Court indicated that the burden of proof shifted to the defendant-employer. In Brazil, the party making the claim generally has the burden of proof. However, Brazilian labor courts are very protective of employees, as they are considered to be the weaker party in any employment relationship. Thus, in some cases, the burden of proof may be shifted to the employer, even though the employee made the claim.[56] In this case, the Court reasoned that the shift in burden to the defendant-employer was justified by the constitutional Right to Work protection against dismissal without cause, since any non-discriminatory justifications

---

law judicial decisions); Catherine A. Rogers (2002), "Fit and function in legal ethics: Developing a code of conduct for international arbitration", *Mich. J. Int'l L.*, **23**, 341, 388–89 (noting that there is a "formulaic, bureaucratic style of civil law judicial opinions").

[54] T.S.T., No. TST-RR-17500-53.2008.5.04.0005, Relator: Min. José Roberto Freire Pimenta, 04.06.2014, http://www.tst.jus.br (accessed 20 September 2017).

[55] Lei No. 9.029, de 13.4.1995 (Braz.) (setting forth the enabling legislation for the constitutional protection against arbitrary dismissal of workers in Article 7 of the Brazilian Constitution).

[56] IUS Laboris (2012), "Human resource lawyers, discrimination law in the Americas", available at: http://www.iuslaboris.com/files/documents/Public%20Files/Publications/2012_Publications/IUS_LABORIS_2012_Discrimination_Law_in_the_Americas.pdf (accessed 20 September 2017).

for dismissal are in the sole possession of the defendant-employer.[57] This is a striking difference to the U.S. racial discrimination jurisprudence where despite having a longstanding system of burden shifting for employment discrimination cases,[58] the mere presence of other employees of color seemingly insulates employers from substantive judicial inquiry.[59]

Another important contrast is that despite the U.S. plaintiff right to discovery, courts still pay great deference to the presumed business judgments of the employer notwithstanding the asymmetry in power and access to information.[60] Despite the absence of procedural devices that are especially helpful to plaintiffs (like automatic burden shifting and rights to discovery), the Brazilian judge in the Ricardo Fagundes Nunes case decided the racial discrimination claim within the broader context of a constitutional Right to Work that then enabled additional contextual elements for judicial decision-making. The realities of the workplace, in which an asymmetry in power and access to information exist for the employee, and employers may act on discrimination even within a racially diverse workplace, were factors that were able to be considered in assessing the case. Stated differently, the constitutional Right to Work focus on workers' just and favorable conditions of employment and protection against unemployment, may center judges on examining allegations within the context of real-world workplaces rather than an idealized workplace where employers are presumed to act rationally and have no greater power than their employees. While the Right to Work influence in Labor Court cases is generally not as overtly stated as in the Ricardo Fagundes Nunes

---

[57] Unlike in the United States, in Brazil, parties do not have automatic rights to discovery. Instead, the discovery phase is conducted by the judge who determines what documents a party should produce. The parties are entitled to request the disclosure of any particular document, and the judge determines whether documents should be disclosed, having regard to whether it is necessary to determine the case. The parties may also request that any documents disclosed are kept out of the public domain if the disclosure may cause damage to a party or the information is confidential. *See* Ronald Meisburg et al. (2011), "International trends in employment dispute resolution – counsel's perspectives", Materials for the Worlds of Work: Employment Dispute Resolution Systems Across The Globe, hosted by St John's University School of Law and Fitzwilliam College, Cambridge University, 21 July, available at: http://www.proskauer.com/files/Event/f4ce52c8-78cb-4634-993f-6a188b827e63/Presentation/EventAttachment/18218ba8-fba8-4d9d-85e7-717a66791533/Agenda.pdf, at 21.

[58] *McDonnell Douglas v. Green*, 411 U.S. 792 (1973).

[59] Tanya Katerí Hernández (2007), "Latino inter-ethnic employment discrimination and the 'diversity' defense", *Harv. C.R.-C.L. L. Rev.*, **42**, 259, 284–88.

[60] *See* Lauren B. Edelman et al. (2011), "When organizations rule: Judicial deference to institutionalized employment structures", *Am. J. Soc.*, **117**, 888.

case described herein, the right still implicitly provides an important backdrop for analyzing racial discrimination allegations.

For instance in the 2008 TST case of Paulo dos Reis Pereira, an employee of Parmalat Brasil, there were no explicit legal citations to the constitutional Right to Work.[61] Nevertheless, the Court affirmed the lower court's conclusion that it was not necessary for the plaintiff-employee to report the racial harassment he experienced to a more senior supervisor as a prerequisite for filing a legal claim. The Court stated it was not necessary because it is the responsibility of an employer to care for the welfare of its employees. The court reasoned that labor law requires that employers be "vigilant" in keeping the workplace environment safe and free from the harms of discrimination. Such vigilance would have made the employer cognizant of all the witness testimony that indicated what a common practice the public racial harassment was against the plaintiff.

This is a judicial perspective that echoes the concern of the constitutional Right to Work aim to care for the social condition of workers. Particularly extraordinary was the TRT Regional Court of Labor lower court's real-world concern that the subordinated status of employees makes official reporting of discrimination difficult in the face of fears of being discharged or further harmed by the harassing supervisor.[62] This helps to explain why an employer's duty to care for the welfare of its employees requires vigilance in being alert to discriminatory behavior. This consideration of how the realities of workplace hierarchies may influence employee reporting behavior, contrasts greatly with the U.S. jurisprudence insulating employer liability for employee harassment by a supervisor when a worker "unreasonably failed to take advantage of the preventive or corrective opportunities that the employer provided".[63]

Another indicator of how the Right to Work may implicitly provide an important backdrop for analyzing racial discrimination allegations, is in the comparison of the labor law plaintiff success rate with that of racial discrimination claims filed outside of the Brazilian workplace context.

---

[61] T.S.T.J. 1011/2001-561-04-00.5, Relator: Min. Carlos Alberto Reis da Paula, 24.03.2008 (Braz.) (available at: http:/www.tst.gov.br).

[62] T.R.T.J. 94.2001.5.04.0561 8 Turma do 4 Região, Relator: Juíza Ana Luiza Heineck Kruse, 30.04.2003 (Braz.) (available: at www.trt4.jus.br).

[63] *Faragher v. Boca Raton*, 524 U.S. 775, 807 (1998). The U.S. framework bars employer liability with this employer affirmative defense when the supervisor harassment is unaccompanied by a tangible employment action (such as dismissal, discipline, failure to promote, transfer or increase wages). In instances of co-worker harassment, the employer is liable only if it was negligent in controlling working conditions. *Burlington Industries, Inc. v. Ellerth*, 524 U.S. 742, 765 (1998).

Specifically, the Brazilian labor law plaintiff success rate is much higher than that for racial discrimination claims filed outside of the Brazilian workplace context.

Like the vast majority of Latin American countries, the focus of Brazilian anti-discrimination law litigation is placed in its criminal law. This is because criminalization symbolically suggests a strong normative commitment to the eradication of discrimination. Unfortunately the criminal law context also situates discrimination as caused by aberrant individuals and is thus an environment in which plaintiffs encounter less receptivity to their claims.[64]

A study of Brazilian racial discrimination criminal cases on file for 2005–2006 found that only 32.9 percent were successful for the plaintiff.[65] Similarly, a study of criminal racial discrimination cases decided in 2007–2008 again found that only 30 percent were successful for the plaintiff.[66] The contrast between the labor law cases and criminal law cases of racial discrimination highlight both the litigation constraints on plaintiffs within the criminal law context with its higher penalty stakes, and the potential benefit of presenting a claim against the backdrop of a Right to Work. The distinction between the contexts is highlighted by the fact that both operate under anti-discrimination laws that parallel each other,[67] and are implemented by jurists emanating from the same elite backgrounds.[68] Such facts would suggest a similar predisposition for viewing anti-discrimination claims in both criminal courts and labor law courts. Yet this is not the case. Nor can the contrast be explained by the development of the labor law courts dating back to the 1930s and the 1943 codification of the Consolidation of Labor Laws (Consolidação das Leis do Trabalho – CLT). Historians of the evolution of Brazilian labor law have long noted the early anti-worker bias that existed in the labor law courts, and how the CLT was in part motivated as a

---

[64] Hernández (n 33), at 104–109.

[65] Maiá Menezes (2008), "Vítimas de racismo perdem 57.7% das ações", *O Globo*, 20 November.

[66] Marcelo Paixão, Irene Rossetto, Fabiana Montovanele and Luiz M. Carvano (2010), *Relatório Anual das Desigualdades Raciais no Brasil; 2009–2010* (Rio de Janeiro: Editora Garamond), p. 264.

[67] Both Lei Número 9.029 de 1995, the employment law, and Lei Número 9.459 de 1997, the criminal law against racism that updated Lei Número 7.716 de 1989, have parallel language prohibiting "discrimination based upon race and color". In addition, the Labor Code C.L.T., Art. 373-A, prohibits discrimination based upon color as of its 1999 amendments.

[68] Maria Angela Jardim de Santa Cruz Oliveira and Nuno Garoupa (2011), "Choosing judges in Brazil: Reassessing legal transplants from the U.S.", *Am. J. Comp. L.*, **59**, 529.

vehicle to defuse and channel class tensions in the government fight against communism and class warfare.[69] Furthermore, the CLT did not begin to specifically address matters of racial discrimination until its 1999 amendments for addressing gender discrimination included language sanctioning color discrimination as well.[70]

Thus, social justice movement actors can work very hard to raise an issue of inequality to the forefront of societal concerns, but some legal contexts appear to be more conducive to responding to those concerns. I contend that the Right to Work context of labor law courts may be that hospitable space, and that with the proliferation and fortification of racial equality social justice movements across Latin America many more labor law courts and other lower courts in the region may begin to parallel the Brazilian example.[71]

On the other hand, U.S. racial equality jurisprudence does not hold such promise. In remarkable contrast to the Brazilian example of plaintiff success rates, the United States is now emblematic of outright hostility to employment racial discrimination claims. In the United States, 94 percent of employment discrimination cases never reach a trial because so many are dismissed outright on preliminary motions to dismiss and later with motions for summary judgment.[72] More than 40 percent of employment discrimination cases in the United Sates are dismissed before trial, and another 54 percent of plaintiffs only receive token amounts to settle their cases out of court.[73] Of the 6 percent that progress to trial in the United States, only one in three has a chance of winning.[74] The absence of a

---

69 John D. French (2004), *Drowning in Laws: Labor Law and Brazilian Political Culture* (North Carolina: University of North Carolina Press), pp. 20–21 and 120.

70 Lei No. 9.799 de 26.5.1999 (Braz.) (adding section 373-A to the CLT).

71 It should be noted that some Right to Work jurisdictions such as France, have so tightly regulated the ability of employers to dismiss employees for cause that it has inadvertently interfered with integrating excluded racial groups into the labor market. *See* Julie C. Suk (2007), "Discrimination at will: Job security protections and equal employment opportunity in conflict", *Stanford L. Rev.*, **60**, 73. Yet a Right to Work does not preordain a heavy bureaucratic burden on employers. Indeed, Brazil's Right to Work context simply mandates notice and a proportionate termination fee. *See* n 45 (above) and accompanying text. *See also* Nicole B. Porter (2008), "The perfect compromise: Bridging the gap between employment at will and just cause", *Nebraska L. Rev.*, **87**, 62.

72 Laura Beth Nielsen, Robert L. Nelson, and Roy Lancaster (2010), "Individual justice or collective legal mobilization? Employment discrimination litigation in the post civil rights United States", *J. Empirical Leg. Stud.*, **7**, 175.

73 Id.

74 Id.

constitutional Right to Work may be part of the reason for the hostility to employment discrimination claims that I analyze in the next section.

III. THE U.S. "RIGHT TO WORK" CONSTITUTIONAL VOID HARM TO RACIAL EQUALITY

The absence of what U.S. labor law historian Sophia Lee calls a "workplace constitution" means that unlike in Brazil and the rest of Latin America, U.S. judges approach labor law cases primed only by their own experience of what it means to be a worker rather than having the cases embedded within a constitutional Right to Work's concern for the realities of the workplace.[75] This is a dynamic that extends itself across the spectrum of judges from the U.S. Supreme Court and lower courts. Yet the potential ill effects of the absence of a constitutional Right to Work are particularly acute in the U.S. Supreme Court context. This is because, for the vast majority of U.S. Supreme Court justices, their primary work histories were as workers with privileged status in hierarchical workplaces. Research on the U.S. Supreme Court has demonstrated empirically that judges' behavior is motivated, in large part, by their individual attitudes as informed by their histories,[76] and elite life experiences.[77] Such data helps

---

[75] Sophia Z. Lee (2014), *The Workplace Constitution: The New Deal to the New Right* (New York: Cambridge University Press), p. 3 (defining workplace constitutions as those that include constitutional protections from arbitrary firings, due process before workers are terminated, and freedoms of speech, association, and privacy).

[76] David W. Rohde and Harold J. Spaeth (1976), *Supreme Court Decision Making* (San Francisco: W.H. Freeman); Jeffrey Segal and Harold J. Spaeth (1993), *The Supreme Court and the Attitudinal Model* (Cambridge: Cambridge University Press); Harold J. Spaeth and Jeffrey Segal (1999), *Majority Rule or Minority Will: Adherence to Precedent on the U.S. Supreme Court* (Cambridge: Cambridge University Press).

[77] Lawrence Baum and Neal Devins (2010), "Why the Supreme Court cares about elites, not the American people", *Geo. L.J.*, **98**, 1515 ("[b]ecause the Justices are 'sheltered, closeted,' and 'overwhelmingly upper-middle or upper-class and extremely well educated, usually the nation's more elite universities,' the views of social and economic leaders are likely to matter more to the Court than to popularly elected lawmakers . . .". The authors use "opinion poll data which suggests that the Court is often more attentive to the views of individuals with post-graduate degrees than it is to the public as a whole"); Mark A. Graber (2013), "The coming constitutional yo-yo? Elite opinion, polarization, and the direction of judicial decision making", *How. L.J.*, **56**, 661 (noting that "Justices tend to act on

to explain why when President Obama presented Justice Sonia Sotomayor as a Supreme Court nominee he commended her "extraordinary journey" from a Bronx housing project to the Second Circuit Court of Appeals, and stated that "it is experience that can give a person a common touch and a sense of compassion, an understanding of how the world works".[78] A natural corollary is that the elite work histories of U.S. Supreme Court justices would thus limit their ability to envision the vulnerabilities of non-elite workers without any other external priming.[79] A review of several key racial discrimination employment cases supports this supposition.[80]

In the 2013 decision of *Vance v. Ball State University*,[81] Justice Alito authored the majority decision in which the Supreme Court narrowed who could be considered a supervisor for the purposes of seeking employer vicarious liability for workplace harassment. A sharply divided five to four Court decided that only employees who had the explicit power to take tangible employment actions (like firing, demoting, transferring or officially disciplining) could be viewed as supervisors whose actions the employer could be held vicariously liable for. Speaking for the Court, Justice Alito stated: "The ability to direct another employee's tasks is simply not sufficient. Employees with such powers are certainly capable of creating intolerable work environments . . . but so are many other co-workers."[82]

In contrast, Justice Ginsburg's dissent observed:

---

elite values because Justices are almost always selected from the most affluent and highly educated stratum of Americans" and that "the direction of judicial decision making at a given time reflects the views of the most affluent and highly educated members of the dominant national coalition"); Benjamin H. Barton (2012), "An empirical study of Supreme Court justice pre-appointment experience", *Fla. L. Rev.*, **64**, 1137 (noting that the Roberts Court justices are outliers compared to prior justices in their deficit in "much needed practical wisdom" and explains that justices "with more real-life experiences" in the past had a prior history of law practice, trial judging, and political experience); Susan Navarro Smelcer (2010), *Supreme Court Justices: Demographic Characteristics, Professional Experience, and Legal Education, 1789–2010*, Congressional Research Service, 9 April (providing a review of the homogenization of the career experiences of Supreme Court Justices).

[78] Jonathan Weisman (2009), "Hispanic picked for top court", *Wall Street Journal*, 26 May.

[79] *See* Michele Benedetto Neitz (2013), "Socioeconomic bias in the judiciary", *Clev. St. L. Rev.*, **61**, 137 (discussion of the privileged socioeconomic status of judges in the United States and their implicit socioeconomic bias).

[80] It should be noted that the comparison between the U.S. Supreme Court employment discrimination cases and those of the Brazilian Superior Labor Court (TST) discussed above is most apt because the TST is the highest court on labor law issues. *See* nn 51–52 and accompanying text.

[81] *Vance v. Ball State University*, 133 S. Ct. 2434 (2013).

[82] Id., at 2448.

> The Court today strikes from the supervisory category employees who control the day-to-day schedules and assignments of others, confining the category to those formally empowered to take tangible employment actions. The limitation, the Court decrees diminishes the force of [precedent on employer liability], *ignores the conditions under which members of the work force labor*, and disserves the objectives of Title VII to prevent discrimination from infecting the Nation's workplaces.[83]

Moreover, Justice Ginsburg also noted that "[*w*]*orkplace realities* fortify my conclusion that harassment by an employee with power to direct subordinates' day-to-day work activities should trigger vicarious liability" and then proceeded to detail concrete examples from cases where a person vested with authority to control employment conditions had used that to facilitate harassment.[84] In other words, Justice Ginsburg's focus on workplace realities of worker vulnerability that foster discrimination influenced her assessment of the proper legal parameters for furthering equality.

Given how pivotal the consideration of workplace realities was for Justice Ginsburg's thicker notion of equality it is important to note that her own experience as a vulnerable worker formed her vision of what the workplace is like for subordinates. Indeed, as President Clinton noted during his announcement of Justice Ginsburg's selection to be a justice of the U.S. Supreme Court, "[d]espite her enormous ability and academic achievements, she could not get a job with a law firm in the early 1960's because she was a woman and the mother of a small child. Having experienced discrimination, she devoted the next 20 years of her career to fighting it and making this country a better place for our wives, our mothers, our sisters and our daughters."[85] Justice Ginsburg herself stated "As the President said, not a law firm in the entire city of New York bid my employment as a lawyer when I earned my degree."[86] Justice Ginsburg's direct experience of discrimination also included being relegated to work as a clerk-typist after having earned a college degree from Cornell University.

Unlike Justice Ginsburg, Justice Alito's work history (apart from

---

83 Id., at 2455 (emphasis added).

84 Id., at 2459–60 (emphasis added).

85 (1993), "The Supreme Court; Transcript of President's announcement and Judge Ginsburg's remarks", *New York Times*, 15 June, available at: http://www.nytimes.com/1993/06/15/us/supreme-court-transcript-president-s-announcement-judge-ginsburg-s-remarks.html?src=pm&pagewanted=1 (accessed 20 September 2017).

86 Id.

college summer internships) was restricted to positions of authority.[87] It is thus not so surprising that Justice Alito's perspective of the workplace from his unitary experience as an elite worker would give him a very different perspective of the power dynamics that affect the majority of lower status workers. In fact, a recent empirical study found that Justice Alito, along with Justice Roberts, are the two most pro-business of all the justices who have served on the Court since 1946.[88]

A similar disassociation with the power dynamics of the workplace is evident in the 2013 case of *University of Texas Southwestern Medical Center v. Nassar*.[89] In *Nassar*, Justice Kennedy authored the majority decision that raised the standard of proof for employment discrimination retaliation claims. The Court again divided five to four in assessing how discrimination can be proved. While the 1991 amendments to Title VII of the 1964 Civil Rights Act specified a "motivating factor" standard for finding liability in cases where discriminatory employer motives are mixed with discriminatory motives, the statute and its amendments were silent regarding retaliation claims.[90] The Court majority refused to extend what it termed a "lessened causation standard" to similar claims of retaliation under Title VII. Instead, it mandated that a plaintiff making a retaliation claim must establish that the alleged wrongful activity was a traditional but-for cause of the unlawful retaliation by the employer even where other causes co-exist and overlap.

The Court majority seemed particularly concerned with the fact that

---

[87] Justice Alito's judicial biography states: "Graduated from Princeton University's Woodrow Wilson School of Public and International Affairs, 1972. Graduated from Yale Law School, 1975. Clerked for Leonard I. Garth of the United States Court of Appeals for the Third Circuit from, 1976–1977. Became an Assistant U.S. Attorney, District of New Jersey, 1977–1981. Was an Assistant to the Solicitor General, U.S. Department of Justice, 1981–1985. Deputy Assistant Attorney General for the U.S. Department of Justice, 1985–1987. Served as the U.S. Attorney for the District of New Jersey, 1987–1990. Was a Judge for the United States Court of Appeals for the Third Circuit, 1990–2006. Became an Associate Justice of Supreme Court of the United States, 2006–present." *See* Clare Cushman (2012), *The Supreme Court Justices: Illustrated Biographies, 1789–2012* (Thousand Oaks: Sage Publications, Inc.), at pp. 499–502.

[88] Lee Epstein, William M. Landes and Richard A. Posner (2013, "How business fares in the Supreme Court", *Minn. L. Rev.*, **97**, 1431.

[89] *University of Texas Southwestern Medical Center v. Nassar*, 133 S. Ct. 2517 (2013).

[90] Under this legal standard sufficient proof of unlawful discrimination can include proof that a prohibited characteristic like race, "was a motivating factor for any employment practice, even though other factors also motivated the [employer's] practice". T. VII Civil Rights Act of 1964, § 703(m) codified at 42 U.S.C, § 2000e-2(m).

retaliation claims had risen in recent years inasmuch as it stressed that the causation issue has:

> central importance to the fair and responsible allocation of resources in the judicial and litigation systems. This is of particular significance because claims of retaliation are being made with ever-increasing frequency . . . Indeed, the number of retaliation claims filed with EEOC has now outstripped those for every type of status-based discrimination except race.[91]

Significantly, Justice Kennedy anchored his concerns about the rise in retaliation claims in hypothetical suppositions rather than in concrete data about the workplace. For instance, he noted that:

> [Lessening the causation standard could also contribute to the filing of frivolous claims, which would siphon resources from efforts by employer [*sic*], administrative agencies, and courts to combat workplace harassment. Consider in this regard the case of an employee who knows that he or she is about to be fired for poor performance, given a lower pay grade, or even just transferred to a different assignment or location. To forestall that lawful action, he or she might be tempted to make an unfounded charge of racial, sexual, or religious discrimination; then when the unrelated employment action comes, the employee could allege that it is retaliation. If respondent were to prevail in the argument here, that claim could be established by a lessened causation standard, all in order to prevent the undesired change in employment circumstances.[92]

Yet, the empirical data indicates that only a small percentage of those who believe they have experienced discrimination actually file a claim given the financial and emotional costs of being considered a "troublemaker" in the workplace.[93] Justice Kennedy's skewed hypothetical suppositions may very well relate to his lack of experience as a vulnerable worker. As the son of a prominent politically connected lawyer and lobbyist, Justice Kennedy's family connections positioned him to be a Senate page at the age of ten.[94] Thereafter his elite education at Stanford College and

---

91 133 S. Ct. at 2531.

92 Id., at 2531–32.

93 *See* Kristin Bumiller (1987), "Victims in the shadow of the law: A critique of the model of legal protection", *Signs*, **12**, 421 (documenting the large extent to which victims of discrimination are disinclined to file claims); *see also* Michael Selmi (2001), "Why are employment discrimination cases so hard to win?", *La. L. Rev.*, **61**, 555, 557 (describing the distorted picture of employment discrimination cases being numerous and easy to win).

94 Robert Reinhold (1987), "Man in the news; Restrained pragmatist Anthony

Harvard Law School ushered him into the professional status of lawyer.[95] Even Justice Kennedy's youthful part-time jobs working in oil fields were connected to his uncle's executive position in the oil business.[96] In other words, being hired as the result of nepotism in a working class job that is meant to be a temporary way station until an elite education is completed, is not conducive to obtaining keen insights about the real extent to which subordinates are exposed to enduring discrimination and retaliation. Moreover, when Justice Kennedy was a practicing attorney, the bulk of his practice was representing businesses as opposed to workers.[97]

In contrast, Justice Ginsburg's dissent focused on what she termed "sensitivity to the realities of life at work".[98] With the realities of the workplace as the focal point, Justice Ginsburg referenced empirical facts about the leading reason for employee silence about discrimination being the fear of retaliation, rather than speculating about the hypothetical possibilities of worker abuse of the legal system.[99] As a result, Justice Ginsburg's dissent concluded that retaliation complaints are "tightly bonded to the core prohibition [of discrimination] and cannot be disassociated from it" as a matter of proof standards.[100]

Further support for the thesis that a judicial focus on workplace realities (whether initiated from a justice's own work history or from the external cue of a constitutional Right to Work) is integral to a robust and effective racial equality jurisprudence, can be found in the contrast to the seminal 1971 employment discrimination case of *Griggs v. Duke Power Co.*[101] In *Griggs*, the Supreme Court ruled that under Title VII of the Civil Rights Act, employment tests that disparately impact racialized groups are in themselves discriminatory unless the businesses demonstrates that such tests are "reasonably related" to the job for which the test is required. Justice Burger drafted the majority opinion which stated in relevant part:

M. Kennedy", *New York Times*, 12 November, available at: http://www.nytimes.com/1987/11/12/us/man-in-the-news-restrained-pragmatist-anthony-m-kennedy.html?module=Search&mabReward=relbias:s,[%22RI:7=%22,=%22RI:12=%22]=&src=pm&pagewanted=1 (accessed 20 September 2017).

95 Cushman (n 87), at 472–76.

96 "The justices of the United States Supreme Court – Justice Anthony Kennedy", Supreme Court Review.com, available at: http://supremecourtreview.com/default/justice/index/id/34 (accessed 10 July 2014).

97 Reinhold (n 94).

98 *Nassar* (n 89) at 2547.

99 Id., at 2534–35.

100 Id., at 2539.

101 *Griggs v. Duke Power Co.*, 401 U.S. 424 (1971).

> Congress has now provided that tests or criteria for employment or promotion may not provide equality of opportunity merely in the sense of the fabled offer of milk to the stork and the fox. On the contrary, *Congress has now required that the posture and condition of the job seeker be taken into account*. It has – to resort again to the fable – provided that the vessel in which the milk is proffered be one all seekers can use.
>
> Good intent or absence of discriminatory intent does not redeem employment procedures or testing mechanisms *that operate as "built-in headwinds" for minority groups* and are unrelated to measuring job capability.
>
> The facts of this case demonstrate the inadequacy of broad and general testing devices, as well as the infirmity of using diplomas or degrees as fixed measures of capability. *History is filled with examples of men and women who rendered highly effective performance without the conventional badges of accomplishment in terms of certificates, diplomas, or degrees*. Diplomas and tests are useful servants, but Congress has mandated the common sense proposition that they are not to become masters of reality.[102]

In short, Justice Burger justified the highly progressive disparate impact standard based upon employment realities of how racially exclusionary employment tests unrelated to business necessity can unfairly exclude good workers even if the employer does not intend to be racially biased. This of course contrasts with the more restrictive intent-based standard that exists for U.S. constitutional inequality claims under the 14th Amendment.[103]

Justice Burger's own work history provided a rich understanding of workplace realities. Because his family's financial circumstances from farming were modest, Justice Burger was delivering newspapers by the age of nine to help with his family of seven siblings.[104] He earned his way through college and night classes at law school working in the accounting department of a life insurance company.[105] This rich employment history from humble origins very likely influenced Justice Burger's active work in racial equality as a young lawyer. He was the first president of the St.

---

[102] Id., at 430–34 (emphasis added).

[103] *Washington v. Davis*, 96 S.Ct. 2040 (1976). The Burger Court did not extend the *Griggs* disparate impact standard to the constitutional context because of the fear that it might have the effect of invalidating a wide range of legislative programs that were not the result of racial discrimination. The Court thought that "extension of the rule beyond those areas where it is already applicable by reason of statute, such as in the field of public employment, should await legislative prescription". Id., at 2052.

[104] *Warren Burger Biography*, Biography.com, available at: http://www.biography.com/people/warren-burger-9231479#growing-up-in-a-working-class-family (accessed 20 July 2014).

[105] "Warren E. Burger", The Oyez Project at IIT Chicago-Kent College of Law, available at: http://www.oyez.org/justices/warren_e_burger (accessed 20 July 2014).

Paul, Minnesota Council on Human Relations.[106] That group, which he helped to organize, sponsored training programs for the police to improve relations with minority groups. For many years, he was also a member of the Minnesota Governor's Interracial Commission.[107] Thus despite having been the Republican appointee of President Nixon, Justice Burger's own experiences of workplace realities trumped his role as the carrier of Nixon's "ideological heritage".[108]

In marked contrast, the contemporary judicial hostility to the relevance of disparate impact which Justice Burger supported in *Griggs*, is demonstrated with the corporate focus of Justice Kennedy in the 2009 case of *Ricci v. DeStefano*.[109] In the five to four *Ricci* decision, the Court ruled that the city of New Haven, Connecticut violated Title VII when it declined to make promotions in the fire department on the basis of a test that disproportionately screened out non-white candidates. The city also had evidence that more fair and effective tests were available. Rather than making promotions on the basis of the discriminatory test, the city declined to certify the results, and sought to explore less discriminatory alternatives, in keeping with its obligations under Title VII of the Civil Rights Act of 1964. When the city declined to make promotions on the basis of the test results, white firefighters who had scored highly on the test filed suit alleging that the city discriminated on the basis of race.

Justice Kennedy, writing for the majority, concluded that New Haven's decision to ignore the test results violated Title VII because the city did not have a "strong basis in evidence" that it would have been subjected to liability if it had promoted the white firefighters instead of the black firefighters. Justice Kennedy asserted that in instances of conflict between the disparate-treatment (intent-based standard) and disparate-impact provisions, permissible justifications for disparate treatment must be grounded in the strong-basis-in-evidence standard. He concluded that "once [a] process has been established and employers have made clear their selection criteria, they may not then invalidate the

---

106 Linda Greenhouse (1995), "Warren E. Burger is dead at 87; was Chief Justice for 17 years", *New York Times*, 26 June, available at: http://www.nytimes.com/1995/06/26/obituaries/warren-e-burger-is-dead-at-87-was-chief-justice-for-17-years.html?src=pm&pagewanted=4 (accessed 20 September 2017).

107 Id.

108 Max Lerner (1994), *Nine Scorpions in a Bottle: Great Judges and Cases of the Supreme Court* (Richard Cummings, ed.) (New York: Arcade Publishing), p. 242 (describing Justice Burger's difficult role as "Nixon's prime appointee, the carrier of his ideological heritage").

109 *Ricci v. DeStefano*, 557 U.S. 557 (2009).

test results, thus upsetting an employee's legitimate expectation not to be judged on the basis of race. Doing so, absent a strong basis in evidence of an impermissible disparate impact, amounts to the sort of racial preference that Congress has disclaimed, §2000e–2(j), and is antithetical to the notion of a workplace where individuals are guaranteed equal opportunity regardless of race." He rejected the respondents' position that "an employer's good-faith belief that its actions are necessary to comply with Title VII's disparate-impact provision should be enough to justify race-conscious conduct".

Once again, Justice Ginsburg's contrasting dissent was embedded in a consideration of workplace realities. Ginsburg's opinion stated that "the Court holds that New Haven has not demonstrated 'a strong basis in evidence' for its plea. In so holding the Court pretends that [t]he City rejected the test results solely because the higher scoring candidates were white. That pretension, essential to the Court's disposition, ignores substantial evidence of multiple flaws in the tests New Haven used. The Court similarly fails to acknowledge the better tests used in other cities, which have yielded less racially skewed outcomes." Thus in considering workplace realities, Justice Ginsburg took notice of other big city fire departments with tests that provide a more racially integrated workplace.[110] In short, Justice Ginsburg's personal experiences of employment discrimination likely prompted her concern with examining the New Haven fire department actions within the actual context of contemporary municipalities striving for integrated workforces.

IV. CONCLUSION

This brief review of significant Supreme Court employment discrimination cases accords with all the existing literature detailing the influence of jurist backgrounds and experiences upon their decision-making.[111]

---

[110] For instance, the Los Angeles firefighting force is 57 percent people of color, Philadelphia's – 51 percent; Boston's – 40 percent; and Baltimore – 30 percent. Center for Constitutional Rights, "In victory for black firefighters, FDNY hiring practices rules racially discriminatory", press release, 22 July (on file with author).

San Antonio, and Chicago both have firefighting forces that are anywhere from 30 to 50 percent African American and Latino. Jane Latour (2001), "Looking for a fire department that looks like New York", *Gotham Gazette*, 2 December, available at: http://www.gothamgazette.com/iotw/firedepartment/doc1.shtml (accessed 20 September 2017).

[111] *See* nn 76–77.

Racial jurisprudence in the United States has decidedly narrowed over the last few decades in ways that permit few racial discrimination cases to survive. The narrowness of the insulated elite work histories of the jurists may have a bearing on the predisposition to articulate abstract analyses divorced from the concrete realities of the workplace. In the absence of a mandate that judges be drawn from a more diverse selection pool, the signal for judicial attention to workplace realities will have to be an external prompt.[112] A constitutional Right to Work could be one such external prompt.

There are those who might argue that there is no need to consider a constitutional Right to Work when the U.S. Constitution already has a fully realized equality provision in the 14th Amendment. In fact, Michael Dorf posits that the U.S. Constitution in its present iteration can be considered "aspirational".[113] Yet the key difference with those Latin American constitutions known to be aspirational and that of the United States, is that Latin American constitutions are overtly aspirational in their inclusion of generous social rights provisions.[114] In contrast, the U.S. Constitution can only be understood to be implicitly aspirational inasmuch as its abstract provisions require judicial elaboration for social rights to be considered legally relevant.

The Brazilian case example suggests that an overtly aspirational constitution may more effectively enable social justice movements to operationalize their concerns. In fact, constitutional scholar Roberto Gargarella notes that significant shifts in the attitudes of Latin American courts regarding disadvantaged groups have arisen since the advent of aspirational constitutions and their inclusion of a plethora of human rights.[115] The shift is particularly noteworthy when one considers that like U.S. jurists the vast majority of Latin American judges are drawn from an elite

---

[112] The lack of racial and gender diversity in U.S. judicial positions has long been observed. *See* Barbara L. Graham (2004), "Toward an understanding of judicial diversity in American courts", *Mich. J. Race & L.*, **10**, 153, 180 (detailing the data that reveal that U.S. courts continue to be occupied overwhelming by Whites at both the federal and state levels); Sally Kenney (2012), "Choosing judges: A bumpy road to women's equality and a long way to go", *Mich. St. L. Rev.*, 1499, 1500 (discussing lack of gender diversity in judgeships).

[113] Michael C. Dorf (2009), "The aspirational constitution", *Geo. Wash. L. Rev.*, **77**, 1631.

[114] Detlef Nolte and Almut Schilling-Vacaflor (eds) (2012), *New Constitutionalism in Latin America: Promises and Practices* (Farnham: Ashgate), p. 26. *See also* Daniel Bonilla Maldonado (2006), *La Constitución Multicultural* (Bogotá: Siglo del Hombre).

[115] Gargarella (n 40).

cadre of society given the historic racial exclusivity of the educational system.[116]

In the specific case of the Brazilian labor courts assessed in this chapter, it has been noted that the judges come "from the well-off classes [and are therefore] psychologically inclined to be better understanding the point of view of the employers than that of the workers" such that workers are likely to lose two to one.[117] One scholar further observes that the TST/ Tribunal Superior do Trabalho (Superior Labor Court) as the highest labor court has traditionally had a propensity to overrule the few TRT/ Tribunal Regional do Trabalho (Regional Labor Court) cases decided in favor of the worker.[118] In addition, of the 26 TST (Superior Labor Court) judges presiding during the 2014 tabulation of this chapter's cases, only two were non-white and five were white women.[119]

Moreover, the vast majority of Brazilian and Latin American law schools provide a conservative legal education focused on educating the region's political elite.[120] Indeed, "traditional legal education in Latin America is under wide attack for its excessive legalism, which promotes the ideal of an autonomous, self-contained legal thinking isolated from social contexts".[121] A culture of legalism where the actual behavior and values of citizens is ignored is still deeply "rooted in Latin American legal culture".[122]

Furthermore, the pre-judicial appointment work histories of the Brazilian judges are similar to the elite work histories of the federal court judges and Supreme Court justices of the United States. This is particularly so given that the basic law degree is earned during undergraduate study after students complete high school at the average age of 18, thereby channeling them immediately into their careers as lawyers. Thus the con-

---

[116] Tanya Katerí Hernández (2005), "To be brown in Brazil: Education and segregation Latin American style", *N. Y. U. Rev. of L. & Soc. Change*, **29**, 683.

[117] French (n 69), at 46–47.

[118] French (n 69), at 51.

[119] Biographies of TST Justices, Tribunal Superior do Trabalho, available at: http://www.tst.jus.br/ministros (accessed 30 October 2014).

[120] Juny Montoya (2010), "The current state of legal education reform in Latin America: A critical appraisal", *J. Leg. Educ.*, **59**, 545, 546.

[121] Id., at 549. Notable exceptions do exist such as the Fundação Getulio Vargas in Brazil, Universidad Metropolitana in Venezuela, Universidad Torcuato di Tella in Argentina, Universidad Diego Portales in Chile, Universidad de Sonora in Mexico, Universidad de los Andes in Colombia, and Universidad Nacional de Córdoba in Argentina. Id., at 551–58.

[122] Rogelio Pérez-Perdomo (2006), *Latin American Lawyers: A Historical Introduction* (Redwood City: Stanford University Press), p. 69.

trasting receptivity to racial discrimination claims cannot be explained as a difference in the demographics of the composition of judiciaries across the Americas, when in point of fact the exclusivity of higher education and the structure of legal education in Latin America fosters a judiciary aligned with privileged interests as is observed in the United States.[123]

What is notable about the contrast between North and South America is the legal positioning of the importance of worker interests. In Brazil for instance, the constitutional Right to Work is complemented not only by having specialized labor law courts but by a particular formation process. Specifically, new judges tend to be appointed to courts in small cities in the countryside with the hope that living so close to the community and being, most of the time, the only labor law judge in the area, the new judge can more fully learn to grasp the contrasting social and economic predicaments in the area.[124] After six to ten years, judges can be relocated to urban centers. To further the Right to Work's principle of promoting a better and more reasonable workplace, each Labor Court has the discretion to innovate greater access to justice. For instance, in the North of Brazil there is a special itinerant Labor Court located in boats to assist with the indigenous populations living along the river.[125] Similarly, in the South of Brazil there are itinerant labor courts located in trucks to service those working in remote areas of the countryside.[126] In short, the Right to Work frames judicial interventions in labor law cases such that judges need not rely upon their own elite work histories for evaluating worker claims in Brazil.

By according constitutional status to international human rights treaties, many Latin American judges have begun to consider more seriously those legal arguments based on the value of human rights.[127] This chapter suggests that the international human rights value of a Right to Work has the same potential for change in the race jurisprudence context across the region as well. The picture for the United States is more somber given the large-scale contemporary challenges to amending the Constitution, and the cultural attachment to the employment-at-will context.[128] Nevertheless,

---

[123] *See* Susan Maloney Smith (1994), "Diversifying the judiciary: The influence of gender and race on judging", *U. Rich. L. Rev.*, **28**, 179.

[124] Email from Glenda Regine Machado, Principal Labor Judge to the 65a Judiciary Section of the City of São Paulo, Regional Labor Law Court (TRT) of state of São Paulo, to author (7 November 2014, 12:23 EST) (on file with author).

[125] Id.

[126] Id.

[127] French (n 69), at 51.

[128] Cass R. Sunstein (2005, "Why does the American constitution lack social and economic guarantees?", *Syracuse L. Rev.*, **56**, 1) (discussing the difficulty of amending the U.S. Constitution). Employment at will is the established law in

the comparative analysis provided herein further illuminates the extent to which the call for diversifying the judiciary in the United States might assist in partially filling the gap that the absence of a constitutional Right to Work creates for emphasizing workplace realities and worker vulnerabilities. While greater attention to matters of racial, gender, and work-history diversity in the judicial selection process will not act as a direct proxy for the absence of a Right to Work, it will certainly place the United States on a better path to recalibrating its race jurisprudence to consider the realities of workplace realities and worker vulnerabilities that racism can create.

---

every state except Montana, which has modified the default rule by statute. *See* Montana Wrongful Discharge from Employment Act, Mont. Code Ann., § 39-2-904(1)(b) (2009) (making discharge wrongful if "the discharge was not for good cause"). *See generally* Lisa J. Bernt (2008), "Finding the right jobs for the reasonable person in employment law", *UMKC L. Rev.*, **77**, 1, 7 ("[E]mployment-at-will is still the default rule in almost every jurisdiction in the United States . . . ."); Mayer G. Freed and Daniel D. Polsby (1989), "Just cause for termination rules and economic efficiency", *Emory L. J.*, **38**, 1097,1097 (explaining that employment at will is the general presumption, and "in the private sector and in the absence of unions, employment is almost always at will").

Name index

Ackerman, Frank 4, 180
Alito, Samuel 275–7
Álvarez, Alejandro 147, 148, 150

Bolívar, Simón 7, 22, 141, 143, 145, 146, 150–52
Burger, Warren E. 279–81

Calvo, Carlos 85
Carpizo, Jorge 148, 149, 150
Castro, Fidel 7
Cepeda, Manuel José 212
Chávez, Hugo 146, 147
Cifuentes Muñoz, Eduardo 212
Clinton, William Jefferson 276
Correa, Rafael 143
Cossio, José Ramón 194

Díaz, Porfirio 158, 159, 160
Dworkin, Ronald 4, 30, 62, 63, 71

Gaitán, Jorge Eliécer 210
García Moreno, Gabriel 113
Gaviria, César 192
Ginsburg, Ruth Bader 4, 247, 275, 276, 279, 282

Habermas, Jürgen 71
Hamilton, Alexander 14, 17
Hart, H.L.A. 30, 62
Hobbes, Thomas 37, 71

Jefferson, Thomas 187
Juárez, Benito 158

Kelsen, Hans 166
Kennedy, Anthony 277–9, 281
Kennedy, Duncan 255, 256
Koh, Harold Hongju 255–7

Locke, John 38, 71

Madison, James 14, 17
Maduro, Nicolás 145, 146, 147, 245

Nozick, Robert 71

Obama, Barack 275

Peña Nieto, Enrique 158, 171, 172, 185
Pinochet, Augusto 8, 144, 224
Posner, Richard 30, 71

Rawls, John 30, 63, 71

Salinas de Gortari, Carlos 171
Samper, Ernesto 212
Sotomayor, Sonia 275
Sunstein, Cass 71

Tushnet, Mark 199

Unger, Roberto 128
Uribe, Álvaro 212, 213

Zedillo, Ernesto 172

Subject index

access to courts, *see* justice, access to
American Convention on Human Rights 141, 144, 146
amparo, writ of 101, 165, 166, 170, 173, 197
Argentina 192, 198, 210, 222, 228
  corralito 198
authoritarianism in
  constitutions 122, 133, 136
  government 6, 8, 9, 96, 124, 149, 231

Belize 224, 225, 227
Bill of Rights 135–7
  Argentine 126
  Bolivian 126
  Brazilian 126
  Costa Rican 126
  Cuban 126
  Ecuadorian 126
  Mexican 126, 168, 174
  U.S. 9, 14, 22, 127, 128, 283
Bolivia 59, 141, 143, 232
Brazil 63, 115, 192, 196, 197, 205, 210, 244, 267–73, 283
  healthcare system 206, 207
BRICS 244
Brown v. Board of Education 15, 203

Calvo Doctrine 85, 86
Caribbean 149
caudillismo 7–9, 232; *see also caudillos*
caudillos 6, 12, 114
Central America 149
Chile 45, 190, 195, 205, 265
Civil Rights Act 277, 279, 281
collective self-government 114, 115
Colombia 30, 45, 48, 72, 192, 194, 196, 198, 205, 232
  economic crisis of the 1990s 209, 211
  healthcare system 206, 207, 212
  vital minimum doctrine 212
colonialism 265
  neocolonialism 17, 19
  post-colonialism 15, 106
colony, *see* Global South
conferences
  Havana Conference of 1928 149
  Montevideo Conference of 1933 149
  Ninth Inter-American Conference of Bogotá 149
  Pan American Conferences 89, 147, 148
constitutions
  Argentinian
    of 1853 219
    of 1857 123
    of 1949 134
    Amendments of 1994 222, 224
  Bolivian of 2009 106
  Brazilian
    of 1891 219
    of 1989 225, 269
    Amendments of 2005 225
  Chilean of 1980 224
  Colombian of 1886 96
  Ecuadorian of 2009 143, 144
  Mexican
    of 1824 219
    of 1857 158, 160, 179
    of 1917 17, 18, 125, 155, 158–60, 163, 164, 169, 171–82, 185, 186, 190
  South African of 1996 246
  U.S. of 1787 3, 5, 11, 79, 117–20, 127–31
  Venezuelan
    of 1811 219
    of 1946 224
    of 1953 224
    of 1961 224
    of 1999 223, 225
  workplace constitution 274

Constitutional Court
  Bolivia, Plurinational of 247
  Chilean 194–5
  Colombian 2, 71, 104, 105, 193, 196, 199–201, 204, 207, 212, 213
  German 71
  Mexican 166
  South African 71, 244
constitutionalism 80
  Bolivarian 143, 145, 146
  checks and balances 113, 119, 123, 124, 126, 130, 131, 132, 137
  critiques
    consistency 112, 113, 116–18, 126, 127, 136
    egalitarianism 114, 116, 117, 126, 127, 128, 136
  drafting 217, 218, 219, 223, 225, 238
  European 7
  global 80, 81, 82, 104, 105, 108
  Latin American 1–3, 7, 8, 13, 16, 20–22, 80, 81, 93–5, 97–100, 103, 104, 107, 108, 111, 112, 114, 122–7, 131–4, 136, 140, 141, 172, 175, 190, 221, 224, 225, 228, 232, 237, 238, 259, 265, 284–6
  liberal 113, 141, 143, 150, 174
  Mexican 156, 157, 172, 183, 184, 185, 190
    reformismo 182, 184
  modern 30, 71, 128
  regional
    conservative approach 115, 116
    liberal approach 116
    republican approach 116
  separation/organization of powers 113, 143, 156, 159, 162, 175, 199, 219
  similarity 220, 221, 224, 225, 228
  structure of rights 113
  U.S. 3, 5, 6, 9, 12, 19–23, 25, 79, 81, 94–8, 100, 104, 111, 112, 116, 124, 127, 132, 188, 196, 202, 213, 258, 280, 285
    influence of 218, 219, 221, 224, 225, 238, 247
Costa Rica 192, 196
court
  Consejo de la Judicatura Federal (Mexico) 166
  labor law courts 267, 272, 273, 285
  Supreme Tribunal Judicial (Brazil) 197, 268

democracy 3, 13, 15, 16, 22, 50, 122, 126, 128, 131, 133, 135, 155, 156, 161, 168, 169, 173, 174, 186, 187
due process 22, 169

Ecuador 113, 141, 143
ejidos 171
emergency powers/rule 96–7, 160
employment at will 263, 267, 285
equality 1, 3, 8, 10, 15, 17, 21, 25, 143, 149, 152, 169, 258–60, 266–73, 275, 279, 280, 283, 285
European
  colonization, *see* European, influence
  Court of Human Rights 71, 246, 253
  Court of Justice 253
  England 114, 115
  France 60, 67, 74, 87
  German 20, 34, 49, 60, 67, 71, 72, 74, 163, 193, 240
  influence 4, 7, 8, 17, 24, 79, 84, 165, 193, 208, 209, 210
  Portugal 60, 74, 115
  Spain 9, 20, 60, 67, 74, 115
  Union 241, 244, 245, 252, 253
executive power 2, 9, 16, 24, 143, 217, 218, 228, 231, 232, 238

federalism 156, 163, 164, 175, 219
Federalist Papers 14; *see also* Hamilton, Alexander; Madison, James
forum non conveniens 91
free market of legal ideas 20, 30–31, 35–8, 41–5, 48, 49, 78

Global North 3, 30–34, 51, 59, 60, 63–5, 71, 74, 75, 77, 80, 101, 104, 105, 106
Global South 30, 32, 33, 34, 36, 59, 60, 63, 64, 68, 69, 70–77, 79, 80, 102, 103, 105, 106, 245

Guantanamo Bay 141
Guyana 224, 225, 227

habeas corpus 249
healthcare systems 199, 200, 201, 211, 212
  Brazilian and Colombian 206, 207
human rights, *see* rights

individual autonomy 114, 115
inequality, *see* equality
Inter-American System 146, 151, 152
  Commission 145
  Court of Human Rights 142, 151
  Human Rights System 17, 23, 140, 151, 252
international commercial arbitration 91
International Labor Organization (ILO) 122, 261
intervention 149
  diplomatic 88, 91
  judicial 207
  militaristic 25, 91, 148
  non-interference/intervention 22, 141, 146, 148, 149, 150, 151, 152
  state 2, 11, 121

judicial
  governance 165
  power 2, 9, 23, 178
  review 165, 181, 183, 197, 205
jurisprudence
  discrimination 258–60, 263, 266–79, 280, 282, 283, 285
  majoritarian and counter-majoritarian 188, 189, 195, 196, 202, 205, 211
justice 9, 11, 21, 23, 25, 31
  access to 43–5
  denial of 21, 82–91, 93, 105

Latin America 43–9, 57, 59–68, 74–6, 79, 83, 86, 149, 218, 221, 228
  constitutions, *see* constitutionalism, Latin American
  courts 89, 90, 93, 101
  democracies 141
  lawlessness 84, 90
  legal dysfunction/failure 91, 92, 95, 96, 105
  legal history 191, 192
  radical constitutionalism 140, 141, 143, 144, 152
law
  comparative 13, 21, 24, 60, 67, 77, 92, 93, 202, 244, 248–50
  international 21, 22, 88, 90, 140, 142, 144, 145, 190, 194, 256, 261
legal academia 35, 44, 49, 58, 65, 68, 70, 71, 72, 76, 77, 241, 248, 252
legal barbarian 31
legal clinics 43, 45, 47, 48, 73, 241, 250
legal diffusion 3, 20, 25, 240, 241, 244, 250
legal education 15, 25, 43–5, 47, 48, 72, 76, 241, 242, 243, 248–57
legal formalism 34, 46, 48, 76–7
legal knowledge and 20, 25, 31
  political economy of 29–31, 50, 77, 157
  production of 240
    colonial model 20, 30–33, 35, 36, 50, 51, 54, 59, 60, 63, 64, 67, 71, 73, 74, 76, 77, 78
  space 29, 31–4, 40, 41, 43, 44, 49, 60, 61, 69, 74
  subject of 31, 32, 37, 38, 40, 41, 50, 51, 66, 71, 73
  time 29–33, 38–40, 43, 44, 54, 57, 59, 63, 74, 78
legal pluralism 79
legal work, *pro bono* 43–5, 250
legislative power 224, 231, 232
legislature 40, 106, 129, 179, 246
liberalism (and liberal legalism) 37, 49, 50, 93, 94, 117, 131
Lochner era 49
Lochner v. U.S. 248

meritocracy principle 32, 35, 42, 43
metropolis, *see* Global North
Mexico 125, 155, 160, 161, 167, 168, 193, 194, 205
  2011 human rights reform 160, 166, 177
  2013 reform 161, 162, 164, 168, 171, 172, 173, 175
  Consejo de la Judicatura Federal 167
  economic constitution 156, 171, 172

energy reform 158, 171, 172, 175, 183
gradualism 156, 157, 183
political class 161

negative injunction model 196, 198, 203, 209–10
neoliberalism 245, 246
Washington Consensus 242, 245
neutrality principle 120
New Deal 49
Nicaragua 60, 143
North America 30, 242

Partido Revolucionario Institucional (PRI) 158, 159, 168
Permanent Court of Justice in the Hague 89
politics and law 1, 2, 5, 6, 8–11, 14–23, 32, 33, 35–45, 47–50, 52, 60, 61, 63–6, 71, 77, 78, 143, 144, 146, 149, 155, 160, 168, 169, 176, 179, 180, 185, 189, 192, 196, 199, 202, 205–11, 213, 214; *see also* legal knowledge, political economy of
presidentialism 3, 126, 132, 133
in Mexico 219, 232
principle of distinction 130

racial discrimination/equality, *see* equality
realpolitik 88, 89, 105
religion 66, 67
and law 114
Roman Catholicism 8, 113, 123, 134
res judicata 88
revolution
Mexican 18, 158, 163, 171, 173
U.S. 11, 115
right to work 259–74, 279, 283, 285, 286
rights 5, 11, 14, 125, 173
civil and political 3, 14, 232
"creep" 223, 224
criminal procedure 224, 232, 234
fundamental 71, 118, 121–5, 142, 169–71
human 17, 22, 24, 66, 140–47, 150–52, 190–91, 218, 236, 256
natural 38
social, economic, and cultural 2, 14, 17, 23, 24, 42, 79, 125, 134, 137, 169, 188–99, 201, 203, 205, 211–14, 224, 232, 265, 266, 283
Roe v. Wade 30, 72, 248
rule of law 150, 157, 183, 185

self-determination 22, 141, 146, 149, 150
social purpose functionalism 240
Supreme Court
Canadian 247
Colombian 212
Indian 71
Mexican 162, 164, 167, 169, 171, 177, 181, 184
U.S. 21, 22, 25, 71, 72, 81, 196, 202, 222, 247, 274, 276, 282
Venezuelan 88

tutela actions 101, 193, 212, 213

United Nations (UN) 147, 261–3
Universal Declaration of Human Rights (UDHR) 261, 262

Venezuela 141, 143, 145, 146, 147, 192, 228, 232

Washington Consensus, *see* neoliberalism
World Trade Organization (WTO) 243, 244